Reading Machines in the Modernist Transatlantic

Reading Machines in the Modernist Transatlantic

Avant-Gardes, Technology and the Everyday

Eric B. White

EDINBURGH
University Press

Edinburgh University Press is one of the leading university presses in the UK. We publish academic books and journals in our selected subject areas across the humanities and social sciences, combining cutting-edge scholarship with high editorial and production values to produce academic works of lasting importance. For more information visit our website: edinburghuniversitypress.com

© Eric B. White, 2020, 2022

Edinburgh University Press Ltd
The Tun – Holyrood Road,
12(2f) Jackson's Entry,
Edinburgh EH8 8PJ

First published in hardback by Edinburgh University Press 2020

Typeset in 10.5/13 Adobe Sabon by
IDSUK (DataConnection) Ltd,

A CIP record for this book is available from the British Library

ISBN 978 1 4744 4149 0 (hardback)
ISBN 978 1 4744 4150 6 (paperback)
ISBN 978 1 4744 4151 3 (webready PDF)
ISBN 978 1 4744 4152 0 (epub)

The right of Eric B. White to be identified as the author of this work has been asserted in accordance with the Copyright, Designs and Patents Act 1988, and the Copyright and Related Rights Regulations 2003 (SI No. 2498).

Contents

List of Illustrations	vi
Acknowledgements	ix
Abbreviations	xii
Introduction	1
1. Dazzling Technologies: Avant-Gardes and Sensory Augmentation in the First World War	28
2. Re-Reading the Machine Age: The 'Audacious Modernity' of the Techno-Bathetic Avant-Gardes	68
3. Excavating the 'Readies': The Revolution of the Word, Revised	118
4. Ghosts in the Machine Age: Rose and Bob Brown's Reading Machines and the Socio-Technics of Social Change	162
5. 'Our Technology Was Vernacular': Radical Technicities in African American Experimental Writing	214
6. Afterword: The Robot Does (Not) Exist	265
Index	270

Illustrations

I.1 Marcel Duchamp, *Encore à cet astre* [*Once More to This Star*], 1911, Graphite on beige wove paper; Philadelphia Museum of Art   20

1.1 Norman Wilkinson, *Plate III* [Dazzle Painted Vessels], illustrates Norman Wilkinson, 'Naval Camouflage', in James Cecil Mottram et al., 'Camouflage', *Encyclopædia Britannica: The New Volumes, Twelfth Edition, Vol. 30* (London and New York: The Encyclopaedia Britannica Company, 1922), pp. 541–57 (pp. 546–7)   29

1.2 Symonds & Co., *H. M. S. Mauretania, dazzle-painted*; Symonds & Co. Collection, Imperial War Museum   30

1.3 Anonymous, Untitled [Photograph of Luigi Russolo, Ugo Piatti, and the *intonarumori* (noise machines)], Milan, 1914–15   46

1.4 Anonymous, *Londre concerto al Coliseum* [News clipping of Russolo and the *Intonarumori* at the Coliseum in London, June 1914]   47

1.5 Eric White, Cillian White and Martina Hallegger, Recreation of Ezra Pound's Vortoscope [1915 Kodak Brownie, pocket mirrors, plywood, and bolts]; view of crystal structures through ground glass   49

1.6 Alvin Langdon Coburn, *Vortograph No. 8*, 1917, Gelatin silver print   51

1.7 Norman Wilkinson, *Ship Being Dazzle Camouflaged by Edward Wadsworth's Crew*, 1918   55

1.8 Edward Wadsworth, *Dazzle-ships in Drydock at Liverpool, 1919*, Oil on canvas; transfer from the Canadian War Memorials, 1921 National Gallery of Canada, Ottawa   56

2.1	Alfred Stieglitz, *Old and New New York, 1910*, Photogravure; Alfred Stieglitz Collection, Art Institute of Chicago	72
2.2	Francis Picabia, *Ici, C'est Ici Stieglitz Foi et Amour*, 291 nos 5–6 (July–August 1915): 1 and *De Zayas! De Zayas!*, p. 5 [gatefold]; Yale Collection of American Literature, Beinecke Rare Book and Manuscript Library	78
2.3	Alfred Stieglitz, *Fountain by R. Mutt* [Marcel Duchamp], *The Blind Man* 2 (May 1917): 4; Yale Collection of American Literature, Beinecke Rare Book and Manuscript Library	84
2.4	Elsa von Freytag-Loringhoven, *Portrait of Marcel Duchamp*, *The Little Review* 9.2 (Winter 1922), following p. 45	94
2.5	Newspaper Enterprise [Mina Loy], 'Would You Be "Different?" Madame Loy Shows How', *The Pittsburgh Press*, 3 April 1921, p. 2	102
2.6	Anonymous [Mina Loy], 'Novel Floral Decorations That Light Up Modern Interiors', *The Daily Telegraph*, 11 October 1929, p. 7	106
3.1	Bob Brown, Flyleaf [Photograph of Ross Saunders's Prototype Reading Machine and Hilaire Hiler's Commercial Design for the Reading Machine], *RFBBM*, p. 4	121
3.2	Bob Brown, Untitled [aka 'Self Portrait'], *1450–1950*, p. 83	126
3.3	A. H. Development Syndicate, *August-Hunter Photo-Composing Machine*, illustrates W. B. Hislop, 'August-Hunter Photo-Composing Machine', *Penrose's Annual* Vol. 28 (1926): 76–80 (n.p.), British Library	128
3.4	Anonymous, 'Bob Brown, Who Used to Write "Diamond Dick" Stories, Debases His Art After Japanese Trip', *The New York Herald (European Edition)*, 27 April 1929, p. 9	131
3.5	Unknown photographer [Bob or Rose Brown], Untitled [Photograph of Ross Saunders's Prototype Reading Machine], B5, F12, SIU Kaplan-Brown	139
4.1	Murray Godwin, 'The Way I See It – [Editorial]', *Science and Invention* 18.6 (October 1930), p. 490	167
4.2	Eric White's annotated version of the Commercial Prototype Reading Machine illustration in *RFBBM* (p. 4)	170
4.3	Bob Brown, [Readies prototype illustration, TS ca. 1932–7], in *Reading Machines V1*, p. 5	173

4.4 Anonymous [Hilaire Hiler], *Bob Brown's Readio*, in
Ezra Pound, 'Deflation Benefit', *Globe* 1.5 (August 1937),
pp. 66–71 (p. 68)   186

4.5 Harris W. Nowell, The Museum of Social Change
[Photograph], in Anonymous, 'A Red College in the Bible
Belt Where Future Labor Leaders Work to Pay Way',
Milwaukee Journal, 5 May 1935, n.p.; clipping from B5,
F3, UCLA Brown   190

5.1 Prentiss Taylor, Cover, in Langston Hughes, *Scottsboro,
Limited* (New York: Golden Stair Press, 1932); Yale
Collection of American Literature, Beinecke Rare Book
and Manuscript Library   227

5.2 Prentiss Taylor, *Christ in Alabama*, in Langston Hughes,
Scottsboro, Limited (New York: Golden Stair Press, 1932),
n.p.; Yale Collection of American Literature, Beinecke
Rare Book and Manuscript Library   228

5.3 Anonymous, *Pete* [Photograph of Pauli Murray], illustrates
Pauli Murray, 'From "Three Thousand Miles on a Dime in
Ten Days"', in *Negro Anthology*, ed. Nancy Cunard
(London: Nancy Cunard at Wishart & Co., 1934),
pp. 90–3 (p. 90)   231

Acknowledgements

The foundations of this book took shape a decade ago when I held a fellowship at the Institute for Advanced Studies in the Humanities at the University of Edinburgh. Laura Marcus, Andrew Taylor and the fellows and staff at IASH were hugely supportive, and I'm particularly indebted to the late Susan Manning, whose inspiring example is warmly remembered and deeply missed. I'm also grateful to the support I received from Fiona Green, Ian Patterson, John Beck, Christopher MacGowan, Patricia Fara, Jean Chothia and David Trotter in the initial stages of this project, and for their enduring influence on my work.

In writing the present text, my most immediate academic debt is to my outstanding colleagues and students at Oxford Brookes University. My thanks go especially to my fellow modernists Alex Goody and Niall Munro, whose generosity and kindness is an inspiration; they both read chapter drafts of this book, and offered rich feedback and encouragement at every stage of its development. Katharine Craik, Simon Kövesi, Daniel Lea, and Nicole Pohl all leant crucial support at important times. A sabbatical provided by the Department of English and Modern Languages and teaching remission from the Faculty of the Humanities and Social Sciences were essential to completing this monograph. Michael Jolliffe provided important research assistance, proof-reading and insightful comments during the final stages of this monograph's production; his contributions have been invaluable and uplifting and I'm extremely grateful for them. I also extend thanks to my former doctoral students, Najla Aldughayem and Nissa Parmar, for their diligence, trust and excellent projects. My brilliant colleagues and collaborators on the Avant-Gardes and Speculative Technology (AGAST) Project have shaped this work more than they may know, and I'm very grateful to John Twycross, Fridolin Wild, Mike Blow, Iain Sinclair, Jay Bernard, David Bullock, Iulian Arcus, Mark Sutcliffe and our fantastic partners at the Ark-T Centre, Oxfordshire County Libraries, EOF Hackspace, Ashmolean Museum, Tesserae and Co-Creation.

I owe a major note of thanks to Craig Saper, particularly for his guidance, insights and great company in our collaborations. I'm also grateful to Helen Burgess and Lynn Tomlinson for their support and insights. Adam Piette, Steven Matthews, Lee Jenkins, Nick Selby and Rebecca Stott all offered important advice and encouragement at pivotal moments, and I remain grateful for it. Sara Crangle, John Gardner, and Jason Watson kindly read drafts of my work and I'm thankful for their suggestions for improving it. It is also a great pleasure to thank the following scholars for their insights and camaraderie: Victoria Bazin, Daniel Burke, Ian Copestake, Georgina Colby, Sue Currell, Andrew Frayn, James Gifford, Stephen Hahn, Faye Hammill, Alexander Howard, Michael Kindellan, Sam Ladkin, Jonathan Martin, Scott McCracken, Michèle Mendelssohn, Richard Parker, Jessica and Stjepan Rajko, Tessa Ronyon, Erin Templeton, Andrew Thacker, Leigh Wilson, and the William Carlos Williams Society; from this last group, I would like to acknowledge especially the late Emily Mitchell Wallace and Gregory Harvey, whose enthusiasm and generosity will be missed.

I presented research on early versions of Chapter 1 at the London Modernism Seminar, and I thank Tim Armstrong, David Ayers and Helen Carr in particular for that opportunity. Efthymia Rentzou and Joshua Kotin kindly hosted me at Princeton's Center for Digital Humanities, and I extend my gratitude to them for a wonderful visit. BAMS, EAMS, MLA, and MSA conferences have all presented valuable opportunities to present and develop early versions of research for this book, and I thank the panellists, chairs and organisers for their support.

I have benefited greatly from invaluable assistance from staff at numerous collections cited in this book, and I would like to thank in particular: the rare books and periodicals teams at the New York Public Library; the Charles E. Young Research Library team at UCLA Special Collections; and Aaron Lisec at the Special Collections Research Center, Southern Illinois University Carbondale. I would like to extend a special note of thanks to Jackie Jones, Michelle Houston, Ersev Ersoy, James Dale and the whole team at Edinburgh University Press for their skill and dedication as well as their enthusiastic support of this project. I'm also grateful to the anonymous readers of this book, whose suggestions undoubtedly improved it.

Early versions of chapters in this book have appeared elsewhere, and I appreciate the following publishers for granting me permission to use that material: *Symbiosis* for '"A Machine of Mirrors": Technology and Identity in the Modernist Transatlantic', *Symbiosis* 17.2 (2013): 69–87; and *Modernist Cultures* for 'Technicities of Deception: Dazzle Camouflage, Avant-Gardes, and Sensory Augmentation in the First World War', *Modernist Cultures* 12.1 (2017): 36–58.

Every effort has been made to obtain permissions and clear copyright for the material collected in this book. Should we have overlooked anyone, notwithstanding good faith efforts, the publishers will be pleased to make the necessary arrangements at the first opportunity. For permission to reproduce copyrighted material in this book, grateful acknowledgement is made to the following people and agencies: Bob Brown's grandchildren and great-grandchildren for permission to reproduce published and unpublished/archival copyrighted work by Bob Brown, Rose Brown and Robert Carlton Brown III, © The Grandchildren and Great-Grandchildren of Bob Brown, 2020; the Estate of Alvin Langdon Coburn; Association Marcel Duchamp/ADAGP, Paris and DACS, London 2020; Roger Connover and the Estate of Mina Loy; Luigi Russolo's Archive, Mart, Archivio de '900; Camilla Wilkinson and the Estate of Norman Wilkinson; quotations from Gwendolyn Bennett are courtesy of the Literary Representative for the Works of Gwendolyn Bennett, Schomburg Center for Research in Black Culture, New York Public Library, Astor, Lenox and Tilden Foundations; quotations from Langston Hughes are © The Literary Estate of Langston Hughes – David Higham Associates Limited, 2020; quotations from Pauli Murray are © by the Estate of Pauli Murray, used herewith by permission of the Charlotte Sheedy Literary Agency, Inc.; and quotations from Gertrude Stein are © The Literary Estate of Gertrude Stein – David Higham Associates Limited, 2020.

My final notes of gratitude are for my wonderful friends and family. Jason and Louise Watson, Anthony Miller and Joanne Daly, John Gardner and Colette Paul, and our friends in Carinthia – my thanks to you all for your warmth and brilliance. My extended family in Canada and the UK, the Halleggers in Austria, my mother Anita, father Brian, sister Genevieve, brother-in-law Jamie, nieces Chloe and Emily, and Kara, Lena and the whole gang in BC are an endless support, and I thank them for their love and kindness. This book is dedicated to the memory of my grandparents, Asta and Raymond Lawry and Robert and Doreen Taylor White. It is written for Martina and Cillian, with all my love, always.

Abbreviations

Archival Collections

Cornell Lewis	Wyndham Lewis Collection, #4612, Division of Rare and Manuscript Collections, Cornell University Library
HRC Cunard	Nancy Cunard Collection 1895–1965, Harry Ransom Center (HRC), University of Texas
LOC Ellison	Ralph Ellison Papers, 1890–2005, MSS83111, Manuscript Division, Library of Congress, Washington, DC
SIU Kaplan-Brown	Philip Kaplan and Bob Brown papers, Special Collections Research Center, Southern Illinois University Carbondale
UCLA Brown	Bob Brown Papers, Collection 723, University of California Los Angeles Library Special Collections, Charles E. Young Research Library
UPenn Farrell	James T. Farrell Papers, 1916–83, Ms. Coll. 886, Kislak Center for Special Collections, Rare Books and Manuscripts, University of Pennsylvania

Books, Periodicals and Unpublished Manuscripts

1450–1950	Bob Brown, *1450–1950*, ed. Craig Saper (Baltimore: Roving Eye Press, 2015 [1929])

6BBB	Bob Brown, 'The Six Books of Bob Brown Vol. 1' [unpublished ms.], 14 June 1923, Box 32, UCLA Brown
Amazing Adventures	Craig Saper, *The Amazing Adventures of Bob Brown: A Real-Life Zelig Who Wrote His Way Through the 20th Century* (New York: Empire State Editions, an Imprint of Fordham University Press, 2016)
B1	*Blast* 1 (July 1914)
B2	*Blast* 2 (July 1915)
Blast	ed. Wyndham Lewis
Body Sweats	Elsa von Freytag-Loringhoven, *Body Sweats: The Uncensored Writings of Elsa von Freytag-Loringhoven*, ed. Irene Gammel and Suzanne Zelazo (Cambridge, MA: The MIT Press, 2011)
CERE	Ralph Ellison, *The Collected Essays of Ralph Ellison*, ed. John F. Callahan (New York: The Modern Library, 2003)
CWLH 1	*The Collected Works of Langston Hughes, Volume 1: The Poems: 1921–1940*, ed. and with an introduction by Arnold Rampersad (Columbia and London: University of Missouri Press, 2001)
FH	Ralph Ellison, *Flying Home and Other Stories, Second Edition*, ed. John F. Callahan (New York: Vintage International, 2012)
Futurism	*Futurism*, eds Lawrence Rainey, Christine Poggi and Laura Wittman (New Haven and London: Yale University Press, 2009)
HHRB	Gwendolyn Bennett, *Heroine of the Harlem Renaissance and Beyond: Gwendolyn Bennett's Selected Writings*, ed. Belinda Wheeler and Louis J. Parascandola (University Park, Pennsylvania: Penn State University Press, 2018)
IFP	*Italian Futurist Poetry*, ed. and trans. Williard Bohn (Toronto: University of Toronto Press, 2005)
IM	Ralph Ellison, *Invisible Man* (London: Penguin Books, 2001)

LLB	Mina Loy, *The Last Lunar Baedeker*, ed. Roger Conover (Highlands, NC: Jargon Society, 1982)
MDComplete Works	Marcel Duchamp and Arturo Schwartz, *The Complete Works of Marcel Duchamp, Revised and Expanded Paperback Edition*, ed. Arturo Schwartz (New York: Delano Greenridge Editions, 2000)
MDEssential Writings	Marcel Duchamp, *The Essential Writings of Marcel Duchamp: Marchand du Sel/ Salt Seller*, ed. Michel Sanouillet and Elmer Peterson (London: Thames and Hudson, 1975 [1973])
METO	Gilbert Simondon, *On the Mode of Existence of Technical Objects*, trans. Cicile Malaspina and John Rogove (Minneapolis: University of Minnesota Press, 2017 [1958 and 2012])
Negro Anthology	Nancy Cunard, *Negro, Edited by Nancy Cunard 1934: Fac-similé*, ed. and with introduction by Sarah Frioux-Salgas (Paris: Nouvelle Éditions Place, 2018)
PEL	Michel de Certeau, *The Practice of Everyday Life, Vol. 1*, trans. Steven F. Rendall (Berkeley and London: University of California Press, 1984)
The Readies	Bob Brown, *The Readies*, ed. and with an introduction by Craig Saper (Baltimore: Roving Eye Press, 2014 [1930])
Reading Machines [V1 and V2]	Bob Brown, 'Reading Machines' [TS, August–September 1937], B5, F13, SIU Kaplan-Brown. The folder contains two drafts of the essay, and I use 'Version 1' (*V1*) and 'Version 2' (*V2*) to distinguish between them where content is unique to that draft.
RFBBM	Bob Brown, *Readies for Bob Brown's Machine: A Critical Facsimile Edition*, eds Craig Saper and Eric White (Edinburgh: Edinburgh University Press, 2020 [1931])
Words	Bob Brown, *Words: A Facsimile*, ed. and with an Introduction by Craig Saper (Baltimore: Roving Eye Press, 2014 [1931])

Introduction

Trudging through a fierce winter evening in Paris with Alice B. Toklas, Pablo Picasso and Eva ('Eve') Gouel, Gertrude Stein witnessed an uncanny encounter between avant-garde aesthetics and military hardware in the darkened streets of Montparnasse. Recounted from Toklas's perspective, Stein illustrated how avant-gardes perceived themselves in relation to technology at the dawn of mechanised total war:

> The first year of the war, Picasso and Eve, with whom he was living then, Gertrude Stein and myself were walking down the boulevard Raspail a cold winter evening. There is nothing in the world colder than the Raspail on a cold winter evening, we used to call it the retreat from Moscow. All of a sudden down the street came some big cannon, the first any of us had seen painted, that is camouflaged. Pablo stopped, he was spell-bound. C'est nous qui avons fait ça, he said, it is we that have created that, he said. And he was right, he had. From Cézanne through him they had come to that. His foresight was justified.[1]

In this famous anecdote, Stein renders Picasso's moment of 'foresight' self-consciously in hindsight. In doing so, she establishes artistic vanguards as cultural prophets, on the one hand, but, on the other, also passive bystanders who are overwhelmed by the scale and ferocity of global events along with everyone else. However, the role of technology here is ambiguous: Stein simultaneously includes and excludes its avant-garde witnesses from its systems of production. Technology emerges yet is also defamiliarised by their work. On a proverbial dark and stormy night, technology becomes a cipher for the avant-gardes' encounter with modernity – a monumental 'black box' that mediates and instantiates the potent forces converging in the First World War.

Nevertheless, Stein's carefully staged scene is itself a work of camouflage, remarkable as much for what it conceals as for what it reveals.

The 'big cannon' arrive suddenly, like infernal apparitions of war, but the setting creates a deeper chronological frame for the encounter. Her reference to 'the retreat from Moscow' alludes to the Napoleonic Wars, while the Boulevard Raspail, previously known as the Boulevard D'Enfer [Boulevard of Hell], skirts Cimetière du Montparnasse. As such, Stein's moment of hindsight contains another dimension of 'foresight' beyond Picasso's revelation – one that connects the city's historical dead to the forthcoming slaughter of its youth (including some of its avant-garde artists). And in this respect, her recollection also includes an oversight.

Stein and Picasso witnessed the camouflaged cannon (and/or transport truck, which replaced the cannon in a later version of the anecdote) between December 1914 and March 1915.[2] In September 1914 the Symbolist portrait artist Lucien-Victor Guirand de Scévola began camouflaging gun emplacements using techniques of crypsis (disruptive patterns, including countershading) and mimesis (disguising one thing as another, for example a gun turret as a tree).[3] By February 1915 he had assembled a small unit experimenting with camouflage technique, which became Scévola's Camouflage Corps by the autumn. The French cubist artist André Mare enlisted in that unit around this time, and was later joined by Jacques Villon, another cubist artist, and brother of Marcel Duchamp.[4] By identifying military technology with an experimental tradition stretching back to Cézanne, Stein and Picasso failed to register that younger avant-garde artists were already embroiled in the war effort. Within a matter of months, the next wave of European avant-garde artists would quite literally 'have created that' camouflage.[5]

In her strategic interplay of geography and syntax – avant-garde praxis and military manoeuvres – Stein uses the camouflaged cannon to comment on technology's capacity both to amplify the range of human abilities and to exploit our limitations. In the Machine Age, the prospect of reading machines, and their increasingly ambiguous role in culture, had become no more straightforward than reading people. Even modernist visionaries such as Picasso had difficulty seeing through the ways in which relationships between people and machines were being camouflaged – and indeed, the ways in which avant-gardes had helped 'create that' effect. He 'was spell-bound' by witnessing something he had foreseen (geometrical designs combined with recognisable objects, and the technicities of augmentation that encouraged such pairings) and something he had not (the military application of these designs). In this respect, Stein's praise for her friend also contains a carefully crafted critique. Although she applauds his 'foresight', she also draws attention to his technological servility. Swept up in his attempt to master his own sense of disorientation, Picasso himself is mastered by the spectacle, and becomes a witness-cum-creator unhinged by his uncanny encounter with a machine that he both recognises and is alienated by.

When Stein wrote her first account of the Boulevard Raspail scene in 1933, however, she had recently inspired, and been inspired by, a convergence between avant-garde art and technology taking shape in expatriate Paris – an exchange that resulted in a more affirmative relationship. The experimental poet, publisher, socialist exile and former stockbroker Bob Brown met Stein in 1929 as he was creating his 'reading machine'. Brown's invention was a mechanised speed-reading system that scrolled micrographically-printed text under a magnifying screen, which he promised would remake everyday acts of reading and writing in the modernist avant-gardes' own image, while simultaneously rendering their work more accessible to a broader reading public. In their first meetings, Brown told Stein how in 1915 (the same year she had witnessed the camouflaged military machines) her experimental writing inspired his invention by inducing a form of sensory overload in him. Brown connected that sensation to the side effects of working with communications technology all day. He felt compelled to use these technologies to transform the everyday act of reading with a new device – the reading machine – and, later, a new medium, the 'readies', a name that deliberately echoed the cinematic 'talkies' (premiered in 1928).[6] Brown's wife Rose (neé Watson) joined him in this endeavour, and their reading machine project reflected a relationship between aesthetic and technical innovation that was neither uncanny nor disorientating, but, rather, a deliberated attempt to recalibrate the human sensorium for the Machine Age.

Stein herself created a 'readie' for the infamous 1931 anthology *Readies for Bob Brown's Machine* (*RFBBM*), which featured Stein and other avant-garde luminaries such as F. T. Marinetti, Ezra Pound and William Carlos Williams, as well as numerous other lesser-known modernists' writing 'samples' for Brown's device. Previously confined to an eccentric footnote in *transition* magazine's 'Revolution of the Word', Brown's reading machine has now been recognised as a major and original (if controversial) convergence of mass culture and avant-garde experimentation – one of the legendary 'unfinished' prototypes of Machine Age modernism, which emerged out of the expatriate enclaves of France in the late 1920s and early 1930s, only to be written off by modernist studies as another casualty of the Great Depression. With only a blurry halftone photo on the flyleaf of the *RFBBM* anthology as evidence, a suspicion has also lingered in critical appraisals of the reading machine: did this device actually exist, and, if so, did it *really work*?[7] And, since it was probably an avant-garde stunt, does it actually matter either way? Drawing on evidence from archives at the University of California, Los Angeles, and Southern Illinois University, Carbondale, including the previously unknown and comparatively detailed photograph of the reading machine prototype featured on the cover of this book, my contention is not only that it *did*, and that it *does*, but that 'it' existed in multiple versions, with multiple co-creators. In this respect, the most fascinating part of the reading machine project has remained completely hidden to modernist studies for nearly a century. As the archives reveal, Brown's wife Rose solved the technical problems with the readies medium that had supposedly sunk the entire project. As well as restoring credit to an overlooked female writer-inventor, this book shows how she co-ordinated efforts to prototype a functional portable device, which the Browns took on a tour to Russia (and then across North and South America).

Interlocutors such as Stein and a legion of other writer-editors adopted the non-servile approaches to technology promoted by the Browns in transatlantic discourse networks, and the idea of machine-assisted reading was debated well past the Second World War. I return to the Browns' reading machines later in this introduction, but the central problem – the ambivalent relationship between avant-garde creative practice and technological innovation – remains. Why do we find it so hard to believe that avant-gardes 'created that'? What cultural narratives have camouflaged their technological interventions, confining them to a nebulous 'black box' of uncanny encounters between related but somehow incompatible fields of expertise?

These questions have many probable answers: the rise of Taylorism and the quasi-utopian values of efficiency, speed and 'functionalism' it expressed in culture;[8] professionalisation and specialisation; industrial and pedagogical apparatuses that discouraged multi-disciplinarity; the tendency to dismiss and overlook women's and ethnic minorities' technological interventions; and a general suspicion of 'amateurism' are all possible reasons why cultural critics are predisposed to distrust artist-led cross-disciplinary innovation. The present book engages with these issues at various points, but it begins by interrogating a prevailing set of assumptions about the socio-technical relations between human and non-human realities, which have been conditioned by specific cultural narratives since the rise of industrial modernity. As David Nye insists on the first page of his popular introduction to technology studies *Technology Matters*, 'Homo sapiens have used tools for at least 400,000 years and seem to have done so from their first emergence. Technologies are not foreign to "human nature" but inseparable from it.'[9] Laura Marcus locates a related sentiment in modernist work, in which 'technological modernity [. . .] did not represent a break with', but 'a continuum and synergy between nature and technology'.[10] Several generations of cultural commentators have re-articulated this point, which I think critics feel compelled to repeat, because Western culture has passively decoupled technics from art and other facets of everyday life over the past two centuries. The result has been that when these fields *do* intersect in a conspicuous way, the encounter appears uncanny, just as it does in Stein's anecdote about camouflaged military equipment.

This process of defamiliarisation has unfolded across a wide variety of cultural practices and narratives but is connected by a coherent and pervasive rhetorical framework that has reduced technology to an almost metaphysical presence in the West: the technological sublime. This framework posits that technology and technics, although attached to human culture, somehow exist beyond it, rather than expressing and defining it. As I will go on to argue, the rhetoric and narrative of the technological sublime – those 'experiences of awe and wonder, often tinged with an element of terror, which people have when confronted particular [. . .] technological achievements'[11] – are bound up in processes of occlusion and mystification. As a result, servile and uncanny relationships to technology, such as those Stein describes in her anecdote, have become standard features of everyday life in the West. As many studies explicitly or implicitly argue, modernism and the technological sublime are coeval phenomena, and together they tell an important story about technology in the Machine Age. It is, however, by no means the only story.

This book explores how avant-gardes probed the intricate relationships between socio-technical ensembles, the human body and the quotidian operations of urban living, which had been camouflaged by sublime cultural narratives that magnify the presence of technology in the public sphere while shrouding key aspects of its operations and functions. In it, I propose a techno-bathetic framework for analysing experimental artists' and writers' engagement with technology and culture. This major but hidden counter-narrative of the technological sublime emerged in the early twentieth century and was articulated most powerfully by the transatlantic avant-gardes. The bathos of technology resides in the messy particulars, the mundane negotiations and the unintended, even ridiculous, consequences of technology's transduction in culture. I use the term 'techno-bathetic' rather than 'technological bathetic' because unlike the sublime, which emphasises the immediate impact of monumental technical *objects* and ensembles bound up in the term 'technology', the bathetic emphasises the transductive *processes* that inhere in terms like 'technics' and 'technicity'. Drawing on this cultural framework, *Reading Machines in the Modernist Transatlantic* articulates several converging technicities that drew on techno-bathetic strategies, which vanguardists used to propose new, non-servile relationships to technology, within and beyond their creative practices.

As with any form of cultural production, technologies do not exist in a vacuum; on the contrary, they are coeval with their creators, users and environments. Accordingly, the stories we tell ourselves about technology condition every aspect of its transduction in culture. The cultural geographers Rob Kitchin and Martin Dodge explain that 'transduction' is a concept 'that understands the unfolding of everyday life as sets of practices that seek to solve ongoing relational problems', while 'technicity' is 'the power of technologies to help solve those problems'.[12] As Adrian Mackenzie notes, '[t]he hallmark of a transductive process is the intersection and knotting together of diverse realities', and it accounts for '*how* things become what they are rather than [explaining] *what* they are' (my emphasis).[13] In my study, I examine the nuts and bolts of those processes from the point of view of cultural vanguardists who included technological experimentation as part of their creative practices. The book explores how these avant-garde figures regularly intersected with fields of technical production, sometimes as artist-inventors, sometimes as tactical saboteurs and sometimes as part of their everyday work. Together, they re-engineered quotidian acts of communication, movement and design – especially those involving processes of reading, writing, perceiving and travelling – as tactical acts of resistance.

I propose three specific technicities in this book which vanguardists incorporated as part of their cultural projects: the first involves sensory augmentation, or the ways in which technology enhances and extends (but also distorts and renders vulnerable) the human sensorium; the second consists of bathetic ripostes to the technological sublime; and the third category takes place within the framework of Rayvon Fouché's model of 'black vernacular technological creativity', or the 'innovative engagements with technology based upon black aesthetics' that range 'from resistance to existing technology' to 'strategic appropriations of the material and symbolic power and energy of technology'.[14] The first and second chapters address sensory augmentation and the techno-bathetic respectively, while the fifth chapter addresses vernacular technicities. Chapters 3 and 4, on the Browns' reading machines, negotiate aspects of all three technicities, and fold them into the individuating spatial practices (tactical actions that create and express the spaces we inhabit) outlined by Michel de Certeau in *The Practice of Everyday Life*.[15]

Chapter 1 investigates the rapid evolution of sensory augmentation technology in the First World War, and avant-gardes' engagement with 'dazzle camouflage', within and beyond the arts. The analysis connects the writing and technicities of Marinetti and other Futurists with the infamous *intonarumori*, or 'noise intoner' machines of Luigi Russolo. It also explores similar strategies connecting technicities of sensory augmentation to avant-garde practice in the Vorticist writing of Wyndham Lewis, Jessica Dismorr and Helen Saunders; in Alvin Langdon Coburn's and Ezra Pound's camera apparatus 'the Vortoscope'; and in Edward Wadsworth's military and modernist 'dazzle painting'. The second chapter traces related technicities emerging on the other side of the Atlantic in the (proto-)Dadaists' attempts to recalibrate relationships between people and machines. However, it emphasises the bathetic technicities that vanguardists detected in America's fragile and unreliable machine ensembles. Exploring the multimodal works of Baroness Elsa von Freytag-Loringhoven, Francis Picabia, Marcel Duchamp and Williams, the chapter uncovers a previously unknown invention by Mina Loy – a thermoplastic she called 'verrovoile'. Together, these figures made a spectacle of the technologically commonplace to propose new, non-servile technicities that they located in the interstitial spaces of socio-technical ensembles.

Chapters 3 and 4 focus on Bob and Rose Brown's reading machines, and the multiple cultural formations that they co-ordinated to develop their prototypes from an avant-garde experiment into an instrument for mass social change. Providing a revisionist and object-orientated analysis of the Browns' project, these chapters challenge critical orthodoxies to reconsider the role of avant-gardes in the Machine Age. The Browns' proletarian class politics and Veblenist technicities articulate a sustained and dialogic engagement between modernist vanguards and mass culture. Developing the diachronic frame of these chapters, the fifth one focuses on African American vanguardists, including Langston Hughes, Gwendolyn Bennett, Ralph Ellison and Amiri Baraka. These writers joined the civil rights lawyer and writer Pauli Murray in recognising illegal rail travel and other appropriations of infrastructure as signifyin(g) spatial practices.[16] Building on research by sociologists, historians of technology and literary critics, the chapter explores how railroads became a signifyin(g) machine for the everyday technicities of black life throughout the twentieth century. The long-running cultural crises sparked by the Scottsboro trials encouraged African American avant-gardes to formulate a vernacular, counter-servile technicity that served as a hinge between rhetorical and spatial practice, which the book's Afterword develops with reference to Ralph Ellison's *Invisible Man*. Drawing on Ellison's sophisticated example, this final section discusses how avant-gardes critiqued the technicities by which hegemonies sustained cultural dominance, while simultaneously introducing alternative approaches. Those unique engagements with socio-technics began by stripping away the cultural camouflage that made a spectacle of technology while concealing key aspects of its social operations. Probing the intricate relationships between socio-technical ensembles, the human body and the quotidian dynamics of urban living, the techno-vanguardists I discuss in this book proposed new, non-servile ways of reading and doing technology in the transatlantic Machine Age.

Camouflaged Canon: How the Technological Sublime Came into Hiding

In his 1934 magnum opus *Technics and Civilization*, the 'Young American' critic Lewis Mumford observed that Western Europeans had imagined 'the "Machine Age"' before it existed; he maintained that '[t]echnics and civilization as a whole are the result of human choices and aptitudes and strivings, deliberate as well as unconscious, often irrational when apparently they are most objective and scientific: but even when they are uncontrollable they are not external'.[17] Like subsequent generations of critics, however, Mumford rejects this conceptual double-bind only to reinstate it, almost in the same breath: he asks, '[h]ow in fact could the machine take possession of European society until that society had, by an inner accommodation, surrendered to the machine?'[18] In his attempts to recalibrate public engagement with technology in the West, Mumford repeatedly configures technics, rhetorically and conceptually, precisely *as* an external force, that people either 'master', or are mastered by.[19] In doing so, he articulated a persistent quirk of narratives of the technological sublime, in which servile dialectics both define and conceal the nature of socio-technical relations in culture. The sheer scale of twentieth-century cities, and the accelerating pace of life within and beyond them, produced a grandiose spatio-temporal framework in which Kantian and Hegelian discourses of the sublime reflected the dynamic, geometric and social operations of technology.[20] By the early twentieth century, these servile technicities evolved in tandem with electrical, communications, transportation and other infrastructure technologies, which had inspired a wide range of cultural agents to consolidate the central tenets of the technological sublime without explicitly naming them.

As Nye reminds us, the term 'technological sublime' was introduced by Perry Miller and Leo Marx in the mid-1960s.[21] Leo Marx described how in the nineteenth century 'the awe and reverence once reserved for the Deity and later bestowed upon the visible landscape is directed toward technology or, rather, the technological conquest of matter'.[22] In fact, that connection was already embedded in language. Early definitions of 'machine' refer to a 'material or immaterial structure', and, in literature, a 'contrivance for the sake of effect' that was frequently 'a supernatural agency, personage, or incident' (*OED*). Rooted in the experience of 'natural grandeur' codified in Romanticism, and primed with an array of cultural resources for bridging metaphysical and physical realms, the sublime, as a concept, is neither difficult nor protracted – on the contrary, it is a phenomenon defined by its immediacy, accessibility and cultural traction. Conceptually, Edmund Burke formulated 'the sublime of the eighteenth century' as 'a permissible eruption of feeling that briefly overwhelmed reason only to be recontained by it'.[23] The source of that feeling is the subject's proximity to power. As one critic has phrased it, 'the sublime entailed a virtual substitution of self for world', which resulted in 'an incestuous twinning of nature back into the self, the NOT ME into the ME' that also mapped onto other aspects of the sublime.[24] Encountered through the senses, the sublime is a power relationship negotiated through the body, and it is bound up with social discourses including sexuality, gender, slavery and other socio-political dynamics. Although it a profoundly visual, material and embodied phenomenon, the technological sublime is also a textual creation; its cross-disciplinary appeal ensured that it became folded into socio-technical practices in virtually all aspects of transatlantic cultural development.

Extending the European Romantic tradition of Burke, Coleridge and others, American Transcendentalists and figures such as Henry Adams codified these encounters in the language of the natural sublime, while documenting the rise of 'the mechanic arts', which Ralph Waldo Emerson described as a Promethean enterprise.[25] As expressions of the natural sublime lost their grip on the public imagination in the nineteenth century, the new, technologically-inflected versions of the sublime began to coagulate in American culture. Using James Watt's double-acting steam engine as a metaphor, Leo Marx documents the inexorable sweep of this transatlantic 'double action', which by the 1840s, through dialogic means, penetrated both the heart of literary canons and political centres of power. From Melville's claim (adapted from a poem by Alexander Pope) that '[s]team is annihilating space', to John Stuart Mill's commentary on Alexis de Tocqueville's *Democracy in America*, figurations of the technological sublime progressed 'directly, imagistically, wordlessly' as a locomotive crossing a landscape.[26] The concept evolved in transatlantic discourse networks coevally with the structures it described, and became embedded in culture as surely as city planners' successive layers of infrastructure. In the Machine Age, engineers explicitly yoked the aesthetics of the technological sublime to monumental structures. As Cecilia Tichi explains, 'from bridges to skyscrapers and Ferris wheels', the 'machines and structures between the 1890s and the 1920s' give the observer 'immediate access to the construction, to the design decisions of the engineers and architects'. Cumulatively, this 'world of girders and gears invites the onlooker to see its internal workings' and 'its component parts', which underscore the sense that 'it is, in fact, an assembly' writ large.[27] Given that the technological sublime thrives on this sense of visibility, however, why does Stein's anecdote about camouflage and the technology of mechanised warfare resonate so powerfully? How does the discourse of concealment that she pinpoints so adroitly resonate with the obverse cultural emphasis on visibility?

The answer is that although the technological sublime is pronounced and immediate, its effects rely on complex, dialectical and drawn-out processes involving visibility and concealment. Through a 'peculiar double action of the imagination',[28] the more *visible* and pervasive technologies such as railways become, the more likely people are to absorb them into their lives, to the point that they become nearly *invisible* parts of daily routines (except, as Alex Goody points out, when things go wrong, such as in the case of train wrecks).[29] In the technological sublime especially, obverse relationships between these sorts of binaries proliferate; far from undermining their traction in culture, technologically sublime effects, when transduced into culture, actually *depend* on such dialectical tensions to function properly. And the reason why they do so is partly down to a Heideggerian process of repression and occlusion described by Malcom Bull as 'coming into hiding'.[30]

Bull uses Joseph Jastrow's famous 'duck-rabbit' illustration – an optical illusion where viewers can see either a duck's bill or a rabbit's ears, depending upon their perspective – to explain how 'one aspect' of a thing can '[disguise] the other', not *despite*, but precisely *because* both alternatives are visible.[31] Bull powerfully connects the process of 'coming into hiding' to the 'Master-Slave Dialectic' in African American literature,[32] with special reference to W. E. B. Du Bois's Hegelian principle of double consciousness, and 'the veil'.[33] One of Du Bois's key insights was to unpick the 'new form of separation in which the old division between master and slave, black and white, becomes an internal division in which one identity is always hidden'.[34] Tim Armstrong has in turn connected those same dialectics to the servile discourses of *technology*, which emerged in dialogue with cultural institutions in Antebellum America, including slavery.[35] These discourses inflect and express technicity at its most basic level, as master-slave dialectics entered technical literature in the nineteenth century to describe hydraulic systems.[36] Again: the stories we tell ourselves about technology shape technology, and vice versa. Like a camouflaged cannon entering a pedestrian zone, technology makes a sublime entrance, radically altering (and reflecting radical alterations) in the socio-technical contexts of the scene. People then incorporate those changes into their daily lives, without necessarily processing the nature of those changes. The technology remains visible, often strikingly so, but its technicity remains hidden. In such discourses, as Mumford (and in her more elliptical way, Stein) demonstrated, people tend to disarticulate technology from the matrix of choices, behaviours and power relations that transduce it in culture, and transform it into either a passive object or an overwhelming force – something either to master, or to be mastered by.

The 'black box' effect is a cultural phenomenon that is analogous to the rhetorical process of 'coming into hiding', and it describes the dialectical means by which technology is integrated into the fabric of everyday life to the point of near invisibility. It involves the active conversion of new, 'unfamiliar' and potentially 'threatening' technologies (for example, a diesel engine or a camera) into a 'stable' and generic 'black box, which can be taken for granted', or (in the case of the Kodak camera) even domesticated and marketed for children – but only through a combination of 'symbolic', 'practical' and 'cognitive work'.[37] Paradoxically, but entirely logically, the technical objects involved attract less attention by becoming more pervasive and 'visible'. Sociological researchers classify these processes as 'domestication', 'diffusion' and 'banalisation'; like Certeau, they do not view such acts as passive consumption, but rather as multiple (and sometimes quite sophisticated) acts of 'innovation', frequently requiring the negotiation of numerous socio-technical ensembles.[38] The complex materialities of a given technical object, such as a radio receiver, may well have appeared disruptive and sublime to early users, who were intrigued and alienated in equal measure as they adapted to its presence in their homes and neighbourhoods; however, habituation cloaked the object's intricacies, and for the user it became simply one black box among many, subsumed in the operations of everyday life.

Stein's intricate staging of the scene on Boulevard Raspail is a brilliant critique of the technological sublime and its cultural operations because it inverts the spatio-temporal effects the phenomenon normally relies on. Disruptive technology normally diffuses (or is camouflaged) in culture over a long period of time: in her anecdote, camouflage is the integral part of an *immediate* spectacle. By collapsing this temporal frame, which foregrounds and suspends Picasso's corresponding disorientation, she exposes the secret of the technological sublime's traction in culture: disruptive and monumental technological objects generate affective responses that suspend critical operations, and that suspension remains in place before their broader effects in culture can be properly appreciated. At that point, the technical objects have joined an ensemble – not by magic, but through processes of diffusion, such as the black box effect, which rely on and perpetuate the rhetoric and practice of techno-servility.

As I have argued, the technological sublime is by some distance the most powerful account of technology in Western culture because it dominates discourses in the public sphere without being named. Having come into hiding, the conceptual framework of the technological sublime underpins critics' complaints about techno-servility without being linked to processes of technicity or transduction. The problem, as Mackenzie points out, is that '[u]ntil we can think of technical objects, machines, [and] ensembles in their own terms, then their role in constituting who or what we are remains shrouded'.[39] In the following two sections, I propose two ways of bringing these objects, processes and relationships out of hiding. The first section triangulates key terms and contexts from recent studies of technology and culture engaging with the work of the French philosopher of technology Gilbert Simondon and applying them to modernist and avant-garde studies. The subsequent section builds techno-bathetic frameworks from those concepts to critique the means by which technology, and the technological sublime, are transduced into culture. In doing so, it outlines the means by which the vanguardists I explore in this study proposed new, counter-servile relationships to technology that exposed and critiqued habituated techno-servility, within and beyond creative practices.

Coming out of Hiding, Part 1: Coming to Terms with Socio-Technics

In his foundational 1958 study *Du mode d'existence des objets techniques* [*On the Mode of Existence of Technical Objects*], Simondon, like Mumford before him, identified an incoherent and unsustainable relationship with technology in Western culture.[40] With a curtly ironic polemic, Simondon stated that in the West, '[c]ulture has constituted itself as a defense system against technics', and 'behaves toward the technical object as man toward a stranger'. The machine is like a metal cipher 'in which something human is locked up, misunderstood, materialized, enslaved, and yet which nevertheless remains human all the same'.[41] As well as providing a classic formulation of the non-human Other, Simondon makes a parallel point about the absurdity of framing culture and technics dialectically. To do so, he argues, 'masks a reality rich in human efforts and natural forces, which constitutes a world of technical objects as mediators between man and nature'.⁴² If humanity accepted the view that technology must either enslave or liberate humanity, then it must also accept a reductive and debilitating binary that not only distorts its relation with the non-human world but also relations between social groups. Simondon's critique was motivated by the rise of cybernetics, a wide-ranging field of research focused on analysing communication, control and feedback mechanisms between humans, animals, machines and organisations pioneered by Norbert Wiener in the aftermath of the Second World War.⁴³ This new cross-disciplinary field held out the promise of recalibrating the ontological status of technical objects and systems in relation to their social contexts. Simondon acknowledged that cybernetics had 'the immense merit of being the first inductive study of technical objects'; however, in his view, cyberneticists were preoccupied with applying biological principles to technology, and vice versa, which meant that they were mainly interested in machines with feedback mechanisms, and in problems of classification.⁴⁴ They also proposed what Simondon believed was a rote equivalency, rather than a nuanced ontological parity, between human and non-human relations.⁴⁵ What Simondon proposed instead, as Henning Schmidgen notes, 'was a dynamic theory of technology, i.e. a theory that would grasp technological objects in their development and their relation to inner and outer milieus or *Umwelten*'.⁴⁶ *On the Mode of Existence of Technical Objects* (*METO*) set out the conceptual framework of that theory by means of detailed observation and polemical critique.

Simondon explained that,

> the most powerful cause of alienation in the contemporary world resides in this misunderstanding of the machine, which is not an alienation caused by the machine, but by the non-knowledge of its nature and its essence [. . .] and its omission from the table of values and concepts that make up culture.⁴⁷

Karl Marx famously located that sense of alienation in the fundamental inequalities that exist between socially stratified classes and ownership. Whereas Marx locates alienation 'at the level of relationships of production as an inextricable mixture of exploitation and domination', however, 'Simondon sees [alienation] in the inadequate relationships that humans, incapable of overcoming the dialectic of domination and submission, maintain with machines'. In her brilliant study of Simondon's philosophy, Muriel Combes argues that Simondon's analysis actually tacks closer to Marx than he admits, because 'Marx simply does not situate alienation in the same place that Simondon does'.⁴⁸ This qualification may not even go far enough, since Marx wrote in 1846 that '[t]he actual application of machines is one of the relationships of our current economic regime, but the mode of utilizing the machines is altogether different from the machines themselves', and that '[m]achinery is no more economic than the ox that pulls the plow'.⁴⁹ Nevertheless, Combes argues, Simondon had a more general, ontological understanding of technological alienation than Marx did, and there are important upshots of their different approaches.

Karl Marx anticipated the emphasis of cyberneticists by positing an equivalency between assemblages in the human and non-human world: put crudely, machines function like organisms, and vice versa. Simondon rejects this emphasis. Thomas LaMarre, a prominent Japanologist, media studies scholar and former biologist, is one of Simondon's most astute critics. LaMarre provides a crisp account of the ontological parity that Simondon's framework proposes:

> when Simondon writes that the role of humans is between machines, his refusal to introduce a dualist divide between humans and machines extends to other registers, such as the relation between mind and body – not only is there no substantialist opposition between mind and body, but there are no hierarchical distinctions between levels of intellectual activity: technical activity is on par not only with biological function, but also with scientific thinking. Rather than fall back on dubious hierarchical rankings and teleological development [. . .] Simondon generates operative analogies across these gradations of complexity, using parity to get at disparity.⁵⁰

LaMarre, like Combes, is alert to the potential pitfalls of Simondon's approach, however, which could seem like 'material determinism', or techno-utopianism, were it not for Simondon's rejection of the dialectical and inherently servile relations that such an emphasis would entail. Indeed, both Marx and Simondon agree that technophobia and technophilia are two sides of the same coin: both express techno-servility. As Amy Wendling argues, for Marx, '[m]achine fetishism is a product of technological alienation' where 'workers use means of production that seem to operate by mystical and occult properties'.⁵¹ Marx, like Simondon, does not explicitly identify technological alienation with the technological sublime, and neither do their critics (as we have seen, the term was coined in the mid-1960s); however, the signature dialectics of that concept suffuse their work – and characteristically for tropes of the technological sublime, they are present without being named.

Like Mumford, both Karl Marx and Simondon advocate a non-servile relationship with technology. For Marx, this meant 'demystify[ing]' the relationship between humans and machines so that 'the historical properties of human labor are [not] mistakenly perceived as belonging to machines themselves'.⁵² For Simondon, this process necessitated a new approach to, and vocabulary for, the ontological relationships between the human and non-human worlds bound up in socio-technics. His framework involves collective and interrelated, or 'transindividual', action to precipitate a 'non-servile relation to nature' and technics.[53] In *METO*, Simondon provides a means of recalibrating those relations. As Alberto Toscano phrases it, Simondon swaps dialectics for 'energetics', or a series of intellectual decouplings that reject dualism and hierarchies in favour of a more dynamic and reticulated set of relations.[54] Energetics involve individual and social interventions that initiate social transformation at the structural level. What emerges in Simondon's work is an emancipatory socio-technics predicated on mutual, energetic exchange rather than discourses of domination and exclusivity.

Modernist and avant-gardes studies have scarcely begun to get to grips with the implications of Simondon's work. However, his concepts and terminologies have entered literary studies indirectly through a range of theorists, including Gilles Deleuze, Félix Guattari, Bernard Stiegler and other poststructuralist thinkers. It is worth clarifying these terms as I apply them in the present study, however, because their meaning has become somewhat elastic as they have crossed disciplines. The sociologist Frank Geels has helpfully explained that in terms of their 'societal functions', technologies work like this:

> a range of elements are linked together to achieve functionality, for example, technology, regulation, user practices and markets, cultural meaning, infrastructure, maintenance networks and production systems. This cluster of elements is called a 'socio-technical' system, thus highlighting that social and technical aspects are strongly interlinked.[55]

Simondon's framework for understanding human and non-human interactions consists of what he calls 'elements', 'individuals' and 'ensembles', which are differentiated (and mediated) according to various modes of being and/or processes of becoming, and which operate in various 'milieus'. Elements are building blocks that can form (and mediate relationships between) individuals, and compose 'sets', which in turn comprise 'assemblages' and 'ensembles', depending on their determinants. As Yuk Hui explains, in this series of interrelations, the 'technical object' in ontological terms 'is a unity of relations' that has two forms: in a technical element, or 'infra-individual', such relations 'are limited to its internal operation'; by contrast, 'when it becomes an individual', a technical object 'extends its relation to an outer milieu and makes these relations an indispensable part of its identity'.[56] This process of 'concretisation', according to Simondon, helps turn 'a collection of organized individuals', which operate in a wider milieu, into an ensemble.[57]

Although distinct from a technical system, a 'milieu' is also systematic and constitutes 'a synthetic grouping of two or more levels of reality'.[58]

The 'assemblage' is a concept related to but distinctive from a milieu. 'Assemblages' are often used in the biological sciences to describe collections of species that interact in particular places over particular durations of time. In Simondon's work, the term describes clusters of site-specific practices germane to a particular culture. Lacking certain bonds of organisation found in a system, an 'assemblage' describes a 'network of relations and associations', broadly conceived, between collectives.[59] As Anne Sauvagnargues notes, the term 'assemblage sets in relation technical, social and natural forces and produces a mode of culture' that over time 'becomes a semiotic system'.[60] This chronological element is crucial: in order to become an 'ensemble', processes of concretisation triangulate such systems and practices across prolonged periods, to the extent that they become interdependent. Wolfgang Schivelbusch's classic example of a 'machine ensemble' is the railroad. This vast system of interconnected parts consisted of specific technical elements directly involved in transporting passengers ('wheel and rail, railroad and carriage'), but also the communications infrastructure (for example the 'telegraph system', which dramatically expanded its scale and capability in response to railways' development).[61] However, rail networks also rely on co-ordinated social ensembles to function, from socio-political and judicial systems (standardised time, regulations and codes of practice), to socio-economic ones, which co-ordinate the interests of groups of workers, users, managers, owners, operators and other interested parties.

As we have seen, technicity is an 'important kind of transduction' that 'pertains to technical objects', and situates them in 'a network of temporal and spatial relays', which express and shape societies.[62] In the transductive processes of machine culture, technology is the *what* and technicity is the *how*, and technical objects, ensembles and assemblages mediate and instantiate those processes of becoming (and, in the process, point us towards the *why*). Human individuals and collectives interact with technical ones to form socio-technical ensembles and assemblages. Machines operate at the intersections of these procedures and realities, and, of course, are inextricable from the social contexts that frame them, to the point that it can be difficult to identify where the technical context ends and the social context begins – and vice versa. However, these fine distinctions are less important than tracking their energetics accurately, especially at moments of accelerated cultural change. In this respect, the preceding terminology helps us triangulate the nature of socio-technical interventions so that we can better understand the stakes of those changes.

Critics and historians of technology have supplied crucial vocabularies and systems for assessing socio-technical change, and, each in their own way, attempt to break down the servile relationships with technology that cultures have transduced over time. In my view, the logic of the technological sublime has an instrumental and ongoing connection to techno-servility, which diffuses in culture not only through narratives but also through techncities that produce phenomena such as the black box effect. Simondon and his critics are clear about the sorts of narratives and procedures that should replace the dialectics of the sublime: they advocate relational, energetic and non-hierarchical engagements with socio-technics. However, they are less clear about why these counter-narratives have less traction than do prevailing ones. How, then, do we challenge the persistence of the technological sublime, and the servile relationships with technics that it engenders? What is needed in the first instance is an intermediate narrative – one that participates actively in the dialectics of the technological sublime while simultaneously unpicking its hierarchical and dialectical structures, and, as part of that work, signposting (or, better, still, *transducing*) energetic alternatives. My argument in this book is that transatlantic avant-gardes in the early twentieth century deployed techno-bathetic strategies which provide that framework. Their work constitutes a major but camouflaged counter-narrative that came into hiding in parallel with, but in the shadow of, the technological sublime. The vanguardists I analyse in this study developed their counter-servile strategies from liminal cultural zones,[63] operating on the periphery of more prominent cultural formations, such as the Naturalists, Pictorialists, Regionalists, Young Americans and High Modernists.

Coming out of Hiding, Part 2: Bathetic Technicities

The conceptual origins of the technological sublime are hardly new. As Leo Marx rightly notes, 'no stock phrase in the entire lexicon of progress appears more often than the "annihilation of space and time," borrowed from one of Alexander Pope's relatively obscure poems' ('Ye Gods! annihilate but space and time, / And make two lovers happy'). Remarkably, Pope's 'obscure' poem, which countless writers, from Melville to Marx, have used to describe 'the *sublimity* of technological progress' (my emphasis),[64] actually derives from Pope's foundational 1728 text on bathos – *Peri Bathous, Or the Art of Sinking in Poetry*.[65] A riposte to the third-century treatise by Longinus, *On the Sublime*, Pope's text articulated both a poetics of bathos and a rhetorical exegesis of processes Bull would later call 'coming into hiding'. *Peri Bathous* unpicks the dialectics of the sublime before satirising them with intricate demonstrations of rhetorical and figurative techniques that writers drew on to create sublime effects. However, Pope's central example is that a 'genuine writer of the *Profound* will take care never to *magnify* any object without *clouding* it at the same time'.[66] 'Ye Gods!', his final poem in *Peri Bathous*, illustrates this principle. In the poem, Pope presents 'a modest request' from 'two absent lovers' who are on a passionate quest to transcend their pain of prolonged separation. The hyperbole of their request is self-evident, but they cloak it by appealing to anonymous classical 'Gods', a non-denominational, amorphous and sublime metaphysical force.[67]

Pope's bathetic exegesis of sublime rhetoric provides a detailed blueprint for the work of uncomfortable revelation. Sara Crangle and Peter Nicholls call this painstaking process '"true" bathos'. They rightly point out that the 'usual understanding of bathos as an unintentional descent "from the sublime to the ridiculous"' ignores 'the huge investment of craft and energy' that Pope performs in bathetic critique.[68] Instead, true bathos 'deflates' the pretension involved in the 'art of the sublime' by 'unmasking' it as such. Part of that revelation draws the sublime 'into potentially disastrous complicity' with the 'bathetic facts of life', such 'work, the body, [and] the commonplace', which 'the coveted grand style strove to transcend'.[69] By making bathetic techniques complicit with the lofty reaches of the sublime, while simultaneously critiquing them as such, Pope's hyperbolic request to 'annihilate but space and time' supports, as well as critiques, sublime technicities. When new technologies began reducing temporal and spatial barriers to communication and transportation in the eighteenth and nineteenth centuries, they did not 'annihilate' the sense of longing that Pope identified in 'Ye Gods' – they merely channelled and re-mediated, and, also, diffused and '*cloud[ed]*', different versions of it.

Bathetic critique evolved tandem with the rhetoric of the sublime, but its practitioners had a clearly defined purpose. As Keston Sutherland reminds us, '[b]athos was, first of all, even in Pope's preconception of it, an instrument of public attack'. In addition, as a meta-linguistic 'instrument', the articulation and nature of that attack is *itself* subject to bathetic processes in 'an instance of the degeneracy it diagnoses'.[70] As an expression and embodiment of culture, technology, like language, is of course subject to the same bathetic procedures. Technology is a product of conscious and unconscious choices, and like language (or a choice) it must be *made*, whether by accident or design. Bathetic frameworks function equally well across both cultural praxes. Although Sutherland does not mention technology specifically in his analysis of bathos, his reading of (faulty) sight, (skewed) perspective and (mishandled) telescopes in Samuel

Beckett's *Endgame* suggests a basis for doing so. Beckett's point 'is that not only the glass itself, but also the sight through the glass, is a production. The manipulator of the perspective is the artificer of the object at the bottom of it.'[71] For Sutherland, bathetic rhetoric does not involve a *how*, but a *what* – not a *process*, but a *destination*. Once that's clear, then so too are the various articulations and diagnoses of the bathetic that we encounter in culture. Crangle's and Nicholls's formulation of 'true bathos' is a great help here, because it folds this bathetic destination into its journey. In the techno-bathetic, the *how* of technicity folds the *what* of technology into its processes of becoming. And like rhetorical bathos, bathetic technicity, in the sense that I use it, is tactical, and it was a strategy that proto-Dadaists such as Marcel Duchamp astutely deployed.

In 1911, Duchamp completed an early study for *Nude Descending a Staircase (No. 2)* entitled *Once More to This Star* (Fig. I.1), which was the third and final illustration for a series of studies of poems by the French Symbolist Jules Laforgue ('*Médiocrité*', '*Sieste éternelle*' and '*Encore à cet astre*'). The series foregrounds the literary foundations of Duchamp's modernist project, while also acknowledging Laforgue's address to the vernacular and the bathetic. '*Encore à cet astre*' nominally charts the gaze of a stargazer towards the heavens, but it quickly descends into an indictment of the quotidian, which rebounds back on the firmament. Laforgue addresses the sun in the language of the 'yellow' press, equating it with an aging blonde model, whose 'growing spots' consume it like 'warts' on '*Un vaste citron d'or*' ['a great gold lemon'].[72] Here, Laforgue encounters celestial light in unabashedly quotidian terms.[73] As Duchamp recognised, this bathetic turn in '*Encore à cet astre*' marked Laforgue's 'exit from Symbolism' and his pivot towards modernism.[74] Duchamp makes that shift central to *Once More to This Star*. In this sketch, Duchamp puns visually on Laforgue's poem, rendering it as an ambivalent climb up a staircase.[75] The legs (and possibly torso) of one geometrical figure face up the stairs while the head faces down, just like the disembodied sections of the second figure (lower body and head) on the left. Duchamp's bathetic *volte face* echoes Laforgue's deflation of the sublime, not with references to food or the body, but with domestic architecture, a mundane expression of spatial vernaculars ('[i]s there not', Pope asks, 'an architecture of vaults and cellars, as well as of lofty domes and pyramids?').[76] Duchamp's bathetic negotiations with Laforgue are crucial literary encounters that chart his shift from architectural subjects to the elaborate technical assemblages of *Coffee Mill, Sad Young Man on a Train, Nude Descending a Staircase, No. 1, Network of Stoppages* and his magnum opus, *The Bride Stripped Bare By Her Bachelors, Even* (aka *The Large Glass*). As

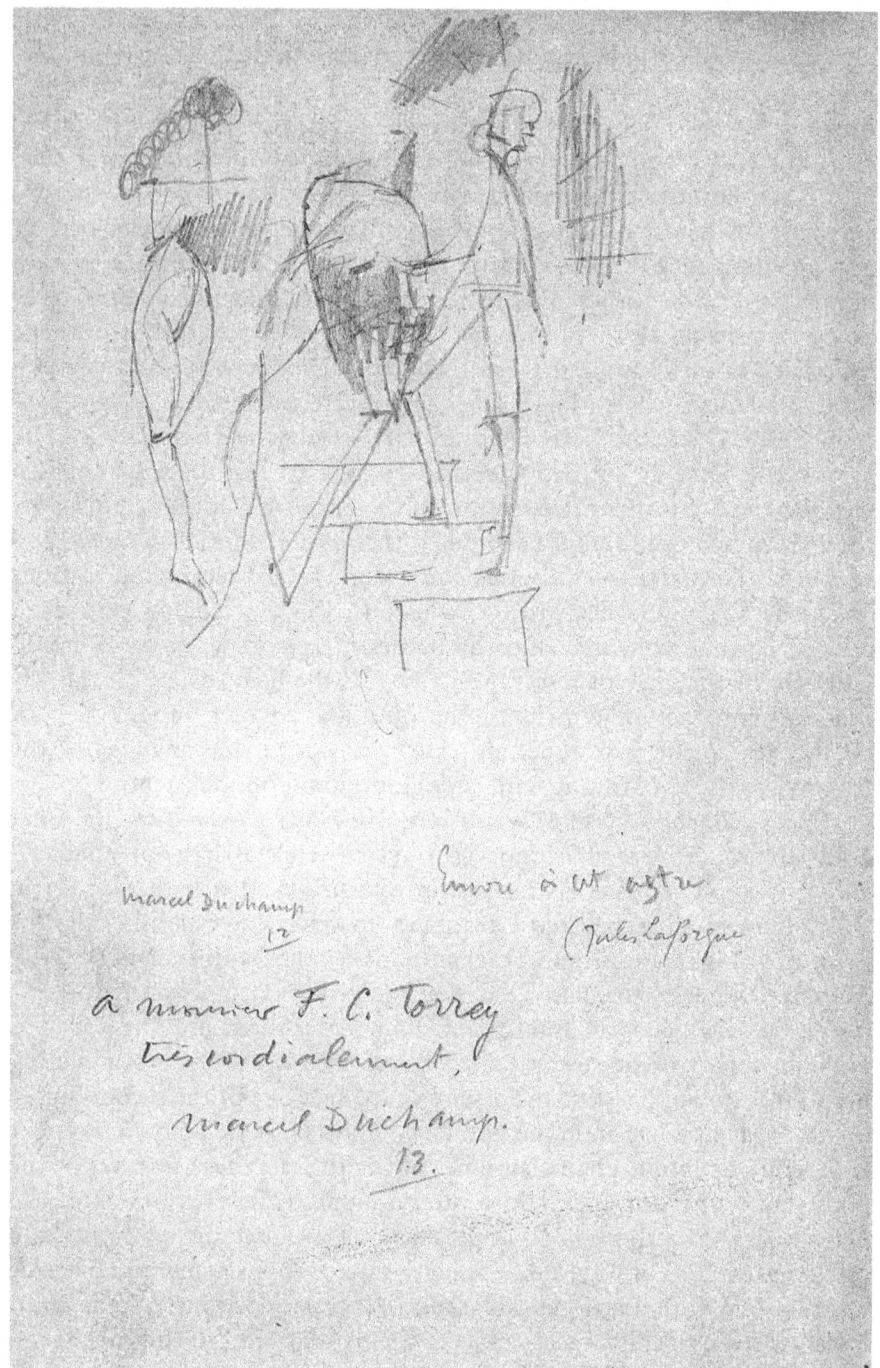

Fig I.1 Marcel Duchamp, *Encore à cet astre* [*Once More to This Star*], 1911, Graphite on beige wove paper; Philadelphia Museum of Art. *Source:* Copyright © Association Marcel Duchamp/ADAGP, Paris and DACS, London 2020.

meticulous schematics of the Machine Age everyday, these works, as I explain in this book, also consist of techno-bathetic analyses of the technological sublime, which Duchamp drew into complicity with the monumental technical objects of the period.

Whether a diagnostic or polemical exercise – a speculative experiment or deliberated strategy – bathetic technicity is a spatial practice that harnesses the semantic power of technology to critique its broader contexts. In 1926, African American vanguardists launched high-stakes critiques of American culture that drew on such practices in *Fire!!*, a self-consciously radical little magazine edited by the queer black modernist Wallace Thurman. Writers in this crucial journal identified valences of race, class, gender and sexuality in transportation and other infrastructure technologies, which they articulated through strategies of techno-signifyin(g) and black vernacular creativity. In 'Wedding Day', for example, Gwendolyn Bennett charts the misadventures of the African American musician and former boxer Paul Watson in Paris, who is left at the altar by Mary, a white American prostitute. While reflecting on this incident, 'the shrill whistle that is typical of the French subway pierced into his thoughts'.[77] In this transatlantic context, rail technology carries a powerful echo of segregationist infrastructure in America, which reveals the extent to which double consciousness became embedded in African Americans' everyday technicities.[78] Hurston's play, *Color Struck*, also reinforced the power of segregationist infrastructure in African American communities by beginning in a Jim Crow rail carriage and ending tragically in *'a one room shack in an alley'*.[79]

Nevertheless, *Fire!!* also explored the more affirmative possibilities of new voices that both crossed and reinforced such divisions. In its dénouement, Richard Bruce Nugent's impressionistic short story 'Smoke, Lilies and Jade' explores how rail technology – the subway and a fairground rollercoaster ride – mediates a bisexual ménage à trois. The characters explore the alternative connections and multiple, non-heteronormative identities made possible in the liminal zones of rail travel, which Nugent constantly evokes with the ellipses that he threads through his prose. As I discuss in Chapter 5, Langston Hughes's 'Railroad Avenue' also harnessed the affective power of disenfranchised black communities to transcend racist zoning laws by hot-wiring the body's circuits with discarded technology. Ralph Ellison later developed similar strategies in his fiction, and his techno-bathetic critique separates his protagonist from America's dominant sociotechnical narrative, before tentatively proposing another: the 'thinker tinker' Invisible Man, who re-imagines American socio-technics quite literally from the (under-)ground up.

Tacitly reinforcing the technological sublime as a normative model, generations of critics have railed against the servile dialectics, rhetoric and erotics that its transduction relies on, while largely ignoring its bathetic origins. Techno-bathetic praxes remain doubly obscured from critical attention, because they are the foil against which sublime tropes accumulate cultural visibility. It's not that sublime narratives explicitly avoid the realms of the bathetic – how could they, given their mutual dependence? It's that the transduction of the technological sublime subsumes the very function of its bathetic counterpart, which is to expose, critique and propose alternative technicities. Rather than a simple deflation of the sublime, then, a true technicity of the bathetic is a critical, tactical and ultimately reformative intervention in socio-technical realities. It is, above all, a counter-servile strategy that forces its practitioners to examine their own complicity in techno-servility. In this way, bathetic technicities require interlocutors to draw banalities, bodies and semi-functional assemblages into dialogue with technicities of the sublime. These operations involve the unpredictable side effects and novel possibilities afforded by specific technologies, and by the consilience of multiple ensembles, or the dissonance across multiple assemblages. Like Pope's satires, techno-bathetic praxes proliferate across generations, venerating the banal and the everyday, not as a means of suppressing the sublime but as an exposition of its fragile, embodied foundations – and potentially, as a method of clearing space for more energetic alternative narratives.

Conclusion: Avant-Garde Socio-Technics and the Everyday

Avant-gardes understood technology not only as a means of analysing and critiquing culture, but as a way of feeding back into it. As networked formations operating on the margins of culture, nevertheless, many of its members had strong contacts with epicentres of cultural activity within industry, education, government and other institutions. They belonged to several cultures of experiment, and multiple formations, which intersected on more occasions than we might suppose. Even so, avant-gardes who sought to reduce the distance between creative practice and everyday life using technology faced a major task in recalibrating debate about technology in the public sphere. As parasites and saboteurs, avant-gardes could become the spanner in the works that disrupted the conceptual fluency of Machine-Age culture; as early adopters and entrepreneurs, they could harness specific technical objects or ensembles for their own purposes, or speculate about possible future uses; as hackers and tinkerers, they could pick and choose between these options, while introducing others. By *reading machines* – as technical objects and 'hinges' that mediate complex cultural relationships – they could deploy technicity as a crucial method of intervening in cultural narratives and promulgating social change as a result.

In their interrelated creative practices, technical inventions and tactical interventions, Bob and Rose Brown, Marcel Duchamp, Ralph Ellison, Baroness Elsa von Freytag-Loringhoven, Langston Hughes, Mina Loy, Luigi Russolo and other figures I examine in this book deployed bathetic technicities to reshape what Certeau calls 'the machinery of representation' – the socio-technical assemblages 'by which a society represents itself in living beings and makes them its representations'.[80] For Certeau, 'tactics', or 'timely intervention[s]' in which 'swiftness of action can affect the organisation of space' and 'differential timescales or rhythms can be advantageous', are important ways of driving social critique.[81] On the one hand, 'the goal' of such interventions 'is to perceive the microbe-like operations proliferating within technocratic structures and deflecting their functioning by means of a multitude of "tactics" articulated in the details of everyday life'; on the other, it is to emphasise 'the clandestine forms taken by the dispersed, tactical and makeshift creativity of groups or individuals already caught in the nets of "discipline"'.[82] Like Simondon, Certeau accurately discerns the tactics by which socio-technical assemblages can be accessed and shaped by non-specialists. However, and also like Simondon, Certeau underestimates the capacity of specialist communities – including engineers and others involved in so-called 'technocratic structures' (including workers) – to undertake similar interventions. The avant-gardes seldom made these kinds of assumptions. In the Machine Age, points of slippage and intersection existed not only between artists and their audiences, but between other specialist collectives and their broader socio-technical assemblages.

When Stein, Picasso and their companions encountered the camouflaged military hardware in Boulevard Raspail in 1915, they stood on the cusp of a major cultural project. The advent of 'dazzle camouflage' in October 1917, in which the Vorticist artist Edward Wadsworth played a leading role, was a rare moment of convergence in which an artistic avant-garde took a leading role in the development of a military technology. By the end of the First World War, tens of thousands of women and men were employed in its design and implementation, and untold hundreds of thousands, perhaps millions, of square metres of equipment, land and people were camouflaged in various forms.[83] Countless lives depended on this new technology, which initially amounted to little more than marks on canvas. The far-reaching impacts of camouflage did not depend on the sophistication of the *materials* used in its fabrication, but on the sophistication of its design – on its *intervention* in the vast socio-technical ensemble of mechanised warfare, and the ways in which the human sensorium negotiated that network. The first chapter peers beneath the 'razzle dazzle' which has disguised and dismissed the rich technicities that emerged from the encounter.

Notes

1. Gertrude Stein, *The Autobiography of Alice B. Toklas*, in *Selected Writings of Gertrude Stein*, ed. Carl Van Vechten (New York: Random House, 1970), pp. 84–5.
2. Gertrude Stein, *Picasso* (Mineola, NY: Dover Publications, 1984 [1938]), p. 11. Eva Gouel died of cancer in December 1915, so the incident would have taken place between December 1914 and March 1915.
3. In America and Britain, the development of military camouflage drew on the work of the American artist and naturalist Abbott H. Thayer and British Professor of Zoology John Graham Kerr, but also from traditional hunting practices in a variety of countries, including 'Scottish deerstalkers known as "ghillies"'; Peter Forbes, *Dazzled and Deceived: Mimicry and Camouflage* (New Haven: Yale University Press, 2011), pp. 85–7, p. 105.
4. Ibid. p. 105. Villon survived, but Duchamp's elder brother, Raymond Duchamp-Villon, was killed.
5. For example, on the British Vorticist sculptor Leon Underwood and German Expressionist artist Frank Marc's involvement in military camouflage, see Patrick Deer, *Culture in Camouflage: War, Empire, and Modern British Literature* (Oxford: Oxford University Press, 2009), p. 44.
6. See Bob Brown, 'Notes for the Life of an American Writer', *Berkeley: A Journal of Modern Culture* 10 (1950): 1–4, 7.
7. See Michael North, *Camera Works* (Oxford: Oxford University Press, 2005), p. 75.
8. See Cecilia Tichi, *Shifting Gears: Technology, Literature, Culture in Modernist America* (Chapel Hill and London: University of North Carolina Press, 1987), p. 78.
9. David Nye, *Technology Matters: Questions to Live With* (Cambridge, MA and London: The MIT Press, 2006), p. 2.
10. Laura Marcus, *The Tenth Muse: Writing About Cinema in the Modernist Period* (Oxford: Oxford University Press, 2007), pp. 214–15.
11. David Nye, *The American Technological Sublime* (Cambridge, MA, and London: The MIT Press, 1994), p. xvi.
12. Rob Kitchin and Martin Dodge, 'Rethinking Maps', *Progress in Human Geography* 31.3 (2007): 331–44 (p. 335).
13. Adrian Mackenzie, *Transductions: Bodies and Machines at Speed* (London: Continuum, 2002), p. 16.
14. Rayvon Fouché, 'Say It Loud, I'm Black and I'm Proud: African Americans, American Artifactual Culture, and Black Vernacular Technological Creativity', *American Quarterly*, 58.3 (September 2006): 639–61 (pp. 639–41).

15. Certeau, *PEL*, pp. 96, 103–10, 115–18.
16. As Henry Louis Gates, Jr. explains, signifyin(g) is a rhetorical and literary strategy deployed by the 'Black Other' that enacts 'chiastic fantasies of reversal of power relationships'; *The Signifying Monkey: A Theory of African-American Literary Criticism* (New York and Oxford: Oxford University Press, 1988), p. 85.
17. Lewis Mumford, *Technics and Civilization* (New York: Harcourt Brace, 1934), p. 6.
18. Ibid. pp. 3–4.
19. Ibid. pp. 6–7.
20. Nye draws on Kant's conception of the 'mathematical sublime (the encounter with extreme magnitude and vastness, such as the view from a mountain), and the dynamic sublime (the contemplation of scenes that arouse terror, such as a volcanic eruption or a tempest at sea)', in his formulation of the technological sublime; *American Technological Sublime*, p. 7.
21. Ibid. p. xv. See Perry Miller, *The Life of the Mind in America: From the Revolution to the Civil War* (New York: Harcourt, Brace & World, Inc., 1965).
22. Leo Marx, *The Machine in the Garden: Technology and the Pastoral Ideal in America* (New York: Oxford University Press, 2000 [1964]), p. 197.
23. Nye, *American Technological Sublime*, pp. 4–5.
24. Bryan Wolf, 'When Is a Painting Most Like a Whale? Ishmael, Moby Dick, and the Sublime', in *New Essays on Moby Dick*, ed. R. H. Brodhead (Cambridge: Cambridge University Press, 1986), pp. 141–80 (p. 155).
25. Marx, *The Machine in the Garden*, p. 192.
26. Ibid.
27. Cecilia Tichi, *Shifting Gears: Technology, Literature, Culture in Modernist America* (Chapel Hill and London: University of North Carolina Press, 1987), p. 4.
28. Nye, *American Technological Sublime*, p. 37.
29. See Alex Goody, *Technology, Literature and Culture* (Cambridge: Polity Press, 2011), pp. 4–5.
30. Malcolm Bull, *Seeing Things Hidden: Apocalypse, Vision and Totality* (London: Verso, 1999), p. 26.
31. Ibid. p. 21.
32. Ibid. pp. 216–17.
33. W. E. B. Du Bois, *The Souls of Black Folk*, ed. Brent Hayes Edwards (Oxford: Oxford University Press, 2007), pp. 8, 11.
34. Bull, *Seeing Things Hidden*, p. 248.
35. Tim Armstrong, *The Logic of Slavery: Debt, Technology, and Pain in American Literature* (Cambridge: Cambridge University Press, 2012), pp. 1–2, 197.
36. See for example James T. White, *The National Cyclopaedia of American Biography*, vol. 55 (New York: James T. White & Co., 1974), p. 240, and Ron Eglash, 'Broken Metaphor: The Master-Slave Analogy in Technical Literature', *Technology and Culture* 48.2 (April 2007): 360–9 (p. 364).

37. Frank W. Geels, *Technological Transitions and System Innovations: A Co-Evolutionary and Socio-Technical Analysis* (Cheltenham: Edward Elgar Publishing, 2005), pp. 47, 51.
38. Ibid. pp. 51–2.
39. Mackenzie, *Transductions*, p. 3.
40. Simondon, *METO*, p. 51.
41. Ibid. pp. 15–16.
42. Ibid. p. 15.
43. See Norbert Wiener, *Cybernetics: Or Control and Communication in the Animal and the Machine* (Cambridge, MA: The MIT Press, 1948).
44. *METO*, p. 51.
45. Ibid. pp. 119–21.
46. Henning Schmidgen, 'Thinking Technological and Biological Beings: Gilbert Simondon's Philosophy of Machines', Revista do Departamento de Psicologia, UFF 17.2 (2005): 11–18 (p. 12).
47. Ibid. p. 16.
48. Muriel Combes, *Gilbert Simondon and the Philosophy of the Transindividual*, trans. with a preface and afterword by Thomas LaMarre (Cambridge, MA and London: The MIT Press, 2013), p. 74. I cite this text as *Transindividual* hereafter.
49. Karl Marx to Pierre-Joseph Proudhon, 28 December 1964, in Karl Marx, *The Letters of Karl Marx*, ed. Saul Kussiel Padover (Eagle Cliffs, NJ: Prentice Hall, 1979), p. 48.
50. Thomas LaMarre, 'Humans and Machines', *Inflexions* 5 (March 2012): 29–67 (p. 33).
51. Amy E. Wendling, *Karl Marx on Technology and Alienation* (Basingstoke and New York: Palgrave Macmillan, 2009), p. 57.
52. Ibid. p. 204.
53. Muriel Combes, *Transindividual*, p. 77.
54. Alberto Toscano, 'The Disparate: Ontology and Politics in Simondon', *Pli: The Warwick Journal of Philosophy Special Volume – Deleuze and Simondon* (2012): 107–17.
55. Frank W. Geels, *Technological Transitions*, p. 1.
56. Yuk Hui, *On the Existence of Digital Objects* (Minneapolis: University of Minnesota Press, 2016), p. 14.
57. *METO*, p. 63.
58. Gilbert Simondon, *L'individuation à la lumière des notions de forme et d'information* (Grenoble: Éditions Jérôme Millon, 2005), p. 30.
59. Yuk Hui, *On the Existence of Digital Objects*, p. 58.
60. Anne Sauvagnargues, *Art Machines: Deleuze, Guattari, Simondon*, preface and trans. Suzanne Verberder and Eugene W. Holland (Edinburgh: Edinburgh University Press, 2016), p. 83 (note 44).
61. Wolfgang Schivelbusch, *The Railway Journey: The Industrialization and Perception of Time and Space in the 19th Century* (Berkeley and Los Angeles, University of California Press, 1986), p. 29.

62. Mackenzie, *Transductions*, pp. 16, 19.
63. Avant-garde figures who included technologies and technicities in their experimentation – for example, Raoul Hausmann, László Moholy-Nagy, Bruno Munari and others – also engaged with facets of the techno-bathetic, as did numerous individual modernists and modernist formations, but they are beyond the scope of the present book.
64. Marx, *The Machine in the Garden*, p. 194.
65. Alexander Pope, *Peri Bathous: Or, Martinus Scriblerus, His Treatise of the Art of Sinking in Poetry*, in *Alexander Pope: The Major Works*, ed. Pat Rogers (New York: Oxford University Press, 1993), pp. 195–238 (p. 219).
66. Ibid. p. 218.
67. Ibid. p. 219.
68. Sara Crangle and Peter Nicholls, 'Introduction', in *On Bathos: Literature, Art, Music*, ed. Sara Crangle and Peter Nicholls (Cambridge: Continuum, 2010), pp. 1–6 (p. 2).
69. Ibid. p. 4.
70. Keston Sutherland, 'What Is Bathos?', in *On Bathos*, pp. 7–26 (p. 13).
71. Ibid. p. 16.
72. Jules Laforgue, '*Encore à cet astre* (Another for the Sun)', trans. Lawrence D. Steefel, Jr. in 'Marcel Duchamp's "Encore à cet Astre": A New Look', *Art Journal* 36.1 (Autumn 1976): 23–30 (p. 29, note 9).
73. Crangle and Nicholls, 'Introduction', in *On Bathos*, pp. 1, 5.
74. Marcel Duchamp and Pierre Cabanne, *Dialogues With Marcel Duchamp*, trans. Ron Padgett (London: Thames and Hudson, 1971), p. 30.
75. See Marcel Duchamp, *Once More to This Star*, in *MDComplete Works*, pp. 555–6.
76. Pope, *Peri Bathous*, p. 199.
77. Gwendolyn Bennett, 'Wedding Day', *Fire!!* 1.1 (November 1926): 25–8 (p. 28).
78. See Eric B. White, *Transatlantic Avant-Gardes: Little Magazines and Localist Modernism* (Edinburgh: Edinburgh University Press, 2013), pp. 165–71.
79. Zora Neale Hurston, *Color Struck*, *Fire!!* 1.1 (November 1926): 7–14 (p. 12).
80. *PEL*, p. 147.
81. Michael Sheringham, *Everyday Life: Theories and Practices from Surrealism to the Present* (Oxford: Oxford University Press, 2009), p. 216.
82. *PEL*, pp. xiv–xv.
83. Deer, *Culture in Camouflage*, pp. 44–5.

Chapter 1

Dazzling Technologies: Avant-Gardes and Sensory Augmentation in the First World War

Introduction

In the First World War, battlefields became zones of technological experimentation. The innovations that engineers developed to address the reality of total war helped armed forces produce carnage on previously unimaginable scales. However, those inventions also influenced and derived from technological developments across a wide variety of disciplines, which shaped everyday life and conceptions of modernity. The introduction of 'dazzle camouflage' by the British Admiralty in October 1917 marked one such invention. Devised by the British painter and naval officer Norman Wilkinson, and implemented by teams of artists, military personnel and at least one member of the London Vorticist movement, 'dazzle painting' was designed to protect military and commercial ships from German U-boat attacks. Rather than attempting the 'impossible' feat of hiding a vessel against the sky and sea, dazzle patterns consisted of starkly contrasting geometric shapes and shades applied strategically to key areas of a ship in order to deceive the enemy rather than to disguise the vessel. Viewed through a periscope, the design could 'break up' a ship's 'form and thus confuse a submarine officer as to the course of a ship', thereby limiting the chance of a successful attack by disrupting the targeting calculations that U-boat crews had only a short time to complete.[1] Wilkinson's illustration for the 1922 *Encyclopaedia Britannica* entry on naval camouflage illustrates how 'violently contrasting' dazzle patterns interfered with 'the laws of perspective', 'making it extremely difficult to judge the accurate inclination of a vessel even at a short range' (Fig. 1.1).[2] In short, although enemies were more likely to notice a dazzle ship, they would be less likely to hit it with their one of their torpedoes.

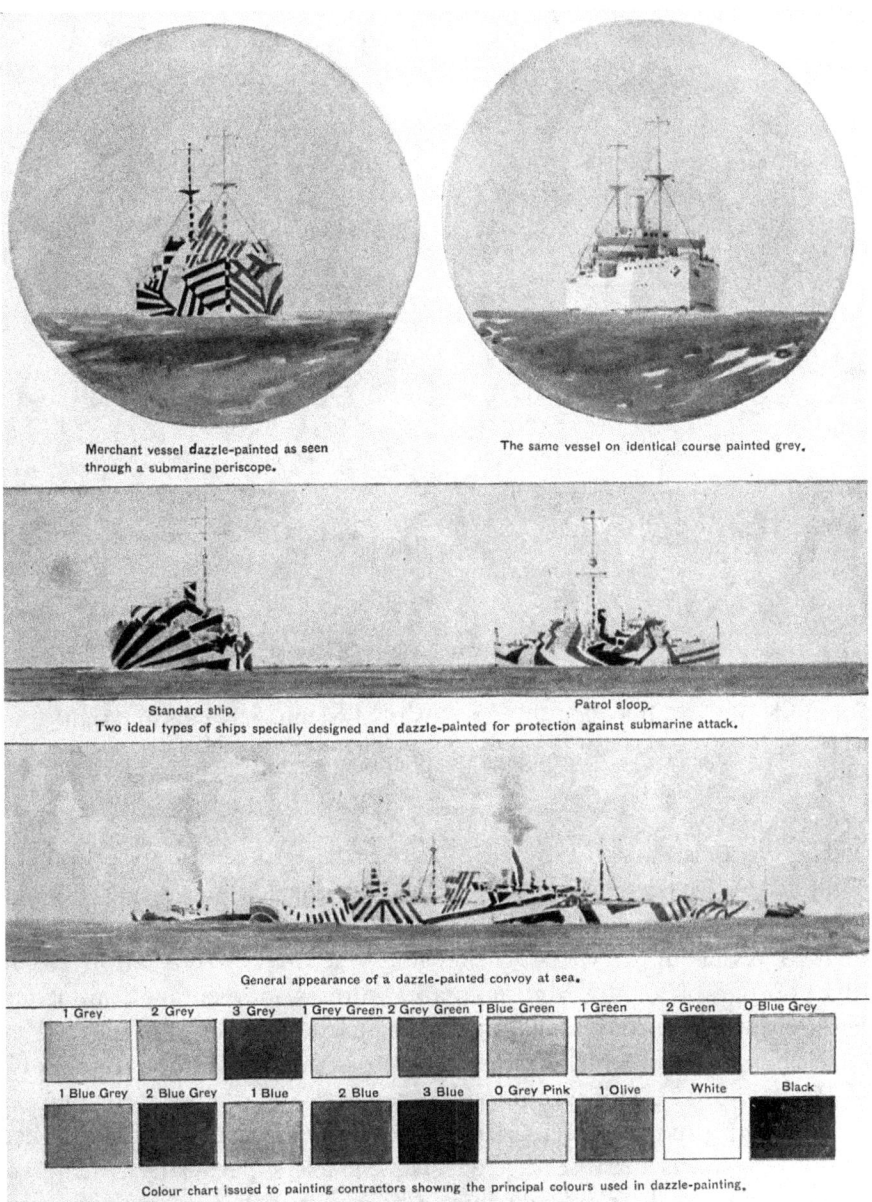

Figure 1.1 Norman Wilkinson, *Plate III* [Dazzle Painted Vessels], illustrates Norman Wilkinson, 'Naval Camouflage', in James Cecil Mottram et al., 'Camouflage', *Encyclopædia Britannica: The New Volumes, Twelfth Edition, Vol. 30* (London and New York: The Encyclopaedia Britannica Company, 1922), pp. 541–57 (pp. 546–7).

Figure 1.2 Symonds & Co., *H. M. S. Mauretania, dazzle-painted*; Symonds & Co. Collection, Imperial War Museum. *Source:* Copyright © IWM (Q 21493).

The Vorticist artist Edward Wadsworth worked as an officer in Wilkinson's Dazzle Section supervising the dazzle painting of ships at Liverpool docks, including the RMS *Mauretania*, one of the fastest commercial vessels in the world at the time.[3] Pictured setting sail in 1918, this photograph of the Mauretania captures a momentary confluence between military, commercial and avant-garde activity that resulted in dazzle camouflage, which first blazed across the world stage from 1917 to 1919 (Fig. 1.2). This technology served as a vital military propaganda tool that captured the imaginations of naval personnel and civilians alike, in many respects because the 'dazzled' vessels superficially resembled avant-garde visual art produced by Cubists, Futurists and Vorticists. For example, one journalist described these vessels as 'floating cubist paintings' and 'a futurist's bad dream'.[4] Playing on avant-gardes' growing reputation for staging cultural stunts, such comparisons encouraged the general post-war opinion that dazzle camouflage may have been a confidence trick played out on a mass scale.[5] However, this was an opinion that the avant-garde figures with knowledge of its production knew to be incorrect (Eastman Kodak Research Laboratories went on to validate the technology in the late 1920s and early 1930s).[6] The interdisciplinary networks which brought this widely-used and (as it turns out) bona fide technology into being have a rich life embedded within and across various cultural formations, before and after the creation of the Admiralty Dazzle Section. My argument in this chapter diverges from most art historical accounts in that it does not treat the similarities between dazzle camouflage and avant-garde art as superficial or coincidental.[7] Rather than claiming a greater instrumental role for avant-gardes in the development of dazzle camouflage – a role which has already been well documented – this chapter explores their centrality to an emergent technicity of sensory augmentation, for which dazzle designs serve as a crucial metonym.

As I discussed in the book's Introduction, the term 'technicity' explains how technology expresses human culture and its relationship to the non-human world. It describes how 'technologies mediate, supplement, and augment collective life' and 'are fundamental to the constitution and grounding of human endeavour', rather than somehow being distinct from it.[8] And as Adrian Mackenzie has argued, technicity situates individual 'technical objects' in 'a network of temporal and spatial relays' that express and shape societies.[9] Dazzle camouflage is a particularly useful example of this 'relay' in action: it can only perform its function as a technical object, i.e. achieve 'course-deception' effects,[10] when *another* technical object, i.e. the enemy's periscope, is in use. In other words, as one military historian has noted, dazzle camouflage was among a host of counter-surveillance initiatives designed 'to fool a glass eye'.[11] These kinds of innovations were based first and foremost on the manipulation of sensory augmentation, imaging and communications technologies used in the hyper-mediated theatres of combat of the First World War.[12]

Sensory augmentation describes the process by which technologies extend, assist or enhance a 'functional' human sensorium, or compensate for limitations or damage to that system.[13] Those augmentations usually involve the controlled distortion of sensory data. For example, periscope lenses bend and amplify light to magnify objects in the field of vision when adjusted correctly – adjusted incorrectly, they distort the field of vision and make those objects indistinct. By contrast, camouflage performs in an opposing way, concealing the intended object from view by disrupting visual pattern recognition. Dazzle camouflage is unique, though, because it is not actually camouflage; as Wilkinson explained, dazzle patterns did not conceal potential targets but attacked the enemy's ability to enhance their senses by overwhelming and confusing them. However, the military applications of sensory augmentation technicities represent only one form of their transduction in culture.

This chapter argues that avant-gardes also deployed dazzle strategies in their creative and spatial practices, which included art, writing and artist-built machines. It explores how the extreme contrasts and geometries which generate the visual logic of dazzle camouflage are analogous to the distorted spatio-temporal fields created by advances in transportation and communications technologies, which emerged as modernism's first movements – and the global conflict of the First World War – took shape. Focusing on the Florentine journal *Lacerba* and the Vorticist magazine *Blast* (and especially its 'War Number'), the first part of the chapter identifies literary networks that explored and exploited technicities of sensory augmentation. In particular it shows how the Futurists F. T. Marinetti, Armando Mazza, Alberto Viviani, Ardengo Soffici and Carlo Carrà, and the Vorticists Wyndham Lewis, Jessica Dismorr and Helen Saunders, developed their 'dazzle poetics' to analyse, critique and exploit the sensory overload that Machine Age socio-technical relations could induce. The second part of the chapter focuses on avant-garde art and performance, and addresses 'dazzle technologies' produced by avant-gardes and the military. It identifies convergences between Luigi Russolo's *intonarumori* (or 'noise intoner' musical performance machines) and Alvin Langdon Coburn's and Ezra Pound's 'Vortoscope' (a reflective apparatus that produced multiple and fragmented photographic images), and it offers new perspectives on their prescient manipulation of sensory augmentation ensembles. The chapter concludes with an analysis of Edward Wadsworth's role in the development of dazzle technicity and the production of dazzle camouflage.

Across the work of these avant-gardes, the crucial role that technicity played was not to annihilate or *transcend* the self, but to *augment* it – not to *escape* the increasingly militarised and commercialised public sphere, but (by making the self multiple, elusive and resilient, embedded in and reconfigured by the technologies transforming everyday life) to *adapt* that self for survival. This tactical spatial practice is the essence of dazzle poetics, and the technicities they express, where the 'razzle dazzle' of technology does not gesture towards the transcendence of quotidian experience but, rather, signals technology's centrality both to everyday life and the unreal experience of total war. As their preoccupations with timing, value and selfhood reveal, Futurists and Vorticists continually refined the relationship between this augmented self and the technicities that were spawned by their guerrilla incursions into military, commercial and political zones.

'Contradictory Magnetisms': Futurist Technicities and the Advent of War

Widely remembered as the first 'mass Avant-garde', Futurism assailed popular imaginations across Europe with a level of coherency that is astonishing given the movement's variety and sources.[14] One common ambition central to Futurist aesthetics was the movement's attempt to schematise the rapidly shrinking distances between various populations and geographical centres in the industrialised world as technology and engineering feats made travel and communications ever more rapid. The militaristic aggression and proto-fascism that emerged alongside this emphasis on speed in Futurist work is well documented. Nevertheless, embedded in some Futurists' need for speed was a sophisticated engagement with the technologies and the historical contexts that fuelled it.[15] For example, in his manifesto 'Destruction of Syntax – Wireless Imagination – Words-in-Freedom', F. T. Marinetti described how 'the earth [had been] shrunk by speed'.[16] Cultural geographers call this phenomenon 'time-space compression', in which technologies dramatically reduce 'spatial barriers' to communication, transport, commercial, military and other interactions.[17] Citing Marinetti's and Le Corbusier's responses to the advent of the aeroplane, however, Dorthe Gert Simonsen observes that 'alternating discursive strategies linking flight, speed and modernity', on the one hand, and the 'flying machine's stabilising [and unifying] effects' on perception, on the other, means that the standard 'time-space compression narrative' is too reductive to capture the full range of technology's impacts on cultural experiences of time and space. Technological infrastructures can speed up, or compress, communications and travel times, but recording technologies can artificially distend the duration of those experiences, with techniques such as 'slow motion' and backwards film effects. I agree with Simonsen's general argument, but I think that Futurists such as Marinetti actually captured a more nuanced range of spatio-temporal phenomena than they are usually given credit for. Like Le Corbusier, many Futurist writers explored instances in which experiences of time and space fluctuate dynamically, and energetically, according to the technology (and/or technicity) under discussion.[18] While Futurist artists such as Umberto Boccioni and especially Giacomo Balla in his *Dynamism* series of paintings had codified such experiences visually, Marinetti was among the first writers to explore fully the perceptual repercussions of what might more accurately be called time-space *flux*. This phenomenon describes the rapid fluctuation between spatio-temporal scales within a particular frame of reference. Futurist writers often performed such oscillations poetically, shifting unpredictably between spatial and temporal fields to create the sorts of disorientating effects essential to dazzle phenomena.

The Futurist manifesto form pioneered by Marinetti provided the crucial schematics of dazzle poetics. In his 1909 screed 'The Founding and Manifesto of Futurism', Marinetti and his colleagues burst from the confines of a bourgeois home into the competitive, liberating zones of streets and roads at a breakneck speed – or so the story goes. In fact, the time-space dynamics and cultural energetics at play in this foundation narrative are a little more subtle than that, since its crucial moment is not the protagonist's heroic departure from the domestic sphere but an unexpected car crash and its aftermath. Marinetti is cut off by two cyclists, 'wobbling like two lines of reasoning, equally persuasive and yet contradictory', which I think signals a more complex, dialectical and self-critical form of Futurist logic at work within the polemical argument.[19] In response, Marinetti continues, 'I spun my car around as frantically as a dog trying to bite its own tail', before careening into a ditch.[20] In the aftermath of the crash, he is rescued by a crowd of onlookers and '[t]he car slowly emerged from the ditch, leaving behind in the depths its heavy chassis'.[21] The death and rebirth central to the Futurist foundation myth takes place in this distended spatio-temporal field, which playfully undercuts the linear thrust of the narrative and the orderly experience of space-time. In the pre-war context, Marinetti's emphasis on the spectacle of potential catastrophe, and on the unintended consequences of a particular course of action, often get lost in his militaristic rhetoric.

Marinetti extended these dialectical tactics in his subsequent pronouncements. His 1912 'Technical Manifesto of Futurist Literature' begins 'astride the fuel tank of an airplane [. . .] two hundred meters above the powerful smokestacks of Milan', and, perhaps as a pay-off for its extensive lists of grammatical and syntactical prescriptions, ends with a wild-eyed promise to use these precepts as the basis for a cyborg-style future that will allow humanity to escape death.[22] The crucial imaginative leap that encouraged this proclamation was that 'aerial speed has multiplied our experience of the world', and, as a result, 'perception by analogy is becoming more natural for man'.[23] In this and other manifestos, Marinetti's dissenting technophilia lurches between a technological sublime – that sense of awe, wonder and terror which technology both provokes and codifies, especially in its relationship to landscape[24] – and a technological bathetic, which, as I explained in the book's Introduction, is a critical response grounded in technology's increasing banality, accessibility and, occasionally, ridiculousness. He reached a similar conclusion in his 1911 tract 'Multiplied Man and the Reign of the Machine', which described 'the imminent and inevitable identification of man and motor, facilitating and perfecting a continual interchange of intuitions, rhythms, instincts, and metallic disciplines'.[25] This anticipated his claim in 1913 that 'the cord of velocity stretched between *contradictory magnetisms*' could produce '*[m]ultiple* and simultaneous states of mind within the same individual' (my emphases).[26] In aggregate, Marinetti's barrages of jargon-heavy hyperbole and frequent attempts to disrupt readers' orderly experience of space-time create the basis for a new Futurist imaginary while attempting to mask the sleights of hand and magical thinking at its core.[27] The external sites of that imaginary, and the dialectical manoeuvres that defined it, allowed Marinetti and other Futurists to add further dazzle to this rhetorical camouflage.

Like the Vorticists, Marinetti and his associates traced out problematic new relationships between the artist, the marketplace, the sexes and a burgeoning military-industrial complex, all of which were framed by a context of time-space flux and a glittering array of technologies and consumer goods. This matrix of preoccupations formed the unstable foundations for Futurist dazzle poetics. Examples of these tactics can be found across a range of Milanese and Florentine Futurist poems, but one of the best examples is '*Transatlantico*', a poem by a Milanese disciple of Marinetti, Armando Mazza. This poem plots a rhapsodic journey in an ocean liner from Cherbourg to New York City using Marinetti's manifesto-driven co-ordinates to induce a kind of synaesthesia in the speaker. The dazzle of a heated sexual-consumerist binge in the ship's dance hall ends in a spluttering combustion of flame and ash, 'syncopated / sparkling musty with joy', until 'slices of the dawning sun dissect / your nudity' and 'the smoking candelabra slowly fizzes out'.[28] Although the motion here is restless, as though Mazza is recreating an angular futurist painting, like certain Marinetti manifestos, that movement is neither constant nor constantly accelerating, but, rather, pitching between temporalities. What's more, Mazza invokes a diachronic sense of technicity: his reference to 'antimony' (a metal used for centuries in the manufacture of both eye make-up and moveable type)[29] and 'iridium' (an extremely strong and reflective metal used in the manufacture of high-end pen nibs) creates a dialogic relationship between the hyperactive pace of mass production/consumption on the ship and the painstaking process of artistic creation rooted in an artisanal tradition embodied in these instruments.[30] In the final lines of the poem, he also distends time, just as he did in the poem's opening, when the speaker is immersed in the process of 'drowning in the liquid air'. As Peter Nicholls has argued, the Futurists 'thoroughly integrated [art] into the fast-moving circuit of commodities', which ultimately 'promised freedom from the limits and incompleteness of a gendered ("pre-modern") identity'.[31] Mazza's strategies also suggest that the pace of these circuits fluctuated, and that the technicities created by this floating international marketplace are ultimately negotiated by and on the body – a point that, as I will argue shortly, the Vorticists also developed in relation to consumer culture in London.

Marinetti and the Milanese Futurists stimulated dialectical fluctuations in human perceptions of time-space. For all of their macho bravado, however, the anxious, contradictory responses to emerging technicities evinced by consumerism and sexuality formed a pronounced but comparatively under-explored part of these Futurists' programme. Mazza's *'Transatlantico'* traced out exactly these sorts of responses, but the *lacerbiani* – the rival Florentine avant-garde associated with Giovanni Papini and Ardengo Soffici's journal *Lacerba* – consolidated them. Founded in January 1913, *Lacerba* initially opposed Marinetti and denounced Futurism, an adversarial stance suggested by title itself (the compression *L'acerba* means 'bitter', 'sour' or 'unripe' in Italian). Yet the journal eventually provided a platform for crucial Futurist manifestos from both camps. In the spring of 1913, Papini colluded with Marinetti to use the public hostilities between the rival Futurist factions as a promotional tactic.[32] As the magazine's backer and publisher Attilio Vallecchi recalled, *Lacerba* frequently used such contrarian tactics, and relied on 'paradox as a means of persuasion' to achieve its impressive circulation figures (which fluctuated between 8,000–18,000 copies).[33] But it also explains how contrast and contradiction worked programmatically across most aspects of Futurist activity, extending from the logic and rhetoric of their manifestos through to their editorial and promotional tactics. Ironically, such tensions created a sense of unity within the movement because it harnessed the spiky factionalism and individualism that existed among Italian Futurists, rather than masking or ameliorating it. The Futurist individual was tested and refined in the heat of such exchanges, and the *lacerbiani* continued to negotiate the enhancement and distortion effects generated by sensory augmentation technologies.

For example, Alberto Viviani's poem *'Partenza aeroplano + concerto vieuxtemps'* ['Airplane Departure + Traditional Concerto'] created a familiar cocoon of time-space flux in which fragility and destructive potential, and male and female anatomy, modify and intersect with each other in the technological chrysalis of the airplane.[34] Soffici's *'Crocicchio'*, or 'Cross-Road', brought these fluctuations down to earth. His poem encodes the ambivalent cross-talk of warfare and commerce in hunting metaphors (the netted 'fish' and 'machine-gunned birds'), which serve as a pointed 'cross-road' of technicities as Italy hovered on the brink of war.[35] Indeed, these shared tactics combined with a general agitation for Italian intervention, which initially helped consolidate the various Futurist avant-gardes' cultural programme in *Lacerba* during the build-up to the First World War. The artist Carlo Carrà was a close associate of Soffici and an enthusiastic nationalist who supported this campaign.[36] Published in his eclectic book *Guerrapitura* [War Pictures],[37] '*Divagazione Medianica No 1*' ['Mediumistic Digression No. 1'] places the vulnerable self – 'MIO' – literally at the centre of the forthcoming war.[38] Carrà's *mise-en-page* set the 'CATASTROPHIC DISORDER' of trench warfare beneath the 'UNIVERSAL REFRIGERATOR' of the 'SKY' as the subject sits 'drinking aniline and selzer'. The result is perhaps a tonic for a Futurist self that was fragmenting in the face of horrors that for some merely formed a distracting background hum to daily life. However, his picture poem also signals the return of a repressed anxiety about the passive individual sustaining a culture of violence fostered by bourgeois commercial and state apparatuses and sustained by consumer behaviour. Many Futurists supported and/or enlisted in the Italian war effort – including Marinetti and his infamous (and in Carrà's view, anachronistic and completely ridiculous) 'bicycle squadron' – but their direct experience of war encouraged many adherents, including Soffici, Carrà, Gino Severini and Luigi Russolo, to repudiate Futurism.[39] Marinetti and the Futurists may have envisaged a 'a Futurist cyborg devoid of interiority',[40] whose body could be 'adapted to the exigencies of an environment made of continuous shocks', including war.[41] However, the anxieties embedded in Futurist dazzle poetry were an essential and widely shared component of Futurist interventionism, which focused on the stubborn vulnerability of the mind and body even as they adapted to and appropriated sensory augmentation technologies.

The temporary harmony between rival futurist camps also enabled the Italian Futurists to reach out to British avant-garde artists and writers, whom they sought to enlist in their cause. In the weeks before open hostilities broke out in July 1914, an Anglo-Italian alliance had been attempted in *Lacerba* following several visits by Marinetti and Futurist artists to England. These Futurist incursions into Britain began in December 1910, when Marinetti delivered his first polemical lecture at the Lyceum Club in London, and they continued throughout his extensive tours of England in the years preceding the war. In July 1914, *Lacerba* reissued Marinetti's and the English Futurist C. R. W. Nevinson's joint manifesto 'Vital English Art', which had appeared in *The Observer* in June.[42] Wyndham Lewis appropriated the dialectical 'Against/We Want' format in the 'blast/bless' arrangement of his Vorticist manifestos, and, equally, the targets that the Futurists attacked (sentimentality, degeneracy and other anti-masculinist/anti-progress forces represented by various institutions) are as recognisable in *Blast* as the principles the Futurists endorsed ('English Art that is strong, virile and anti-sentimental').[43] The 'powerful advance guard' that Marinetti and Nevinson call for in their manifesto reaffirms Futurist individualism, but ties it to an uncritical evocation of modernity that the London avant-gardeists of the Rebel Arts Centre (whom Nevinson enlisted as signatories without their permission) found anathema. The furious response that 'Vital English Art' drew from Lewis and Ezra Pound was one of the catalysts for Vorticism – and yet the content of *Blast* 1, its most important publication, closely followed Marinetti's and Nevinson's prescriptions in almost all other respects. For both avant-gardes, the war was devastating, as key individuals (including the Futurists Antonio Sant'Elia and Umberto Boccioni and the Vorticist Henri Gaudier-Brzeska) died in combat. Nevertheless, the battlefield ultimately extended and informed their debates about modern technicities rather than ended them, and it tested their pre-war suppositions against the brutal realities of mechanised combat in the process.

Blast's 'War Number': Dazzle Refractions, Mechanised Warfare and Multiple Selves

Blast, like *Lacerba*, used polemic and sarcasm programmatically in its editorial strategy. Indeed, like the stinging title of *Lacerba*, the name *Blast* suggested sensory overload, disorientation and danger, likening the magazine to a kind of dazzle attack. Yet for all their hyper-competitive bluster, both journals' editors laced their polemics with careful argument and satire, on the one hand, and strategic self-contradiction and collusion, on the other. For his part, Wyndham Lewis usually took pains to differentiate the emphases of his Vorticist avant-garde while continuing to acknowledge the aesthetic territory it shared with Futurism, particularly in its negotiation of art, modernity and technology. Published on 20 June 1914, just before the outbreak of war, *Blast* 1 (*B1*) had firmly established the Vorticists' relationship with technology and militarism, and then enumerated the ways in which they were distinct from the Futurists' related concerns. The key distinction in Lewis's approach was not to focus on the *what* of technology, as the Futurists had done, but on the *how* of technicity. This focus became even more pronounced in the magazine's War Number, published in July 1915, when contributors became especially invested in problems of technicity and selfhood posed by the reality of industrialised warfare.

Although the outbreak of the First World War significantly delayed the second issue of *Blast*, to a certain extent it also cut through some of the tribalist tensions in its first issue. For example, C. R. W. Nevinson, who was pointedly excluded from *B1* due to his Futurist affiliation, appeared and received praise from Lewis the following year in *Blast 2 (B2)*.[44] Lewis still attacked Marinetti in the second issue, but toned down his polemics significantly, and overall he engaged more openly with Futurist art and theory. 'Surrounded by a multitude of other Blasts of all sizes and descriptions', Lewis was now able to focus on 'the serious mission' Vorticists had 'on the other side of World-War'.[45] Part of that 'mission' was to issue a definitive statement of Vorticist technicity,[46] which reflected the Futurists' dazzling poetics off the famously 'polished sides' and clean angles of Vorticist art.[47] Accordingly, in works by Lewis, Jessica Dismorr, Helen Saunders, Ezra Pound and Edward Wadsworth, *B2* downplayed the satiric bombast of the first number of the journal and refined its augmentation of the multiple, modern self. Despite Lewis's cavalier attitude towards technology and feats of engineering in the issue, the War Number as a whole actually reinstated Futurist anxieties about the limits of human-mechanical interaction. Its contributors also worried about the vulnerability of the human body as it was transformed by contact with commercial and military technicities of sensory augmentation. Even so, the Vorticists found ingenious ways of channelling those anxieties in this issue and adapting emergent technicities to the artist's cause.

In *B1*, Lewis had argued that since machinery was a long-standing part of Britain's culture, and an acknowledged part of its new art, there was no need to get quite so worked up about it: 'AUTOMOBILISM (Marinetteism) bores us', he declared, affecting a patronising tone to explain the difference between the fetishisation of technical objects and the exploration of technology's relationship to culture.[48] Lewis declared that 'Machinery is the greatest Earth-medium', and that artists should make their works 'MACHINES OF LIFE, a sort of LIVING plastic geometry'.[49] Vorticists, he argued, 'hunt machines, they are our favourite game. We invent them and then hunt them down.'[50] The pun on 'game' not only deflates the technological sublime that Futurists associated with machinery, but also shows how Lewis situates technology, and *techné*, as a crucial ligature between human experience and culture. This strategy places artists and technologists on a level plane, so that '[e]ngineer or artist might conceivably become transposable terms, or one, at least, imply the other'.[51] In *B2* he set about negotiating that shift.

As Günter Berghaus has noted, the Futurists imagined 'a symbiotic relationship' between humanity and machines that would eventually result in a mystical fusion of the two.[52] However, this relationship was based on a form of techno-mysticism that Lewis found to be sentimentally utopian. So in *Blast*'s War Number, he praised the Futurists who 'rejected the POSED MODEL, imitative and static side of CUBISM, and substituted the hurly-burly and exuberance of actual life'.[53] To this he added a dualistic Vorticist logic that playfully encouraged readers to 'become mechanical by fundamental dual repetition', a tactic that he believed would help 'invent [themselves] properly'.[54] In 'becom[ing] mechanical', Lewis's writing in *Blast* envisages a transductive process of individuation. Contemporary cultural geographers describe this kind of technicity as a process in which 'the distinction between living and nonliving (technological)' does not proceed on substantialist or dualist terms, so that 'instead of there being an interface between humans and technology, they become entwined as hybrids'.[55] Lewis's use of machinery in *Blast* forms a ligature between the living and the non-living best described as a technicity, rather than (as the Futurists would have it) a mystical fusion of humans and technology. In *B2*, for example, he insists that '[a] machine is in a greater or less degree, a living thing', on the one hand, and on the other, he associates the machine with the 'the unhuman character [. . .] of art itself'.[56] However, I don't think that Lewis is implying a base equivalency here: rather, anticipating Gilbert Simondon's arguments, Lewis understands the distinctions between humans and machines but proposes a kind of ontological parity.[57] The difficulty, as ever, was to identify a praxis that could accurately embody this technicity. Lewis's critique of Jacob Epstein's iconic *Rock Drill* in the War Number comes close. In it, Lewis enthusiastically notes that 'the nerve-like figure perched on the machinery, with its straining to one purpose, is a vivid illustration of the greatest function of life'.[58] Because Epstein used alabaster for the bust and torso, however, Lewis felt 'that the combination of the white figure and the rock-drill is rather unfortunate and ghost-like'.[59] The result is that despite its powerful address to the forthcoming Machine Age, for Lewis, the version of *Rock Drill* displayed at the Goupil Gallery in March 1915 *approached* the model of ontological parity between humans and machines that he envisaged, but it fell short of that ideal because it abstracted rather than reinforced the intricate technicities that he and other Vorticists had used to connect the human and non-human world. Nevertheless, Lewis's critique of Epstein served to identify technicity as a vital subject and cultural project for artists, which was developed by other Vorticists as the war raged on.

In the War Number, technicities were alternatively presented as heroically aggressive or flippant (usually in the work of Lewis), but, elsewhere, increasingly defensive, a response driven by a sense of the body and the city's vulnerability to attack. The Central Powers began Zeppelin bombing raids on London in January 1915, which provoked terror and defiance in equal measure. Jessica Dismorr and Helen Saunders in particular managed to balance these emphases exquisitely, and to produce some of the most forceful yet intricate examples of modernist dazzle tactics extant. Both artists trained at the Slade, but they were also incisive writers who embraced the contradictory aesthetics of the vortex. As Miranda Hickman argues, they 'enlist[ed] the semiotics and imaginative strategies of Vorticist masculinity, both in their visual art and public affiliations, in order to pursue professional advancement as New Women artists'.[60] In the process they reinvigorated the commercial tropes common to Futurist poetry, while ramping up the military discourses introduced by Lewis in *Blast*.

In Dismorr's 'Monologue', fashion is simultaneously a weapon, victim and victimiser of the Vorticist model/designer/soldier:

> I ache all over, but acrobatic, I undertake the feat of existence.
> Details of equipment delight me.
> I admire my arrogant spiked tresses, the disposition of my perpetually
>   foreshortened limbs,
> Also the new machinery that wields the chains of muscles fitted beneath
>   my close coat of skin.
> On a pivot of contentment my balanced body moves slowly.
> Inquisitiveness, a butterfly, escapes.
> It spins with drunken invitation.[61]

As it enters the public sphere, the speaker's bodily 'machinery' experiences a gradual chrysalis, from inquisitive sentient automaton, to cornered fighter, to accidental explorer. This is consistent with Vorticist aesthetics, which, like certain Futurist works, often treated the marketplace as an arena for competitive spectacle. At first subsumed by its capacity for sensory disorientation, the speaker then turns the experience of synaesthesia to her advantage by dazzling her enemies in the commercial sphere. As her 'eyes dilate and bulge' in 'pursuit of shapes', she turns her gaze against her 'sick opponents dodging behind silence' by using a form of 'echo' location, which 'shrills an equivalent / threat'. Dismorr's early warning system makes explicit the connection she identifies between commercial culture and war as 'pampered appetites and curiosities become blood-drops', unequivocally linking acquisitive greed and an imperialist state that 'yells war'. In doing so, Dismorr shows how the polyphonic public sphere in which these discourses intersect becomes drowned out by this brutal 'gong' or droning 'Monologue'. Her literary tactics provide a way of waging guerrilla warfare in and against this monologic field, even in a state of temporary vulnerability, when 'Striped malignities spring upon' her. As Dismorr writes in her 'London Notes' in the same issue of *Blast*, the 'many perspective lines, withdrawing, converging' in the city 'indicate evidently something of importance beyond the limits of sight', which the augmented Vorticist sensorium could perceive, exploit and, crucially, sustain amid the new realities of mechanised warfare, and in an increasingly mechanised society.[62] In this way, Dismorr's multiple and mechanised self deploys her dazzle camouflage in constantly shifting surroundings, striking out against her opponents unexpectedly even while they target her.

Saunders injected similar strategies into her poem 'A Vision of Mud', which was haunted by the filth and attrition that had come to characterise trench warfare by the time *B2* was published. Against this abject, 'antediluvian' formlessness, Saunders aligns various tools, shapes and implements that betoken modernity, which engulfs and disorientates the speaker with its contradictory properties.[63] This poem, when it is read at all, is usually framed as though it were addressed exclusively to the 'mud' of First World War battlefields, but it is actually about a 'Hydro', or 'health-resort', a space for the sort of luxury 'pampering' that Dismorr addresses in 'Monologue'.[64] Like Dismorr, then, Saunders explicitly connects war and consumer self-indulgence: the 'poisoned arrows' in the poem do not counterpoint, emerge from or interject against a backdrop of consumer desire, but are synonymous with it. However, unlike the Futurists (and to a certain extent, unlike Dismorr), she does not conflate consumer activity and the lure of sexual satisfaction – there is nothing *petit* about the *mort* she alludes to, and nothing trivial about the parallels she draws between a luxury spa and trench warfare. Saunders also carefully recalibrates the relationship between the human sensorium and modern technicities. 'A Vision of Mud' replaces the gemstones, crystals and reflective surfaces that typically litter Futurist dazzle poetry with large-scale leisure and warfare technology, which produce mundane 'ashen kaleidoscope[s]' rather than a storefront of dazzling products.[65] In doing so, she makes the point that modern technologies and technicities can stultify and fix the subject, as well as mobilise and liberate it, and, thus, make it a vulnerable target.

Saunders introduces the war in 'A Vision of Mud' via the 'olive branch', 'recruiting band' and 'iron bar' with sharp 'edges', which produces a pleasurable sensation of pain and conflates consumer pleasure with the anticipation of harm. The Hydro's leisure technology disrupts spatial norms ('How is it that if you struggle you sink') and temporal fields, which link the 'antediluvian sounds' of Old Testament history with the 'drums' and 'fifes' of a 'recruiting band' pursuing conscripts for a future skirmish in the quintessentially modern war. A sensory disorientation accompanies this time-space distortion, as 'A crowd of india-rubber-like shapes swarm [. . .] like an ashen kaleidoscope'. The resulting 'dream' state pairs London consumers wallowing in 'medicinal' mud with the lethal filth that lubricates the industrial-scale slaughter taking place on the continent. The speaker has 'just discovered with what I think is disgust, that there are hundreds of other / bodies bobbing about against me'[66] – 'Every now and then one of these fellow-monstrosities bumps softly against me'.[67] Unlike in Dismorr's poem, however, in which the speaker is stimulated and even regenerated by her struggles against various threats, Saunders's multiple self remains a 'monstrosit[y]' that is somewhat defeated by its encounter with modernity. Unable or unwilling to transmute the contexts of pain and death that surround it into anything potentially stimulating, Saunders's persona 'think[s] of my ancestors' as 'Rain falls in the grave distance'. This drift signals a retreat into time and space, as the self is 'too proud and too lazy' to resolve the dichotomy of death and desire, and hands the problem over to the addressee.[68] Nevertheless, that self survives a violent moment of time-space compression by slipping away from the entropy, attrition and deadening noise that surrounds it, preserved by its own unique twist on dazzle tactics.

Such tactics were essential in analysing and exploiting blind spots in the technologies and technicities developed by military and commercial engineers. Yet, as *Blast*'s War Number reveals, artists took advantage of those perceptual loopholes at the same time as, or even before, the engineers did. And prior to the advent of dazzle camouflage, Futurist and Vorticist artists experimented with new ways of manipulating technicities of sensory augmentation by developing technologies themselves. In Luigi Russolo's *intonarumori* ['noise intoners'] and Alvin Langdon Coburn's and Ezra Pound's 'Vortoscope', 'engineer' and 'artist' did indeed become 'transposable terms', in which avant-gardes adapted representational technology for public exhibition.[69]

Aesthetic Distortion: *Intonarumori* and Vortoscopes

Following the publication of *Blast*'s War Number in July 1915, Vorticism, like Futurism, experienced a lull. Despite both avant-gardes having been effectively cut short by the war, however, 1916 represented a crucial juncture in the evolution of Vorticism and Futurism as each movement produced a key innovation that year. Alvin Langdon Coburn and Ezra Pound developed the Vortoscope, a photographic apparatus meant to achieve special and non-representational visual effects, in September 1916. That same year, a seminal text by the Futurist artist-cum-musician

Luigi Russolo, *The Art of Noises*, was published, gathering together his writing about the infamous *intonarumori*, or 'noise intoner' machines, and his spectacular performances with them in Italy and London. As Marinetti, Russolo and Ugo Piatti noted in *Lacerba*, 'all of London' was aware of these performances. Although the events eventually won acclaim from British audiences, the first ones were 'violently opposed by the public', to the point where the musicians were actually drowned out by the audience's booing.[70] The Vorticists may not have been aware of the publication of *The Art of Noises*, but they were certainly aware of Russolo's and Marinetti's projects and performances.[71] Accordingly, Pound and Coburn followed Russolo's strategy of inventing machines that could interpolate their avant-garde's technicities for various audiences. These inventions may have lacked technical sophistication, but the machines and their performance/exhibition contexts elegantly demonstrated how technicities of sensory augmentation had opened a new front in the modernist conflict between representation and abstraction, and new possibilities for the artist-engineer.

Russolo first described his plans for the *intonarumori* in his 1913 tract 'The Art of Noises: A Futurist Manifesto', but in his 1916 book *Art of Noises* he provided a detailed account of their construction. Most of the instruments looked like a cross between an enlarged gramophone and a blunderbuss, and their imposing design deliberately evoked military and recording technologies. While their internal mechanisms were concealed, they generally took 'the form of boxes of various sizes, usually constructed in a rectangular base' with 'a trumpet' on 'the front end [. . .] to collect and reinforce the noise-sound' and 'a handle' on the back end 'to produce the motion that excites the noise'.[72] When performing as an ensemble, Russolo intended the effect to resemble the sensation of 'wander[ing] through a great modern city with our ears more alert than our eyes', 'creating mental orchestrations' of mechanically-generated noise.[73] The sounds the *intonarumori* generated could be purely percussive, or pitched, siren-like tones. They all produced specific categories of sounds associated with industrialised cities and warfare – for example 'Howlers (*Ululatori*)' for sirens, 'Roarers (*Rombatori*)' for engines, 'Bursters (*Scoppiatori*)' for heavy machinery, and so on.[74] But although he wanted his machine 'noise to remind us brutally of life', Russolo insisted that 'the art of noises must not be limited to an imitative reproduction'.[75] Instead, he sought to augment the range of sounds and timbres represented in traditional musical notation and performance, and, beyond that, to use his 'network-of-noises' to challenge the expectations of Machine Age audiences.[76]

As Russolo argued, from their first demonstration to their most infamous performances,[77] it was 'the *strange, bizarre,* and *incomprehensible* thing that is the orchestra of noise instruments' rather than the volume or ferocity of their performances that he believed would dazzle audiences.[78] That was no surprise, because as Luciano Chessa notes, technologically, the machines were little more than updated versions of the 'hurdy gurdy', an instrument dating to medieval times that also used strings and rotating discs (some of them mechanised) to produce pitched sounds.[79] Arndt Niebisch has noted that, given the limitations of this design, it would have been impossible for Russolo to 'overwhelm his audience' with volume; instead, Niebisch argues, Russolo's major ambition was 'to train the sensorium of the listeners, so that they became accustomed to the art of noises and able to adjust more efficiently to the noise of war and traffic'.[80] In this respect, the *intonarumori* and *The Art of Noises* fit into the Futurists' broader pedagogical programme to recalibrate the human sensory apparatus to align it with the movement's aesthetics. However, I don't think that Russolo limited his project to acoustics and music: my argument is that he created a multimedia, multisensory spectacle with the *intonarumori* by drawing on a range of Futurist dazzle tactics to hyper-stimulate the *imaginations* of his audiences. Russolo achieved this by manipulating audience expectations in advance of his performances in three main ways: firstly, with his ingenious manifestos, which linked his project to military contexts and the Futurists' literary enterprises; secondly, with the design and staging of the *intonarumori* themselves; and, finally, with the advanced press and publicity photos for his ensemble performances.

Given that Russolo was primarily a visual artist and a talented manifesto writer, the literary, visual and media contexts of *The Art of Noises* and his musical performances are crucial, but surprisingly overlooked, aspects of his project. Russolo was arguably even more adept than Marinetti at lacing nuanced arguments about sensory augmentation among his militaristic polemics, and he achieved this across several mediums. For example, the second chapter of his book *The Art of Noises* likens the first *intonarumori* performances to 'Battles',[81] and the fifth describes 'the Noises of War', discussing how battlefields served as his sonic laboratories.[82] Chapter 5 in particular is an overt piece of military propaganda that demonstrates how Russolo's s research and art of noises could help train civilians to detect threats on the battlefield, so that 'the soul of the soldier is suspended' and the body is transformed into a technologically-enhanced biological radar.[83] Although Russolo's constant references to military assault encouraged audiences to expect an aural equivalent when his 'noise orchestras' performed, he was actually more interested in engaging them in the Futurists' pedagogical assault on the human sensorium. As he declared in his original 1913 manifesto, '[o]ur multiplied

Figure 1.3 Anonymous, Untitled [Photograph of Luigi Russolo, Ugo Piatti, and the *intonarumori* (noise machines)], Milan, 1914–15. *Source:* Courtesy of Mart, Archivio del '900, Luigi Russolo's archive.

sensibility, having already been conquered by the eyes of the Futurists, will at last have Futurist ears'.[84] But in order to accomplish this transformation, the Futurist publicity machines primed their imaginations with a series of manifestos and press announcements.

Russolo and his assistant Ugo Piatti staged numerous publicity photographs in their laboratory (Fig. 1.3), versions of which appeared in multiple newspapers, including the front page of *Le Matin* on 16 January 1915. In these photos, the quasi-military array of *intonorumori* crowd the inventors, creating a forest of 'black boxes', while the wiring evokes an electrical sublime. These composition features suggest that this technology could also dominate and overwhelm audiences. The hybrid aesthetic suggests an oversized gramophone, but their coincidental resemblance to military hardware suggests associations with guns, sirens and other communications equipment that Russolo discusses in *The Art of Noises*.[85] Other photographs, such as the example from a performance at the Coliseum (Fig. 1.4), show the *intonarumori* supplanting the instruments of a traditional orchestra while preserving its basic structure and attire (i.e. performers and instruments clustered in a semicircle in front of a conductor).

Figure 1.4 Anonymous, *Londre concerto al Coliseum* [News clipping of Russolo and the *Intonarumori* at the Coliseum in London, June 1914].

Rather than destroying the present musical culture, then, the noise intoners radically defamiliarised it. Russolo's 'Howlers', 'Roarers' and 'Bursters' certainly proposed new ways of combining and articulating sounds, but they did not fundamentally reimagine or even reclassify their basic categories.[86] Similarly, the visual spectacle of technical objects muscling in on reified cultural spaces primed his audiences for a sonic confrontation, which was itself a synecdoche for a broader encounter between Futurists and established cultural institutions. Russolo's main dazzle tactic was to use this confrontation as a distraction from his more subtle ambition, which was to distort and modify, rather than to destroy and recreate, the cultural points of reference he targeted. In this way, his programme exaggerated, manipulated and transfigured the materials and environments of everyday life into a series of hyper-stimulating encounters with them.

Whereas Marinetti, Russolo and the Milanese Futurists in particular relied on strategies of radical mimesis and defamiliarisation to supplant existing orthodoxies with their own Futurist ones, Vorticists tended to revel in creating ironic, satiric and contradictory relationships between their avant-garde and the public sphere, preserving their position as detached interlocutors while simultaneously jostling for the same sorts of cultural spoils that the Futurists pursued. Jacob Epstein's *Rock Drill* suggested the kinds of hybrid projects that might result from this fusion, but two Americans, Ezra Pound and Alvin Langdon Coburn, actually produced a working Vorticist machine. In fact, their Vorticist machine art marked the next, and essentially final, phase of the movement's overt public activity. The January 1917 Vorticist Exhibition at The Penguin Club in New York was followed in February by Coburn's solo exhibition in London's Camera Club. This modest exhibit of thirteen watercolours and eighteen 'Vortographs' suggested a major development of Vorticist technicity, and for the complex negotiation of representational and non-representational art that obsessed both the Futurists and Vorticists.[87] As Pound noted in the programme notes, Coburn's 'desir[e] to bring cubism or vorticism [sic] into photography' was only possible 'with the invention of a suitable instrument': the Vortoscope.[88]

A painter, photographer, amateur musician and temporary Vorticist, Coburn had regularly taken portraits of key London-based vanguardists between 1913 and 1916, including Roger Fry, Max Weber and the Vorticists. During this period, his growing enthusiasm for non-representational art made him realise that his 'own medium' had begun to 'lag behind' other art forms.[89] Following the outbreak of war, Coburn also became interested in the role that technology might play in art. He developed an obsession with mechanical player pianos and their possibilities for avant-garde composition and wondered whether some similar technical innovation might allow photographers to concentrate on 'arrangements of form for their own sake, just as a musician does'.[90] By 1916, Coburn had begun a collaboration with Pound to recreate the geometric spectacle of Vorticist painting using photography, and together they invented the Vortoscope.[91] Despite its flashy name, the device itself was little more than a staging apparatus – a reflective diorama composed of 'three mirrors fastened together in the form of a triangle', which 'resembl[ed] to a certain extent a kaleidoscope' (indeed, Pound suggested that there was more than one version, and he was very probably involved in their construction).[92] The original objects do not survive, but my reconstruction of Pound's model in Figure 1.5 gives a reasonable approximation using a contemporaneous portable camera. The device created multiple reflections of the subject, which Coburn captured with a standard manual single-lens-reflex camera. Despite its simple construction, however, the system was actually quite a powerful intervention in the technical relay of SLR photography. It produced fragmented and strategically distorted images that could only otherwise be produced through time-consuming multiple exposure developing techniques.

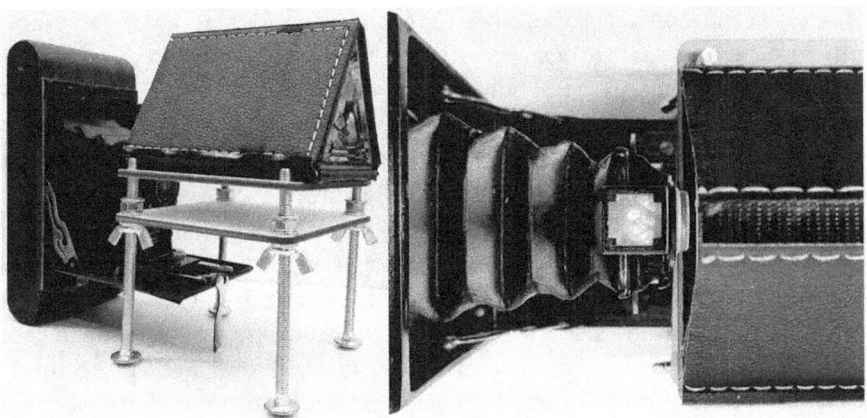

Figure 1.5 Eric White, Cillian White and Martina Hallegger, Recreation of Ezra Pound's Vortoscope [1915 Kodak Brownie, pocket mirrors, plywood, and bolts]; top view of crystal structures through ground glass.

Like the *intonarumori*, the device was not especially sophisticated, but based on Coburn's descriptions the Vortoscope probably would have been quite fragile and cumbersome, and not as visually striking as Russolo's machines. So when Pound announced to his parents that he and Coburn had 'invented vortography', the compositional possibilities of the process, rather than the technology itself, were his chief interest. He explained that their 'idea is that one no longer need photograph what is in front of the camera, but that one can use one's element of design'; in other words, they could 'take the elements of design from what is in front of the camera, shut out what you don't want, twist the "elements" onto the part of the plate where you want 'em, and then fire'.[93] The Vortoscope helped Coburn and Pound compose the design elements so that fragmentation, reflection and distortion effects could be composed on the camera's sheet of ground glass (the surface used by the photographer for focusing and composing the real image) before the shot was taken, rather than laboriously achieved with exposure effects in the developing process.

The technicity of the Vortoscope embodied the Vorticist credo of 'being dual'. Coburn's Vortographs of Pound in particular literally reflected the sense of multiple selfhood that technologies of sensory augmentation and photochemical reproduction encouraged in the Machine Age.[94] In this respect it is hardly surprising that Coburn's Vortographs of objects almost exclusively featured crystals as their subjects, since they refracted light and were used in wireless communication devices as well as other technologies. As Anne McCauley points out, for all Coburn's claims to the contrary, these Vortographs were not actually 'abstract, but represented real things – crystals, reflected and refracted under the influence of strong artificial lights that flared into the lens'.[95] The objects themselves enhanced the reflective properties of the Vortoscope, referring back to the means of the Vortographs' production in a kind of conceptual feedback loop. This was only one way in which the dazzle effects generated by Vortographs depended more on their referentiality than on any sense of abstraction. Another was the manner in which Vortography could simulate the crystalline structures typical of Vorticist paintings, which used a geometric interplay of forms to negotiate strategies of mimesis and representation. Heavily mediated by technology, Vortographs were in some senses uncanny re-presentations of these paintings, and Pound added the final dazzling 'twist' to the mimetic games by restoring a contextual detail that haunted the Vortographs' inception.

In September 1916, when Coburn and Pound invented Vortography, the Zeppelin raids over London that had begun in January 1915 intensified. Pound restored this context in his anonymous preface to the catalogue for Coburn's February 1917 Camera Club exhibition through a formal fallacy:

> the modern will enjoy Vortograph No. 3, not because it reminds him of a shell bursting on a hillside, but because the arrangement of forms pleases him, as a phrase of Chopin might please him. He will enjoy Vortograph No. 8, not because it reminds him of a falling Zeppelin, but because he likes the shape and arrangement of its blocks of dark and light.[96]

As Mike Weaver rightly points out, thanks to Pound's prompt in the catalogue 'we will never again look at "Vortograph No. 8" without thinking of a Zeppelin', not *despite* its instruction to the contrary, but precisely *because* of it (Fig. 1.6).[97] However, I think that Pound's fallacy was entirely deliberate. The comparison to munitions and especially the airships produced by the Luftschiffbau Zeppelin Company connected Vortography indirectly to the technologies of warfare, evoking not only mass destruction but also aerial transportation and the time-space dynamics it represented. Like Russolo before him, Pound combined the allure of a new technological 'instrument' and its connection to military contexts to produce a spectacle by means of a classically Vorticist double bluff.[98] Using this rhetorical dazzle tactic to complement the Vortographs' pictorial dazzle, Pound demonstrated how he and Coburn had realised a distinctively Vorticist technicity, which was intimately bound up with Machine Age technologies of warfare and commerce.

Figure 1.6 Alvin Langdon Coburn, *Vortograph No. 8*, 1917, Gelatin silver print. *Source:* Copyright © Estate of Alvin Langdon Coburn.

Unlike Russolo's art of noises, the disruptive impact of Vortography would be limited to bourgeois gallery spaces. And although experiments with 'abstract' photography would be continued by Man Ray and others, the Vortography experiment finished shortly after its 1917 debut. Following his initial surge of enthusiasm, Pound grew disenchanted with the machine, and told Quinn that 'the vortescope [*sic*] is an *attachment* to enable a photographer to do sham Picassos' [my emphasis].⁹⁹ The Vortoscope simply introduced a further technical object into the photographic process, and, like dazzle camouflage, could only perform its function as a technical object when another technical object (i.e. the camera) was in use. Nevertheless, and as predicted by Lewis, this invention enabled the Vorticists to bridge the worlds of art and engineering with a technical object that produced spectacular aesthetic objects. The relationship between Coburn and Pound imploded when Pound included only lukewarm appraisals of Coburn's work in the introduction to the Vortograph Exhibition catalogue, which also heavily qualified the photographer's participation in the Vorticist movement. Coburn had enjoyed a close friendship with Edward Wadsworth, and as Mark Antliff has noted, Coburn shared Wadsworth's measured, meditative approach to composition; however, when Wadsworth, like Lewis, entered military service in 1916, Coburn lost a strong connection to Vorticism.¹⁰⁰ For Wadsworth, however, this period marked the beginning of a startling new chapter in the history of Vorticism. Rather than avant-gardes parasitically appropriating military and commercial technology (as Niebisch, adapting an argument by Friedrich Kittler, persuasively characterises Futurist and Dada relationships with media technologies),¹⁰¹ the advent of dazzle camouflage in 1917 appeared to reverse the roles in that relationship.

The War Engine: Edward Wadsworth's Dazzle Designs

Blast's War Number and Vortography showcased the ways in which Vorticists could use new technicities and technologies to disrupt 'perceptive powers' as well as enhance them – and to exploit the perceptual 'gap between perceiver and perceived' that various technologies of the First World War had attempted to 'close'.¹⁰² Drawing on Futurist precedents, Vorticist projects helped anticipate and develop the technicities that culminated in the advent of dazzle camouflage just two years later – not, I think, because of any 'subliminal' influence from the artists on the military (or vice versa), but because of the Vorticists' acute grasp of a new battlefront that had opened, in which technicities of augmentation could be attacked. Dazzle designs, pre- and post-camouflage, deliberately interrogated the boundaries between representational and non-representational forms. In doing so they signposted the escalating capacity of technology both to enhance and distort the human sensorium. This new emphasis on sensory augmentation coincided with the Vorticists' engagements with technicity, making it no surprise that one of the unsung architects of that movement, Edward Wadsworth, became centrally involved in the Admiralty Dazzle Section.

Despite being a crucial organiser and proponent of Vorticism, Wadsworth is often overlooked in critical appraisals of this avant-garde.[103] Just as he had done for the first issue, Wadsworth played a crucial role in engineering the second number of *Blast*, and it was he who first proposed the idea for a War Number with leaner typography in August 1914. His correspondence with Lewis indicates that he knew exactly which buttons to push in order to motivate his collaborator. He suggested that it would 'sell like hot-cakes',[104] but warned him that 'no other paper has ceased to appear' because of the war; 'if "Blast" were the first that couldn't keep its end up', Wadsworth continued, 'it would be regarded by everyone – especially the enemies – as a sign of lack of stamina'.[105] Wadsworth's goading was clearly an effective stimulant, but this was merely one strand of the measured diplomacy that, combined with his calculated aesthetics, forensic intellect, translation skills and international contacts, made his presence crucial to Vorticism's programmatic dualism.[106] Pound wrote that '[t]he Vorticist movement is a movement of individuals, for individuals, for the protection of individuality'; although the work of 'Mr Lewis and Mr Wadsworth' is 'quite different', he continued, together, their presence in *Blast* 'arranges itself almost as a series of antitheses. Turbulent energy: repose. Anger: placidity, and so on.'[107] In statements such as these, Vorticists made it clear that competitive 'antithesis', and not consistency, was responsible for the group's dynamic, collective identity, and any significance it laid claim to. Wadsworth's unique contributions to *Blast*'s War Number served as a foil for the work of Lewis and other Vorticists, but it also formed telling similarities with it. Like Saunders and Dismorr, he explored how Vorticist technicities could enable the individual to negotiate the cultural impact of industrial-scale warfare and the contradictory energies of modernity.

In his woodcuts *Rotterdam* and his engraving *War-Engine* for B2 Edward Wadsworth revisited the aerial perspectives he had used in B1 (e.g. in *A Short Flight*) from an overtly military perspective. *War-Engine* resembles an overhead view of a port, which focuses a vortex of mechanical energy into a trumpet blast, projecting from the clean angles and saw-tooth designs patterns that anticipate certain dazzle camouflage schemes. For Richard Cork, the tactics and subjects used in these woodcuts help 'explain why Wadsworth became so readily involved in the dazzle-camouflage of ships'.[108] However, Wadsworth took an important step in the intervening period that made the match perfect: he enlisted with the Royal Naval Volunteer Reserve in 1916, which provided both the contacts and military experience necessary for the Dazzle Section in time for its launch in the summer of 1917. As Jonathan Black summarises,

> [a]fter 18 months service with Naval Intelligence and the Royal Navy Air Service at Mudros, on the eastern Aegean island of Lemnos, Wadsworth was invalided back to Britain in December 1917 with a combination of dysentery and sunstroke. Two months later he was snapped up by marine artist and RNVR officer Norman Wilkinson to serve as a 'port officer' attached to his 'dazzle camouflage' department within the Ministry of Shipping.[109]

Among art historians there is a general perception that the connections between Vorticism (and other experimental art movements) and the development of dazzle camouflage was largely circumstantial, and any influence of modernist art on the Dazzle Section probably 'subliminal' at best.[110] However, *Blast*'s contributors expressed a sense of shared purpose with the military by using naval warfare and ports as subjects, as well as in their negotiation of the emergent technicities that resulted in the invention of dazzle camouflage. As Black argues, while 'the first issue of *Blast* bullishly promoted Britain's seemingly unchallengeable maritime supremacy literally built upon high-technology manufacture', there was also 'a growing sense that Britain was being remorselessly outclassed economically and in terms of technological innovation by Imperial Germany and by that manifestly even greater industrial behemoth, the United States'.[111] In popular accounts of its military, commercial and Vorticist applications, dazzle painting amounted to a nationalist techno-aesthetic counter-blast against continental opposition. Responding to an urgent letter by Norman Wilkinson, the British Admiralty finally launched 'controlled, preliminary full-scale trials' of 'Dazzle Painting' on 'the Admiralty storeship *HMS Industry*' in the summer of 1917.[112] Coincidentally – although in the context of my argument, it is a very telling coincidence – Wilkinson intended the Transport Camouflage Section (as the first Dazzle Section was originally known) to focus on merchant shipping, as the name of the first test vessel, the HMS *Industry*, clearly indicates. It is therefore appropriate that dazzle camouflage ultimately was an acquisitive technology: it bought time.

As a trained draughtsman, highly skilled artist, naval officer and heir to a wealthy industrialist, Wadsworth was perfectly placed to interpret and implement Wilkinson's dazzle strategies for mass production. Each system designed and tested by Wilkinson and his team of male and female artists at Burlington House had to be adapted for each specific vessel by officers at eight British ports. The brilliance of Wilkinson's dazzle system was its adaptability, and it quickly evolved into a standardised (if not altogether consistent) system with clearly defined designs, each for a specific category of vessel, to achieve specific objectives.[113] The scale of the operation was enormous, with as many as 100 ships being 'camouflaged in a British port such as Liverpool, Bristol, Southampton, and Newcastle, at any one time', totalling '2,300 British Merchant ships' by June 1918, and 1,200 American ships by November.[114] Wadsworth was stationed at Liverpool docks and, just as he had done in his earlier work, he chronicled the tactical role played by ports and their crews in his art. A photograph of his crew dazzle-painting a docked vessel taken by Wilkinson in 1918 foregrounds the dynamic activity of the painters (Fig. 1.7). Their movements and rigging are accentuated by the shadows on the vessel, and it is this design, rather than the dazzle camouflage, that the shot accentuates. This emphasis subtly but importantly inflects Wadsworth's best-known works relating to dazzle camouflage, which include his monochrome woodcut *Dry-docked for Painting and Scaling, Liverpool (1918)* and his monumental 1919 oil on canvas *Dazzle-ships in Drydock at Liverpool* (Fig. 1.8). In each case, the figures performing the maintenance are diminutive. However, in the woodcut, they recollect the angular, mechanised forms associated with Lewis's representational Vorticist figures, as well as his energetic technicities, and they also resemble the support mechanisms

Figure 1.7 Norman Wilkinson, *Ship Being Dazzle Camouflaged by Edward Wadsworth's Crew*, 1918. *Source:* Copyright © and courtesy Camilla Wilkinson/The Estate of Norman Wilkinson.

Figure 1.8 Edward Wadsworth, *Dazzle-ships in Drydock at Liverpool, 1919*, Oil on canvas; transfer from the Canadian War Memorials, 1921 National Gallery of Canada, Ottawa. *Source:* Photo: NGC.

used to hoist the ship. The 1918 photograph achieves this effect by using shadows cast by the crew and their rigging (a technique that Coburn also uses in his portraits of Wadsworth).[115] In *Dazzle-ships in Drydock at Liverpool*, the figures are more organic but, equally, more obscure than in the woodcut. Like Dismorr's and Saunders's camouflaged bodies, and

Mazza's floating marketplace in '*Transatlantico*', they are both engulfed by the technological apparatus that surrounds them, while subtly dominating it. The focus is of course on the dazzle ship, and to a lesser extent the other vessels in the background. However, the infrastructure is just as important as the ships themselves. The intricate dock ramps, scaffolding and other intersecting lines are essential to the painting's epic scale, which is ultimately (and subversively) determined by the diminutive figures painting diligently at its base.

Wadsworth's dazzle-themed works more than any others suggest the strident Vorticist foundations of his project. At the same time, they establish the subtle convergence of technicities that helped produce a collaboration between avant-garde artists and a burgeoning military-industrial complex, in which technology, and especially 'weapons systems', became 'grand symbols of sovereignty'.[116] The Dazzle Section highlights the crucial role that commercial interests played in developing this symbolic order, and the vexed position of the avant-garde artist in its creation and material execution. Wadsworth's representations of dazzle seem obsessed with such intersections, and this may be the reason why his depictions of dazzle camouflaged ships are all rooted to ports. These points of mediation between sea and land, movement and stasis, and commercial and military contexts capture the ambivalence of an individualistic experimental artist plying his trade in a highly regulated system of mass production for organised conflict. In his introduction to a series of woodcuts by Wadsworth published in April 1921, which included an illustration of another dazzle ship *In Dry Dock (1918)*, O. Raymond Drey remarked that Wadsworth's 'irregular black and white mosaics do not yield up all their secrets to the first glance'. However, Drey continued, the 'designs are full of a brilliant movement which at first may seem an end in itself, but which is quickly seen to be controlled by a clearly formulated logic of arrangement which is only at a short remove from literal accuracy'.[117] Drey was discussing the tension between representational and non-representational forms in the woodcut series, but he also identifies a tension central to dazzle camouflage and to Futurist and Vorticist technicities. For these avant-gardes, technological advances in commercial and military spheres created opportunities for both critique and collusion – for attack and defence – and for evasion.

Conclusion

The correlation of dazzle camouflage with Vorticist and Futurist art and literature represents just one strand in a broader cultural narrative about cross-disciplinary innovations that emerged in response to a world increasingly viewed through 'a glass eye'. This new world was heavily mediated by sensory-enhancing technologies and the military, commercial and aesthetic strategies formulated in response to them. Dazzle camouflage is an especially instructive example of how these technicities emerged across multiple spheres of production. Popular accounts of the technology continued to appear in the immediate aftermath of the Armistice on November 1918, although then, as now, usually in a valedictory context.[118] By that stage, however, the public and Establishment alike were beginning to appreciate the Vorticists' contribution to national life. In an ironically-titled article 'The Death of Vorticism', Pound noted that 'the government has at last put a Vorticist lieutenant [Wadsworth] in charge of the biggest port in England', and that 'after trying all kinds of war painters [. . .] [it] has [also] taken on Mr. Wyndham Lewis' and 'Mr. [William] Roberts'.[119] Pound's point, of course, was that Vorticism emphatically was *not* dead, but had been assimilated by the British Establishment (which, in an unintentional irony, actually represented a form of cultural 'death' for a supposedly oppositional avant-garde) and was garnering new interest across the Atlantic.[120] Indeed, in May 1917 he admitted using his newly acquired position as Foreign Editor of *The Little Review* to continue the Vorticist project by stealth, writing to the critic Edgar Jepson that his 'corner of the paper [was now] *BLAST*, but *BLAST* covered with ice, a literary and reserved camouflage'.[121] Dazzle camouflage remained a highly visible part of his continuing strategy to reinvigorate the fading Vorticist avant-garde for a new American audience by citing its Establishment credentials. Unfortunately for Pound, even as he did so, the Establishment and various mainstream publications were busy consigning the dazzle project to history.

One of the most prescient accounts of dazzle camouflage's legacy was published in *The Sphere* in March 1919, and Norman Wilkinson quoted it at length in his autobiography to conclude his chapter on the Dazzle Section. The article accurately represented dazzle technology and its value to the war effort, but it also chronicled its rapid slide from high visibility into memory and legend, at a time when '[a]ll this welter of colours is fast vanishing from the world'.[122] The British Admiralty pushed this decline a step further: shortly before the Armistice, a Committee on Dazzle Painting 'produced a report that called into question covering camouflaged ships which were attacked or sunk by submarines'; ultimately, the Admiralty concluded that as well as being expensive to maintain, 'dazzle camouflage of capital ships' did not represent any real tactical advantage.[123] Nevertheless, the Admiralty was 'not averse to the dazzle camouflage of other ships as evidence suggested that such camouflage was not harmful and might at least have intangible benefits in aiding morale'.[124] As such, the report concluded that the effectiveness of dazzle designs was subjective. In making his final appraisal of dazzle in his autobiography, Wilkinson's stylistic tack somewhat supports this reading: for all his emphasis on statistics and procedure, he tends to rely on the subjective testimony of military, industrial and political leaders rather than empirical evidence in his discussions of dazzle camouflage. So, was dazzle camouflage really just an unproven (and unprovable) sleight of hand after all, a mass spectacle that boosted morale with a 'razzle dazzle' of techno-nationalist propaganda designed to resemble, rather than execute, proven technological innovations?

If so, then the narrative would seem to be neatly concluded: Futurism died with the Futurists in the War, and the Futurist 'cult of the machine' along with it; Pound's sardonic epitaph declaring the 'Death of Vorticism' was eventually drained of its irony; the avant-garde artist-engineer was an unsustainable experiment, at least in the short term; and dazzle camouflage faded into history, condemned as a confidence trick on a grand scale. Except that none of these things is really true: Futurists and Futurism persisted well (and problematically) into the 1940s; Pound identified a proponent of Vorticist music in *George Antheil and the Treatise on Harmony* (1924), and, as Douglas Mao has noted, the movement experienced 'many afterlives' in many spheres;[125] Marcel Duchamp, Mina Loy, Baroness Elsa von Freytag-Loringhoven, Francis Picabia and others revitalised the figure of the artist-engineer in the 1920s (as I shall discuss in the next chapter); and the British Admiralty was wrong about dazzle camouflage. Tests conducted in the Physics Department of the Eastman Kodak Research Laboratories in Rochester, New York in the 1920s and 1930s proved conclusively that, in the limited contexts for which it was originally intended, 'Dazzle Painting was perfectly sound and valid as confirmed by the subsequent adoption of refined versions in the Second World War'.[126] In other words, when applied correctly, it worked exactly as it was intended to do, not *despite* (as the British Admiralty would have it) its connections and similarities to avant-garde art, but in important (though not, as Pound would have it, decisive) ways, *because* of them.

The shock of avant-garde techniques suddenly attaining instrumental value produced a dazzle effect in multiple spheres of discourse, from mass print culture to the specialised networks of military strategy and aesthetic production, often via chicken-and-egg narratives that marvelled at these unexpected confluences of technicities. The First World War created the rare – though as we shall see in subsequent chapters, certainly not unique – conditions that jammed these strands together into genuine collaborations. Once those conditions faded, the common purpose that justified those partnerships was removed, and collaboration would begin to look suspiciously like collusion, on both sides. Pound's final encounter with dazzle designs appears to acknowledge this tension even as he sought to break his ties with Britain. The decorated capitals in the Vorticist alphabet created by Wadsworth, which appeared in the 1920 Ovid Press edition of *Hugh Selwyn Mauberley*, added hierarchies of crystals to the dazzle designs commonly found in his woodcuts. In *Mauberly*, Pound reclaims this aesthetic innovation from the military and turns the technology back against it by tacitly evoking the strategies of deception that ultimately lay behind the dazzle project. By doing so, he commemorates those who 'walked eye-deep in hell / believing in old men's lies' and calls upon the survivors to train their gazes on the 'old lies and new infamy' that awaited them at home.[127] Throughout *Mauberley*, Pound both invokes and indicts nineteenth-century empiricism to insist that *techné* and *episteme* must circulate through culture, and not ossify among corruptible hegemonies. Indeed, his organising persona, Mauberley, evokes the Italian word for movement, *'mobile'*. The translinguistic resonances of the name recall the cosmopolitan Futurists and Vorticists, whose mobility, adaptability and technological savviness enabled them to negotiate the conflicted spaces of modernity. The Vorticists understood that America would be the next frontier in the avant-gardes' engagement with technicity.[128] Accordingly, the next chapter criss-crosses the Atlantic to explore the mechanics of that process, in which modernist vanguardists similarly struggled with representation and selfhood in the post-war Machine Age. In New York especially, the techno-bathetic vanguardists were determined to prove that in the American Machine Age, '[e]ngineer or artist might conceivably become transposable terms, or one, at least, imply the other'.[129]

Notes

1. Norman Wilkinson, *A Brush With Life* (London: Seeley Service & Co. Ltd, 1969), p. 79.
2. Norman Wilkinson, 'Naval Camouflage', in James Cecil Mottram et al., 'Camouflage', *Encyclopædia Britannica: The New Volumes, Twelfth Edition, Vol. 30* (London and New York: The Encyclopaedia Britannica Company,1922), pp. 541–7 (pp. 546–7).
3. First pressed into military service as a troop transport for the Gallipoli campaign after the infamous sinking of her sister ship the *Lucitania* by German U-boats, the *Mauretania* was previously a commercial passenger ship owned by the British Cunard Line; see Humfrey Jordan, *Mauretania: Landfalls and Departures of Twenty-Five Years* (London: Hodder & Stoughton, 1936; Wellingborough: Stephens, 1988), pp. 13–25.

4. Charles DeKay, 'Ships That Fade Away', *Nation* (27 July 1918): 105; quoted in Roy R. Behrens, 'The Role of Artists in Ship Camouflage During World War I', *Leonardo* 32.1 (1999): 53–9 (p. 57).
5. In addition to many articles and photos featuring these dramatically painted vessels, novelties such as dazzle bathing suits and other fashions began to appear in 1919; see Roy R. Behrens, *Camoupedia: A Compendium of Research on Art, Architecture and Camouflage* (Dysart, IA: Bobolink Books, 2009), pp. 132–4.
6. David Williams, *Naval Camouflage 1914–1945: A Complete Visual Reference* (London: Chatham Publishing, 2001), p. 36.
7. In his influential study *Vorticism and Abstract Art in the First Machine Age*, Richard Cork argues that although Wilkinson developed dazzle painting from 'optical theories about the distortion produced by violent colour contrasts and heraldic patterns than from any engagement with the avant-garde', nevertheless, 'the camouflage designs do possess extraordinary subliminal links with the concerns of Vorticism'; *Vorticism and Abstract Art in the First Machine Age, Volume 2: Synthesis and Decline* (London: Gordon Fraser, 1976), p. 523.
8. Martin Dodge and Rob Kitchin, 'Code and the Transduction of Space', *Annals of the Association of American Geographers* 95.1 (March, 2005): 162–80 (p. 169).
9. Adrian Mackenzie, *Transductions: Bodies and Machines at Speed* (London: Continuum, 2002), pp. 16, 19.
10. David Williams, *Naval Camouflage*, p. 36.
11. Roy M. Stanley II, *To Fool a Glass Eye* (Shrewsbury: Airlife Publishing Ltd, 1998), p. 5.
12. Other such camouflage systems were designed to disrupt aerial surveillance and 'photo intelligence'; Ibid. pp. 5–25.
13. Kurt A. Kaczmarek, 'Sensory Augmentation and Substitution', in *The Biomedical Engineering Handbook, Fourth Edition*, ed. Joseph D. Bronzino and Donald R. Peterson (Boca Raton, FL: CRC Press, 2014), pp. 46-1–46-10 (p. 46-1). 'Augmentation' is a problematic term; although it evokes a utopian promise of risk-free technological enhancement, it is understood that any augmentation carries risks, costs and unintended consequences (for example, dazzle designs exploited the exaggerated perspective of range-finding technologies). I use the term in its technical sense, but also fold in the counter-servile contexts established in the book's Introduction.
14. See Germano Celant, 'Futurism as Mass Avant-Garde', trans. John Shepley, in *Futurism and the International Avant-Garde*, ed. Anne d'Harnoncourt (Philadelphia: Philadelphia Museum of Art, 1980–1), pp. 35–42.
15. See Günter Berghaus, 'Futurism and the Technological Imagination: Poised between Machine Cult and Machine Angst', in *Futurism and the Technological Imagination*, ed. Günter Berghaus (Amsterdam and New York: Rodopi, 2009), pp. 1–39.
16. F. T. Marinetti, 'Destruction of Syntax – Radio [Wireless] Imagination – Words-in-Freedom' (1913), in *Futurism*, pp. 143–51 (p. 144).

17. David Harvey, *The Condition of Postmodernity: An Enquiry into the Origin of Cultural Change* (Oxford: Blackwell, 1989), p. 232.
18. Marjorie Perloff describes the Futurists' general interest in 'spatial and temporal distortions' as a characteristic feature of their work in *The Futurist Moment: Avant-Garde, Avant Guerre, and the Language of Rupture, With a New Preface* ([1986]; Chicago: University of Chicago Press, 2003), p. 8. Walter Benjamin would observe similar spatio-temporal dynamics at play in his later discussions of close-ups in cinema; see 'Art in the Age of Mechanical Reproduction', in *Illuminations*, ed. Hannah Arendt, trans. Harry Zorn (London: Pimlico, 1999), 211–244 (pp. 229–30). On 'energetics', see my discussion of Alberto Toscano's use of the term in the book's Introduction.
19. F. T. Marinetti, 'The Founding and Manifesto of Futurism' (20 February 1909), in *Futurism*, pp. 49–53 (p. 50).
20. Ibid.
21. Ibid.
22. F. T. Marinetti, 'Technical Manifesto of Futurist Literature' (11 May 1912), in *Futurism*, pp. 119–25 (p. 119).
23. Ibid. p. 120.
24. See David E. Nye, *American Technological Sublime* (Cambridge, MA, and London: The MIT Press, 1994).
25. F. T. Marinetti, 'Multiplied Man and the Reign of the Machine', in *Futurism*, pp. 89–92 (p. 90).
26. F. T. Marinetti, 'Destruction of Syntax – Radio [Wireless] Imagination – Words-in-Freedom' (1913), in *Futurism*, pp. 143–4.
27. As Berghaus notes, the Futurist technological imaginary 'involved a new concept of a New Humanity of the Machine Age, where people were not only friends, masters and allies of the machine, but fused with it in a symbiotic relationship' ('Futurism and the Technological Imagination', p. 26). I will argue later that the Vorticists developed this imaginary in sophisticated ways.
28. Armando Mazza, '*Transatlantico* [Oceanliner]', in *IFP*, pp. 44–7 (p. 47).
29. See Frederick G. Kilgour, *The Evolution of the Book* (New York and Oxford: Oxford University Press, 1998), pp. 41, 86.
30. See L. B. Hunt 'A History of Iridium: Overcoming the Difficulties of Melting and Fabrication', *Platinum Metals Review* 31.1 (January 1987): 31–41 (pp. 36–8).
31. Peter Nicholls, *Modernisms: A Literary Guide, Second Edition* (Basingstoke and New York: Palgrave Macmillan, 2009), pp. 98–9.
32. See Claudia Salaris, 'Marketing Modernism: Marinetti as Publisher', trans. Lawrence Rainey, *Modernism/Modernity* 1.3 (1994): 109–27 (p. 115).
33. Attilio Vallecchi, *Ricordi e idee di un editore vivente* (Florence: Vallecchi, 1934), p. 119; cited and trans. Walter L. Adamson in *Avant-Garde Florence: From Modernism to Fascism* (Cambridge, MA: Harvard University Press, 1993), p. 171.
34. Alberto Viviani, '*Partenza aeroplano + concerto vieuxtemps*' ['Airplane Departure + Traditional Concerto'], *IFP*, pp. 76–81.

35. Ardengo Soffici, '*Crocicchio* [Cross-Road]', *IFP*, pp. 82–3.
36. See David Mather, 'Carlo Carrà's Conscience', in *Nothing but the Clouds Unchanged: Artists in World War I*, ed. Gordon Hughes and Philipp Blom (Los Angeles: Getty Research Institute, 2014), pp. 88–95 (pp. 90–1).
37. Carlo Carrà, *Guerrapitura* (Milano: Edizioni Futuriste di 'Poesia', 1915).
38. Carlo Carrà, '*Divagazione Medianica No 1*' ('Mediumistic Digression No.1'), *IFP*, pp. 92–3 (p. 93).
39. See Christine Poggi, 'Introduction to Part 2', in *Futurism*, pp. 305–30 (pp. 323–4).
40. Ibid. p. 319.
41. F. T. Marinetti, 'Multiplied Man and the Reign of the Machine', in *Futurism*, p. 91.
42. F. T. Marinetti and Christopher Nevinson, 'Futurism and English Art' (*The Observer*, 7 June 1914), in *Futurism*, pp. 196–8; 'Vital English Art', *Lacerba* 2.14 (15 July 1914): 209–10.
43. *Futurism*, p. 198.
44. See Wyndham Lewis, 'The London Group', *B2*, pp. 77–9 (p. 77).
45. Wyndham Lewis, 'Editorial', *B2*, pp. 5–6 (p. 5).
46. Ibid.
47. Wyndham Lewis, 'Our Vortex', *B1*, pp. 147–9 (p. 149).
48. Wyndham Lewis, 'Long Live the Vortex', *B1*, pp. 7–8 (p. 8).
49. Wyndham Lewis et al., 'Manifesto', *B1* (20 June 1920), pp. 30–42 (p. 39); Wyndham Lewis, 'Relativism and Picasso's Latest Work', *B1*, pp. 139–40 (p. 140).
50. Wyndham Lewis, 'Relativism and Picasso's Latest Work', p. 140.
51. Wyndham Lewis, 'Futurism, Magic and Life', *B1*, pp. 132–5 (p. 135). Martin Heidegger's 1955 definition of *techné* connects 'the skill of the craftsman' to 'the arts of the mind and the fine arts', and the notion of 'bringing-forth'; *The Question Concerning Technology and Other Essays*, trans. William Lovitt (New York: Harper & Row, 1977), p. 13.
52. Günter Berghaus, 'Futurism and the Technological Imagination', p. 26.
53. Wyndham Lewis, 'A Review of Contemporary Art', *B2*, pp. 38–47 (p. 40).
54. Wyndham Lewis, 'Vortex No. 1', *B2*, p. 91.
55. Martin Dodge and Rob Kitchin, 'Code and the Transduction of Space', *Annals of the Association of American Geographers* 95.1 (March, 2005): 162–80 (p. 169).
56. Wyndham Lewis, 'A Review of Contemporary Art', *B2*, pp. 43–4.
57. Simondon, *METO*, pp. 15–16.
58. Ibid. pp. 43–4.
59. Ibid.
60. Miranda Hickman, 'The Gender of Vorticism: Jessie Dismorr, Helen Saunders, and Vorticist Feminism', in *Vorticism: New Perspectives*, ed. Mark Antliff and Scott W. Klein (Oxford: Oxford University Press, 2013), pp. 119–36 (p. 124).
61. Jessica Dismorr, 'Monologue', *B2*, p. 65.

62. Jessica Dismorr, 'London Notes', *B2*, p. 66.
63. Helen Saunders, 'A Vision of Mud', *B2*, pp. 73–4 (p. 73).
64. Ibid. p. 73.
65. Ibid.
66. Ibid.
67. Ibid. p. 74.
68. Ibid.
69. Wyndham Lewis, 'Futurism, Magic and Life', *B1*, p. 135.
70. F. T. Marinetti, Luigi Russolo and Ugo Piatti, '*GL'intonarumori Futuristi triofano a Londra* [Futurist Noise Intoners Triumph in London]', *Lacerba* 2 (15 July 1914): 218 (I am grateful to Martina Hallegger for help with my translations; any errors are my own). The article is a response to negative press in Italy and England which labelled the performances at the Coliseum a failure. The authors countered that only the first performance was 'opposed', in part due to the use of Coliseum staff musicians, and that the other eleven events 'at the Coliseum' were 'all applauded' (p. 218). Indeed, their perseverance was rewarded, because in 'the last two performances [. . .] some of the results were good [. . .] and the public was aware of it'; Luigi Russolo, *The Art of Noises* (New York: Pendragon, 1982), p. 36.
71. Wyndham Lewis, Ezra Pound, Edward Wadsworth, Jacob Epstein, Henri Gaudier-Brzeska and T. S. Eliot all attended a reading by Marinetti, which was accompanied by Christopher Nevinson on percussion at the Doré Galleries in May 1914; see Wyndham Lewis, *Blasting and Bombardiering: An Autobiography (Revised Edition)* (London: John Calder, 1982 [1937]), pp. 32–5.
72. Russolo, *The Art of Noises*, pp. 75–6.
73. Luigi Russolo, 'The Art of Noises: A Futurist Manifesto', in *Futurism*, pp. 133–9 (p. 135).
74. Russolo, *The Art of Noises*, p. 75.
75. Ibid. pp. 136–7.
76. Luigi Russolo, '*Dalla rete di rumori: risveglio di una citta*', *Lacerba* 2 (1 March 1914): 72–3.
77. See Russolo, *The Art of Noises*, pp. 32, 35–6.
78. Ibid. p. 36.
79. See Luciano Chessa, *Luigi Russolo, Futurist: Noise, Visual Arts, and the Occult* (Los Angeles: University of California Press, 2012), pp. 185–6. A few *intonarumori* used motors powered by 'a small current of 4–5 volts provided by a pile battery or a storage battery', but these only powered motors, and the results were no louder than traditional instruments; Russolo, *The Art of Noises*, p. 76.
80. Arndt Niebisch, *Media Parasites in the Early Avant-Garde: On the Abuse of Technology and Communication* (New York: Palgrave Macmillan, 2012), p. 125.
81. Russolo, *The Art of Noises*, p. 31.
82. Ibid. pp. 49–53.
83. Ibid. p. 53.

84. Russolo, 'The Art of Noises', in *Futurism*, p. 138.
85. See especially Russolo, *The Art of Noises*, pp. 49–53.
86. Ibid. p. 75.
87. Ezra Pound to John Quinn, 29 February 1916, *The Selected Letters of Ezra Pound to John Quinn, 1915–1924*, ed. Timothy Materer (Durham, NC, and London: Duke University Press, 1991), pp. 62–5.
88. Ezra Pound, 'The Vortographs', in *Ezra Pound and the Visual Arts*, ed. Harriet Zinnes (New York: New Directions, 1980), pp. 154–7 (p. 154).
89. Alvin Langdon Coburn, *Alvin Langdon Coburn, Photographer: An Autobiography*, ed. Helmut and Alison Gernsheim (New York: Praeger, 1966), p. 102.
90. Coburn, *Alvin Langdon Coburn*, p. 104.
91. Ann McCauley has documented Coburn's experience with multiple exposure techniques in his portraiture from 1907 in 'Witch Work, Art Work, and the Spiritual Roots of Abstraction: Ezra Pound, Alvin Langdon Coburn and the Vortographs', in *Vorticism: New Perspectives*, pp. 156–74 (pp. 161–4).
92. Pound claimed partial credit for inventing the device as well as the process in Ezra Pound to John Quinn, 13 October 1916, *The Selected Letters of Ezra Pound to John Quinn*, p. 88. According to Pound, other versions of the apparatus existed. He explained to Quinn that 'the present version happens to be rectilinear, but I can make one that will do any sort of curve, quite easily'; Ezra Pound to John Quinn, 24 January 1917, *The Selected Letters of Ezra Pound 1907–1941*, ed. D. D. Paige (New York: New Directions, 1971), pp. 103–5 (p. 105). There is little reason to doubt Pound's account, given the Vortoscope's basic components and design.
93. Ezra Pound to Homer L. Pound, 22 September 1916, in *Ezra Pound and the Visual Arts*, p. 293.
94. Mark Antliff has noted that Coburn produced three categories of photographs based on his experiments with Pound: 'a series combining multiple exposures of Pound with mirror effects; a group of two-dimensional profiles of Pound's silhouette; and the famous series of abstractions he later exhibited as "Vortographs" at the London Camera Club' (see Fig. 1.6); 'Alvin Langdon Coburn Among the Vorticists: Studio Photographs and Lost Works by Epstein, Lewis and Wadsworth', *The Burlington Magazine* 152 (September 2010): 580–9 (p. 584).
95. McCauley, 'Witch Work', p. 166.
96. Pound, 'The Vortographs', p. 155.
97. Mike Weaver, *Alvin Langdon Coburn, Symbolist Photographer, 1882–1966* (New York: Aperture Foundation, 1986), p. 68.
98. Pound, 'The Vortographs', p. 154.
99. Ezra Pound to John Quinn, 24 January 1917, *The Selected Letters of Ezra Pound*, p. 103.
100. That rupture marked the beginning of Coburn's long retreat not only from Vorticism but from photography more generally, as he began to embrace spiritualism and the mystic philosophy of Georges Gurdieff; see Antliff, 'Alvin Langdon Coburn Among the Vorticists', p. 589.

101. See Niebisch, *Media Parasites*, pp. 8–9. Niebisch draws mainly on Friedrich Kittler's claim that the entertainment industry appropriated and 'abused' military technology, in *Gramophone, Film, Typewriter* (Stanford: Stanford University Press, 1999), pp. 94–105.
102. Ryan Bishop and John Phillips, *Modernist Avant-Garde Aesthetics and Contemporary Military Technology: Technicities of Perception* (Edinburgh: Edinburgh University Press, 2010), p. 4.
103. Wadsworth's letters to Lewis indicate that he worked tirelessly behind the scenes to organise and edit *Blast*, and that he secured the services of Leveridge & Co., the printer for the journal, as well. See especially Edward Wadsworth to Wyndham Lewis, 22 December 1913; 1 January 1914; 4 February 1914, WL Cornell.
104. Edward Wadsworth to Wyndham Lewis, 29 August 1914, WL Cornell.
105. Edward Wadsworth to Wyndham Lewis, [n.d., ca. 1914–15], WL Cornell.
106. Wadsworth translated extracts and provided synopses of Kandinsky's seminal work, *Uber das Geistige in der Kunst*, in Edward Wadsworth, 'Inner Necessity', *B1*, pp. 119–25.
107. Ezra Pound, 'Edward Wadsworth, Vorticist', *The Egoist* 1.16 (15 August 1914): 306–7 (p. 306).
108. Richard Cork, 'Wadsworth and the Woodcut', in *A Genius of Industrial England: Edward Wadsworth 1889–1949*, ed. Jeremy Lewison (Hatfield: Arkwright Arts Trust and Bradford Art Galleries and Museums), pp. 12–29 (p. 24).
109. Jonathan Black, '"Constructing a Chinese-Puzzle Universe": Industry, National Identity, and Edward Wadsworth's Vorticist Woodcuts of West Yorkshire, 1914–1916', in *Vorticism: New Perspectives*, pp. 89–101 (p. 101).
110. Cork, 'Wadsworth and the Woodcut', p. 24.
111. Jonathan Black, '"Constructing a Chinese-Puzzle Universe"', p. 96.
112. Williams, *Naval Camouflage*, p. 232.
113. See Williams, *Naval Camouflage*, pp. 230–47.
114. Jonathan Black, '"A Few Broad Stripes": Perception, Deception and the "Dazzle Ship" Phenomenon of the First World War', in *Contested Objects: Material Memories of the Great War*, ed. Nicholas J. Saunders and Paul Cornish (London: Routledge, 2009), pp. 190–202 (pp. 195–6).
115. Antliff notes that in a 1916 portrait of Edward Wadsworth, Coburn captured 'a series of striped shadows on the back wall [. . .] to emulate the abstraction of Wadsworth's Vorticist prints and paintings'; 'Alvin Langdon Coburn Among the Vorticists', p. 587.
116. Mackenzie, *Transductions*, p. 212.
117. O. Raymond Drey, [untitled introduction], *Edward Wadsworth: Modern Woodcuts 4* (London: The Little Art Rooms, 1921), n.p.
118. See for example Pound's review of John Everett's December 1918 exhibition 'Paintings & Drawings of the Camouflage of Ships' at the Goupil Gallery: B. H. Dias [Ezra Pound], 'Art Notes', *New Age* 24.8

(26 December 1918): 126–7. Also see his review of the 'Sea Power' Exhibition at Grosvenor Galleries: B. H. Dias [Ezra Pound], 'Art Notes', *New Age* 24.15 (13 February 1919): 240–1.
119. Ezra Pound, 'The Death of Vorticism', *The Little Review* 5.9 (January 1919): 45–8 (p. 48).
120. See Eric B. White, *Transatlantic Avant-Gardes: Little Magazines and Localist Modernism* (Edinburgh: Edinburgh University Press, 2013), pp. 78–9.
121. Ezra Pound to Edgar Jepson, 29 May 1917, *The Selected Letters of Ezra Pound 1907–1941*, pp. 112–13 (p. 112).
122. 'Dazzle-Painting and its Purpose', *The Sphere*, 22 March 1919, in Norman Wilkinson, *A Brush With Life* (London: Seeley Service & Co. Ltd, 1969), p. 83.
123. Williams, *Naval Camouflage*, p. 11.
124. Ibid.
125. Douglas Mao, 'Blasting and Disappearing', in *Vorticism: New Perspectives*, pp. 235–55 (p. 249).
126. Williams, *Naval Camouflage*, p. 36. As Camilla Wilkinson incisively points out in her forthcoming article, dazzle camouflage systems were developed in a rigorous testing regime involving periscopes, models, and a variety of real and simulated environments. The finished designs 'could disrupt the vertical elements' of ships' 'superstructure by painting the bridge, poop deck and masts in highly contrasting tones' so that 'the U-boat Commander would struggle to calculate the ships length and course when using the periscope estimater'. Crucially, this technology was part of a larger tactical and socio-technical milieu, in which ships travelled in convoys (and often in zig-zag patterns). Dazzle camouflage should not be considered separately from such tactics (as some military and art historians are inclined to), but rather, following Camilla Wilkinson's proposal, as an integral part of them; see 'Distortion, Illusion and Transformation: the Evolution of Dazzle Painting, a Camouflage System to Protect Allied Shipping from Unrestricted Submarine Warfare, 1917–1918', (forthcoming 2020). This level of technical integration in no way diminishes the importance of dazzle camouflage as a discrete technology – on the contrary, it reinforces the sophistication of its technicity, and the strategic vision of its inventor and technical development teams. I am grateful to Camilla Wilkinson for sharing her research with me; any errors in its interpretation are my own.
127. Ezra Pound, 'IV', *Hugh Selwyn Mauberley* (London: The Ovid Press, 1920), p. 12.
128. See Wyndham Lewis, 'A Soldier of Humour (Part I)', *The Little Review* 4.8 (December 1917): 32–46 (pp. 41–2); Ezra Pound to Edgar Jepson, 29 May 1917, *The Selected Letters of Ezra Pound 1907–1941*, p. 112; and Edward Wadsworth to Wyndham Lewis, 29 August 1914, WL Cornell, in which he wrote of *B2*, 'A war number would go well in America I think.'
129. Wyndham Lewis, 'Futurism, Magic and Life', *B1*, pp. 132–5 (p. 135).

Chapter 2

Re-Reading the Machine Age: The 'Audacious Modernity' of the Techno-Bathetic Avant-Gardes

Introduction

As the Machine Age accelerated on both sides of the Atlantic, modernists grappled with the languages that might properly describe it. The sprawling proliferation of new socio-technical assemblages seemed to lack a coherent focal point, but as I argued in the Introduction to this book, they had inherited a coherent system for thinking about them. The metaphysics of the 'American technological sublime' supplied a cultural narrative that emerged coevally with transatlantic discourse networks addressing technology and modernity. By the early twentieth century, the Naturalists and Pictorialists had articulated the central tropes of that quasi-mystical language, evoking the 'awe', 'wonder' and 'terror' associated with railways, electricity, megastructures, automotive power, automated production and various technical objects in their writing and art.[1] However, for many avant-garde figures, particularly those who came to be associated with Dada, the monumental technical objects of the Machine Age were not as important as the assemblages and ensembles that they emerged from, and the tense negotiations involved in their transduction in culture. This insight enabled avant-garde figures such as Marcel Duchamp, Baroness Elsa von Freytag-Loringhoven (aka the Baroness), Mina Loy, Francis Picabia, William Carlos Williams and others to produce innovative prototypes, and even new technical objects, as well as visionary creative responses to these systems. Experimentalists who converged in New York in the early decades of the twentieth century had a uniquely intimate encounter with technology, and in particular with the mundane technicities of quotidian life. Fully aware that the technological sublime dominated most discourse networks in the Machine Age, their technicities charted an alternative route: an aesthetic counter-narrative that I call the techno-bathetic, which interlaces bathetic strategies and technical processes and subjects. Techno-bathetic cultural productions tend to critique servile relationships with technology, while proposing new, more energetic ones.[2]

The previous chapter explored the ways in which avant-gardes harnessed processes of transduction and technicity for alternative ends. Counter-surveillance technologies like dazzle camouflage elegantly demonstrated the interdependence of socio-technical ensembles, or infrastructures, by disrupting them for defensive purposes. Like the Futurist poets I discussed in Chapter 1, the proto-Dada artists of New York City began to propose new ways of reading Machine Age America. One of the figures who stimulated that process was the Swiss experimental writer Arthur Cravan. Born Fabian Avenarius Lloyd, the boxer, poet, editor and 'master of disguise' was a con artist as much as an avant-garde one, and he is now best known for his tragic marriage to Mina Loy.[3] Yet his brief career helped articulate an alternative way of reading modernism's relation to technology. Cravan's poem 'New York' identifies how the orthodox technicities of the technological sublime could be reconfigured to negotiate the built environments of modernity. In 'New York', as the 'dazzling' spectacle of the modern city made by 'science' and 'industry' fades, Cravan's speaker begins to identify technology as a means of inhabiting and domesticating, rather than conquering, space. He peers into the intimate interiors of cityscapes and reconnects them to the circulations of the natural world. By accentuating the 'softness', or accessibility and intimacy, of its technologies (including 'the American telephone' and 'elevators'), he reconfigures orthodox technicities of the sublime to negotiate the conflicted spaces of modernity. In this sense, the 'audacious modernity' of Cravan's poem – and of the techno-bathetic avant-gardes – does not reside in its 'dazzling' description of urban 'palaces' but, rather, in the domestication and diffusion of the technologies that built and sustained them.

In this chapter, I explore how the avant-gardes affiliated with the New York Dada movement identified their creative practices with the bathetic technicities unfolding in Machine Age America. My argument is that their techno-bathetic works decrypted the scrambled codes that sprung up between socio-technical ensembles. Splicing these codes onto and into the language of (failed) love, (thwarted) desire and (unstable) gender and sexuality, the techno-bathetic vanguardists' polemic was to ground technical and commercial communications systems within the fraught biomechanical, neuro-chemical and cognitive processes of human experience. The bathos of these gestures demonstrated at once the intrinsic humanity rather more than the uncanny otherness of socio-technics, especially as configured in narratives of the technological sublime. But these interventions also attest to the cross-disciplinary innovation and extraordinary technological literacy of the techno-bathetic avant-gardes, which sprung up across transatlantic discourse networks in the 1910s and 1920s.

Making a spectacle of the technologically commonplace, this avant-garde counter-narrative has eluded modernist studies because, like its subject, it has become so deeply embedded in more dominant narratives (particularly the technological sublime). Tracing a roughly chronological arc from 1913–30, this chapter gives a focused analysis of those underexplored stories, which have previously been dominated by Fordist and Taylorist principles, on the one hand, and sublime aesthetics, on the other. The first parts of the chapter detail the divergent aesthetics of two key modernist formations: in the first section, the Pictorialist-inflected mystical nationalism of Alfred Stieglitz and his 'Young American' literary acolytes (including Waldo Frank and Lewis Mumford); and, in the second section, the radical proto-Dadaists of the magazine *291*, exemplified by the 'mechanomorphic portraits' of Francis Picabia, which satirised (among other things) the technological sublime of Stieglitz, the journal's founder. The third section analyses Duchamp's involvement in the emergent infrastructures of New York's modernist avant-gardes, beginning with the infamous Armory Show, and the salons of Walter Conrad and Louise Arensberg and Allen and Louise Norton. However, it also discusses crucial readings of his projects by the Baroness, Loy and Williams, who used Duchamp's work as a foil for their technicities of reading and writing modernity. The fourth section focuses on the work of the Baroness, whose writings, artworks, inventions and fashion designs interrogated the implications of socio-technics for problems of sex, gender and nationality. Concluding with an analysis of Mina Loy, section five examines her recently uncovered fashion designs from the early 1920s, and, for the first time, unveils her invention 'verrovoile', her commercial sobriquet for 'glass fabric'. Experimenting with the newly discovered organic compound cellulose acetate, Loy created a translucent thermoplastic material with which she constructed elaborate lighting designs and profiled it in a previously unknown 1929 article in a London newspaper. I argue that Loy helped inaugurate the advent of the artist-engineer in the mid-1920s, and her use of 'verrovoile' in her home lighting designs combined materials from the early days of mass production with the latest thermoplastic technology to signpost a diachronic sense of technicity grounded in the rhythms of everyday life.

For Loy, as for the avant-gardes coalescing in New York in the mid-1910s, technical objects were not necessarily totemic emblems of a new age but motley patchworks of schematics, speculative technologies and unreliable machines, rooted in the mundane rhythms of everyday life by their attachments to language and routine. The self-consciously provisional, ephemeral, and even deliberately unfinished nature of their projects revealed how in the modernist transatlantic, America's cultural production was conceived as both a functioning dynamo and a mountain of scattered blueprints – an immense project perpetually under construction, and an unstable collection of assemblages. Rather than invoking the power and efficiency of its machines and infrastructure, these vanguardists emphasised their delicacy, intricacy and fragility. Nevertheless, their work thrived in the shadows of the technological sublime, and one of its key modernist proponents, Alfred Stieglitz.

Alfred Stieglitz and the Rise of the Nationalist Technological Sublime

Stieglitz documented the rise of the American metropolis through his dialectical urban studies, which held Naturalist realism and symbolic abstraction in dynamic tension. Works like *The Steerage* (1907), which anticipated his precisionist work of the 1920s–1930s, articulated a stark, realist clarity that explored the social reorganisations expressed and imposed by monumental technologies, from transatlantic ocean liners to skyscrapers. Yet as William Sharpe argues, Stieglitz and the Photo-Secessionists were first and foremost Pictorialists, who 'favored a suggestive, symbolist vagueness [. . .] to find new solutions to the old problem of extracting an artistic ensemble from the urban hodgepodge'. Their use of techniques to create shadow and soft-focus effects (which included 'gauze or petroleum jelly over the lens, or even kick[ing] the tripod during a time-exposure') helped drape their subjects in indeterminacy.[4] In turn, Stieglitz bolted this symbolic scaffolding onto the language of the sublime. His grand industrial structures evoked metaphysical awe just as they dwarfed the human subject and its quotidian rhythms, and often squalid surroundings. Steiglitz's *Old and New New York* (1910) shows a partially constructed skyscraper emerging from a mist, detached and towering over its urban contexts (Fig. 2.1). The human subjects are divided and displaced, and the older structures reduced to backdrops. Stieglitz's strategic use of blurring renders the newer structure emergent and primordial, and the structure on the far right of the picture fragile and crumbling. This photograph anticipates Stieglitz's 'skyscraper sublime' of the 1920s but lacks his later precisionist clarity. *Old and New New York* captures a sublime in transition, its encroaching unfamiliarity generating tension and fear as much as

Figure 2.1 Alfred Stieglitz, *Old and New New York, 1910*, Photogravure; Alfred Stieglitz Collection, Art Institute of Chicago.

awe. Stieglitz was not an uncritical utopian – like the Young Americans, his photographs sometimes incorporated narratives of social deprivation, and, perhaps, in the evanescence of his late-nineteenth- and early-twentieth-century nocturnes, even hinted at the eventual decline of industrial modernity's most totemic structures.

From 17 February until 15 March, the 1913 'Armory Show' intrigued audiences in New York and across the United States. Owing to its venue, the Sixty-Ninth Regiment Armory building, the event consolidated an enduring association between military hardware and avant-garde spectacle in the public imagination. Stieglitz was not involved in organising the show, possibly because its scale and cultural exposure were out of keeping with his own artisanal approach, but he did help promote it.[5] However, in the show's aftermath, Stieglitz's vanguardism, and the nationalist technological sublime it advanced, became diffuse and unfocused. Alert to his declining reputation, he re-energised the 291 Gallery network by launching *291* magazine with the Mexican illustrator, writer-editor and gallery owner Marius De Zayas. They edited the journal with writer-patron Agnes E. Meyer and critic-patron Paul Haviland to rejuvenate New York's post-Armory visual arts scene, which had also begun to stagnate with the advent of the First World War. By the mid-1910s, however, the proto-Dadaists had hijacked *291* magazine to attack Stieglitz's techno-nationalist sublime, largely thanks to De Zayas. As I discuss in the next section, Francis Picabia used his mechanomorphic 'portraits' of Stieglitz and others to characterise the Pictorialist avant-garde's attempt at rejuvenation as a further symptom of its decline. However, Stieglitz launched a counter-offensive to restore his reputation and re-articulate his aesthetic principles. Spearheaded by Waldo Frank, the new group of Young American writers associated with the little magazine *The Seven Arts* fused the literary nationalism of the Chicago Renaissance with the technological sublime of Stieglitz and the Pictorialists in an effort to restore the normative hierarchies threatened by industrialisation – and by the bathetic tactics of the avant-gardes. Together, these modernist formations created one of the most potent but (in terms of their relative levels of cultural scrutiny) most lopsided dialectics of the American Machine Age: the technological sublime vs. the techno-bathetic.

Although he founded *291*, Stieglitz's status as a Machine Age auteur owes more to his first journal, *Camera Work*. From 1903–17, this exquisitely produced little magazine consolidated a Symbolist lexicon for American modernity grounded in the technological sublime. The problem was that it was almost too successful. De Zayas noted that by 1915 Stieglitz's distinctive techniques, and his reputation as an artistic moderniser, had long since descended into cliché. In a *291* editorial De Zayas acknowledged that Stieglitz 'wanted to discover America. Also, he wanted the Americans to discover themselves.' De Zayas acknowledged that Stieglitz had successfully 'married Man to Machinery and he obtained issue', and that his address to the sublime was central to his encounter with America.

Although he praised the 'importance' of Stieglitz's cultural contribution, however, De Zayas also pointed out that it was largely being ignored. This was because in the contemporary 'milieu', Stieglitz's approach represented a shortcoming rather than a strength: 'in pursuing his object, [Stieglitz] employed the shield of psychology and metaphysics' – classic tactics of occlusion that Alexander Pope frequently associated with the sublime. De Zayas argued that this evasive approach had 'failed' because it did not encourage 'the individualistic expression of the spirit of the community'. De Zayas insisted that in America '[o]ne lives here in the present. In a continuous struggle to adapt oneself to the milieu', and that this relationality would be the key to the 'complex mentality' that united the country with the 'true modern artist'. He concluded that '[a]ny effort, any tendency, which does not possess the radiation of advertising remains practically ignored'.[6] In other words, Stieglitz's vision failed because he did not recognise the individuating potential of socio-technical assemblages, and, instead, used them to inspire metaphysical awe.

However, Stieglitz was adept at harnessing the power of cultural formations, and he understood the danger of becoming trapped in an outmoded one. When his 291 Gallery closed and *Camera Work* folded in 1917, he saw the potential for an emerging cultural formation to regenerate his more established one. The Young Americans had embraced the work of Stieglitz as a supreme expression of the nationalist technological sublime. Through the auspices of Sherwood Anderson, Stieglitz engaged with this new generation of literary nationalists, who included Randolph Bourne, Van Wyck Brooks, Lewis Mumford, Louis Untermeyer and Waldo Frank. In his major prose work, *Our America*, Frank argued that 'the Machine' had become 'the god of the American world', a malign and uncontrollable force. Frank concluded that 'if the machine [was] the fresh product of the outpouring human soul, [then] it soon became its master, and the soul that made it could not cease to feed it'.[7] Here, Frank captures the servile dread articulated across the sublime imaginary of the Young Americans. And yet, citing Stieglitz, he also identified its curiously unifying potential. As David Nye argues, 'when experienced by large groups, the sublime can weld society together', united by the 'fundamental hopes and fears' that the sensation – an 'essentially religious feeling' – engenders.[8] In the first issue of *The Seven Arts*, Paul Rosenfeld explicitly connected Stieglitz's programme for cultural renewal with precisely this kind of religious mission, in which technology serves merely as a platform for his 'dynamic' nationalist art.[9]

The Young Americans reflected widespread anxieties about industrial modernity, ranging from urban 'ethnic chaos' to runaway automatism under 'the clamped dominion of Puritan and Machine'.[10] However, they reinforced the strategies by which Stieglitz redirected the metaphysical awe generated by this servile technicity away from a malign industrialism, and towards an organicist sense of nationalism. As Marcia Brennan rightly notes,

> Stieglitz and his critics countered the idea of the camera as a disembodied, mechanical eye, detached and precise in its movements, with the image of Stieglitz's organic incorporation of the camera into himself. With this rhetorical move, man became re-centred, and was restored to a position of control and mastery.[11]

As well as affirming the basic structure of techno-servility (which, as I discuss in the book's Introduction, configures technophilia and technophobia as two sides of the same coin), the Young Americans' gendered language was deliberate: for them, Stieglitz's work restored the masculine hegemony that technology threatened to disrupt (a disruption that the New York proto-Dadaists delighted in). Frank, like Lewis Mumford, believed that technics and civilisation were not incompatible,[12] and that the worship of the machine could be corrected by artists (and, specifically, by Alfred Stieglitz) within the framework of the technological sublime.

Despite the Young Americans' boosterism, from the mid-1910s, Stieglitz's 291 Gallery continued to struggle, and, to their chagrin, a variety of other intersecting avant-gardes began to capture its niche – and, ironically, under its own auspices. Picabia, Duchamp, Man Ray and the various intersecting avant-garde circles of the Arensbergs, as well as the cultural localists associated with the Greenwich Village free verse movement (including Loy and Williams) began to infiltrate and mimic some of the strategies of the 291 scene. When he founded *291* magazine, Stieglitz wanted to create a place for dialogue between science, technology and the arts. As Michael North has noted, Stieglitz's approach, both in aesthetic and critical terms, repeatedly 'demonstrated how new inventions could require a wholesale reorganization of the artistic and cultural apparatus'.[13] *291* was an experiment that Stieglitz hoped would re-energise this 'reorganization', but he lost control of it and instead produced a rogue infrastructure.[14] The journal's tendency to hybridise abstract and representational forms owed a good deal to Agnes E. Meyer and her conception of 'the SCIENTIFIC INFLUENCE IN ART'.[15] Critics and artists, she insisted, must take their lead from the 'experimental' impulse in science and engineering that had been articulated by the key modernist 'isms': 'impressionism, cubism, futurism', and other group art formations. Adapting these 'experimental' methods, critics should analyse the products of the 'new art' and retain only those accomplishments from which 'would arise a new art'.[16]

In some respects, Meyer's argument anticipates Theodor Adorno's reflections on avant-garde art movements. According to Adorno, '[t]he subject, conscious of the loss of power that it has suffered as a result of the technology unleashed by himself, raised this powerlessness to the level of a program', i.e. an 'ism'.[17] The drive to foster group experimentation is both a product and re-articulation of this sense of 'powerlessness', but it also has a fascinating upshot. For Adorno, '[i]sms are scandalous because they do not fit into the schema of absolute individuation'.[18] In other words, 'isms' stress the *relationality* of creative production, and put *ensembles*, rather than individuals, centre stage. In the 1910s both 'isms' and socio-technical ensembles proliferated symbiotically, and co-constructed that subjective disenfranchisement Adorno identifies. Stieglitz's response was to convert that sense of 'powerlessness' into a sense of awe – the sublime aesthetic that pervades his subjects. In the first issue of *291*, he configured this trope as a gothic rather than technological sublime in his literary vignettes 'One Hour's Sleep – Three Dreams'.[19] Thereafter, his contributions to the journal were largely administrative, and he became a subject in rather than a shaper of its aesthetic development. Ironically, this exclusion prompted Stieglitz and his acolytes to reformulate a far more coherent version of the American technological sublime, and with a far broader reach, than he could have achieved in the specialist publication *291*. For example, in *Our America* Frank held up Stieglitz's work as an example of 'mystic' nationalism that produced an affective bond between metaphysics, nationalism and technology in urban America.[20] Nevertheless, by displacing rather than confronting society's servile relationship with technology, Stieglitz and the Young Americans had simply swapped one set of hierarchies for another. They had diminished even further the interest that existed in the messy negotiations that unfolded beneath and between the monumental subjects addressed in their work. In *291*, however, the proto-Dadaists had precisely the opposite emphasis.

291 vs. *291*: Sublime Vistas and Bathetic Machines

The notorious fifth issue of *291* (July–August 1915) contained an overt rebellion against its founder. In his editorial, De Zayas acknowledged that although Stieglitz had found a system for incorporating technology into the arts, he 'did not succeed in bringing out the individualistic expression of the spirit of the community'. De Zayas had cautioned that 'any tendency' that 'does not possess the radiation of advertising remains practically ignored'. In America, he felt that the *ensemble* was the important subject, not the transcendent subject or genius, as Stieglitz did, since these emphases shaded out the collective with a servile focus on the individual. As such, the monumental technological sublime that Stieglitz presented had become moribund, but De Zayas immediately recognised an antidote – an artist who 'does not protect himself with any shield'.[21] Francis Picabia articulated his intensely relational and overtly experimental approach in a series of 'mechanomorphic' portraits for *291*. Resembling electrical schematics of individuals and cultural archetypes, they exposed the complexities of American socio-technical ensembles, and their intricate engagements with bathos, rather than their overweaning articulations of the sublime. Of course, Picabia's machines are deliberately incomplete caricatures of blueprints and schematics, but this is not the essence of their bathetic critique: they all 'work' at some level, and all invite intellectual and/or biomechanical ignition to resist the production of technologically induced stupefaction, and return it to the reality of work, the body and the commonplace. Like Duchamp, and to a lesser extent, Stieglitz, in his mid-1910s 'American' phase, Picabia seeks to re-evaluate (or re-start) the terms by which artists could describe the new relationships forming between the machine, the body and language, as well as the increasingly mundane theatres for their encounter. As such, the joke on his subjects and the readership of *291* – that they have failed not only to execute but even to comprehend the reciprocal cycles of generating art in 'the Age of the Machine' (which Haviland would describe in the next issue of the journal) – is an important cultural product of these machines.[22]

The cover of *291*'s fifth issue featured Picabia's 'mechanomorphic portrait', *Ici, C'est Ici Stieglitz Foi et Amour* (*Here, Here This Is Stieglitz / Faith and Love*), as its cover.[23] The illustration is a caricature of a schematic, which ostensibly supplants the photographer with his tools (Fig. 2.2). Despite Paul Rosenfeld's subsequent attempt in *The Seven Arts* to spin Picabia's portrait as an affectionate tribute, De Zayas's polemical editorial in the same issue of *291* erased any sense of doubt that the 'portrait' was a prank at Stieglitz's expense.[24] De Zayas had argued that American society uniquely articulated the advanced ensembles of modern industrial complexes. By way of parody, Picabia's *Ici, C'est Ici Stieglitz* does not depict an isolated genius but instead reminds the viewer of a serial networker. Accordingly, Picabia's design splices two apparently unrelated machine ensembles together: an SLR camera and the electrical and transmission systems from an automobile. These systems embody the complexly interdependent chains of production emerging in the art as well as the industry of the Machine Age. Looking under the bonnet of Stieglitz's technological sublime, Picabia evokes

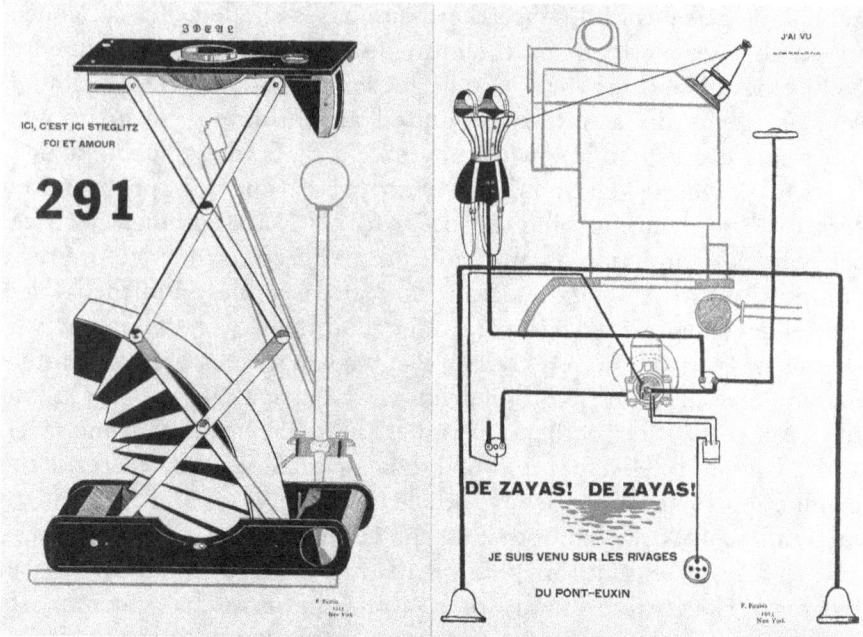

Figure 2.2 Francis Picabia, *Ici, C'est Ici Stieglitz Foi et Amour*, *291* nos 5–6 (July–August 1915): 1 and *De Zayas! De Zayas!*, p. 5 [gatefold]; Yale Collection of American Literature, Beinecke Rare Book and Manuscript Library.

the intricacy of these machine ensembles, but focuses on their fragility rather than their power. As William Rozaitis points out, *Ici, C'est Ici Stieglitz* depicts a system in which a 'brake is engaged' and a 'gearshift is stuck in neutral' – in other words, these interlocking ensembles *don't actually work*.[25] Although Picabia's detailed design captures Stieglitz's 'respect for the primacy of the visual object', the elaborate technical joke pokes fun at the photographer's 'pretentions'.[26] However, like Picabia's other mechanomorphic portraits, the non-functionality he depicts in *Ici, C'est Ici Stieglitz* should not be understood as *failure*, but as a different kind of *product*.

In the July–August 1915 issue of *291*, Picabia produced a whole series of bathetic machines – sophisticated multimodal ensembles that generated cultural criticism, humour and productive creative entropy. In these proto-Dada works, Picabia draws technology into the realms of the banal and everyday from which they emerge. However, he also relies on concurrent processes of sublation (in which a concept is both preserved and changed through its dialectical exchanges with another) to evoke public awe of machine ensembles – and in the case of Stieglitz, the artist who evokes that awe. As I discussed in this book's Introduction, the 'black box' effect is a process by which unfamiliar technical objects 'normalise' in culture through a process of diffusion over time. This phenomenon elides symbiolitcally with sublime processes of abstraction and mystification, which, like petroleum on a camera lens, help translate the operations of those technical systems into the language of the sublime. Opening that black box returns us to its details, but also to its functionality, operations and social relations. The bathetic impulse of Picabia's mechanomorphic portraits always alludes to its obverse: to peer into the 'black box' is simultaneously to dismantle it, and also to affirm its power. In this respect, it reveals how Picabia and his fellow proto-Dadaists understood technicity as a spatial practice kith and kin with reading and writing.

As a tactical spatial practice, the techno-bathetic cleaves closely to Dada's aesthetics, which, as Sara Crangle argues, 'bring the sublime into the realm of the everyday, and simultaneously [elevate] happenstance'.[27] The rich semantics of technography and advertising culture provided Picabia with fitting subjects for his mechanomorphic portraits, which revel in the bathetic interplay between these socio-technical ensembles. Language and technicity are fundamentally conjoined in these processes, and in Picabia's negotiation of them, so it is surprising that his critics tend to overlook the importance of written texts in these illustrations. Words and language do not merely provide titles, or prompts, but form crucial parts of the schematic: printed language transforms his seemingly inoperable or merely parodic apparatuses into functional, meaning-making machines. Picabia's radial logic culminates in his final and most complex mechanomorphic illustration, and his most elaborate polemic, *De Zayas! De Zayas!*, which also appeared in the fifth issue of *291*.

In *De Zayas! De Zayas!*, Picabia engineers a deliberately incomplete mechanism that invites readers to complete it with their own expressive and libidinal input (Fig. 2.2). Spoken with a New York City accent, *De Zayas! De Zayas!* sounds like 'Desires! Desires!', a klaxon that unsubtly announces (and warns of) the subject's sexual proclivities.[28] For Picabia, the bathetic drift of language forms the blueprint for his machine. The schematic depicts an empty corset connected to an automotive electrical system and mediated by various phrases.[29] The chassis and major components connect to the central starter motor, while the corset is also connected to a phallic bobbin on the upper right-hand side of the apparatus. Lauren Kroiz argues that '[i]f this engine were actually to start, the female undergarment would be pulled in'.[30] So is this a machine for stimulating male desire? Not quite, because the corset actually connects to a switch, and not to the motor itself. But tracing the circuit path is not at all straightforward, because the lines depicting electrical connections do not feature circuit jumps (i.e. half-circle lines indicating that intersecting lines on a diagram do not form a point of electrical contact) or points of contact (full stops at the centre of a four-way intersection). As such, these intersections could be interpreted as crossed wires and/or parallel connections, which would either short each other out or entangle the operations, despite the various switching mechanisms in the circuit. In that case, the whole apparatus would not only loosen and 'pull in' the corset, but also shock the heart and crotch of the garment while self-destructing.[31] In *De Zayas! De Zayas!*, Picabia effectively hot-wires the soul and loins of American culture, destroying its erotic and aesthetic circuity as a generative act, so that it can be remade. It is clearly a playful portrait, but nevertheless it generates dark humour, and the potential for dangerous malfunction and/or abuse in this system should not be overlooked, not least because the garment factories were notorious sites for the exploitation of young working-class women (as the 1913 Paterson Silk Strikes had illustrated).[32] In his satire of his patron-advocate De Zayas – and consumer desires in American culture – Picabia observes that attempts to channel sexual desire to consumer (or patronage) activity can potentially cross into predation and exploitation, potentially resulting in (self-) destruction.

Picabia's mechanomorphic portraits trace the Icarian fall of language and technology, but also patch them together to make working ensembles. As Kroiz rightly argues, in *De Zayas! De Zayas!*

> [t]he inscription at upper right, J'ai vu, et c'est de toi qu'il s'agit, ['I have seen / and it is you that this concerns'], identifies this seducing machine as De Zayas, and suggests that, unlike Stieglitz, the caricaturist was indeed able to mate with America and produce a new art as his offspring.[33]

However, the other, more cryptic, text statement also implicates the Old World gaze in this figuration of the New. The phrase 'Je suis venu sur les rivages du pont-euxin' appears beneath the work's title and a sketch resembling an inverted triangle. Willard Bohn translates the text as 'I have come to the shores of the Black Sea', an allusion to *Anabasis* in which the Greek warrior-philosopher Xenophon retreats home from an unsuccessful campaign in Persia.[34] However, Kroiz identifies Jules Verne's adaptation *Kéraban the Inflexible* as another source of this classical reference, which narrates a merchant's absurd attempts to evade a tax collector on the Bosporus.[35] Both arcane points invoke the technobathos of Picabia's machine. In *De Zayas! De Zayas!*, he suggests that the ambiguities and jarring meanings of specialist registers extend from electro-mechanical and literary milieus to the commercial sphere (the corset design is copied from contemporary adverts for *Persephone* undergarments).³⁶ All components of the machine break down, and the sum of these parts presents a travesty of Machine Age Taylorist efficiencies. If transduction consists of 'sets of [everyday] practices that seek to solve ongoing relational problems in society' and technicity is 'the power of technologies to help solve those problems', then Picabia's mechanomorphic portraits also revealed the power of technology to *compound* those 'relational problems', rather than solve them.³⁷ As commentaries on the bathos of technicity, his machines worked perfectly.

In this sense, Picabia's portrait of De Zayas is neither despairing, nor anarchic, but grounding, in a strategically literal sense. The inverted triangle mediating the title *De Zayas! De Zayas!* and the French phrase in the lower-left corner tend to be read as the Black Sea in *Anabasis* 'extending to the horizon'.³⁸ However, an inverted triangle comprised of lines of decreasing length closely resembles the electrical symbol for *earth ground*, a common return path or a physical connection to the earth in an electrical circuit. (In mains-powered systems, the earth point serves as a kind of 'fail-safe' in the event of overloads, while in other systems it can reduce the build-up of static electricity.) Located at the base of the illustration, the earth/ocean composite is simultaneously a conductor and an insulating fail-safe, and the common meeting point for this elaborate circuitry. For Picabia, bathos is the rhetorical equivalent of that common ground. It resides both within and beyond technical systems, and is embedded in the partially compatible ensembles, and the multimodal languages, of the Machine Age. For the proto-Dadaists, these ensembles existed in a perpetual state of becoming – and, therefore, in a persistent state of instability, vulnerability and exposure – '*L'État de Nudité*', to quote another of Picabia's mechanomorphic portraits.³⁹

'A Machine of Mirrors': Marcel Duchamp, *The Blind Man* and William Carlos Williams on Vernacular Technicities

Intensely ironic and dizzyingly variegated, Duchamp's 'engineered' aesthetics explored identity and language as well as the status of art and the image in the modern, technology-driven world. As I discussed in the book's Introduction, in Duchamp's early work on machine forms ca. 1912–14, technology mediates the dialectics of the Machine Age everyday. Diagrams of technical objects and exposed technical ensembles spark and grind against the sensory apparatus of human biology with a disjunctive sexual pulse. It was during this period that he conceived of *The Bride Stripped Bare by Her Bachelors, Even*.[40] An eroticised depiction of a mechanised bride and her adoring, competing bachelors, the work was also known as *The Large Glass*, a mirror in which the technological languages of modernity re-processed the socio-technics as well as the biomechanics of reproduction, and identity. Like Picabia's mechanomorphic portraits, *The Large Glass* was an extended exercise in bathetic prototyping that both anticipated and epitomised the Machine Age techno-bathetic. And like Picabia's work, Duchamp's magnum opus was a literary as well as a visual creation. Building on his interventions in *The Blind Man* and *The Little Review*, other Dada-inspired vanguardists such as the Baroness, Mina Loy and William Carlos Williams helped identify their implications for reading and writing in the Machine Age. For avant-gardes inhabiting this New World, discourses of technology and technicity were generating new languages with which to conduct transatlantic aesthetic debates, and new ways of folding vernacular culture into creative practice.

First conceived in Munich in July–August 1912, Duchamp's *Large Glass* became a sprawling transatlantic composition that ranged across and ironised multiple modalities and defined the visual language of modernist avant-gardes. Yet appropriately for a professional librarian, it was an intensely literary work, articulated across reams of notepaper. The elaborate visual puns of the bachelors' domain in the completed *Large Glass* nearly match the technical detail of the blueprints that Duchamp drafted in his initial designs for the *Bachelor Apparatus (Plan and Elevation)* of 1913.[41] However, the literary and linguistic aspects of the work are concentrated mainly in the domain of the Bride (as well as the brief aphorisms and notes in the *Box of 1914* and later boxed collections). In these early sketches especially, such references are paradoxically notable by their absence. The incomplete aperture of the 1913 sketches – part of the 'alphabetic units' and 'triple cipher' of 'nets' in the Bride's 'cinematic blossoming', which in turn 'govern [the] alphabet and terms of the Pendu Felelle's [female hanged body's] commands' – gestures at her secret messages in the final (unfinished) work.[42] In the work itself, however, those languages are implicit, and almost invisible.

Duchamp's writings and literary sources were only unveiled as publications in his various 'boxed' collections of designs. The work of articulating the literary elements of Duchamp's relentless prototyping is performed by the machine ensembles embedded in *The Large Glass* – and then only in schematic form. Some of Duchamp's greatest conceptual gestures in the piece are his references to incompletion, especially in terms of the communications processes which, in their suggested presence but glaring absence, are a key focal point for the piece. Yet Duchamp included them in several installations associated with the masterpiece, or 'published' them as 'boxes' of notes, which reveal the inner workings of his complex project. This vast panorama of ideas persistently featured technology's relationship to language, and especially the language of mirroring, doubling and reflection – but also processes of omission, incompletion and illusion. Appropriately, he deployed the linguistic equivalent of mirrors – puns and double-entendres – to accrue ever increasing levels of aesthetic capital for his project (and of course, the 'Glass' of its popular title is an archaic synonym of 'mirror'), while constantly deferring any definitive 'return' or reading.

In his notes for the project, Duchamp describes 'the Bride stripped bare by her bachelors' as an 'agricultural machine',[43] which, like a 'green house', could foster the '[b]reeding of colors', accelerating economic production and biological reproduction by means of Machine Age engineering.[44] But he was also fascinated with breeding new languages. His search for the 'prime words' with which to express the fourth dimensional meta-languages of the new physics leads Duchamp to concoct a kind of translinguistic computer.[45] He planned to make 'this dictionary by means of cards' and 'films', rehearsing various systems for ordering and transfiguring linguistic data throughout his *Notes and Projects*.[46] Using a form of technological synæsthesia, at one point Duchamp proposes a 'color dictionary' to broadcast messages from the bride to her bachelors, 'breeding' and hybridising both colours and language, and folding his eroticised technologies into a machine that has little to do with biological reproduction and everything to do with textual (re-)production. And yet, the messages never reach their intended recipient, and exist only as ghosts in the machine – a form of bathetic haunting that is one of his major products in *Notes and Projects for the Large Glass*. Like other techno-bathetic avant-gardists, Duchamp performs rather than explicates his strategies for reading and writing the Machine Age in these works. The elusive connections that *The Large Glass* both describes and withholds require completion beyond the boundaries of its own circuitry. Other Dada-inspired artists and writers were only too willing to collaborate in that process, including the Baroness, Mina Loy, William Carlos Williams, and his collaborators on *The Blind Man*.

Edited by Duchamp with Walter Conrad Arensberg, Henri-Pierre Roché and Mina Loy, *The Blind Man* was a focal point for the second major New York modernist axis (the first being the Stieglitz circle of the 291 Gallery), and its important second issue was published in May 1917. Discussions of this issue tend to be overshadowed by the debate around 'R. Mutt's' readymade *Fountain*, the urinal controversially rejected by the jurors for *The Society of Independent Artists'* Exhibition of April–May 1917 (Fig. 2.3).[47] The readymade is of course attributed to Duchamp,[48] but 'Fountain' is undoubtedly a co-created work. *The Blind Man* featured 'Buddha of the Bathroom', Louise Norton's famous defence of the piece, and an uncredited editorial 'The Richard Mutt Case', which was probably written by Duchamp.[49] Duchamp's close friends Roché and Beatrice Wood were also involved in the logistics

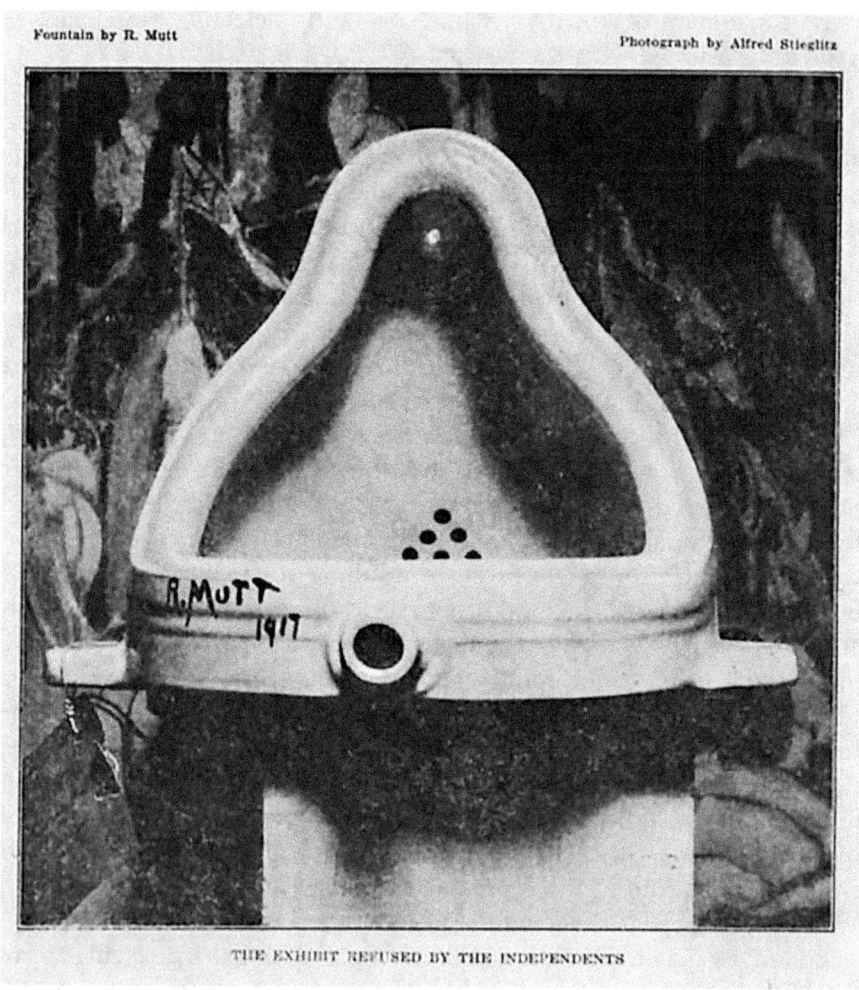

Figure 2.3 Alfred Stieglitz, *Fountain by R. Mutt* [Marcel Duchamp], *The Blind Man* 2 (May 1917): 4; Yale Collection of American Literature, Beinecke Rare Book and Manuscript Library.

and staging, and, recently, critics have also speculated that the Baroness may have been involved in its creation.⁵⁰ Indeed, in 1917 the Baroness produced another *objet trouvé* with the artist Morton Schamburg, which focuses on the pipes rather than the base of a plumbing fixture. A sheered-off cast-iron plumbing trap mounted on a carpenter's mitre box, *God* is the first salvo in the Baroness's ongoing critique and sabotage of American infrastructure and discourses of hygiene. It is a brilliant negotiation of the bathetic and the sublime, but it emerged on the fringes of New York's avant-garde exhibition scene, unlike *Fountain*, which relied on an extensive discourse network to generate public attention.

Stieglitz's collaboration with Duchamp on *Fountain* in *The Blind Man* is an important but somewhat under-explored feature of the readymade's infamy. Stieglitz not only photographed the work, but also wrote an oblique defence of it in *The Blind Man*.⁵¹ It is ironic but entirely fitting that *Fountain* involves both the lead engineer of bathetic technicity and a major architect of the American technological sublime. As Wood later recalled, Stieglitz 'took great pains with the lighting, and did it with such skill that a shadow fell across the urinal, suggesting a veil. The piece was renamed "Madonna of the Bathroom."'⁵² The halftone reproduction of *Fountain by R. Mutt* accentuates Stieglitz's well-worn use of shadows to evoke metaphysical ambiguity.⁵³ However, the cheap paper tilts the readymade closer to the everyday and the bathetic, suggesting that the exaggerated shading and abstractions are artefacts of mass production rather than artifice. The spectacle of two modalities – two technicities – competing for the same detached piece of radically-recontextualised, gender-specific sanitation equipment is perhaps the supreme Dada gesture of *The Blind Man*. Dada-bathos wins this contest, of course, but Stieglitz's 'amusement' with the piece, and his support for its creators' attempts to 'fight bigotry' in the American arts scene, acknowledges the interdependency of the bathetic and sublime.⁵⁴ However, the image points to another crucial project of New York's proto-Dada scene. Found art and readymades were above all testaments to the power of the city's artistic infrastructure every bit as much as to its technological and civic infrastructure. Punning on the 'black box' effect, in which technology becomes less visible as it becomes more pervasive, *The Blind Man* revelled in paradoxes created by the intersection of America's socio-technics ensembles.

Mina Loy produced a work that was also connected to the Arensberg's New York salon in the same issue of *The Blind Man*. Entitled 'O Marcel - - - Otherwise I Also Have Been to Louise's', and riffing on his coupling of machines and language, Loy's work incisively addressed the inscription and decryption of Machine Age technicities. As Alex Goody has argued, the font of this prose piece deliberately resembles the courier-style fonts of typewriters.⁵⁵ Indeed, it looks like a linear paste-up of fragments discarded from a series of dialogues, while the dashes suggest a malfunctioning ticker-tape machine that transcribes the discussions of salonnieres from the post-*Rogue* Arensberg circle rather than stock market quotations (which Loy's friend Bob Brown later claimed had influenced his reading machine). But rather than a reading machine, Loy creates a *writing* machine to record and redeploy Machine Age cross-talk like a Dada switchboard operator. The results generate a violently disembodied ensemble of ocular, oral and reproductive organs. Uniquely, however, Loy's work also concerns haptic sensations and tactile organs. One subject 'has a pencil in her hair – very impressionistic', while another asks 'Mina are you short-hand?' 'Absolutely', Loy seems to answer, emphasising how new inscription techniques and technologies folded back into the everyday language of getting and spending.

Loy's intention is ironic, and it is satirical, but it also portends a desperate urgency. I think that this is no accident: the second issue of *The Blind Man* appeared one month after the United States entered the First World War, and Loy's piece is laced with violent and sometimes explicitly military language. For example, she cites 'a very old French story about "the English man must shoot first"', and alludes constantly to consuming or detaching body parts ('Waiter! tongue sandwiches').⁵⁶ Acts of interruption, silencing and erasure connect these vignettes and compound the sensation of severance. 'Don't write, he is going to leave you for a minute', Loy notes, and in light of future events it seems nervously to anticipate her enforced separation from her husband-to-be Arthur Cravan, who was already making plans to flee America to avoid conscription and prosecution for sedition.⁵⁷ Over the next few months, Loy, the Browns and Allen Norton would all prepare to join him as 'Battery J', a 'self-proclaimed faux army unit' that joined other politically-motivated exiles known as 'slackers'.⁵⁸ In 1917–18, these dissidents fled the United States into Mexico as anti-sedition enforcement became increasingly oppressive, especially in the Greenwich Village radical scenes. Leaving New York in December 1917, Loy eventually embarked on a five-day train journey to Mexico, where she joined Cravan early in 1918.⁵⁹ Viewed in retrospect, 'O Marcel', with the throwaway line, 'how do you light a match? Did you, well it is not dangerous at all', conveys a forced breeziness that masks real cultural flashpoints.⁶⁰ One interlocutor comments, 'Are you an American representative –. I am sorry', while another (ostensibly referring to a 'tongue sandwich') insists that 'you must suck it - - - Censorship!'⁶¹ Even in Loy's encrypted writing, her intention here is to unmask the oppressive nationalist forces resurgent in wartime America. Like Anthony Comstock's previous crusade against

Alfred Kreymborg's *Others* magazine, which strongly championed Loy's work, the censorship and anti-sedition agencies had begun targeting little magazines.[62] Loy conveys her sense of personal risk across the disjunctive assemblages that she inscribes with her writing machine.

In his review of *The Blind Man*, William Carlos Williams singled out 'Du Champs' [sic] "chocolate grinder"', which appeared in the first issue, for particular praise, recognising at once its strategic apposition of quotidian subject and insouciant sexuality in a technological instrument.[63] Williams made his most famous address to Duchamp in *Kora in Hell: Improvisations*,[64] but his most important one in 'Writing(s)'. He composed this unpublished tract of improvised prose between 1923–6; in it, he connected the bathetic technicity of American culture to the institutional frameworks of its avant-garde networks, and the vicissitudes of writing in American.[65] He is particularly invested in moments in which apparent disjunctions of timing and representation throw up new, unpredictable possibilities for avant-garde practice, and in this respect the manuscript forms an important techno-bathetic prototype. Although he does not identify them explicitly, Williams describes the language machines sketched out by Duchamp in his *Notes and Projects for the Large Glass*, the *Monte Carlo Bond* project and *Anémic Cinéma*, the short film that he created with Man Ray, which emerged from his experiments with optical illusions, language and 'mirroring'.[66] For instance, Williams refers to 'Marcel's color machine that invents sentences [;] a thing makes the machine that makes the chance sentence'.[67] This manufactured game of chance forces '[us] to define ourselves against chaos and make a little --- chaos all colored and revolving so that we can be made up of I-I-I-I [. . .] like taking a photo of a machine'. These shards of aggregated prose clatter through the manuscript, and concoct a 'We' that refers both to an American literary avant-garde, and to Machine Age America as a whole.

Williams's translinguistic punning on the French affirmative 'oui' evokes the hybrid, transatlantic character of his network and nation, but how much diversity really exists in an age of mechanical reproduction? Well, he reasoned, 'we are made up in the first instance of I': Williams's modernist selfhood becomes refracted through his artistic sense organ ('e-y-e'), which in turn has been augmented by the artistic and engineering feats that coalesced in the pages of the transatlantic little magazines, pamphlets, anthologies and unfinished projects in the modernist archive. His key insight in 'Writing(s)' was that processes of reading and writing had been folded into processes of transduction and technicity. Like other avant-garde figures, he understood that technology was a new vernacular, echoing off the reflective surfaces of the technological sublime. Williams's argument was that 'I' and 'We', part and whole, had become co-constructing parts of a faintly ridiculous machine. His dizzying critique of its socio-technical assemblages emerges from his desire to peer into and take seriously its inner workings. And in this respect, Williams felt Duchamp had a unique insight into his own backyard.

Jane Heap announced Duchamp's *Monte Carlo Bond* project in the autumn 1924–winter 1925 'Juan Gris Number' of *The Little Review*.[68] That piece 'advertised' a roulette system designed to convert small amounts of money into larger sums, multiplying equity in a quasi-mystical process involving the transfiguring power of the artist's *techné*. And, of course, Duchamp embedded an elaborate pun within the poster he created in response, which depicted the artist in the guise of the Roman god Mercury, who was also known as Quicksilver – in this case, rendered bathetically as the god of the fast buck. However, Duchamp's *Discs Inscribed with Puns*, which he produced for the short film *Anémic Cinéma* with Man Ray and his own *Precision Optics* experiments, is equally applicable to Williams's critique.[69] The *Discs*' most forceful pun is that in the Machine Age, transductive processes of reading quite literally revolved around technology, producing a new technicity of literacy. The French critic Michel Charles proposed that 'every reading modifies its object';[70] by extension, technicity folds textual procedures into technology's transduction in culture. The disorientating effects produced by Duchamp's installations are achieved by alternating graphic designs of spirals with spiralling texts, which are mounted on a modified gramophone motor. In the project, Duchamp makes explicit the technical means by which (as Certeau phrases it) 'reading operations manipulate the reader by insinuating their inventiveness into the cracks in a cultural orthodoxy'.[71] As Williams recognised, Duchamp's ambivalent role as an artist-engineer helped thread discourses of technology into the American vernacular.

Throughout 'Writing(s)', Williams dissects and reconstitutes the alphabetical components of language and creates incessant, multiplex puns in the process, recursively probing the relationships between producer and reproduction, individual and collective, chance and design, which Duchamp negotiates in his art machines. Although Williams's localist avant-garde shared the European Dadaists' conception of technicity as a bathetic spatial practice, his anxieties about the 'chaos' that such approaches create veer back into the discourses of the sublime, particularly in his discussions of national identity. Young American critics such as Waldo Frank feared the chaotic heterogeneity that was a by-product of Puritan intellectual legacies – an emotionally repressive, technologically-driven society that produced cultural incoherence. Williams's anxiety represented the flipside of this predicament: he was apprehensive about the cultural *homogeneity* engendered by the Machine Age. In this configuration, his 'machine of mirrors' was not kaleidoscopic or cinematic, but, rather, a hall of mirrors, presenting warped homogeneity.[72] As *transition*'s editor Eugene Jolas later phrased it, the 'machine worship' produced by the 'Calvinist Mentality' in America risked producing stock personalities and tired clichés rather than artistic revolution.[73] However, Duchamp provided a way out of this conceptual trap, and in this respect Williams anticipated Certeau's arguments by about half a century. In *The Practice of Everyday Life*, Certeau argues that Duchamp's works confront 'the myths of an incarceration within the operations of a writing that constantly makes a machine of itself and never encounters anything but itself'. In this configuration, '[t]he machine producing language is wiped clean of history, isolated from the obscenities of reality, absolute and without relation to the "celibate" other'. However, Duchamp does identify 'ways out' in his work, 'through fictions, painted windows, mirror-panes'.[74] In 'Writing(s)', Williams comes to a similar conclusion as Certeau.

Although works such as *In the American Grain* developed Williams's anxieties about the homogeneity generated by America's technological sublime, in 'Writing(s)', he implies that US culture is certainly a product of its techno-vernacular, but it is not a machine gone rogue. He insists that since Duchamp can 'invent machines that accurately make chance', it proves, counter-intuitively, that 'chaos has not made us'.[75] In this respect, the bathos of 'Writing(s)' is neither an expression of despair nor a diagnosis of failure. Instead, it is a prescription for a new way of reading across disciplines and socio-technical assemblages – and a new way of writing. Writing, in 'Writing(s)', becomes an individuating practice born of collective cultural production. The 'American' avant-gardes – the 'We' that Williams envisages – do not subordinate the individual 'I' to the collective, but rather, use creative dialogue as the basis for a process of radical de-hierarchisation: a camera 'I-I-I'. In this configuration, writers, like readers, become cultural tinkerers who re-present and interpolate the chaos of America's proliferating socio-technical assemblages, rather than being subsumed by them. Williams was a literary prototyper of the Dada techno-bathetic, rather than an artist-engineer, like Duchamp. Yet he detected in Duchamp's work the blueprints for a new way of writing through the 'chaos' of the Machine Age that drew on Americans' preoccupation with technology, and their various forms of technical literacy, as intellectual resources, rather than fetishes that inhibited their culture's development. However, it is also true that Williams and Duchamp both helped embed masculinist anxieties about the disruptive counter-normativities latent in the age of mechanical reproduction. The Dada-inspired artist-engineers Baroness Elsa von Freytag-Loringhoven and Mina Loy confronted these anxieties by drawing them more forcefully into the arenas of everyday life – and the institutions of the transatlantic avant-gardes.

'Outside Machinery': The Dada Designs of Baroness Elsa von Freytag-Loringhoven

In her 1925 'Machine-Age Exposition' manifesto, Jane Heap declared that 'there is a new race of men in America: the Engineer'.[76] However, in contradistinction to the heroic model of the Futurist man-machine resuscitated by Heap in her manifesto, a new, and far more ambivalent, figure also appeared: the *artist*-engineer. As Michael Mackenzie has noted, Machine Age writers had begun representing 'the engineer [. . .] as a kind of apolitical dandy, an exalted figure whose elegance and esprit was expressed in his solutions to practical problems'.[77] Linda Dalrymple Henderson has convincingly argued that Marcel Duchamp in particular cultivated the persona of the engineer-technician rather than that of the traditional artist.[78] The phallogocentric assumptions behind this hybrid professional (and equally, the potentially derogatory readings of the figure's artistic and non-normative cultural position) are readily apparent, but there is no reason why the artist-engineer should continue to be associated with masculinist tropes about the heroic 'genius'. The Baroness (and, as I will go on to argue in the next section, Mina Loy) certainly matched the job description, and reappraising her practice helps in the task of challenging historical normativities associated with what we would now call STE(A)M professions (the 'A' is for 'Arts'). Deploying the 'arid clarity' frequently associated with Americanist poetics,[79] the engineer-as-artist analysed the disjunctive contours of modernity dispassionately and adapted them to the human psyche with a clinical, detached precision. However, Dadaists such as the Baroness also tapped into the affective power of machine ensembles. In this section, I show how the Baroness deployed Dada-inspired technicities to reshape what Certeau calls 'the machinery of representation' – the ensembles 'by which a society represents itself in living beings and makes them its representations'.[80] By re-engineering everyday acts of design and communication, the Baroness expressed new modes of reading, and writing, modernity. She also alligned the role of the artist-engineer with Dada's interventionist aesthetics in her broader struggle to negotiate technicities of the sublime and bathetic, as well as the practical demands of a transatlantic life.

In *The Little Review*, John Rodker declared that 'Paris has had Dada for five years, and we have had Else [sic] von Freytag-Loringhoven for quite two years. But great minds think alike and great natural truths force themselves into cognition at vastly separated spots. In Else von Freytag-Loringhoven Paris is mystically united [with] New York.'[81] For Rodker, and many writers, the Baroness embodied the transatlantic connections and cultural paradoxes that Dada embraced, and in her works in *The Little Review* she also articulated them. Her work paid close attention to bathetic, quotidian and corporeal themes, but she also challenged the demotic and democratic conventions of her adopted home. An actual Baroness by marriage, she declared that true '[a]rtists are aristocrats', not 'plain working people, mixing up art with craft, in vulgar untrained brains'. She compared her own body and creative practice with those of an 'engineer', while at the same disparaging America's embrace of engineered 'machinery' and the 'high scientist'.[82] In 'A Modest Woman', for example, the Baroness mocks the Puritan impulse behind innovations in American plumbing and sewer infrastructure (and their connotations of 'sanitation—outside machinery'), while exalting her aristocratic right 'to mention my ecstasies in toilet room'.[83] As Goody argues, 'the Baroness's externality travesties the working machines of American modernity, whilst also embracing the technicity of individuation and human creativity'.[84] In the Baroness's work, the discipline of engineering serves as both the means of and metaphor for achieving states of sublime ecstasy, on the one hand, and performing bathetic critiques of American culture, on the other. In doing so, she subverted the nationalist depictions of engineering in 1920s' American literature, and explored the hierarchies expressed in socio-technical infrastructure.[85]

As we have seen in her 1917 *objet trouvé* entitled *God*, the Baroness's early work detaches and recontextualises technical objects from their ensembles. Her *Enduring Ornament* (1913) anticipated this approach: the fist-sized metal ring she found en route to her wedding with Baron Leopold Friedrich von Freytag-Loringhoven was originally part of a large industrial rigging system.[86] Its shape suggests a wedding ring, which echoes in the word 'Endu*ring*', but its battered form suggests that the object and the union will eventually corrode, leaving only the large 'zero' at its centre. In the context of its newly ennobled creator's personal history, *Enduring Ornament* serves as a synecdoche for both a patriarchal and aristocratic system now detached from its moorings and re-presented defiantly as a battered sigil. In the Baroness's early oeuvre, technology binds her creative practice to those moorings, while technicity offers a means of challenging the hierarchies that they represent. However, although she passionately subverted some hegemonies in her work – particularly patriarchal ones – as I and other critics have argued elsewhere, she also reinstated others, including ones based on class, race and ethnicity.[87] In particular, she defended what she perceived as the entitlements of the Old World artist-aristocrat, which she frequently used to shore up her subject position as a culturally marginal female artist in male-dominated avant-garde scenes.

The Baroness was clearly fascinated by America's flexible class hierarchies, fluid racial and ethnic categories, and emergent mass culture, but she was also in some ways repelled by them. In a poetic screed against William Carlos Williams, for example, she used anti-Semitic, racist and class-based tropes to attack him and, more broadly, the North American cultures that he represented (which she did not restrict to his own bourgeois class).[88] She clearly thrived on these sorts of cultural polemics in her art. As Irene Gammel and Suzanne Zelazo rightly argue, however, her contradictory subject positions should be contextualised by her entanglements with the American state in her life; although they do not mitigate her prejudices, they do 'situate the Baroness's ethnoracial utterances in the context of the geopolitical anxieties on both the national and international stage'.[89] Those positions also altered as the Baroness continually recalibrated her intellectual exchanges with Machine Age technicities over the course of her career.

Like many avant-garde artists, the Baroness was caught up in the repressive climate of the First World War. She had made national headlines after police arrested her for wearing men's clothes in Pittsburgh, but in 1917, just prior to her association with *The Little Review* in New York, she was accused of being a German spy.[90] Although the charge had no basis in fact, she was arrested and imprisoned for three weeks in Connecticut. Her antipathy towards aspects of American culture emerged from this immediate grievance, but her enduring outrage at her treatment at the hands of officials (and lovers) often feeds into her horror at the general inhumanity of industrialised warfare. For example, her infamous 1919 poem 'Cast-Iron Lover' addressed the Baroness's failed love affair with the art instructor Robert Fulton Logan. The poem splices national tragedy with personal pain, disrupting the normative codes of heterosexual relationships with military violence imported from bayonet battles. The 'bloody scythe' that she associates with her lover unites bodies and machines in death, a common transcendent trope of the technological sublime (especially in its allusion to the grim reaper).[91]

Another polemic against a male artist who spurned her advances – in this case 'Marcel (A Futurist)' – the Baroness's 1918 poem 'Love – Chemical Relationship' also reinstates a thwarted sublime. Although it lacks the gothic ferocity of military conflict, in its deliberately arcane language, the poem reduces its addressee to a reflective 'glass' mirror that promises transcendence but produces only mechanistic purgatory: 'I must bleed', she exclaims, and 'weep – laugh – ere I turn to glass and the world / around me glassy!'[92] Here, the speaker is able to recreate herself in the subject's reflection, but she violently rejects the illusory results. Instead, she asserts her corporeality to escape Duchamp's self-reflexive machine of mirrors, in which the subject, as Certeau warned, 'never encounters anything but itself'.[93] The Baroness, like Duchamp and Williams, escapes this potential trap, but does so by deploying the language of the body and somatic practice, rather than socio-technical vernacular, 'fictions' or reflective surfaces.[94] However, she had no desire to escape Duchamp as a subject.

The Baroness's sculpture/assemblage *Portrait of Marcel Duchamp*, photographed by Charles Sheeler, also creates a cautionary parable about its subject's fragile machines.[95] The version published in *The Little Review* (Fig. 2.4) accentuates the gears and coiled friction motor spring because it is shot from the opposite angle of a better-known archival photograph from the Bluff Collection, featured in Gammel's and Zelazo's edition *Body Sweats: The Uncensored Writings of Elsa von Freytag-Loringhoven*, which foregrounds the wine glass and feathers.[96] The *mise-en-page* of the *Little Review* photograph suggests a more lively interplay of decorative machinery, while its dramatic shading (accentuated by the halftone printing) reinstates the visual language of the technological sublime in Stieglitz's photograph of Duchamp's *Fountain* in *The Blind Man*, which used shadows to create a metaphysical frame for the bathetic object. In this particular *Portrait of Marcel Duchamp*, the feathers evoke neither the camp glamour of Duchamp's transvestite alter ego Rrose Sélavy nor a transcendent ascent to the sublime, but instead describe an Icarian fall – a sly jab at the would-be Daedalian artificer of the American Machine Age. The shadows, which merge with the drooping feathers, embody both the sublime heights that Icarus failed to reach and his watery grave in the Aegean when the sun melted his waxwork wings. In this way, the Baroness consigns Duchamp to the originary scene of bathetic allegory, while taunting him with the sublime regions that they might have ascended together.

The Baroness eventually concluded her gloriously failed love affair with America in 1923, when she returned to Berlin in a state of abject poverty. Nevertheless, she continued to negotiate competing Machine Age technicities in a series of unpublished poems, but in the socio-political climate of a defeated nation recovering from the horrifying repercussions of total war. Rather than identifying technology with that sense of horror, however, she identified its potential for renewal, in multiple

Photograph by Charles Sheeler

PORTRAIT OF MARCEL DUCHAMP
BY BARONESS VON FREYTAG-LORINGHOVEN

Figure 2.4 Elsa von Freytag-Loringhoven, *Portrait of Marcel Duchamp*, *The Little Review* 9.2 (Winter 1922), following p. 45.

forms. Her 1924–5 work 'Narcissus Icarus' recalls the thematic terrain and wry energetics of *Portrait of Marcel Duchamp*, pitting biology, spirituality and creative generation against technologically-induced entropy and mechanised reproduction. She aligns the 'potential germs' of 'spiritual matchlessness' against 'Incest's infinite circuits', in which 'each periodclick [devours] each' in 'sterile succession'. Like *Enduring Ornament*, these interactions across socio-technical ensembles, as well as biological ones, appear to result in a sublime negation: 'Allsum of allconception = O (naught – / Spinning cell)'.[97] The 'neurasthenic' conditions she diagnoses and performs in the poem appear and disappear with 'mechanical incessancy', yet despite the existential despair these oscillations produce, the Baroness folds their 'madness' into the 'shadowcarousel' of 'human intellect'. She is describing a bathetic Icarian fall here, certainly, but also a system with fail-safes, which achieves a state of metastability, or 'the provisional equilibrium established when a system rich in potential differences resolves inherent incompatibilities by restructuring itself topologically and temporally'.[98] Like *Portrait of Marcel Duchamp*, 'Narcissus Icarus' becomes a robust and self-sustaining instrument of bathetic critique. The Baroness's systems can reprise multiple tragic descents by performing a series of imaginative oscillations within and between her intersecting technical, mental and biological ensembles.

In her 1920s works especially, the Baroness's point is not that human life and culture is a 'paradigm of the machine', and that the confusion of boundaries between human and non-human realities results in some rote equivalency, or an effacement of crucial differences, as it would in the cybernetics theory of Norbert Wiener. Indeed, as Goody has argued in her definitive readings, the transgressive juxtaposition, crossing and collapsing of boundaries in the Baroness's technological discourses aligns her project convincingly with cyborg theory. This model emerged from cybernetic paradigms and Heideggarian ontology, 'as well as its deconstruction' in poststructuralist theory.[99] Cyborg theory frequently posits binary relations between various subjects and hierarchies in order to deconstruct and transgress them. In Donna Haraway's originary formulation, the cyborg is a model of relationality in which 'transgressed boundaries, potent fusions, and dangerous possibilities' inhere in 'oppositional, utopian' strategies of deconstruction and reconnection.[100] Haraway argues that '[l]ate twentieth century machines have made thoroughly ambiguous the difference between natural and artificial [. . .] and many other distinctions that apply to organisms and machines'.[101] Although these ambiguities have powerful critical valences, however, the forms of parity that the cyborg model proposes between human and non-human realities often re-articulate the servile dialectics of the technological sublime.

As Thomas LaMarre has noted, '[w]hat counts in the cyborg model is the blurring of the law, what renders law ambiguous or transgresses it'. One important side effect of this '*de jure* distinction' is that it articulates a dualist and substantialist emphasis that can *reinforce* a servile relationship with technology instead of supplanting it. As a result, cyborg theorists can appear 'ambivalent about, or even indifferent to, the de facto relations between humans and machines, that is, the actual techniques that couple human and machine'.[102] Such strategies can inadvertantly reinstate the very hierarchies that the cyborg model sets out to subvert. As we have seen, these effects are evident in the Baroness's most oppositional works, where she self-consciously reinstates various hierarchies, including those of class, race and ethnicity, as well as aesthetic categories of the sublime and bathetic, in order to perform her social critiques from a position of strength. The servile dialects which inhere in such moments are consistent with the cyborg model, and illustrate its pitfalls as well as its strengths.

However, unlike LaMarre, I don't think that cyborg theory necessarily 'forecloses' the chance of 'finding new points of departure' in human and non-human relations.[103] Posthuman configurations such as those articulated by N. Katherine Hayles '[recognise] the mutuality of our interactions with [machines]' and 'the complex dynamics through which they create us even as we create them'.[104] Hayles's position is compatible with Simondon's own formulations of technicity, since she focuses on disaggregating hierarchical ontologies so that new ones can be proposed. Nevertheless, the servile dualism that LaMarre has identified with the cyborg model still remains in hiding. Techno-bathetic critiques offer a specific route through this problem, since they expose and undermine the dialectical operations of technology in culture, while attempting to supplant servile technicities with energetic, non-hierarchical ones. And I think that the Baroness came to a similar conclusion. In her later, unpublished work, the Baroness evinces an escalating impatience with the dualist, substantialist and, ultimately, servile logic of the cyborg. The 'fantasies of disembodiment' that the cyborg model can engender[105] became increasingly anathema to a poet so invested in the somatic possibilities of technicity, in which technology augments and facilitates the construction of knowledge through the human body (rather than by transcending or subordinating it).[106] Accordingly, in her final unpublished poems in Paris, the Baroness began to identify 'new points of departure' that she had experimented with in her techno-bathetic works of the early 1920s.

Perhaps stimulated by her contact with other expatriates, such as Djuna Barnes, Baroness Elsa's relocation to Paris in 1926 seems to have kindled a nostalgia for America's Machine Age. This turn was in keeping with her other 'pro-American leanings' during this stretch of increasingly dire poverty, in which she sought financial assistance from New York patron of the arts Peggy Guggenheim.[107] The Baroness's 1926–7 manuscripts 'Filmballad' and 'Stagnation' in particular signal a late technobathetic turn towards a vernacular, somatic technicity, which involved an intellectual armistice with the American Machine Age. 'Filmballad' fuses biology and socio-technics, as 'Blood throbs' with a youthful pulse, and 'reel[s] / once more' through a 'screen' that becomes a productive 'womb' rather than the sterile expanse of the works addressed to Duchamp.[108] Arranged in three handwritten columns of equal length, and punctuated with connective dashes, the poem encourages relational strategies of reading cribbed from the *mise-en-scène* of cinema, forming new channels of reading horizontally and vertically across the page.

Similarly, in 'Stagnation', the motif of technology forms a bond with, rather than drives a wedge between, the Baroness's vernacular strategies for reading the Machine Age. The radical parity that she expresses in the poem not only preserves ontological distinctions between her subjects, but also carries a political dimension. 'Stagnation' establishes a heroic sense of creative penury rather than proletarian solidarity with the working classes, but, nevertheless, her technicity transforms 'Poverty' into a 'Psychological x-ray', which she aligns against those who occupy a 'monotony vacuum in affluence'.[109] She deployed a similar strategy in her late poem 'X-Ray'. Published in *transition* in 1927, this poem appears to target the rise of Mussolini, and/or other masculinist 'Brilliant boss[es]', satirising his Futurist affiliations and reasserting the power of 'Nature' to shape, as well as be shaped by, technical activity ('Nature', she reminds us, 'causes brass to oxidize').[110] In 'Stagnation', she sustains her techno-bathetic 'X-Ray', but focuses its critical work on her own poverty, isolation and socio-technical contexts. Paradoxically – yet in keeping with her abiding sense of prerogative – this tack grants her a privileged insight into socio-technical relations, particularly as they apply to her own creative practices. Finally, the Baroness seems to reconcile the frenzied automation she associated with the American Machine Age with her autonomous, embodied poetics, and combines them in an expression of 'industry': 'All ind. is imagination / All im. ind'.

The Baroness's use of abbreviations in the poem does not represent a capitulation to Taylorist efficiency, or to a dualistic technological sublime; rather, the final lines of 'Stagnation' articulate a radical assertion of ontological parity between humans and machines – between creative practice and technical activity. It also suggests a recalibration of language, in which human and machine communication combine unpredictably to generate new meanings, and new ways of thinking about language ('All im. ind' could also be read as 'All i mind'). In this sense, the poem points towards a new vernacular technicity. Her compressed language in 'Stagnation' reclaims corporatist notions of efficiency as expressions of *techné*, an exercise in (linguistic) economy and self-discipline. Masculinist associations bound up in that Taylorist sublime are repackaged and returned to sender as 'mailemballage – posted to eternity'. The port*man*teau pun on 'mail'/male and 'emballage'/embellish exposes and casts off capitalist excess and phallogocentric discourse as a form of 'Senility'. Instead, the Baroness proposes a new 'Life circumference', a technicity that repackages 'industry' as an exercise in restraint and tactical focus that can thrive in sympathy with a socialist and feminist poetics.

In 'Stagnation', she embraces a counter-servile bathetic technicity that dispenses with the technological sublime she had encountered (and re-processed) in America, while retaining a heightened awareness of its power to shape socio-technical relations. In doing so, she identified a pragmatic and demotic impulse that configured 'Each cell same size'.[111] Although 'unnoticed by [the] habit blunt perception' prevailing in her own time, her insight was to acknowledge that, in its accessibility, socio-technical discourse could express her poetics in collaboration with (as well as in opposition to) Machine Age ensembles. Niall Munro has eloquently described 'technology/*techné*'s power to reveal and make present' deeply embedded creative resources in everyday surroundings.[112] In 'Stagnation', the Baroness mined the banal techniques of Taylorese to exploit those resources, but her later projects applied these strategies more broadly. Ultimately, the Baroness hijacked the linguistic and technical infrastructures of the New World, in order to reformulate her technicity in the Old.

It is tragic, but entirely in keeping with her oeuvre, that the Baroness left her project unfinished. She died by asphyxiation when she left her gas heater on at night in an unfamiliar hotel room.[113] Whether by accident or design, she ended her life by means of malfunctioning infrastructure, which consigned her later work to the archives for the rest of the twentieth century. The Baroness's works, on and off the page, re-presented technical objects as performance props, which interrogated the interstitial spaces and temporal slippages between socio-technical ensembles, and the hierarchies they expressed. Through the flux of her poetics and somatic practices, her key insight was to identify the potential of technicity to recalibrate the power dynamics in Machine Age culture. Yet her technicity, like other elements of her practice, was not static, and as a self-proclaimed 'engineer' she altered it to respond to her volatile circumstances. Her final refusal of dualist and substantialist paradigms helped articulate an emergent vernacular technicity that reclaimed technological resources for the culturally marginalised (albeit in keeping with her delimited sense of that marginality). Rooted in the diachronic rhythms of everyday life but committed to redressing some of the social inequities stemming from techno-servility, her continuing journey from this 'point of departure' was cut short. Baroness Elsa's unpublished works remain an essential, but characteristically hidden, contribution to the techno-bathetic avant-gardes, whose narratives often thrive in forgotten corners of the modernist archive.

Verrovoil[a]: Mina Loy's Inventions and Diachronic Techno-Poetics

Like the Baroness, Mina Loy travelled relentlessly through the 1910s and early 1920s, and her attentions were similarly divided by the demands of her creative practice and dire financial circumstances. Drawing on her artistic training and reputation as a celebrated painter, Loy had turned to the decorative arts to support herself when she arrived in New York in 1916. She worked in a studio that produced lampshades initially (a business that she would later develop in earnest), but she was a mainstay of the fashion world as well as the avant-garde literary scene, a balancing act epitomised by her appearances in Allen and Louise Norton's *Rogue* magazine. However, as we have seen, she was forced into exile in 1917 during her travels in Central and South America with 'Battery J' and Arthur Cravan. She referred to this period euphemistically as her 'itinerancy', in which she travelled extensively under the shadow of deprivation and eventually tragedy.[114] Undertaking processes of both literary and commercial invention during her absence, in the spring of 1920 Mina Loy returned to New York from London via Florence, and turned to design work and invention as a means of supporting herself and her family. Her work in this field focused on the body, and on augmenting its mechanics and coverings to adapt to and transform urban environments.

Focusing on Loy's interdisciplinary creative practices in the 1920s, but drawing on a range of work outside this period, this section of the chapter considers how Loy honed her multimodal poetics across a range of forums. From her publications in modernist journals to her fashion writing in mass market periodicals, the section shows how her inventions and Paris workshop creations both reflected and informed those texts. It also introduces a previously unknown 1929 article by Loy that asserts her intellectual property claim for her invention 'verrovoile', her own formulation of a thermoplastic material that she used for her interior lighting designs. Loy's inventions were a strategic amalgam of durable products from a previous era of mass production and strikingly new, ephemeral and fragile materials associated with planned obsolescence and rationalised production. As well as shedding new light on Loy's career as a serious inventor, these discoveries reveal that she had not been 'defeated' by her interventions in the marketplace but, rather, continued to find new ways to fight for her creative and financial autonomy. In her fashion designs and inventions, Loy sought to unite these intersecting demands in the unremarkable crucibles of everyday life.

When Loy returned to New York in 1920, she broadly aligned herself with its Dadaist proponents, and retained her reputation as a serious vanguardist. Hardened by her exertions and the presumed death of her husband, she picked up where she left off, and began to sharpen her knives against the competing avant-gardes who hoped to make inroads in Machine Age America.[115] For example, in her 1920 play, *The Pamperers*, Loy targets imagists, Cubists and 'vitalist[s]', but like her early dramatic work, *The Sacred Prostitute* and her poem 'Lion's Jaws', it identifies the Futurists for particular scrutiny.[116] As well as honing her feminist poetics, these works signalled a re-engagement with technology as a subject matter, but a reputational break from her former Futurist affiliations. For Loy, technicity was a guerrilla tactic of disguise and misdirection, which could be harnessed to rewire socio-technical relations in her favour, whereas for Futurists like F. T. Marinetti it had been reduced to a 'prismatic locomotive', i.e. a vehicle for flamboyant self-promotion.[117] Drawing on her feminist critiques of transatlantic avant-gardes, by the 1920s Loy had become one of the most astute techno-bathetic critics of the Machine Age.

Given the gruelling challenges of her peripatetic life, Loy drew relentlessly on her creative practice as an intellectual and emotional resource to meet those challenges of material production. Loy's interrelated investments in technology, the body and everyday spatial practices form a ligature between these fields of creative activity. She announced her first 'invention', 'Auto-Facial-Construction', in Florence in 1919, which offered potential clients 'the chance to become masters of their own facial destiny'.[118] As Jessica Burstein rightly argues, Loy's idea is '[l]ess product than process', and, in a sense, 'presents invention in its pure form, for it rests solely on the status of the idea'.[119] However, Loy probably had financial motives for this invention as well. In the pamphlet, she marketed herself as a personal trainer with a high-value proposition based on an 'esoteric anatomical science'. Her course mainly involved calisthenics and postural practices, which were 'expensive but economical'. Ironically, her market included the type of patron-salonnière she parodied in *The Pamperers*, as well as other wealthy professionals and actors.[120] Clearly, the 'Auto-Facial-Construction' project did not solve her financial hardships in Florence, but after putting her creative work on hold for nearly two years, it did lead her back to the material arts via its focus on the body, and shaping its social performances from the inside out. Accordingly, when she relocated to New York in March 1920, Loy moved into fashion design. As Certeau notes, clothes are part of a 'disciplinary apparatus' that 'displaces and corrects, adds or removes things' from 'malleable' bodies.[121] Mirroring tactics she used in her writing, Loy turned her attention from the body to that 'apparatus', creating designs 'for several houses' in New York, but also marketable copy for mass market periodicals.[122]

Her nationally syndicated article, 'Would You Be "Different?" Madame Loy Shows How', distributed by Newspaper Enterprise, included three sketches by Loy, including her remarkable, recently discovered 'Horse Ear Hat' design (Fig. 2.5).[123] The article is anonymous, but is very probably written (in whole or part) by Loy herself. The lucid, elliptical style and rich technical detail in the piece are characteristic, and given her contacts in the field of journalism (via Djuna Barnes and Bob and Rose Brown) she had the network available to place it. As well as providing payment for the copy, the article gave Loy a remarkably wide exposure for her designs, reaching hundreds of thousands, perhaps even millions of readers. During the period, 'short-lived fashion designs' could not be protected effectively by patent law, copyright law or 'misappropriation theory', and generally were covered by legislative schemes alone.[124] The lifestyle pages of mass-circulation newspapers could therefore serve as an informal assertion of intellectual copyright as well as a marketing tool. In her article, Loy consistently emphasises the novel features of her work, and in doing so promotes cultural vanguardism to the American mainstream. Thus, 'Would You Be "Different?"' forms a ligature between producer and consumer using avant-garde practice as a form of legitimation: 'difference' is not actually the equivalent of dissent, but by buying (into) Loy's designs, the reader endorses a dialogic relationship between modernist art and everyday life.

Loy styles commercial fashion as a wearable, transformative technology, painstakingly itemising the materials, stitching and aesthetics in each piece. The article highlights Loy's capacity for 'innovation' but identifies her 'Horse Ear Hat' design as 'the very smartest'. With its self-referential 'strap of real horsehair', she insists that the design will appeal to 'those who seek to be different'.[125] Invoking the form of the horse as she does so is a particularly compelling gesture, particularly after the advent of New York Dada. One translation of 'dada' is 'hobby horse', but there are

Figure 2.5 Newspaper Enterprise [Mina Loy], 'Would You Be "Different?" Madame Loy Shows How', *The Pittsburgh Press*, 3 April 1921, p. 2.

wider symbolic registers at work in this example too. As Crangle argues, in Futurist and Dadaist writings, 'horses are both vulgar and esteemed'.[126] For example, in his Futurist manifestos, Marinetti celebrates 'a superior machine-cum-horse', but in Dada writing, 'the horse is more base, multivalent, and ultimately, vulnerable'.[127] Crangle is correct to point out that European Dadaists especially aligned 'far-too-logical machine technology' with the terror and destruction of mechanised warfare, which folds into the symbolic terrain of the technological sublime;[128] however, as we have seen, it is also true that Dadaists continually subsumed a range of technologies, including military ones, into their expressions of bathos.

In keeping with Loy's Futurist background, and the avant-gardes' penchant for engaging the non-human world in their art, the oversized horse ears on the hat also contain echoes of Futurist dazzle tactics. Beyond their functionary masquerade, these decorative features suggest an aural early warning system that relies on sensory augmentation, echoing Luigi Russolo's strategies in *The Art of Noises* (which I discussed in Chapter 1). Horses rely on their enhanced senses to evade predators, and as Jussi Parikka has rightly argued, scientists and engineers have routinely cited 'animal ensembles' in theories of technology since the late nineteenth century. In the twentieth century, '[a]nimals were at the core of the cybernetic interest and the turn toward the informatic biopower of network society'; indeed, 'cybernetic zoology relied on the embodied and contextual animality of both machines and nature' to describe how feedback mechanisms worked (among other things).[129] Avant-gardes proposed similar strategies: for example, Marinetti's 'Centaur', the automotive cyborg he describes in 'The Founding and Manifesto of Futurism' suggests a hybrid that folds the mythical and animal worlds into Machine Age socio-technical ensembles.[130] For all its bathetic playfulness, Loy's horsehair hat participates in that gesture, while using fashion and costume to protect and conceal the new woman in an androcentric public sphere. However, if her fashion designs articulate a form of this 'cool modernism', then it is a version forged in the heat of profound physical and emotional strain, grinding poverty and near-total despair.

Loy's designs represent an avant-garde practice kindled by a warm spirit of collaborative ingenuity as well as individual effort born of necessity. During their exile in South and Central America, Loy and the Browns were forced to live 'by the show-me trades', and when their period of immediate post-war crisis passed, they folded those skills into their avant-garde practice, in fits and starts – and, as I discuss in the book's later chapters, this engagement occurred over a surprisingly long duration.[131] Yet like Duchamp, with whom the Browns crossed paths in

Buenos Aires in 1919, Loy was a vanguardist who anticipated the rise of the artist-engineer by more than a half a decade. For her, as for the Baroness, fashion could be re-processed into a performance that confronted the irresolvable, parasitic dialectics between avant-gardes, mass culture and cultural elites. As in the proto-Dada work of Cravan, Picabia and Duchamp, Loy's fashion designs, and 'Horse Ear Hat' especially, fold bathetic discourses of technological innovation quite literally into the fabric of the everyday, and with an urgency and even desperation that belie the breezy commercial contexts in which they were disseminated.

When she relocated to Paris, Loy published the first section of *Anglo-Mongrels and the Rose* in *The Little Review* and *Lunar Baedecker* [sic] with Robert McAlmon's newly launched Contact Editions Press. To maintain this creative momentum, Loy planned to launch an interior design business that could subsidise her writing and art. She moved to Paris in 1923, and with the financial backing of Peggy Guggenheim and Laurence Vail she set up a specialist 'lampshade business' on 52 rue de Colisée that eventually opened in 1926.[132] As well as finding ways of funding her poetry, she also returned to the visual arts, and exhibited works with floral themes, including *Jaded Blossoms* and other cut-out and flower paintings in American galleries (thanks to Peggy Guggenheim's promotion).[133] By 1927 she had a manufacturing workshop with six staff and extended her productions to include decorative glass lights and novelties.[134] The operation was an artisanal meeting point between the retail, design, manufacturing, and research and development fields – and between the liberating imaginative realms of her creative practice and the fraught engagements with business partners/patron-investors and family. She made it a commercial success but earned little money from it. Although she sold designs to a range of prestigious French companies and American department stores, well-documented interference from her patrons and the constant theft of her intellectual property (which she fought frequently in the French courts) took a heavy toll on her time, health and finances. As Burstein rightly notes, the shop soon became 'a burden to the artist it had been meant to liberate'.[135] However, it was also a vehicle for Loy's creativity, both as a proving-ground for the assemblages she would later create in America, and as a means of embodying her poetics.

As Caroline Burke explains, Loy's lampshade and lighting designs 'seemed to have materialized from the pages of *Lunar Baedecker*'.[136] 'Ova Begins to Take Notice', from *Anglo-Mongrels and the Rose*, signposts this aesthetic, as the speaker recalls 'the souvenir / of the delirious ball', which had been 'deleted' and consigned to 'the ivied / dust'. Loy describes how it redirects an 'optic-ray' towards a 'cat's eyes horseshoe' ornament,

> And instantly
> this fragmentary
> simultaneity of ideas
>
> embodies
>   the word.[137]

As material objects, Loy's lighting designs embody the word, and achieve an extraordinary redeployment of apparently disconnected socio-technical ensembles. Her lamps often featured ornate nineteenth-century glass bottles that she bought in Parisian market stalls. Burke rightly notes that the results seem slightly anachronistic, more reminiscent of 'Art Nouveau' than the more 'geometric' modernist forms emerging in the late 1920s. However, Loy's use of ultra-modern materials such as Crystal Lux (a kind of durable cellophane-like substance) and Rhodoid (a thermoplastic) attest to her interest in mass-production techniques.[138] Indeed, her main innovation in her lighting designs was to produce diachronic hybrids of manufactured products that endured from the previous century and ultra-novel materials created for the socio-technics of planned obsolescence and disposability.[139] Loy's technicity actively subverted manufacturing practices that encouraged consumers to replace functional goods with new ones based mainly on aesthetic and (frequently distorted) technical criteria, while at the same time retaining her vanguardist emphasis on novelty and innovation.

By 1928, Loy held copyrights for 'several inventions in lighting and decoration' and was firmly established and in demand as a designer in Paris.[140] However, by the time she sold her shop in March 1929, she was financially, physically and emotionally depleted after becoming embroiled in multiple legal disputes to protect her designs. Nevertheless, Loy was not the defeated figure Peggy Guggenheim describes in her memoir, with her resources drained and 'ideas [. . .] stolen'.[141] A previously unknown article by *The Daily Telegraph*'s 'Paris Fashion Expert' about Loy's 'Novel Floral Decorations That Light Up Modern Interiors' was published on 11 October 1929, well after Loy had sold her interior design shop in Paris (Fig. 2.6). Given its level of technical detail and thematic richness, as well as its stylistic similarities with 'Auto-Facial-Construction' and 'Would You Be "Different?"', the article is almost certainly written by Loy herself.[142] The piece is reproduced here for the first time since its original publication, and, just as she had done in 'Would You Be "Different?"', Loy uses the piece to assert her intellectual property rights without filing patent or copyright claims. It also suggests that she was beginning to emphasise her credentials as an artist-engineer as well as a designer. Accordingly, 'Novel Floral Decorations' showcases

Figure 2.6 Anonymous [Mina Loy], 'Novel Floral Decorations That Light Up Modern Interiors', *The Daily Telegraph*, 11 October 1929, p. 7.

her methods as well as her creations, particularly her development of a new thermoplastic 'verrovoile, invented by Mina Loy – an artist of repute', which delivered 'new and original results' in lighting.

The lighting designs pictured in Loy's article develop her well-known floral lamp creations (featuring arum rather than canna lilies in this case) for the London market, emphasising their fashionable Parisian provenance. She also uses the piece to circulate the trade name 'verrovoile', which she describes as 'New Substitutes for Glass' in the same class as the cellophane product 'Crystalline', but with slightly different properties. A sobriquet that loosely translates as 'glass fabric', in Loy's account, 'verrovoile' is a 'new medium' that she developed as a 'substitute for glass', particularly for creating foliage effects. 'The material is non-inflammable', the piece continues, 'and instead of having the transparency of glass it is made opaque with a white paint during the process of development to achieve a semi-tone that diffuses light perfectly'. No

French or English patent or trademark seems to exist for the product, but her description sounds quite similar to Rhodoid, a thermoplastic made from cellulose acetate, at that stage a biopolymer derived mainly from tree pulp cellulose with 'incombustible' and light-diffusing properties (*OED*).[143] As such, Loy's discovery seems to have been a new method of processing cellulose acetate (which usually involves dissolving the substance in a solvent and spinning or casting it) to achieve unique consistency, pigmentation and light diffusion properties. Further novelties may have been 'verrovoile's' malleability, which allowed it to 'be moulded to shape before settling into a solid composition', preferable to other materials. The 'voile' that forms the second half of her material's name implies a more delicate, fabric-like result than she could have achieved using, for example, Rhodoid. Indeed, she seems to have developed 'verrovoile' specifically 'to imitate the leaves' in her lamp designs.

Loy achieved the 'most striking results' by using other 'opaque substances' to create the green tints and optical characteristics of these leaf decorations, including the arum lily lamp design pictured in the upper-right corner of the article.[144] However, Loy's previously unknown *Mexican Bloom* design in particular showcases the effects she could achieve with 'verrovoile' leaves. Even the monochromatic photograph in the article suggests a detailed and delicate form, particularly in the lighter leaf design to the right of the '*single beautiful bloom*'; but it also engages with a traumatic moment of recreation. Loy wrote that '[a] white flower glowing in the moonlight of Mexico City inspired [her] to create the floral lamp' *Mexican Bloom*. Although she accentuates the novelty and whimsicality of this creation narrative in 'Novel Floral Decorations', the design is also an elegy for Cravan. Instead of the literal and spiritual wasteland that she creates in her poem 'Mexican Desert', where 'Vegetable cripples of drought / thrust up' among 'stump-fingered cacti' and 'hunch-backed palm trees', the single blossom in *Mexican Bloom* creates a poignant memorial to a lost life (including her son Giles, who died in 1923), but, also, the creation of a new one (Fabienne, Loy's and Cravan's daughter).[145] As a decorative object, the memorial diffuses into domestic spaces, seeding Loy's tribute organically into everyday life without the client being aware of its origins.

With its 'verrovoile' leaves and associations with mourning, Loy's arum lily design also suggests that in some respects she used her lighting creations as memorials to an itinerant life with Battery J in Mexico. In 'Novel Floral Decorations', she compounds the reference to this post-war context in her choice of materials for the lamps. Since 'all the metal moulds were confiscated during the war for ammunition', she uses glass, and particularly 'old blown glass bottles' repurposed 'into stands for her attractive lampshades'. Blending technical detail and self-promotion, original manufacturing processes and *objet trouvé* aesthetics, the sublime and bathetic traces of mourning in her lighting designs bear all the hallmarks of a Loy composition. Collectively, they negotiate a tense middle ground between the necessity to create and to earn a living; 'to solve the problem of keeping alive', as she wrote to Mabel Dodge Luhan, 'without prostituting art';[146] and to keep ahead of present trends while tending to the traumas of her past.

When Loy returned to the 'iris circus of Industry' of the United States in 1936, her creations remained both prescient and anachronistic.[147] By then, as she wrote in her later poem 'Mass Production on 14th Street', electric lights had assumed a near-botanical role of flowers in the ecology of manufacturing. The 'ruby neon' blossoming 'among a foliage of mass production' resembled a 'mobile simulacrum' rather than a hybrid of compatible ensembles – the 'horticulture / of her hand labor' she had perfected in Paris.[148] Of course, Loy identified a niche for herself among the 'foliage of mass-production' in America. Here, 'The consumer [. . .] jostles her auxiliary creator / the seamstress'. Conjoining the language of consumer and sexual desire in the human and non-human worlds, Loy creates her own machine of mirrors from 'the conservatories of commerce' and their 'long glass aisles'.[149] The references to automata, insects and biological feedback mechanisms in 'Mass Production on 14th Street' anticipate the language of the cyberneticist sublime, but Loy's 'ironic' sideways glances to the ephemeral world of fashion and the daily routines of 'the garment worker' recall the bathetic distortions of technological duration that she created in her lighting designs.

Loy's return to the United States and her urgent need to earn money prompted her (forced) return to the craft of invention. There, she set about documenting her creations in a number of patent applications for a suite of technologies that combined her enthusiasms for reading, writing, the body and everyday tasks. Her inventions included: the 'Corselet', a protective posture-correcting brace that she described as 'Armour for the Body'; a 'Blotter Bracelet' for writers to wipe excess ink from their pens; an ergonomic broom with swivel-mounted cleaning attachments;[150] fabric designs; new technology-themed lampshade designs; and a modular alphabet in which parts of letters could be detached and reassembled.[151] During the 1940s she also attempted to copyright another plastic invention, a reflective multi-layered material she named *Chatoyant*, which evoked the 'changeable lustre or colour' of 'a cat's eye in the dark'. In her meticulous technical drawings for the material, Loy identified how a 'metallic layer' could be 'embedded in plastics' so that it was either 'coextensive with [an] area of plastics or glass', or 'form[ed] patterns' with it.[152] She also attached a wax and foil model to the patent application.[153] In Loy's archive at Yale University, these formal intellectual property documents may appear to be a late-career oddity; however, as we have seen, she had been working with cutting-edge plastics designs for over a decade previously. Her 1920s journalism also indicates that her later inventions were an extension of a career-spanning engagement with technology and technicity, not a new direction.

Across the arc of her career, Loy combined feminist poetics and techno-bathetic critique as the supreme artist-engineer of the Machine Age. Her work articulates a counter-servile technicity that actively modified the semiotic processes Certeau describes as the body's social 'codes' – the 'instruments through which a social law maintains its hold on bodies and its members, regulat[ing] them and exercis[ing] them through changes in fashion as well as through military manoeuvres'.[154] Loy sought surreptitiously to modify 'these tireless inscriptions' by resisting 'instrumentality' through bathetic strategies of technicity and transduction.[155] Her technical objects form strategic dialogues with her texts, and both diffused in culture through specialised cultural channels. Indeed, Loy's credibility as an artist-engineer emerges not *despite* her avant-garde practice and hardships but, rather, precisely *because* of them. Loy should be regarded a serious inventor with an excellent grasp of socio-technics and (though seldom successful in defending her claims to it) intellectual property law. In her extraordinary designs as well as her writing, she redeployed disconnected socio-technical ensembles to fashion an energetic and diachronic counter-servile technicity.

Conclusion

Alfred Stieglitz, the Pictorialists and the Young Americans had established a remarkably coherent lexicon for the American technological sublime as a key doctrine of their mystical nationalism. As we have seen throughout this chapter, this cultural narrative gained valency as it circulated through transatlantic discourse networks of the 1920s. However, as I have argued, the conceptual framework evolved alongside a bathetic counterpart, in which mirror images of the technological sublime took the form of backfiring machines, unstable infrastructures and intricate vernacular technologies that prototyped new relationships between socio-technical ensembles. Sometimes working in desperate circumstances, figures such as the Baroness, Duchamp, Loy, Picabia, Williams and others imagined the American Machine Age as a *Large Glass*, through which a dazzling array of identities and languages might be refracted. The techno-bathetic avant-gardes focused intently on the cultural infrastructures they themselves helped to create, and on how those networks interfaced with the socio-technical ensembles proliferating in the 1910s–1920s. Those points of contact became the subject of broader considerations about the role that technology and technicity might play in the production of art and spatial practices. In short, the techno-bathetic avant-gardes created new ways of reading – and writing – machines.

As the 1920s drew to a close, the surging techno-utopianism of the post-war boom comingled with a sense of pre-Depression malaise. This convergence surfaced most visibly in new modernist formations taking shape in expatriate artists' colonies in France. Based in Paris, Eugene Jolas's influential journal *transition* captured late modernist conflations of utopia and dystopia as expatriate modernists turned their gazes from urban geography to the mass cultural spaces suggested by technologies such as cinema and photography. Jolas described this ad-hoc movement as a 'Revolution of the Word'. The utopianism that many critics identify with this 'Revolution' was sustained across other strands of late modernist writing for a remarkably long period.[156] Yet these accounts frequently omit the counter-narratives of the techno-bathetic vanguardists, who understood that technology was just one of modernity's many conflicted inscriptions on the modernist self. After remaining silent throughout much of the 1920s during their exile in South America, Bob and Rose Brown re-emerged as some of the most strident American voices in *transition*'s 'Revolution of the Word'.[157] Combining a new literary form (the 'readies') with a prototype invention, Bob Brown's 'reading machine' has long been considered a crucial if short-lived experiment that encapsulates the utopian naivety of the modernist avant-gardes. However, as I will discuss in the next chapters, the Browns' project was not only technologically viable, but the work it spawned also articulated vernacular, counter-servile technicities that several avant-garde formations deployed as instruments of social critique (as well as literary experimentation). Like Loy's dissenting technicities, the Browns' 'readies' demand a diachronic re-reading, across the *longue dureé* of modernist cultures.

Notes

1. David Nye, *The American Technological Sublime* (Cambridge, MA, and London: The MIT Press, 1994), p. xvi.
2. As I discuss in the book's Introduction, I use the term 'techno-bathetic' as a general description that includes the 'technological bathetic' (a bathetic

engagement with a technological subject) and especially 'bathetic technicity' (a bathetic spatial practice articulated by technical means).
3. Roger Conover, 'Introduction', *LLB*, pp. xv–lxvi (p. xlvii).
4. William Sharpe, *New York Nocturne: The City After Dark in Literature, Painting, and Photography, 1850–1950* (Princeton: Princeton University Press, 2008), p. 200.
5. See Charles Brock, 'The Armory Show, 1913: A Diabolical Test', in Sarah Greenough et al., *Modern Art and America: Alfred Stieglitz and His New York Galleries* (Washington, DC: National Gallery of Art in association with Bullfinch Press, 2000), pp. 127–43.
6. Marius De Zayas, [untitled editorial], *291* 5–6 (July–August 1915): 6.
7. Waldo Frank, *Our America* (New York: Boni & Liveright, 1919), p. 45.
8. Nye, *American Technological Sublime*, p. xiii.
9. Peter Minuit [Paul Rosenfeld], '291 Fifth Avenue', *The Seven Arts* 1.1 (November 1916): 61–5 (p. 61).
10. Frank, *Our America*, p. 135.
11. Marcia Brennan, 'Alfred Stieglitz and New York Dada', *History of Photography* 21.2 (1997): 156–61 (p. 158).
12. See Jennifer L. Lieberman, *Power Lines: Electricity in American Life and Letters, 1882–1952* (Cambridge, MA, and London: The MIT Press, 2017), p. 197.
13. Michael North, *Camera Works* (Oxford: Oxford University Press, 2005), p. 40.
14. As Sascha Bru insightfully comments, avant-gardes were adept at producing their 'own "institutions", that is their own material infrastructure for art education, production, distribution and reception'; *The European Avant-Gardes, 1905–1935: A Portable Guide* (Edinburgh: Edinburgh University Press, 2018), p. 27.
15. Agnes E. Meyer, 'How Versus Why', *291* 1 (March 1915): 2.
16. Ibid.
17. T. W. Adorno, *Aesthetic Theory*, ed. Gretel Adorno and Rolf Tiedemann and trans. C. Lenhard (London, Boston, Melbourne and Henley: Routledge & Kegan Paul, 1984), p. 33.
18. Ibid. p. 35.
19. See Alfred Stieglitz, 'One Hour's Sleep – Three Dreams', *291* 1 (March 1915): 3.
20. Frank, *Our America*, p. 186.
21. Marius De Zayas, [untitled editorial], *291* 5–6 (July–August 1915): 6.
22. Paul Haviland, Untitled ['We are Living in the Age of the Machine'], *291* 7–8 (September–October 1915): 1.2.
23. Francis Picabia, *Ici, C'est Ici Stieglitz Foi et Amour*, *291* 5–6 (July–August 1915): 1.
24. Peter Minuit [Paul Rosenfeld], '291 Fifth Avenue', p. 61.
25. William Rozaitis, 'The Joke at the Heart of Things: Francis Picabia's Machine Drawings and the Little Magazine *291*', *American Art* 8.3/4 (Summer–Autumn 1994): 42–59 (p. 48).

26. Ibid. pp. 47–8.
27. Ibid. p. 43.
28. Francis Picabia, *De Zayas! De Zayas!*, 291 5–6 (July 1915): 5.
29. As Rozaitis notes, critics tend to agree that the design is based on a 'Delco starting and lighting system'; 'The Joke at the Heart of Things', p. 56.
30. Lauren Kroiz, *Creative Composites: Modernism, Race, and the Stieglitz Circle* (Los Angeles and Berkeley: The University of California Press, 2012), p. 87.
31. Rozaitis favours this interpretation; see 'The Joke at the Heart of Things', pp. 53–4.
32. See Steve Golin, *The Fragile Bridge: Paterson Silk Strike, 1913* (Philadelphia, PA: Temple University Press, 1988), pp. 65–71.
33. Kroiz, *Creative Composites*, p. 87.
34. See Willard Bohn, *The Rise of Surrealism: Cubism, Dada, and the Pursuit of the Marvelous* (Albany: State University of New York Press, 2002), p. 65.
35. Kroiz, *Creative Composites*, p. 87.
36. See Jennifer Wild, *The Parisian Avant-Garde in the Age of Cinema, 1900–1923* (Oakland: University of California Press, 2015), p. 98.
37. Rob Kitchin and Martin Dodge, 'Rethinking Maps', *Progress in Human Geography* 31.3 (2007): 331–44 (p. 335).
38. Bohn, *The Rise of Surrealism*, p. 65.
39. Francis Picabia, *Portrait D'une Jeune Fille Américaine Dans L'État de Nudité*, 291 5–6 (July 1915): 4.
40. Marcel Duchamp, *The Bride Stripped Bare by Her Bachelors, Even*, in *MDComplete Works*, p. 111.
41. Marcel Duchamp, *Bachelor Apparatus (Plan and Elevation)*, in *MD Complete Works*, p. 579.
42. Marcel Duchamp, Michel Sanouillet and Elmer Peterson, 'Bride Machine', in 'The Bride's Veil', in *MDEssential Writings*, p. 20. In *The Green Box* of 1934 ('The Bride's Veil', pp. 26–71), Duchamp's notes on the Bride are concentrated on pp. 38–9 and 42–8.
43. Ibid. p. 44.
44. Ibid. p. 70.
45. Ibid. p. 31.
46. Ibid. pp. 31–2. The best primary source for examining the evolution of *The Large Glass* is Marcel Duchamp, *Notes and Projects for the Large Glass*, ed. and introduction by Arturo Schwartz and trans. George H. Hamilton, Cleve Gray and Arturo Schwartz (London: Thames and Hudson Ltd, 1969).
47. Alfred Stieglitz, *Fountain by R. Mutt*, *The Blind Man* 2 (May 1917): 4.
48. See William Camfield, *Marcel Duchamp: Fountain* (Houston: Houston Fine Art Press, 1989), pp. 13–28.
49. Louise Norton, 'The Buddha of the Bathroom', *The Blind Man* 2 (May 1917): 5–6, and Anonymous, 'The Richard Mutt Case', p. 5. See Robert Kilroy, *Marcel Duchamp's Fountain: One Hundred Years Later* (London: Palgrave Pivot, 2018), pp. 61–4.

50. See Irene Gammel, *Baroness Elsa: Gender, Dada, and Everyday Modernity* (Cambridge, MA, and London: The MIT Press, 2002), pp. 218–29. Although entirely circumstantial, as she acknowledges, Gammel's evidence presents a fascinating possibility.
51. Alfred Stieglitz, [letter to the editors], *The Blind Man* 2 (May 1917): 15.
52. Beatrice Wood, *I Shock Myself* (Ojai, CA.: Dillingham Press, 1985), p. 30.
53. Alfred Stieglitz, *Fountain by R. Mutt* [Marcel Duchamp], *The Blind Man* 2 (May 1917): 4.
54. Stieglitz, [letter to the editors], *The Blind Man* 2: 15.
55. Alex Goody, *Modernist Poetry, Gender and Leisure Technologies: Machine Amusements* (New York: Palgrave Macmillan, 2020), p. 109.
56. Mina Loy, 'O Marcel - - - Otherwise I Also Have Been to Louise's', *The Blind Man* 2 (May 1917): 14–15.
57. Ibid. p. 15.
58. Craig Saper, *Amazing Adventures*, pp. 114, 112. Brown described their harrowing journey in his semi-autobiographical novel *You Gotta Live*, and although they took different routes, all ended up in Mexico City.
59. Caroline Burke, *Becoming Modern: The Life of Mina Loy* (New York: Farrar, Straus and Giroux, 1996), p. 251.
60. Ibid.
61. Ibid.
62. See Eric B. White, *Transatlantic Avant-Gardes: Little Magazines and Localist Modernism* (Edinburgh: Edinburgh University Press, 2013), pp. 24–31, 87.
63. William Carlos Williams, 'America, Whitman, and the Art of Poetry', *The Poetry Journal* 8.1 (November 1917): 27–36 (pp. 33–4).
64. See William Carlos Williams, 'Prologue' to *Kora in Hell*, in *Imaginations*, ed. Webster Schott (New York: New Directions, 1970), pp. 6–28 (pp. 8–10).
65. William Carlos Williams, 'Writing(s)' [unpublished typescript], in *The Manuscripts and Letters of William Carlos Williams*, The Poetry Collection of the University Libraries, University at Buffalo, The State University of New York, B123–C, p. 2. Internal evidence suggests that Williams composed the text in 1924, but possibly as early as 1923, or as late as 1926.
66. Ibid. p. 3. Duchamp and Williams would have had several opportunities to meet and discuss these ideas at galleries and salons in New York between 1915–26.
67. Williams, 'Writing(s)', p. 3.
68. Jane Heap, 'Comment', *The Little Review* 10.2 (Autumn 1924–Winter 1925): 17–22 (pp. 18–19).
69. See Duchamp, *Rotary Demisphere*, in *MDComplete Works*, p. 392; *Discs Inscribed with Puns* (pp. 393–5); and *Anémic Cinéma* (pp. 396–401).
70. Michel Charles, *Rhétorique de la lecture*, trans. Stephen F. Rendall (Paris: Seuil, 1977), p. 83.
71. *PEL*, p. 172.

72. Williams, 'Writing(s)', p. 3. See Frank, *Our America*, p. 164, and Emmy Veronica Sanders, 'Fourth of July Firecrackers', *Broom* 2.4 (July 1922): 287–92 (pp. 288–9).
73. Eugene Jolas, 'The Machine and Mystic America', *transition* 19–20 (June 1930): 379–83 (p. 379).
74. *PEL*, p. 150.
75. Ibid. p. 3. On Williams's anxieties about cultural homogeneity, see William Carlos Williams, *In the American Grain* (New York: Charles & Boni, 1925; repr. New York: New Directions, 1956), p. 68.
76. Jane Heap, 'Machine-Age Exposition', *The Little Review* 11.1 (Spring 1925): 22–4 (p. 22). The Machine Age Exposition was planned for autumn 1925 but was eventually held at Steinway Hall in New York in 1927.
77. Michael Mackenzie, 'Marcel Duchamp and the Antinomies of Art Historical and Art Critical Discourse', *Modernism/Modernity* 7.1 (2000): 153–63 (p. 160).
78. Linda Dalrymple Henderson, *Duchamp in Context: Science and Technology in the 'Large Glass' and Related Works* (Princeton and Oxford: Princeton University Press, 1998); see especially chapter 3, 'From Painter to Engineer, I', pp. 31–9.
79. Ezra Pound applied the term 'arid clarity' to the work of Mina Loy and Marianne Moore in 'A List of Books', *The Little Review* 4.11 (March 1918): 54–8 (p. 56).
80. *PEL*, p. 147.
81. John Rodker, '"Dada" and Else von Freytag-Loringhoven', *The Little Review* 7.2 (July–August 1920): 33–6 (p. 33).
82. Elsa von Freytag-Loringhoven, 'The Modest Woman', *The Little Review* 7.2 (July–August 1920): 37–40 (p. 37).
83. Ibid. p. 38.
84. Goody, *Modernist Poetry, Gender and Leisure Technologies*, p. 2.
85. See Cecilia Tichi, *Shifting Gears: Technology, Literature, Culture in Modernist America* (Chapel Hill, NC, and London: University of North Carolina Press, 1987), pp. 117–31.
86. Gammel, *Baroness Elsa*, p. 160.
87. See Adam McKible, '"Life Is Real and Life Is Earnest": Mike Gold, Claude McKay, and the Baroness Elsa von Freytag-Loringhoven', *American Periodicals* 15.1 (2005): 56–73, and White, *Transatlantic Avant-Gardes*, pp. 132–3.
88. See Elsa von Freytag-Loringhoven, 'Thee I Call Hamlet of the Wedding Ring', *Body Sweats*, pp. 291–313.
89. Irene Gammel and Suzanne Zelazo, 'Introduction', *Body Sweats*, pp. 1–39 (p. 21). Gammel and Zelazo do not go into much detail about the Baroness's statements on class.
90. See Ibid. p. 1.
91. Elsa von Freytag-Loringhoven, 'Mineself – Minesoul – And – Mine – Cast-Iron Lover', *Body Sweats*, pp. 277–89 (p. 283).

92. Elsa von Freytag-Loringhoven, 'Love – Chemical Relationship', *Body Sweats*, pp. 253–5 (p. 255).
93. *PEL*, p. 150.
94. Ibid.
95. Elsa von Freytag-Loringhoven, *Portrait of Marcel Duchamp*, *The Little Review* 9.2 (Winter 1922), following p. 45.
96. Elsa von Freytag-Loringhoven, *Portrait of Marcel Duchamp*, *Body Sweats*, p. 254.
97. Elsa von Freytag-Loringhoven, 'Narcissus Icarus', *Body Sweats*, pp. 264–6 (p. 264).
98. Adrian Mackenzie, *Transductions: Bodies and Machines at Speed* (London: Continuum, 2002), p. 103.
99. Thomas LaMarre, 'Humans and Machines', *Inflexions* 5 (March 2012): 29–67 (p. 30).
100. Donna Haraway, 'A Cyborg Manifesto: Science, Technology, and Socialist-Feminism in the Late Twentieth Century', in *Simians, Cyborgs and Women: The Reinvention of Nature* (New York: Routledge, 1991), pp. 149–81 (pp. 154, 151).
101. Ibid. p. 152.
102. LaMarre, 'Humans and Machines', pp. 29–67 (p. 30).
103. Ibid. p. 31.
104. N. Katherine Hayles, *My Mother Was a Computer: Digital Subjects and Literary Texts* (Chicago: University of Chicago Press, 2005), p. 243.
105. LaMarre, 'Humans and Machines', p. 30.
106. Thecla Schiphorst and Kristina Andersen define somatic practice as 'the experience from within the lived body', which incorporates affect and embodiment as a central component of cultural performance; 'Between Bodies: Using Experience Modeling to Create Gestural Protocols for Physiological Data Transfer', *CHI* 2004 (2004): 1–12 (p. 3). I am grateful to Jessica Rajko for drawing this work to my attention.
107. Gammel, *Baroness Elsa*, p. 373.
108. Elsa von Freytag-Loringhoven, 'Filmballad [Ms. version]', *Body Sweats*, pp. 256–61 (p. 260).
109. Elsa von Freytag-Loringhoven, 'Stagnation', *Body Sweats*, pp. 255–6 (p. 256).
110. Elsa von Freytag-Loringhoven, 'X-Ray', *Body Sweats*, p. 195.
111. Elsa von Freytag-Loringhoven, 'Stagnation', *Body Sweats*, pp. 255–6 (p. 256).
112. Niall Munro, *Hart Crane's Queer Modernist Aesthetic* (Basingstoke: Palgrave Macmillan, 2015), p. 164.
113. Gammel, *Baroness Elsa*, p. 383.
114. See Sandeep Parmar, *Reading Mina Loy's Autobiographies: Myth of the Modern Woman* (London and New York: Bloomsbury Academic, 2009), pp. 1–2.

115. See Eric White, '"A Machine of Mirrors": Technology and Identity in the Modernist Transatlantic', *Symbiosis* 17.2 (2013): 69–87 (pp. 76–7).
116. Mina Loy, *The Pamperers*, in *Stories and Essays of Mina Loy*, ed. Sara Crangle (Champaign, Dublin and London: Dalkey Archive Press, 2011), pp. 162–82 (pp. 162–3), and *The Sacred Prostitute*, in *Stories and Essays of Mina Loy* (ca. 1919), pp. 188–215.
117. Mina Loy, 'Lion's Jaws', *LLB*, p. 57.
118. Mina Loy, 'Auto-Facial-Construction', *LLB*, pp. 283–4 (p. 283).
119. Jessica Burstein, *Cold Modernism: Literature, Fashion, Art* (University Park, PA: The Pennsylvania State University Press, 2012), p. 184.
120. Loy, 'Auto-Facial-Construction', *LLB*, p. 284.
121. *PEL*, p. 147.
122. Anonymous [Mina Loy]/Newspaper Enterprise, 'Would You Be "Different?" Madame Loy Shows How', *The Pittsburgh Press*, 3 April 1921, p. 2.
123. The article is available on Suzanne Churchill's excellent online resource *Mina Loy: Navigating the Avant-Garde*; Linda A. Kinnahan, 'Loy's Italian Baedeker: Mapping a Feminist En Dehors Garde', in *Mina Loy: Navigating the Avant-Garde*, ed. Suzanne W. Churchill et al., Davidson College, 2017 <https://mina-loy.com/chapters/italy-italian-baedeker/5-italian-retreats/> (accessed 10 May 2019).
124. Richard A. Epstein, 'The Basic Structure of Intellectual Property Law', in *The Oxford Handbook of Intellectual Property Law*, ed. Rochelle Cooper Dreyfuss and Justine Pila (Oxford: Oxford University Press, 2018), pp. 25–56 (p. 45).
125. Loy, "Would You Be "Different?"'
126. Sara Crangle, 'Dada IS Bathos', in *On Bathos: Literature, Art, Music*, ed. Sara Crangle and Peter Nicholls (Cambridge: Continuum, 2010), pp. 27–48 (p. 29).
127. Ibid. pp. 37–8.
128. Ibid. p. 36.
129. Jussi Parikka, *Insect Media: An Archaeology of Animals and Technology* (Minneapolis: University of Minnesota Press, 2010), p. 123.
130. F. T. Marinetti, 'The Founding and Manifesto of Futurism' (20 February 1909), *Futurism*, pp. 49–53 (p. 49).
131. Bob Brown, *You Gotta Live* (London: Desmond Harmsworth, 1932), pp. vi, 372.
132. Burstein, *Cold Modernism*, p. 187.
133. Roger Conover, 'Time-Table', *LLB*, pp. lxiii–lxxix (pp. lxxii–lxxiii).
134. Ibid., and Burke, *Becoming Modern*, p. 365.
135. Burstein, *Cold Modernism*, p. 189.
136. Burke, *Becoming Modern*, p. 343.
137. Mina Loy, 'Ova Begins to Take Notice', *LLB*, pp. 135–42 (p. 141).
138. Burke, *Becoming Modern*, p. 342.
139. See Giles Slade, *Made To Break: Technology and Obsolescence in America* (Cambridge, MA, and London: Harvard University Press, 2006), p. 5.

140. Roger Conover, 'Time-Table', *LLB*, pp. lxiii–lxxix (p. lxiv).
141. Peggy Guggenheim, *Out of This Century: The Informal Memoirs of Peggy Guggenheim* (New York: Universe Books, 1979), p. 71.
142. Anonymous [Mina Loy], 'Novel Floral Decorations That Light Up Modern Interiors', *The Daily Telegraph*, 11 October 1929, p. 7. The article bears especially telling resemblances to 'Auto-Facial-Construction', including a shift to the passive voice to accentuate the objective tone of the jargon-heavy sections. I am grateful to Roger Connover for discussing Loy's article with me. Any errors in its interpretation are my own.
143. See Paul Rustemeyer, 'History of CA and Evolution of the Markets', *Macromolecular Symposia* 208.1 (2004): 1–6, and Rachel C. Law, 'Cellulose Acetate in Textile Application', *Macromolecular Symposia* 208.1 (2004): 255–66.
144. Loy, 'Novel Floral Decorations', p. 7.
145. Caroline Burke, *Becoming Modern*, p. 251.
146. Mina Loy to Mabel Dodge Luhan, February 1920, in Roger Conover, 'Textual Notes', *LLB*, pp. 323–9 (p. 328).
147. Mina Loy, 'Mass Production on 14th Street', in *The Lost Lunar Baedeker: Poems of Mina Loy*, ed. Roger L. Conover (New York: Farrar, Straus and Giroux, 1996), pp. 111–13 (p. 111).
148. Ibid. pp. 112–13.
149. Ibid. p. 112.
150. For reproductions and sharp analyses of Loy's designs for 'The Corselet' (ca. 1940s), the 'Blotter Bracelet' (1946) and her ergonomic broom (1946), see Burstein, *Cold Modernism*, pp. 179–85.
151. See reproductions and insightful discussions of Loy's lampshades, fabric and alphabet designs in Tara Prescott, *Poetic Salvage: Reading Mina Loy* (Lewisburg, PA: Bucknell University Press, 2017), pp. 79–83.
152. Mina Loy, *Chatoyant* (ca. 1940s), YCAL MSS 6, B7, F186, Mina Loy Papers, Beinecke Rare Book and Manuscript Library, Yale University Library.
153. See the facsimile of Loy's *Chatoyant* in Prescott, *Poetic Salvage*, p. 84.
154. *PEL*, p. 147.
155. Ibid. pp. 147, 150.
156. See for example Barnaby Haran, 'Machine, Montage, and Myth: *Experimental Cinema* and Politics of American Modernism During the Great Depression', *Textual Practice* 25.3 (2011): 563–84 (p. 563).
157. See Eugene Jolas et al., 'The Revolution of the Word Proclamation', *transition* 16–17 (1929): 1.

Chapter 3

Excavating the 'Readies': The Revolution of the Word, Revised

Introduction

Bob Brown's Reading Machine promised to transliterate the visual and temporal energies of the Machine Age in a new reader-focused textual space, within the modernist avant-gardes, but also far beyond them. Although Brown's idea reached across multiple fields of cultural production in complex ways, the central concept for his reading machine and corresponding textual medium 'the readies' was quite straightforward. His first surviving sketch for the project is a 1923 holograph manuscript he wrote in Brazil, which describes 'a simple machine run by a motor to carry a tape under a reading glass'.[1] Following a period of development in 1929, Brown expanded the idea in 1930, explaining that the reading machine itself would be 'as handy as a portable phonograph, typewriter or radio; compact, minute, operated by electricity, the printing done microscopically by the new photographic process on a transparent tough tissue roll which carries the contents of a book and is no bigger than a typewriter ribbon'.[2] The micrographic 'contents' printed on that 'tough tissue roll' were known as 'the readies'. Brown described the readies as 'a moving type spectacle' that involved 'reading at the speed rate of the day with the aid of a machine, a method of enjoying literature in a manner as up-to-date as the lively talkies' in cinema.[3] This simple idea rapidly evolved into a co-created vision for an entirely new media ecology, which became the focal point for multiple avant-gardes and other specialist professions in a global cottage industry spanning decades and continents. Experimentalists from a variety of fields produced 'sample' texts in full-sized print that Brown collected in his 1931 anthology *Readies for Bob Brown's Machine*.[4] The contributors included F. T. Marinetti, Ezra Pound, Gertrude Stein and William Carlos Williams, but also influential figures such as Kay Boyle, Nancy Cunard, Hilaire Hiler, Eugene and Maria Jolas, Norman Macleod, Samuel Putnam,

Rose Brown (née Watson, Bob's wife), and many other writers associated with *transition*'s 'Revolution of the Word'. Despite their utopian ambitions to transcend space and cultural barriers (which frequently cropped up in *transition*, particularly among the Jolas' coterie), the technicity of reading Readies, and the palpability of the prototype reading machine, pulls us relentlessly back to earth. This chapter combines literary-historical close reading and object-orientated materialist analysis to identify the cultural and socio-technical ensembles involved in the production of the readies project, and, more broadly, to begin a fundamental reconsideration of key modernist, media, engineering and commercial formations in the transatlantic Machine Age.

After some initial scepticism, Brown's work has now been recognised as a major and original (if sometimes controversial) contribution to the modernist project in a slow but steady stream of important critical studies.[5] Nevertheless, the current consensus among literary and media scholars is that 'Brown never managed to transform his enthusiasm into an actual, working machine'.[6] Drawing on previously-unknown evidence from Brown's archives at UCLA Special Collections and SIU Carbondale Special Collections, and a range of French newspapers and specialist periodicals, this chapter and the next present a revisionist account of this infamous modernist project that upends these assumptions. In all probability, Brown's reading machine worked exactly as he described it, and its development provides a compelling and long-running modernist counter-narrative, which profoundly alters how we conceive of avant-gardes' cultural work in the 1930s and beyond. From its conception in Greenwich Village in 1915, to its development during the Browns' exile in South and Central America in the mid-1920s, to its first major articulation and prototyping in expatriate France in 1929–32, this chapter fills in gaps in the historical record while providing new documentary evidence about the reading machine. These documents include previously unknown articles and manuscripts by Brown and others, and a detailed, never-before published photograph of the first working prototype model, which is reproduced for the first time in this chaper (Fig. 3.6). The untold story of the readies project spans five decades of modernist history and transforms the endeavour from a solo enterprise into a collaborative effort involving Bob's wife Rose, the American surrealist artist and 'engineer' Ross Saunders, his fellow expatriate painter Hilaire Hiler, and a team of engineers and writers in the US.[7]

In Craig Saper's most recent account of Brown's work, he explores how Brown and other avant-garde figures 'used the networking and publishing processes as a canvass' and helps establish a clear vocabulary for discussing Brown's project. Saper explains that when referring to the term '"readies" as a style, then one might call it readies. If it is a name of [the *RFBBM* anthology's] contributions, then perhaps each individual chapter is one readie, and the plural is readies. If it is a genre, or perhaps a brand name, then one might capitalise it as Readies or put it in quotes as "Readies"'.[8] Building on these terms, I use 'readies project' to describe the Browns' overarching plans for reading 'machinewise' in a new media ecology encompassing the devices, media and genre Brown designed (and indeed, the wider socio-technical ensembles needed to support these).[9] The 'reading machine' refers to a generic description of the technical object itself. However, that object took three distinct forms. The first version, the 'Saunders Prototype', refers to the working patent model reading machine built in Cagnes-sur-Mer in the summer of 1931, which I discuss in this chapter. The second form is the 'Commercial Design', which was sketched by Saunders, Hiler or the Detroit-based engineer Albert Stoll, and was reproduced on the flyleaf of *RFBBM* along with Saunders's device (Fig. 3.1). Brown described this version in an article and sample of readies for the Southwestern little magazine *Morada*, where he announced that '[i]n Detroit a simple, portable, electrically-driven device as compact, practical and cheap as a kodak [*sic*] is being perfected to present a continuous line of type in motion before the reader's eye'.[10] The third form is the 'Readio', a working prototype built by Rose Brown, Stoll, the lithographer Hugo Knudsen, and Brown's cousin Clare Brackett. Named after a 1937 sketch by Hilaire Hiler in *Globe* magazine, which depicts a similar device, the Browns took this version of the reading machine to Russia in 1935 (I discuss the production of this model in the next chapter).

Following a revisionist account of the reading machine's foundation narrative, this chapter focuses on three strands of the distinct but complexly interdependent matrix of cultural formations that contributed to the evolution of Bob and Rose Brown's reading machines: the transatlantic avant-garde writers and artists who fostered Brown's project in journals such as *transition*, *The Morada* and *The New Review*; expatriate publishers such as the Black Sun and Hours Press; and American expatriate newspapers such as *The New York Herald (European Edition)* and *The Chicago Tribune European Edition* (aka *The Paris Tribune*). The American print and publishing trade journal *The Publishers' Weekly*, where Brown published an influential essay on his reading machine, acts as a bridging point to the non-literary specialist publications I address in Chapter 4. Rather than breaking down the conceptual barriers between literary vanguardists and other specialised practices, Brown sought to synchronise their operations. The texts and technicities of the readies project – and the crises of form, identity and hierarchy that its co-creators

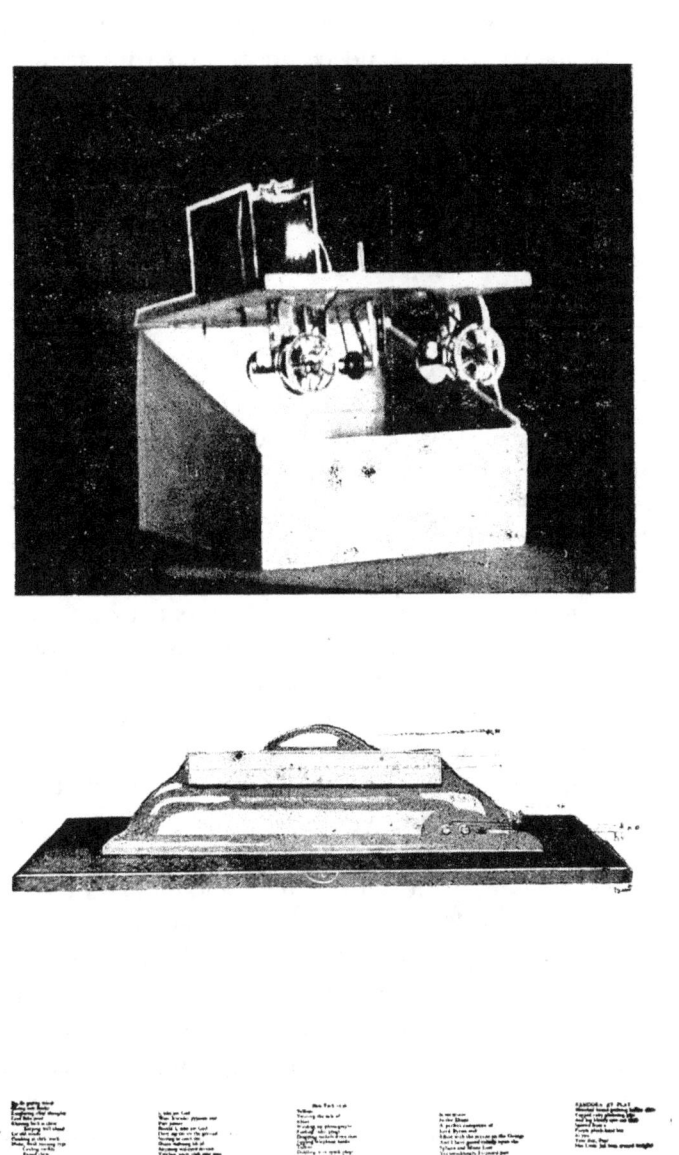

Figure 3.1 Bob Brown, Flyleaf [Photograph of Ross Saunders's Prototype Reading Machine and Hilaire Hiler's Commercial Design for the Reading Machine], *RFBBM*, p. 4.

and contributors sought to engage with – provide a legible blueprint for this socio-technical enterprise. Instead of an apolitical and reactionary scion of the expatriate avant-garde, re-reading Brown's project, from its origins in Greenwich Village to its first completed prototype, vastly widens the chronological, cultural and socio-technical frames of an episode previously confined to the historical avant-garde. As Gilbert Simondon argued, 'a great many technical objects are unfinished inventions that remain as an open virtuality and could be taken up again, according to their deep intention, their technical sense'.[11] The Browns' reading machines remained 'an open virtuality', and 'unfinished', but the archive reveals how their evolution produced new, counter-servile encounters between aesthetic and technological vanguardism.

The Foundations of the Readies Project: Re-Reading Bob Brown's Machine

Brown's reading machine, like so many transatlantic avant-garde projects, has its roots in post-Armory Show Greenwich Village. A fixture in both its arts and political scenes, Brown was also a contributing editor of the socialist journal *The Masses*, and wrote Imagist free verse, which he published in *Bruno Chap Books* and *Others: A Magazine of the New Verse*.[12] He also pursued a variety of freelance careers, which included pulp fiction writing, rare book dealing, entrepreneurship, events promotion and stock market trading.[13] According to his foundation narratives, a number of which he produced between 1930 and 1950, the reading machine was the inevitable result of these cross-disciplinary activities. Most accounts begin in 1915, when he claimed that 'I had to think of the reading machine' because 'I read Gertrude Stein and tape-tickers in Wall Street. Once I worked for some weeks with the head printer of *Munsey's* [*Magazine*] who was experimenting with steel-faced type, [and] later I owned a monotype and watched molten letters pour through it into an endless stream of words.'[14] Here, Brown compresses eight years into two sentences, from the inception of his idea for the readies project in 1915 to its first articulation in print in Brazil in 1923. Brown's reading machine narratives frequently involve such elisions – not only between discourse networks, but also cultural formations, socio-technical ensembles and even time periods. Inspired by Dada-Surrealism and marketing tactics in equal turns, his juxtapositions are techno-bathetic strategies designed to shock, surprise and capture readers' attention in order to shake them from their habituated ways of reading (and the technicities bound up in those practices). Brown carefully engineered his foundation narratives to produce such effects – but he also used them to camouflage a complicated and, at times, acutely painful history surrounding the development of the readies project.

Although no direct record of Brown's readies project from the 1910s survives, he spends eight pages of the *RFBBM* 'Appendix' explaining how the readies ensemble emerged from and merged with the Greenwich Village zeitgeist. He insists that the idea found its first expression in the publication of his optical poem (or calligramme) 'Eyes' in the second issue of Marcel Duchamp's little magazine *The Blind Man* in May 1917.[15] As I discussed in the previous chapter, *The Blind Man* was a crucial modernist document, which William Carlos Williams associated with the techno-bathetic 'chaos' of American culture. Williams detected a predatory version of this impulse in 'Eyes', and he admired how Brown's poem 'cleverly likened cocotte's eyes to oysters'.[16] Vaguely alluding to Shakespeare's *The Tempest*, Brown's poem transfigures the cocottes' eyes into pearls, which are served like oysters 'on the half-shell', but also arranged like the dancers at a louche cotillion ('cocottes' can mean sweethearts, or prostitutes, in French, as well as appetisers). Here, the organs of perception are re-presented for visual consumption as aphrodisiac hors d'oeuvres. They gaze inwards, refracting, monitoring and proliferating, recreating their own distorted stares after the third line of text: 'My God † / What Eyes'.[17] For Brown, the body began to mimic the machine, simulating a 'camera eye' by zooming in on an unseen object of desire. Like Duchamp's *Nude Descending a Staircase, No. 2*, 'Eyes' recreates a bathetic technicity from the perspective of both the subject and the reader/viewer. In the *RFBBM* 'Appendix', Brown identified the hand-drawn versions of 'Eyes' in *The Blind Man* and *1450–1950* (one of which is included in Fig. 3.2) as 'the link that reached out into space for me and surprisingly coupled with the reading machine. Brought it down to earth as Ben Franklin's kite string brought electricity'.[18] His insight was that in the Machine Age, literary forms could re-present the radical disembodiment produced by sensory augmentation and recording technologies. Brown's optical poetry performs that dissection, and in its radical compression of language, his readies project intensified that process.

As we have seen in Chapter 2, however, the proto-Dada experiments in Greenwich Village came to an abrupt halt in the summer of 1917, and, with them, Brown's readies experiments. As Brown recalled, '[t]he war came along' – or rather, the United States intervened in the First World War – and the resulting suppression of anti-war and/or culturally subversive activities in New York scattered and disrupted the Browns' avant-garde network. Bob and Rose Brown and their group of friends were coming under increased scrutiny and made plans to flee the United States. The group included Arthur Cravan, Mina Loy and Allen Norton, who came to be known as the mock-battalion 'Battery J'. From that point on, Brown recalls that he 'did nothing about [his] machine except try to explain it to an occasional friend'.[19] This account, though broadly accurate, omits the flight of his band of political exiles to Mexico. Many of Brown's associates on *The Masses* had already been indicted as the federal government clamped down on anti-war sentiment. Although Brown was not among them, he hadn't done himself any favours by hosting a 'Censorship Ball' in tribute to Anthony Comstock, the US Postal Inspector who became the public face of censorship in the 1910s.[20] However, his new wife Rose was 'in real immediate danger' because of her feminist activist 'work with Emma Goldman's group' (Goldman herself had already been arrested for denouncing the war).[21] Following Cravan into Mexico, Battery J joined the migration of 'slackers' in the autumn of 1917, who survived by drawing on their enormous ingenuity, resourcefulness and co-operative energies.[22] They lived a precarious life south of the border until they disbanded following Cravan's disappearance and probable death at the end of 1918.[23]

By September 1918, Battery J had threaded their way through South America, eking out a poverty-level existence which saw Brown briefly serving as Cravan's boxing promoter. In September, a thief stole a suitcase containing the only copies of 'a whole manuscript full of free verse to make a follow-up volume for *My Margonary* [1916] when we arrived at the huge station in Buenos Aires and I threw my arms around Mina Loy'.[24] If there was a reference to the reading machine among those papers, then it was lost to history at that moment. Following Cravan's disappearance, and a grief-stricken Loy's departure, the Browns sustained themselves through odd jobs until they managed to obtain new (forged) documents. In an audacious but grimly ironic manoeuvre, they both found posts in the American propaganda service Compub – an agency sponsored by the same forces that caused Battery J to flee the United States.[25] The Browns could keep tabs on the organisation and earn a comfortable living during this period, but they left their posts as quickly as possible. Using their modest capital and contacts, they began publishing a series of successful business magazines. Launched in 1920, their flagship journal, *The Brazilian American*, was an astonishing success and quickly became a template for a new publishing empire that expanded to *The Mexican American* and *The British American*. Brown often found himself gazing at 'a monotype' in its press plant, which he recalled in his *RFBBM* 'Appendix'.[26] Watching his impressive new print works in Rio de Janeiro, he recorded the first surviving evidence that describes his experimental reading machine.

On 14 June 1923, Brown composed a holograph manuscript entitled 'The Six Books of Bob Brown'. Only one page of this document survives, but it outlines the basic design of the reading machine and the readies, which would 'gradually [eliminate] unnecessary vermicelli, conjunctions, etc'.[27] This process of textual compression anticipates the approach he would later propose for the readies medium, which he literally sketches out on the page with a crude illustration. Brown later reproduced that sketch in his 1929 collection of calligrammes *1450–1950* as part of his untitled 'self portrait', which he labelled 'my reading machine' (Fig. 3.2). The calligramme visually schematised Brown's embodied poetics, and positions both 'eyes' and the 'reading machine' as the foundation of his life's work, while suggesting a common point of origin.[28] The title of the volume, *1450–1950*, also contains an echo of 'The Six Books of Bob Brown', where he complained that 'more modern reading and writing must be achieved. Very little has been done since 1450.'[29] Brown may well have had the idea for his reading machine in 1915, and early sketches might have survived his journey south, but I have not located any references to the project prior to 1923. Whether it was an idea he recalled from his Greenwich Village days, or an innovation inspired by his new publishing empire in Brazil, it was during this period that Brown began exploring publishing technologies in earnest.

In November 1920, Rear Admiral Bradley Fiske, a retired naval officer, author and serial inventor, filed a patent for a non-motorised micrographic reading device. During the First World War, he developed several telescopic range-finder and targeting devices for various weapons, as well as a design for an early version of 'dazzle camouflage' for the US Navy.[30] After the war, he turned to writing and inventions, particularly information technologies, and received his patent for his device in March 1922. The invention received widespread press coverage (but few sales) later that year.[31] His machine resembled a hand-held microfiche reader, with micrographic texts arranged in columns on printed paper 'tape' (approximately two inches wide and thirty inches long) read through a monocular magnification lens. Fiske went on to patent and produce numerous versions of his machine until the late 1930s, but they were all variations on his original idea.[32] Once adjusted with the manual scrolling rollers, the text itself was static. 'A family friend' sent Brown the patent documents for Fiske's machine in 1925, and he clearly studied them carefully.[33] In doing so, he better understood the novelty of his own invention, which was primarily to do with the scrolling text medium (i.e. the readies), the mechanised system and the user interface. In addition, his international travels had also helped him identify a new opportunity for producing micrographic print.

In March 1923, a few months before Brown wrote his 'Six Books' manuscript, the British print trade journal *Caxton Magazine* published an

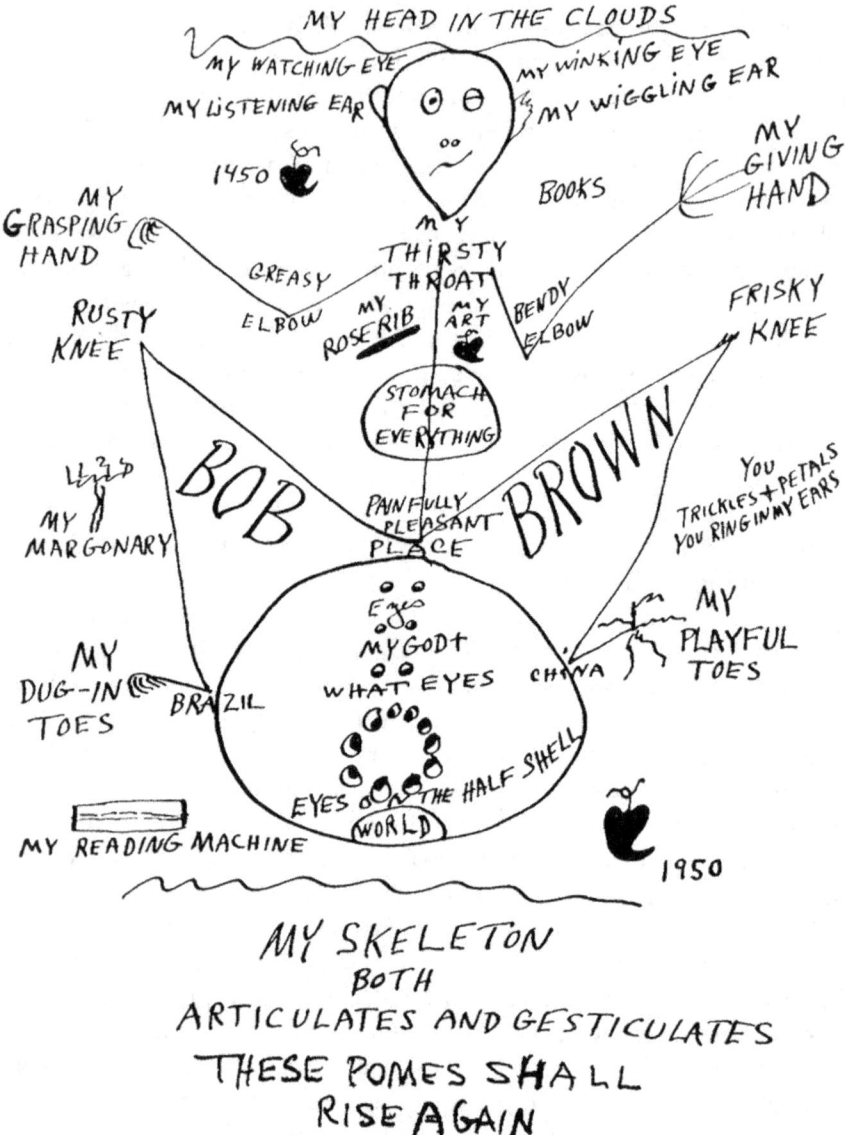

Figure 3.2 Bob Brown, Untitled [aka 'Self Portrait'], 1450–1950, p. 83.

article about the revolutionary but highly experimental August-Hunter Photo-Composing machine, and followed that up with a second article in December (Fig. 3.3).[34] Using this machine, 'type of any style can be composed in the form of a latent image on a roll of film, as quickly as an operator can manipulate a keyboard, similar to that on a typewriter'.[35] Photo-compositing was a revolutionary new technology that dramatically improved the efficiency and flexibility of typesetting for publishers, and J. R. C. August and E. Kenneth Hunter, the machine's inventors, frequently speculated about its potential developments. A news clipping in Brown's archives proposed that by using 'telegraphy and wireless telegraphy' in conjunction with the machine, 'an operator at a keyboard in London could [. . .] set up "copy" simultaneously in provincial towns, or in, for example, Paris and Edinburgh'.[36] Brown was clearly inspired by the possibilities of producing the readies medium with this machine, and the dramatic but technically plausible prospect of a new globally-connected medium that harnessed the latest networked communications technology. Brown visited J. R. C. August as part of his work with *The British American* in 1925, which they followed up in their correspondence. August's November 1925 letter to Brown suggests that the pair had formed tentative plans to develop the readies project using the photo-compositing machine.[37] Although Brown enthused about this potential partnership across his readies publications, their plans were never realised; however, this association opened doors for him.[38]

Shortly after he corresponded with August, Brown finally sought out Admiral Fiske as a potential collaborator during a business trip to New York.[39] In the winter of 1926, Brown was preparing to negotiate with General Electric about a million-dollar investment in his company at the opulent Waldorf Hotel. Although only an amateur inventor at this stage, Brown had considerably more success in writing and business than Fiske did, and being resident at the Waldorf, Brown held a slight 'home turf' advantage for the meeting. Despite his resources and connections with August, Brown's proposal for a mechanised apparatus did not inspire Fiske's confidence. Fiske believed that streaming texts would cause eye strain, and that Brown would eventually run into patent problems (indeed, as I discuss in the next chapter, Fiske's objections were valid and shared by others).[40] Yet Brown also had justifiable reservations about Fiske's device, which he dismissed as 'uncomfortable', 'awkward', static and restrictive.[41] Their meeting did not result in a partnership, but the upshot was that his encounter with Fiske not only helped Brown to clarify his own niche but also to learn a great deal (though not quite enough) about technical and intellectual property development. And although Brown's discussions with General Electric did not yield an investment,

Figure 3.3 A. H. Development Syndicate, *August-Hunter Photo-Composing Machine*, illustrates W. B. Hislop, 'August-Hunter Photo-Composing Machine', *Penrose's Annual* 28 (1926): 76–80 (n.p.), British Library.

they did set the stage for Brown's future sale of his publishing business, which in turn funded the development of his reading machine.

In his writing about his invention, Brown continually associates his idea with avant-garde innovation. He often emphasises that his reading machine was not a mere augmentation of someone else's brainwave, but at the same time he makes numerous references to contemporary technological innovations, some of which were highly experimental. Nevertheless, his foundation narratives downplay Brown's greatest strength: his capacity for collaboration. He recognised his own limitations ('I can't even drive a nail straight', he admitted, 'so I can't help in making the machine, but I hope to drive home [the idea]') but had a heightened awareness of others' strengths.[42] He expressed this by consistently tapping the unrealised potential of multiple socio-technical ensembles and forming strategic, if sometimes unlikely, partnerships. Characteristically, Brown pressed ahead with the readies project despite Fiske's warnings and continued to refine it with other collaborators in France and America once he left his South American business behind. When the Browns sold their international publishing empire in September 1928, they travelled through the South Pacific and Asia, China and Africa before arriving in Marseilles on 31 March 1928, and settling briefly in Paris on 6 April.[43] Sustained by these funds, Brown returned to avant-garde writing with a vengeance among a thriving expatriate print culture. He adapted his reading machine idea to these new circumstances and investigated ways of harnessing and transforming mass print culture at the same time.

Expatriate Publishing in Paris: Galvanising the Readies Project

Brown's output between 1929–31 was volcanic, and it included eight collections of experimental writing as well as numerous contributions to modernist journals.[44] Harry and Caresse Crosby's influential Black Sun Press published Brown's seminal book *1450–1950* in August 1929, which featured not only his first ideas about the reading machine but also his optical poem 'Eyes'. He wrote a version of his foundational essay 'The Readies' shortly thereafter and published the final version in the June 1930 issue of *transition*. This essay became the third and fourth chapters of his famous pamphlet that he self-published the following month, also entitled *The Readies*, which was the first publication by his own Roving Eye Press. 'Writing Readies', a selection of extracts from *RFBBM* introduced by Brown, was collected in *Morada 5* in December 1930. His experiments in micrographic printing with Nancy Cunard ca. October 1930–January 1931 anticipated a 'reading-machine future', and appeared in a book of poetry as miniature gloss-poems entitled

Words, which was published by Cunard's Hours Press in the spring of 1931.[45] Brown had collected all of the contributions to his anthology *Readies For Bob Brown's Machine* by November 1931, and he published a prospectus for this anthology shortly before its final publication on 31 December.[46]

These avant-garde print contexts are of course crucial to the development of the readies project, but they are not the first, or even perhaps the most important, forums in which he published his ideas about the reading machine and optical writing. For example, *The New York Herald (European Edition)* meticulously recreated his calligramme 'Eyes' with strategically placed conventional type, as well as part of 'Japanese Print Rain Storm', also from *1450–1950* (Fig. 3.4).[47] In addition, Brown unveiled his first fully-fledged plans for the reading machine, not in his famous essay for *transition*, but in an interview for *The Paris Tribune* in January 1930. In fact, 'The Readies' was not even his first essay for a specialist audience: 'My Reading Machine' appeared in the American publishing trade journal *The Publishers' Weekly* in May 1930, one month before the summer 1930 'Revolution of the Word' issue of *transition*. As crucial as Brown's contributions to that expatriate 'Revolution' were, in some respects, the scholarly attention that they have received deflects attention from his far more ambitious project: to engage both literary and non-literary specialist formations in the creation of a new media ecology. Brown's strategic interventions in expatriate news forums reached across the relevant specialisms of writers, publishers and avant-garde artists he targeted while prototyping the readies ensemble.

When Brown arrived in Paris, *The New York Herald (European Edition)* announced the arrival of a cosmopolite writer-collector who had renounced his mainstream career writing pulp fiction and embraced experimental writing: 'Bob Brown, Who Used to Write "Diamond Dick" Stories, Debases His Art After Japanese Trip'. The headline and tone of the article recycled many tropes common to expatriate newspaper stories on Left Bank artists and writers, which appeared regularly in the international editions of *The New York Herald* and the *Chicago Tribune and the Daily News New York* (better known as *The Paris Tribune*). These articles usually consist of a polemical headline, a tongue-in-cheek (if slightly scandalised) tone that both mocks and extols the subject, and an insider 'scoop' on a fascinating fringe of American expatriate life, and how it becomes transformed by cross-cultural contacts. Brown's arrival presents an especially eye-catching version of this narrative. His contact with (and appropriation of) Japanese responses to American culture via its unique print culture spurs a re-evaluation of his own practice, and encourages him to embrace a new, extemporaneous and visual form of writing at the expense of his much-loved potboilers.[48] Brown uses a 'carved jade fish'

Bob Brown, Who Used to Write 'Diamond Dick' Stories, Debases His Art After Japanese Trip

A man who helped write "Diamond Dick" into immortality, and at the same time could turn out sonnets for the sedate pages of the "Century" magazine, has just arrived in Paris, bag and baggage, with his mind made up to give up collecting—at least for the moment—and settle down to writing.

This person of a thoroughly ambidexterous nature is Mr. Robert Carlton Brown, founder in 1919 of the "Brazilian American," the business builder of Brazil, who when he decided to come to Paris to settle down and write decided that he would like also to see a bit of Japan.

The result was that for 63 days he and his family, son, wife and mother, coursed about from Rio de Janeiro to Cape Town, and then to Malay and thence to Yokohama. It was a nice, leisurely trip. To get to Paris Mr. Brown and the various Browns got on another ship and for thirty days more they went through tropic seas to Marseilles.

Yesterday, shortly before sundown, in a quiet little hotel in the rue des Capucines, Mr. Brown was found in his lavender pyjamas, deep in the luxury of his beds, books, Japanese prints, jade and poems. All except the beds and the poems represent the fruit of rapid, but highly selective collecting in the Far East.

* * *

"In Japan, it is so beautiful," Mr. Brown said, offering a French cigarette, of which he had a small collection, "everybody collects something. I went in for Japanese prints, but very special prints. I got about three hundred and fifty showing the Japanese reaction to the first Americans who arrived there in numbers with Admiral Perry.

"I brought back a number of books —thirty trunks of books, I should say —some are still in Marseilles—because a person can pick up more interesting old books in Tokio than anywhere in the world unless it is Paris. There is one section of the town with five miles of old book shops."

Mr. Brown's prints, some on silk several hundred years old, and some done in simple black and white at the time when, before newspapers, these wood block prints were issued with a notable's picture on them and a few words of "news" and sold like tabloids, are probably the most complete Japanese Americana ever to arrive in Paris.

"The people I've shown them to want me to have an exhibition of them in Paris. And I might. It would be fun, probably. But right now I'm interested more in writing."

Mr. Brown explained that he was through with all the old forms of writing, and the public could expect no more "Diamond Dick" stories out of him.

"I wrote a thousand stories in a couple of years," he said. "When I was twenty I went to London and wrote feuilletons for Munsey. I edited "Pearsons." I wrote for the old "Masses." I was the editor of the first book of free verse which Mencken said got the spirit of that movement. I wrote myself out. So I went into commerce in South America and last September I sold out my three papers down there and now I'm going to write."

Mr. Brown seems at the moment to have a somewhat similar idea of words and art as Wagner had of words and music.

"I want to combine art with words. Not only drawings with poems, but perhaps even color. For instance, see this?"—He drew a carved jade fish out of a pocket in the pants hanging near the bed—"Well, that is beautiful. The artist there availed himself of those two deep green spots in the stone to make them fish eyes.

"Here, I'll show you what I mean. I have a poem called

Eyes
(.) (.)
My God +
(.) (.)
What Eyes.
(.) (.)
(.) (.)
(.) (.)
(.) (.)
· (.) (.)
(.) (.)
(.)
Eyes on the Half Shell.

* * *

"Here's another:
/ / / / / / / / /
/ / / / / / / / /
/ / / / / / / / /
/
Japenese print Rain Storm:
/ / / / / / / /
/ / / / / / /

Rice Growing in a Swamp:
I I I I I I I I I I I I
I I I I I I I I I I I I

The Hairs on Esau:
I I I I I I

Sanitary tooth brush:
|||||||||||||||||||

and

The whiskers on a gnat:
' ' '

Mr. Brown gathered his lavender pyjamas around his throat and placing a hand-made eye-shade over his bronzed brow, said:

"Wait a moment
(half-rest)

"I think I can do one on Varèse, the composer I heard this week. Great music. In Brazil all we have in picture music..."

But outside the maws of the press (.) ( ) were waiting with open mouths, and the reporter was forced to toddle on . . and on. . . into the night.

GENARO TO DEPART ON ALBERT BALLIN

Frankie Genaro, having regained his world's fly-weight title from Spider Pladner, will start for New York today for old worlds to conquer, sailing on the Hamburg-Amerika liner Albert Ballin from Boulogne. The Albert Ballin's boat-train leaves the Gare du Nord at 8.25 this morning.

Al Shane, Broadway entertainer, will be another prominent passenger on the

---

Figure 3.4 Anonymous, 'Bob Brown, Who Used to Write "Diamond Dick" Stories, Debases His Art After Japanese Trip', *The New York Herald (European Edition)*, 27 April 1929, p. 9.

by a Japanese artist to make his point. 'The artist there availed himself of those two deep green spots in the stone to make them fish eyes', he explains, and connects that practice with his transcribed poem 'Eyes'. This improvisational practice is reminiscent of Marcel Duchamp's 'readymades' and recalls Brown's appearance in *The Blind Man* over a decade earlier. In this respect, the piece also has a connection to the reading machine's foundation narrative.

Writing about his hand-drawn optical poem 'Eyes' in the *RFBBM* 'Appendix', Brown exclaimed that '[h]ere are Black Riders for me at last actually galloping across a blank page. They'll gallop faster when I print them on the tape of my reading machine.'[49] However, Stephen Crane's poem 'Black Riders' refers to a *typewriter* pounding out characters across a blank page, not a stylus, so this association initially appears quite oblique. *The New York Herald* article makes the connection clear. The article reproduces Brown's calligrammes using standard type (Fig. 3.4). The transliterated text disrupts the linear flow of the page, which creates a visual spectacle. Yet the newspaper also brokers an important exchange of methodologies. After the samples of Brown's optical poetry, the journalist adopts the same visual language, depicting the 'maws of the press ( ) ( )' with parentheses, and a 'half-rest' and the 'night' with shapes.[50] The effect echoes Brown's work in its elision of humour and lyricism, and avant-garde writing and expository prose. In the process, this collaborative production suggested a model for radically expanding the optical vocabulary of print media while indicating simultaneously how it might be compressed using the same strategies. This two-way collaboration helped Brown establish the circumstances in which 'Eyes' 'coupled with the reading machine', not only as an inspiration for the readies medium, but for the co-creative practices it inspired. Restoring the journalistic context suggests how he hybridised avant-garde writing and journalism, or what Gertrude Stein would later describe as 'the missing link between [H.L.] Mencken and [Brown]'.[51]

While collating (and probably still creating) his calligrammes in the spring of 1929, Brown also began the second stage of his work on the readies project. *1450–1950* not only reproduced his 1923 sketch of the readies medium, which I discussed in the previous section, but also produced the clearest micrographic 'sample' of the dash-laden readies format, which appeared at the beginning of the collection. Caresse Crosby of the Black Sun Press created this text using tiny 3-point diamond type that required a magnifying glass to read.[52] In his micrographic sample readie, Brown promised that 'writing will be readable at the speed of the day – 1929 – not 1450'. Name-checking Gutenberg, Crane, Stein and Joyce,

Brown described future generations of 'eye-writers – – – writing-in-an-endless-line-for-my-reading-machine – – – simple-foolproof-machine-with-printed-tape-like-typewriter-ribbon-running-on-before-readers-eyes'.[53] Although it was larger than his planned medium, Crosby's miniature type showed that micrographic printing was at least plausible. As a text, this 1929 readies prototype provided a ciphered preview of his broader project as well as an advanced-footnote for the 'reading machine' Brown depicted in his 'Self Portrait'. Yet it also signposted Brown's networking tactics. He refused to sell copies of *1450–1950*, and instead sent them to many contacts across the world, fifty-six of whom he listed on its dedication page, including his old friends Stuart Davis, Charles Demuth, Duchamp, Loy, Pound, Man Ray, Carl Sandburg and Williams. Brown also sent the book to numerous editors and publishers, as well as to new contacts such as Stein and Cunard, with whom he became good friends when he arrived in France. Most of these figures responded with rich praise for the book, and his gesture had primed an influential group of specialists to lend support for his readies project, which he continued to flesh out over the summer of 1929.

In his 1 October 1929 letter to Caresse Crosby, Brown mentioned that he had sent a manuscript about his reading machine to *transition*, suggesting that he had fully developed his plans for the readies project by this point.[54] However, he first unveiled them in an interview with the pseudonymous journalist Montparno on 13 January 1930 in *The Paris Tribune*, half a year before *transition* published 'The Readies'. With characteristic ironic hyperbole, Montparno announced that Brown's device would help readers 'Absorb [A] Dozen Gertrude Stein Novels in [An] Afternoon', while Brown focused on practical details. Brown explained that his machine would 'resemble a typewriter in shape', but 'be much smaller'. He planned to print the text on 'a ribbon of tough impressionable material' using 'type so small the human eye cannot read it'. The medium would scroll across a magnification screen with 'the speed and direction controlled by pressing buttons' and stored in a 'pill box'-sized container between uses. As well as delivering a suite of Taylorist efficiencies, Brown promised that his reading revolution would also ensure that 'modernist writers will have some praise in their own day'.[55] Whether or not his wares could actually decode modernist novels for the masses was almost beside the point. Brown had effectively proposed a new relationship between specialist and mass market readerships brokered by a key feature of this new (if at this stage, speculative) technology: mechanically-assisted speed-reading.

As Sue Currell has pointed out, '[b]y the mid-twentieth century, the "mechanization" of reading had evolved into a huge business that focused on training to increase reading pace, often with the aid of machines'.[56] Following Brown's lead, *The Paris Tribune* article ingeniously grafted the production of American modernist literature (notably in the work of Gertrude Stein) onto this mechanised articulation of modernity. Jessica Pressman has noted that the article held out the simple promise that 'the reading machine [would] make difficult modernist works more absorbable by speeding them up'.[57] In the article, Montparno explains how Brown's new medium, aided by his device, would achieve this: 'only major words would assault the mind' and 'all punctuation marks and articles – will be minimized, slaughtered, made entirely useless. And with the public accustomed to such reading, surrealism will be more understandable.'[58] For Brown, it is 'the rapid reading that will count and the corollary that writing will be revolutionized after the surrealist manner'.[59] The promise seems counter-intuitive, but draws on four underlying assumptions: firstly, that applying Taylorist principles of speed and efficiency to new and existing texts could result in a novel, more efficient reading medium (the readies); secondly, that those efficiencies both informed and emerged from a wide range of modernist techniques, ranging from narrative representations of the Jamesian stream of consciousness to Dada-Surrealist visual prosody; thirdly, that these cultural movements were complementary and would result in new forms of reading and writing; and finally, that mechanical and literary systems were complementary.

The Paris Tribune article is fairly typical in its pre-emptive anticipation of the 'black box' phenomenon I discuss in the book's Introduction, where complex technical objects diffuse into the scene of everyday life through habituation. The strategy is frequently associated with the American technological sublime, and, as we will see, Brown draws on these tropes (and their techno-bathetic counterparts) throughout his readies writings to capture readers' attention. However, like Luigi Russolo and the Futurists I discussed in Chapter 1, Brown thought that a central part of the readies project involved augmenting the human sensorium through both technological and pedagogical means, over an extended period of time. By engaging with this media ecology conceptually, via various print forums, Brown hoped to retrain readers to become more receptive to modernist praxes.[60] In this respect, as Robbie Moore astutely argues, Brown's ideal 'machinereader would require careful training of the kind required by expert tickertape readers. Brown talks of the "practiced reading eye" and the "intelligent, experienced eye"', and retraining these readers could help 'collaps[e] the opposition between modernism and mass culture'.[61] However, Brown usually identifies such readers as a vanguard of early adopters, rather than the sole or even the primary market that he targets. Moore rightly argues that Brown's 'vision drags high modernism into a sleepless, accelerated, 24-hour marketplace' in which '[m]odernist culture's resistance to commodification would be broken down simply by routing it through a novel delivery mechanism'.[62] However, that process worked both ways – mass culture's resistance to modernism could also be broken down through these economic and technical exchanges. This transition could not happen overnight, which is why Brown focused on implementing his 'Revolution of the Word' by targeting specialist communities, but also by identifying ways of branching out into mainstream print culture. In this respect, *The Paris Tribune* was the ideal platform, because many Left Bank writers and specialists with whom Brown collaborated on the readies project (including Wambly Bald, Theodore Pratt and Walter Lowenfels) produced journalistic copy for mass markets in America and Europe. However, in his initial specialist works on the readies project, Brown cleanly divided his audiences into two camps: firstly, the avant-garde readership of *1450–1950*, *transition* and *Morada*; and, secondly, his peers in the American publishing trade in *The Publishers' Weekly*.

The Readies Manifestos in *The Publishers' Weekly* and *transition*

Brown published his first full account of the readies project in 'My Reading Machine', an essay printed in *The Publishers' Weekly* in May 1930, a month before it appeared in *transition*. With a substantial and influential readership consisting of thousands of publishers, booksellers, writers and legislators, this article appeared just as activity in the American publishing industry neared its peak, with the annual Publishers' Convention taking place in New York City at the end of May. Its readership dwarfed the avant-garde audience of Brown's modernist publishing contexts, which rarely exceeded a few hundred individuals.[63] Echoing his 'preview' in *The Paris Tribune*, Brown's *Publishers' Weekly* article appeared with the strap line 'Perhaps We are on the Verge of a Machine Which Will Enable Us to Read Hundred Thousand Word Novels in Ten Minutes'.[64] Notably, this strips the readies project of its association with reading modernist *writing*, and focuses instead on modern *reading*. Brown used the article to assert his intellectual property, much as Loy did with her newspaper articles the previous decade, and potentially to attract investors and partners, as well as collaborators for his anthology *RFBBM*. He calibrated his essays for *The Publishers' Weekly* and *transition* to appeal to each respective specialist audience, while subtly encouraging closer collaboration instead of further differentiation between them.

Although his register was typically jocular, the technical detail in Brown's essay for *The Publishers' Weekly* was appropriate to the trade journal's readership. In 'My Reading Machine', Brown described how the 'reading film will unroll beneath a magnifying glass set in a reading slit which will bring the invisible type up to comfortable reading size and the reader will not have to hold a cumbersome book or juggle his eyes back and forth'. Proposing a sort of electro-mechanical proto-intranet (albeit a less sophisticated version than the telegraphic signalling system envisaged by J. R. C. Hunter), he imagined a new publishing ecology evolving around the machine ensemble. His system could make reading 'as simple and automatic as shaving with a Schick razor, [with] refills sent by mail or through pneumatic tubes all over town by enterprising publishers'.[65] Brown balanced the Taylorist rhetoric of efficiency, convenience and elimination of 'waste' by citing related technological achievements such as the 'English August-Hunter Camera Composing Machine', '[e]xperiments with diamond type' and even Fiske's 'hand reading machine'.[66] Only towards the end of the article does he discuss the machine's potential effects on the practice of reading and writing itself. In a marked distinction from the blood and thunder of his modernist manifestos, in 'My Reading Machine' he stages a 'bloodless battle' between 'real words' and 'punctuation marks'. Again, Brown cites a precedent – 'Carl Van Vechten has done away with quotes in the French manner' – but that is the extent of his engagement with modernism.[67] Instead, Brown advocates repackaging 'the classics' as micrographic readies editions, a process that was already well under way in the publishing trade with such popular series as the Modern Library (launched by Boni & Liveright in 1917, run by Brown's associate Bennett Cerf, and later associated with Random House) and J. M. Dent's Everyman's Library, albeit using conventional print.[68]

As the title suggests, Brown's article 'My Reading Machine' provided a succinct description of the technical object, the machine ensemble and the media ecology it might produce, in that order. 'The Readies', published in *transition*, reversed that emphasis, and restored his attention to the task of making modernist writing accessible to a wider readership, just as he had done in Montparno's *Paris Tribune* article – but he also emphasised the readies' possibilities for modernist writing. The article is the most accomplished exposition of his project, which Brown had discussed with Eugene and Maria Jolas since October 1929, when Brown first reached out to *transition* with an early version of his manifesto.[69] By January 1930, Brown had announced his idea for the project that would become the 1931 anthology *Readies For Bob Brown's Machine* to Jolas, and invited a contribution from him.[70] In turn, Jolas actively incorporated Brown's readies project into the lexicon of his 'Revolution of the Word' – literally in one case, where the term 'readies' appeared in '*Transition*'s Revolution of the Word Dictionary'.[71] Brown's advert in the March 1932 issue of *transition* reasserted the readies' avant-garde credentials, claiming 'the book presents a revolutionary step forward in the mechanics of reading and writing'.[72]

Brown remained good friends with Jolas, but although he was in many respects a typical *transition* cosmopolite Brown's technicity and poetics were fundamentally at odds with those of Jolas. *transition*'s 'Revolution of the Word' was an attempt by literary modernists to produce a transnational language of the arts, infused with their Jungian conceptions of a collective unconscious and the aesthetic cosmopolitanism of James Joyce's late 1920s/early 1930s writings that would later be collected in *Finnegan's Wake*. For the *transition* editor, technology and technicity played a largely metaphorical role in this vision of transcendent utopianism, which was steeped in the figurative sleights of hand common in the technological sublime. Jolas wrote that 'Poetry, using the word as mechanics, may, like the film, produce a metaphoric universe which is a sublimation of the physical world.'[73] Brown, however, insisted on a tactile, sensual technicity in which the human body and sensorium was augmented rather than replaced or transcended. In his *transition* essay 'The Readies', his attention to speed and efficiency, though somewhat utopian, remains importantly tethered to 'daily necessity'. Although he sends his texts into the 'ether', his machine ensemble still renders them palpable.[74]

'The Readies' began with a succinct account of the machine and medium, which Brown wove into a freewheeling version of the venerable modernist manifesto. He invited the readers to fix their 'mental eye for a moment on the ever-present future and contemplate a reading machine which will revitalize this interest in the Optical Art of Writing'. Splicing together technological modernity and modernist aesthetics, he continued,

> In our aeroplane age radio is rushing in television, tomorrow it will be a commonplace. All the arts are having their faces lifted, painting (the moderns), sculpture (Brancusi), music (Antheil), architecture (zoning law), drama (Strange Interlude), dancing (just look around you tonight), writing (Joyce, Stein, Cummings, Hemingway, *transition*). Only the reading half of Literature lags behind[.][75]

Here, Brown cajoles *transition*'s contributors and readership into a partnership to modernise reading so that it keeps up with and spawns further modern, modernist and avant-garde cultural production. His punning and word games focus on the bathetic relationship between language and its material form – and between writers and the publishing trade. Brown entreated *transition*'s avant-garde readership to 'look for literary renaissance through the Readie; a modern, moving, word spectacle' so that they might 'be rapidly read and quickly understood by their own generation at least'.[76] Like his interview for *The Paris Tribune*, he also enticed his audience with speculative features of the readies project, while pre-emptively banalising them:

> The Readies are no more unusual than the Talkies, and not a scratch on television. As soon as the reading machine becomes a daily necessity certainly it will be out of date. Pocket reading machines will be the vogue then; reading matter probably will be radioed and words recorded directly on the palpitating ether.[77]

In fact, these interface and connectivity features were not especially speculative because they were grounded in existing wireless and telecommunications technology, including the RCA Thereminovox, the wireless, television and the August-Hunter Photo-Composing Machine, all of which were mentioned in his readies writing.[78] Such inventions were part of a burgeoning and globally-connected electronic communications ensemble, which later developed into the infrastructures of the Information Age. However, in Brown's own Machine Age, these trajectories were well underway. 'The Readies' distilled Brown's research, readie-writing and proselytising into a manifesto that deployed humour, pastiche and polemics against practical observation and contextualisation, piquing his readership's interests with his multiple frames of reference, while challenging their presumptions. His strategies subtly built readers' trust, but also fuelled their suspicions. Readers and critics, then and now, are not predisposed to believe Brown's claims, because the very qualities that align his readies writing with the utopian/dystopian dialectics of late modernism also discourage audiences from associating the project with the real business of technological prototyping. However, new archival evidence helps us distinguish between the accomplished and speculative features of the reading machine. While Brown was busy gathering contributors for *RFBBM* from October 1929 to the autumn of 1931 (all the while writing and publishing furiously), his collaborators – the artist-engineer Ross Saunders and the artist and industrial designer Hilaire Hiler – were busy blueprinting and building prototype reading machines.

'Ready Now': Ross Saunders's Working Prototype Reading Machine

When Brown finally published pictures of the prototype reading machine and the commercial design he proposed for it, the blurry, spectral images on the flyleaf of *RFBBM* did not seem entirely real (Fig. 3.1), even to Brown's friends. For example, the journalist Frank Scully, who later

Excavating the 'Readies' 139

reported on the machine in *Variety*, thought that they might have been 'phony'.[79] Scully's suspicions anticipate the contemporary critical consensus, which maintains that 'the Readies remained a conceptual rather than an actual machine',[80] and equates that status, ultimately, with Brown's and the project's 'failure'.[81] In some ways, this is a more convenient narrative – one in which the messy intersections of avant-garde and technological experimentation remain cleanly divided. It just does not happen to tell the full story. This section seeks to correct prevailing scepticism about the reading machine's functionality by exploring the Saunders Prototype as a technical object using newly available evidence. Brown insisted in the *RFBBM* 'Appendix' that the machine is 'ready now [. . .] and you can come to Cagnes-sur-Mer any day and see it in the flesh. It doesn't stand still any more than life does.'[82] Archival evidence strongly suggests that he was telling the truth, on both counts. The uncatalogued and never-before-published photo of the Saunders Prototype reading machine pictured in Figure 3.5 and on the cover of this book is from the Philip Kaplan and Bob Brown papers at the Special Collections Research Center of Southern Illinois University Carbondale, which has received little attention in modernist studies, as most scholars use Brown's archives at UCLA.[83] Although similar to the version published on the *RFBBM* flyleaf, and shot from a similar vantage, the lid of the Saunders Prototype

Figure 3.5 Unknown photographer [Bob or Rose Brown], Untitled [Photograph of Ross Saunders's Prototype Reading Machine], B5, F12, SIU Kaplan-Brown.

opens at a larger angle in the SIU photograph, exposing more of the mechanism, and with far greater clarity. In addition, the SIU collection contains a wealth of manuscripts and correspondence by Brown, his son Robert Carlton ('Carlton') Brown III, and their collaborators, plus contextual evidence from newspapers and other periodicals. These materials and evidence from other archives help clarify the prototyping protocols and timeline for the reading machine ensemble.

Wambly Bald, a Left Bank writer, journalist and *RFBBM* contributor, reported that the Saunders Prototype reading machine was 'in the process of construction' in May 1931.[84] The machine is very probably the 'picture of the readie machine' to which Kay Boyle refers in her 18 July 1931 letter to Brown.[85] This strongly suggests that the Saunders Prototype was built in the spring and finished by the early summer of 1931 (by July at the latest). Theodore Pratt, a prolific writer, correspondent for *The New York Sun* and *RFBBM* contributor who lived mainly in Paris from 1929–31, also recalled in his correspondence with Brown's friend and collaborator Philip Kaplan that he 'knew Bob in Cagnes, France, and saw the first model of the machine built there'.[86] According to other archival evidence, Saunders apparently kept this model in Cagnes until at least 1940, after which it – and he – appear to have been lost to history.[87] Nevertheless, the existence of the Saunders Prototype, and the time it was created, is fairly certain. But apart from the collaborators' and Pratt's testimony, how can we know whether it worked or not? Two unpublished accounts of the readies project provide a guideline for describing Saunders's prototype as a technical object, and using the picture in Figure 3.5 as a reference it is possible to make a reasonable evaluation. The first document is a draft typescript by Bob entitled 'Reading Machines', which he wrote in the summer of 1937 in response to an article by Ezra Pound.[88] I discuss the rich and complex context of this essay's creation in the next chapter, but here I focus on the insights those drafts provide into Saunders's prototype. The second document is an unpublished article about the readies project by Carlton intended for the British market entitled 'Reading By Machine', which he wrote in the winter of 1931–2 to promote the recently published *RFBBM* anthology.[89] Starting with the enclosure and working through the internal components and their functions, this new evidence not only helps assess the Saunders Prototype's functionality, but also re-situates the socio-technics of the readies project within a culture of technological, as well as literary, experimentation.

In 'Reading Machines', Bob noted that he and his collaborators made 'the first model of a reading machine out of a cracker box' – and, indeed, the Saunders Prototype chassis closely resembles the hinged wooden boxes used by companies such as Kraft to store and ship crackers and biscuits.[90] The wooden enclosure has an angled top, like a drafting desk, and in both photos it is propped up with a screwdriver. In 'Reading by Machine', Carlton explains how the prototype was assembled from other scavenged components. He wrote that Saunders's 'little working model of the machine [. . .] runs by gramophone motor, and is most ingeniously constructed'. He cautions that the device 'is merely for demonstration purposes, and it serves its purpose very well. The text of a story by Bob Brown has been typed on a roll of serpentine, such as is used at carnivals, and it unrolls by motor before your eyes.'[91] The metal rectangular enclosure mounted on the top of the box resembles a wide range of electric and clockwork gramophone motors, as well as other similarly-sized units used in other devices, available ca. 1915–30, which would have been readily accessible.[92] The transmission system in the Saunders Prototype is robust enough to change directions, however, which suggests that it was designed to work with a reversible electric motor.

The underside of the Saunders Prototype's box lid contains two spools, each attached to a small cog by an axle. In the second version of 'Reading Machines', Bob disclosed that the model used two 'typewriter [ribbon] spools', possibly from a Woodstock Model 5 or similar mass-market unit. In both photographs of the Saunders Prototype, these spools are the most prominent feature of the reading machine. The framing of the exposed mechanism invites comparisons to typewriter adverts from the same period.[93] The emerging field of consumer information technology also tapped into the 'gear and girder' aesthetics of the American Machine Age, in which exposed gears articulated the object's power and efficiency and correlated mechanical efficiency with aesthetic harmony. On the reading machine, the metal support straps, pulleys, bevelled gears and pinions are from either Gilbert or Meccano sets, which were widely available toy systems marketed to aspiring (and almost exclusively male) engineers, and manufactured in England and France since the early twentieth century.[94] By 1919, Meccano had provided instructions for complex electric and clockwork motorised models of working looms, derricks, printing machines and other industrial equipment using its intricate gear and pulley systems.[95] These parts could also be used to build far more sophisticated devices. For example, in 1934, two theoretical physicists at the University of Manchester, Professor Douglas Hartree and his doctoral student Arthur Porter, created a working differential analyser from standard Meccano parts and other materials. The device was an 'early analogue computer designed to solve equations using a wheel and disk mechanism', and could solve complex differential equations.[96] The basic mechanics of Brown's reading machine were nowhere near as sophisticated as this difference engine (or, indeed, many of Meccano's own designs), but Saunders, like many professional engineers, clearly understood the practical value of using Meccano components for rapid prototyping projects and proof-of-concept models.

The operation of Saunders's system is comparatively simple, but it is robust enough to perform several functions.[97] Metal Meccano perforated strips affix each of the reading machine's assemblies to the lid, and those holes would both support the rods connecting the take-up and supply reel assemblies, allowing them to spin freely. On the left-hand side, two of these straps protect the belt drive, which extends through an opening in the lid to the motor, and drive the left take-up reel. The take-up reel assembly on the left side of the box consists of a spool, transmission rod and contrate gear (a gear with angled teeth generally used to connect with other gears at 90-degree angles). This drives the supply reel mechanism on the right side via a horizontal transmission rod. The metal rod is stabilised by a free-spinning metal pulley, which is in turn supported by further rigging made of bent Meccano straps, and possibly leather or some other flexible materials. This drives the supply reel via a pinion (a smaller metal gear) on the rear of the right side of the box, which then connects to the bush wheel, possibly via another pinion (this connection is obscured, but it would have been a fairly straightforward transmission point). Together, the mechanism would have created a stable, even motion for unwinding the supply reel into the take-up reel. Although it would be perfectly suitable for demonstration purposes, however, it would not have travelled well even over short distances and would have needed constant fine-tuning.

The reading apparatus on the upper side of the prototype's lid – what we would now call the user interface – is obscured and was probably not photographed because it was either unfinished or not as impressive as the reel assemblies. Nevertheless, the richer details in the SIU photo now reveal how the 'readie' viewer might have functioned. Two roughly chiselled apertures in the wood allow the 'serpentine' medium Carlton described in his essay (which appears to be standard half-inch paper tape wound around the spools, half the size of standard stock market ticker tape) to scroll through. A bolt and washer near the right-hand supply reel aperture suggests that Saunders fashioned and affixed some kind of viewing apparatus to the top of the lid. The photograph reveals only a short protrusion in the reading area, however, so if the machine did include lenses then they would have been minimal, and either fixed or capable of only minor adjustments, since anything more elaborate would have been taller and therefore visible in the photograph. The viewer was probably only a cover with a central slit for viewing the text and guides to keep the medium level and correctly aligned. However, the content of the prototype readies themselves, like the medium used in their production, involves less speculation.

Based on Carlton's description, the Saunders Prototype was probably loaded with either Bob's 'Story to be Read on the Reading Machine', which appeared in both *The Readies* and his 'Appendix' to *RFBBM*, or the 'sample readie' from *1450–1950* (micrographic) and *transition* essay (full size).[98] Although a micrographic sample 'readie' would technically have been possible, the version produced for the Saunders Prototype was probably standard-sized type, as it appeared in *transition*, which would have been more easily produced. A non-micrographic reading machine prototype might seem like a damp squib in terms of Brown's proof-of-concept, but he included several miniature examples in other readies project texts: his *1450–1950* 'sample readie' and his micrographically-printed poems in *Words*, which he and Nancy Cunard produced using a rough but ingenious copper-relief intaglio printing method. In *RFBBM* he included ten of those micro-poems from *Words*, which formed a textual border for the illustrations of the reading machines on the anthology's flyleaf. These micro-texts not only provide a proof-of-concept for the readies medium, but also gloss the possible futures for their media ecology, which in 'New York 1930' Brown imagines joining the mechanised transportation and communications infrastructure of the Big Apple.[99]

In combination, Brown had assembled a nearly-complete package of technical proofs-of-concept for the readies project: the Saunders Prototype; micrographic sample readies printed in *1450–1950*, *RFBBM* and *Words*; the technical descriptions supplied in Hiler's detailed 'Preface'; and the extraordinary endorsements collected in Brown's *RFBBM* 'Appendix'.[100] Mechanically, the device almost certainly functioned exactly as the Browns and Hiler described. Whether or not the scrolling text 'worked' in the way Brown said it should (that is, as an efficient means of mechanically-assisted speed-reading) is another matter, and without formal testing this remains rather subjective, and speculative. Brown's cousin, Clare Brackett, would suggest a more practical, articulated version of the continual text stream in 1932, but regardless, for specialised readers (such as stock market analysts) at least, Brown's technical concepts, elements and ensembles were robust and largely proven.[101] As Carlton Brown claimed, Saunders's 'model' made it 'very easy to see what a boon the reading machine will be when perfected', because its basic mechanics are sound.[102] However, there remained only one stumbling block: a translucent medium suitably flexible and robust with which to convey his micrographic texts through the compact, high-specification machine that Brown and his collaborators were developing with Brackett's National Machine Products Company in Detroit. He was not able to locate one, and most critics agree that this problem eventually sunk the readies project; as I argue in the next chapter, however, Rose Brown and Hugo Knudsen eventually did find a solution. Nevertheless, a poignant personal connection might have made that process more efficient, had it not been missed.

In his January 1932 letter to Fiske, Brown asked the Admiral if he had tried reproducing 'microscopic type' by 'printing on cellophane'. This was a material Brown was considering for the readies medium at the time. As I discussed in Chapter 2, in the late 1920s Brown's friend Mina Loy had worked extensively with cellulose acetate, the biopolymer used in the commercial product cellophane, and other thermoplastics such as Rhodoid and Loy's own material, 'verrovoile'. Loy may have found a suitable solution using cellulose acetate where Brackett could not, or she may have advised against further research. Though they retained their affection for each other, Loy and the Browns do not seem to have had much contact in Paris.[103] However, Brown and his collaborators were right to show interest in cellulose acetate: as I discuss in the next chapter, that material eventually replaced nitrate-based film in commercially produced microfilm by the end of the 1930s. Far from being technical naïfs, in this respect, Brown and his collaborators were actually ahead of industry competitors in identifying the future of micrographic reading technology.

In some ways, Brown's missed connection with Loy illustrates how his considerable economic resources paled in comparison to the human resources he had accumulated in expatriate Paris. For example, Hiler was an industrial designer as well as a modernist artist, nightclub owner and musician. He had a detailed interest in the applied science behind painting, and (as I discuss in the next chapter) he opened a radical art school, Atelier Hiler, in 1931. Kay Boyle had studied architecture at the Ohio Mechanics Institute in Cincinnati and had a BA in Sociology and Economics from Barnard College and a BE from Teacher's College. Like Rose Brown, she had amassed considerable professional skills in art, photography and interior design in the 1920s, and could also contribute to discussions of design and fabrication. Nevertheless, these contacts also came with complications. Boyle's husband (and fellow *RFBBM* contributor) Lawrence Vail had been married to and later acrimoniously divorced from his wife Peggy Vail Guggenheim, who was Mina Loy's well-intentioned but interfering and exasperating patron. Eventually, Bob fell out with Vail after he and Rose left Paris, which strained the close friendship between the families. And Hiler's crucial involvement with the readies project was curtailed when he was arrested for accidentally killing a cyclist on 6 December 1930. He was jailed several times during the trials and worked with Brown only sporadically before the case was eventually dropped in January 1932, around the time that *RFBBM* finally appeared.[104] Unlike Saunders, who seems to have lost all contact with the Browns when they left France, Hiler would resume contact with the Browns in New York – and, as we shall see in the next chapter, in 1937 he sketched the 'Readio', possibly based on the prototype built by Rose.

Reflecting on the Saunders Prototype in his 1937 'Reading Machines' essay, Brown complained that the invention 'doesn't repose in the Louvre alongside Marcel Duchamp's and Man Ray's machine for producing an endless spiral, but is kicking around in the cellar of Saunders' shack with a lot of other arty junk and Venus de Milo manikins with their arms off. Such is fame!'[105] Coupling the Duchamp-Ray collaboration *Anémic Cinéma* with his own experiments, Brown (only partially ironically) lamented that his more famous artist friends were able to surmount the apparent incongruities between literary and technological experimentation by confining their work to the art world. Tacitly, however, he implied that his own efforts might be more impressive, because they were not only avant-garde productions but functional proofs-of-concept. Although he cultivated the impression that his invention might have been a 'performance-art stunt',[106] the Saunders Prototype also slots neatly into the venerable field of patent models.[107] Inventors, including Admiral Fiske, often included photographs and sketches of such models with patent applications, and Brown's flyleaf for *RFBBM* closely matches such formats (Fig. 3.1). As Hiler explained, Saunders's model did not address the full range of features Brown described, but simply it 'satisfied the mechanical requirements' of the project, which allowed the artists to experiment with its potential for speed-reading.[108]

Hiler also explained how the machine related to the anthology's contents, and especially its visual pyrotechnics. He noted that '[t]he use of hyphens, arrows, other connectives and punctuation is solely to suggest that the reading matter is to pass in a pleasant reading size at a pleasing speed before the reader's eye on a tape unrolled by a motor' and 'visualize the experiments in optical reading in spite of the fact that they are not in motion'.[109] He also noted that the omission of small connective words and other elements of language was a Taylorist efficiency. However, these instrumental features were by no means the extent of the readies' visual prosody, as Hiler well knew, and the contributions themselves frequently undercut his descriptions, despite his assurances. In fact, the *RFBBM* contributors undertook a pitched battle over competing technicities and their vexed identitarian contexts, which were being negotiated by avant-garde and mainstream writers alike in the modernist transatlantic.

Intersections and Collisions: The Readies in *Morada*

The Taylorist efficiencies that Brown correlated with 'reading machine-wise' have led critics to identify *RFBBM* as a cautionary tale about the oppressive uses to which Machine Age aesthetics could be applied.[110] As Saper notes, the readies project encouraged contributors to give free reign to impulses normally considered taboo, as if 'baiting a fantasized censor with sexually explicit and racist language'.[111] In some cases, Brown was all too keen to play up these features as a promotional tool, because the censorship and anti-sedition persecution he experienced prior to his departure from the United States, and the ongoing contexts of mail censorship and Prohibition, made standing up for freedom of expression a political imperative. Reaching back into the radical traditions of American print culture, Brown's primitivist trope of racial essentialism simultaneously claimed and rejected racial and ethnic difference as the basis of a 'liberated' American identity:

> Stephen-Crane's-Black-riders-----Crash-by-hell-bent-for-leather-uppercase-LOWERCASE-[. . .]Print-in-action-at-longlast - - - - - - moveable-type-at-break-neck-gallop-Cummings----Cossacks-astride-mustang-bronco-vocabularies----leaning-farout-into-inky-night-picking-up-carefully---placed-phrases-with-flashing-Afric-teeth.[112]

In this string of metaphors, Brown alludes to Stephen Crane's Black Riders – printed type on the page – and transfigures them into a racial analogue, an irrepressible impulse that surfaces alongside his American revolutionaries with alarming frequency and worrying intensity throughout the readies. This impulse folds into a broader, universalist project in Eugene Jolas's and *transition* magazine's 'Revolution of the Word'. As Michael North points out, Brown's attempts to represent '[t]he drive toward a purified, universal language', both in *RFBBM* and in his violently racist colophon of *1450–1950*, could not make 'specificities such as race disappear into the abstraction of a universal sign system'.[113] Rather, the opposite was true: 'the persistence of race as a subject in the readies [. . .] demonstrates how difficult it is to transmute the actual and incidental into pure form. Race, in this sense, is the subject that refuses to be formalized.'[114] The same pattern repeated in other modernist articulations of identity in the 'Revolution of the Word', including sex, gender, sexuality and ethnicity. Machine Age technology codified social normativities, but also broke them down, and transatlantic institutions such as *transition, Morada* and *RFBBM* showcased emergent late modernist anxieties about these indeterminacies. In the readies, the bigotry, normativities and essentialist fantasies on display are as clear as the contibutors' explosive visual wit. While some of Brown's expatriate avant-garde reinforced these prejudices, however, others responded to and pushed back against them.

A matrix of increasingly politicised and progressive avant-garde writers who published in *Morada* and *transition* complicate long-standing critical traditions that frame the readies project, and, more broadly, transatlantic avant-gardes, as either 'political' or 'aesthetic' experimentalists. As well as the reactionary high modernism sometimes associated with the 'Revolution of the Word', contributors from *transition* and Norman Macleod's Southwestern little magazine *Morada* helped showcase a late modernist counter-narrative that sprung up among the dominant modernist formations – one embedded in the emergent left-wing politics of the new localism and American superrealism. Combining the formal experimentation of *transition* with the vernacular aesthetics of *Contact* and *The Little Review*, these complementary expressions of late modernism had begun to *détourne* high modernist anxieties about Machine Age socio-technics. In doing so, these writers created bathetic snapshots of the hierarchies of urban life, which articulated a latent localist Americanism and, in some cases, a politically progressive emphasis that critiqued the high modernist strategies and sublime technicities of some contributors.

Between the publication of Brown's *Publishers' Weekly* and *transition* essays in the spring of 1930 and the final production of the *RFBBM* anthology in November–December 1931, Brown had assembled an impressive collection of readies, stimulated in part by the promotional copies of *1450–1950* he sent to his writing and publishing contacts. He published a sample of the first tranche of these writings in the fifth and final issue of *Morada* in December 1930, based on a lukewarm recommendation by William Carlos Williams.[115] Operating from Albuquerque from an office in the University of New Mexico, *Morada* was Macleod's second journal. He had previously edited *Palo Verde* (originally *Jackass*), and after *Morada* folded would go on to edit *Front* (1930–1), which combined left-wing politics and modernist experimentation. What began as a Southwest localist and regionalist modernist journal quickly evolved into a multilingual 'attempt to tie Southwestern writing to international modernism and labour issues'.[116] By its final issue, it provided an outlet for an important group of American experimentalists who operated mainly on the periphery of the *transition* network. These localist modernists and American superrealists also published in the close-knit but geographically dispersed journals

Blues (published in Mississippi by Charles Henri Ford) and *Pagany* (based in Boston and New York and edited by Richard Johns), as well as in the Parisian journal *Tambour* and Samuel Putnam's Italy-based periodical *The New Review*.

In this respect, *Morada* was the perfect home for the multiple formations Brown attempted to correlate in the readies project. Many *Morada* subscribers also received *transition*, and would have already seen 'The Readies', so Brown provided only a brief reminder of the readies project's core concepts in his introduction 'Writing Readies'. Instead, he focused on how the project had developed since the summer, particularly as he could showcase the extraordinary range of modernist talent involved in co-creating this new literary genre. Like the advertisement for the first issue of *Pagany*, which appeared in the same issue of *Morada* and featured a similarly diverse collection of American and European modernist and (super-) realist writers, Brown put his roster of contributors centre stage. 'Writing Readies' featured a selection of the anthology's modernist writers, including Boyle, Putnam, *Morada* co-editor Donal Mackenzie, librarian and experimental writer J. Jones, F. T. Marinetti, avant-garde writer Abraham Lincoln Gillespie, Jr, Rose Brown, (*Pagany* editor) Johns, Walter Lowenfels, Hiler, Cunard and George Kent, an occasional contributor to modernist expatriate journals who helped run Brown's magazine *The Brazilian American*.

Brown boasted that his 'anthology of readie scripts, specially written to be read on the reading machine', consisted of 'thirty modern minded writers' (by 1931 the total had increased to forty-three) who created 'snappy evidences of speeding-up for the new medium'.[117] The majority of the texts used dashes, equals signs, capitalisation and unique spacing strategies to simulate the readie effects, but Walter Lowenfels arranged his contribution in vertical lines because he felt this 'gives the effect of tape better than horizontal' ones.[118] Marinetti's text 'Olfactory Poetry' was similarly eye-catching, not only because of its erratic spacing but because of the 'big name' it attached to the readies. Putnam arranged for this contribution, and though it was extracted from another work he declared that Marinetti's submission was 'actually made for the readies',[119] since the readies project had clearly drawn on Futurist experiments with language, form and sensory augmentation technicities. But, unwittingly, Putnam also invited connections with Marinetti's far-right politics. Even though Putnam's own extract in 'Writing Readies' was from a longer work intended to expose rather than endorse reactionary politics and prejudices, the n-word in its racist title, and the indeterminate context generated by the compressed readies format, puts his intentions in doubt. The fact that Putnam also endorsed Marinetti's fascist politics in an editorial row with

The New Review scarcely helped this perception (but it is worth remembering that Putnam recanted this position in the 1930s, when he shifted his affiliations to communism).[120] 'Writing Readies' in *Morada* anticipates these reductive effects, versions of which would play out across the entire *RFBBM* anthology.

North rightly characterises Putnam's piece as 'a quasi-photographic glimpse into the mind of a bigot'.[121] However, as North also points out, and Saper elaborates on, Putnam's contribution is one example where the readies format exposes and satirises rather than simply facilitates the bigotry of its subject (such as in the case of Laurence Vail).[122] The brutal misogyny and homophobia that frequently surfaces in *RFBBM* also forms indelible subjects, but in some cases (though certainly not all) they can be framed in the same way. In this respect, North is certainly correct when he argues that 'the stripped-down telegraphic form of the readies' make it 'very difficult to distinguish authorial comment from first-person narration'.[123] The incomplete and reformatted extracts in *Morada* compound this issue and exaggerate the readies' already-diminished contextual frames. In their desire to shock audiences with their controversial language and aggressively modernist techniques, they risked endorsing the bigoted viewpoints that they processed with their speculative reading machine medium. This is especially true of the expatriate writers, and most notably Putnam, Boyle, Cunard and Brown himself. As we have seen, Brown prominently used racialist, sexist and phallocentric language to explicate his readies project in *transition*. Brown's selections in *Morada*, rather than his writing, articulate these controversial tactics.

For example, Brown included an extract from 'Nancy Cunard's poem-length racial slur "Dlink"'.[124] Cunard's racialist and racist caricature of a first generation working-class Chinese American reduces the subject purely to an economic unit of production (and implies that the speaker would be right to take offence when the subject does the same thing in reverse).[125] However, Brown's *Morada* edit omits the phrase that gives the poem its meaning, 'No ticky no lan'dy', a fact that upset Cunard. In a disappointing irony for someone working to oppose racial bigotry against black people, she was more concerned about her work's form than about insulting other marginalised groups.[126] Yet Cunard's stance was a common theme that emerged in the readies' bathetic turn: a descent into the everyday guarantees neither authenticity nor a levelling of hierarchies. In fact, such manoeuvres can simply reinstate asymmetrical power structures in different ways. Brown's editing mitigates these effects in the case of Cunard's readie, but it unfairly amplifies them in Boyle's. In its full form, Boyle's readie 'Change of Life' celebrates an indomitable working-class mother, whose *joie de vivre* helps her face the hardships of life in rural France. However, the extract in 'Writing Readies' focuses attention on the story's single use of the n-word.[127] Here, we encounter a more severe version of the problem faced by Cunard. Brown presumably selected this line to complement Putnam's piece, which featured the racist, censor-baiting racial epithet in its title. However, it is impossible from the context to determine Boyle's main intention – however flawed to contemporary eyes – of representing working-class speech accurately, energetically and in sympathy with (rather than opposition to) experimental formal strategies. Like many burgeoning American superrealists, Boyle had begun exploring how people living near the bottom of social hierarchies treated those further below them.

First identified by Nathaneal West and later theorised by Jonathan Veitch, the 'American Super-realist' mode formed part of an interwar late modernist project. Although it did not constitute a distinctive late modernist formation per se, American superrealism articulated a more earnest and politicised strain of these practices. It emerged in the United States and various expatriate outposts in the late 1920s and early 1930s, and included writers as diverse as Erskine Caldwell, Robert Coates and John Dos Passos, as well as *RFBBM* contributors James T. Farrell, Charles Henri Ford, Peter Neagoe and William Carlos Williams; in fact, the term could be applied convincingly to many of the anthology's other contributors, especially Boyle, B. C. Hagglund, Herman Spector, Robert McAlmon, Macleod and Kathleen Tankersley Young.[128] Although Veitch cautions that it 'never constituted a separate movement', nor a distinct modernist formation, he uses this specific 'translation' of *'surrealisme'* 'in order to distinguish it from the depoliticized phenomenon that surrealism eventually became in America'.[129] 'In addition', he continues, the term 'caricatures-burlesques-deconstructs the mimetic codes and conventions upon which more traditional forms of realism rely. It is, as its name implies, an "excessive realism" that aspires to turn its particular kind of joking into a distinct mode of social criticism.'[130] These practices also dovetail with what I have termed the new localism, a late modernist formation in America that combined post-Imagist aestheticism, regionally-specific idioms and partisan social realism with an experimentalist and satirical Dada flair.[131] Although rarely acknowledged as such, *RFBBM*, like *Morada*, was a pivotal forum in which writers experimented with late modernist practices. The readies project was especially valuable for exploring the relationship between the ways in which technicity reinforced, and potentially subverted, prevailing cultural hierarchies.

Negotiating precisely this matrix of concerns, Boyle's readie addressed how technology and technicities expressed the dominant hegemonies of the Machine Age. Like other readies contributors, in this piece she accepted uncritically the essentialist prejudices of her day, which conditioned such responses as she explores in it (and like many of those writers Brown included, she later rejected them as she engaged more urgently in political activism). Nevertheless, many contributors, including Boyle, clearly understood and challenged such Machine Age hegemonies, though it was not always clear from the context that they were doing so. In the *Morada* readies, Macleod's 'Ready: Revelation' is the best example of this conundrum. Brown's edited version focuses on a single, brutal depiction of the ritual abuse of Native American women by Catholic priests. The extract describes 'Red orgiastical-with padres-calling - one girl-to-another-in-midnight-confessional', and concludes with the dominant 'phallus-of-mind' conspiring to 'shut-this-woman-slut'.[132] By foregrounding only the sexual brutality of the piece, Brown largely strips Macleod's readie of the subtle social critiques in the full version. In its complete form, 'Ready: Revelation' confronts the cultural fall-out produced by successive colonisations of this land, where the new mythologies of industrialisation do not *supplant* those of previously dominant nations, but, rather, re-process them for their own ends.

Macleod's reference to 'navajos-stolen-blanket-of-sky' evokes both an original creation myth and its appropriation by the Southwestern tourist economy, which traded in actual and reproduction Native American artefacts.[133] The readies format reinforces this process of myth making. Macleod uses the new, highly visual machine language to rewrite the Southwest 'with-kodaks', producing a narrative that pits an imperialist lust for exploitation against the regenerative sexuality of the landscape and its inhabitants, past and present. The readie culminates in an awkward effusion of northern lights, 'aurora-borealis-in-stark-mythos', and southern fecundity, 'a-globe-of-tre-terrestial-cactusbloom', before abandoning the narrative with a series of ticking dashes.[134] In doing so, 'Ready: Revelation' both reinstates and critiques the American technological sublime. For Macleod, the reading machine and the readies present a means of reconceptualising disparate regions and cultures in the United States, in which the human body is neither transcended nor necessarily diminished, but, like the human imagination, remodelled with machines. The cultural fall-out of this spectacular encounter, though unresolved, was ultimately bathetic, because it presented a state of persistent ambivalence that inherently critiqued Machine Age technicities, and the systematic injustices they facilitated, which keep ticking way as background noise. This failure is the essence of Macleod's 'Ready: Revelation', which the 'Writing Readies' version could only hint at.

It would be wrong to suggest that misogyny in various readies – whether overt and violent examples by Vail, casual articulations of sexism in contributions by Johns and Marinetti, or critiques of these attitudes in Macleod's extract – went unanswered, even in the *Morada* readies. While Boyle's extract in 'Writing Readies' only hints at her major ambitions in this direction, however, Rose Brown's readie 'Dis' was a pithy synopsis of it. 'Dis' suggests both the negative/privative prefix and a city containing the lower circles of hell in Dante's *Divine Comedy*, which she evokes by setting the story in New York's Hell's Kitchen. Like Boyle's readie, Rose's concerns working-class women's struggle to survive the daily grind in the neighbourhood. Despite remaining politically, economically and corporeally oppressed by the relentless demands of the mechanised city, Elaine, the protagonist, finds the moral courage to persevere and care for her family. Even in the truncated *Morada* version, the social critique of 'Dis' is difficult to miss because, although violent, the conflicts it depicts are not sensationalised by sexually or racially explicit language. Rose tallies up and commodifies every aspect of the women's day in the story, which she indicates with the persistent use of equals signs: '= Paul-didnt-mind-his-mark-upon-her-youcansee-shes-minenow-putting-his-dis-upon-her-disillusioned-discouraged-dissemblingdiafigured-disabled-living-womans-life-by-mans= maxims='.[135] Playful and formally experimental, 'Dis' performs the excoriating social critique that Veitch associates with American superrealism, while at the same time developing the techno-bathetic feminist satire pioneered by Loy and the Baroness. In the full *RFBBM* version, Rose's readie charts the constant oppressive rhythm of minor cash transactions that delimit the lives of its working-class subjects. This creates a restless purgatory of 'WAITING- - -' punctuated by constant failure, be it in the Catholic education system, on the delimited job market, or in marriage.[136] Like Gertrude Stein's contribution to *RFBBM*, Rose deploys mathematical symbols to deconstruct the economic and social assemblages of American culture, using the accreted syntactic and symbolic capital to bolster and explicate her subjects, as well as sympathetically render the conditions of their everyday life.

In *RFBBM*, American superrealist writers such as James T. Farrell and B. C. Hagglund used similar tactics to Rose Brown when exploring the contours of American working-class life, and, in particular, its sexual, gender, ethnic and racial hierarchies (which I discuss further in the next chapter). However, Macleod's and Rose Brown's texts were the first detailed examination of these hierarchies to appear in print. At this stage in the 'Revolution of the Word', the techno-bathetic and technological sublime, like the professional and avant-garde spheres, could brought into ever-closer relation in the process of 'modernizing reading and writing'.[137] In this emerging media ecology, writers of the modernist transatlantic could articulate their differences from other specialist and mass cultural formations while reinforcing their mutual dependence and shared frames of reference. The readies. extracts in *Morada* hint at the unintended fall-out of such exchanges, but, also, the ingenious responses that the readies form could stimulate from modernist writers, and modern readers, alike.

Conclusion: Modernist Avant-Gardes in Transition

In the end, it was *transition* and its 'Revolution of the Word', and not *Morada, The Publishers' Weekly* or the American expatriate newspapers of Paris that became most associated with the readies. In many ways the association with *transition* is most appropriate, even if the other publications generated a wider and more variegated audience for Bob Brown. Jolas's editorial strategies provided a powerful example to Brown, which he extended to multiple formations within and beyond the arts. In some respects, Brown's readies ensemble exacerbated the journal's paradoxical, 'almost schizophrenic discourse', which, as Céline Mansanti argues, relied on 'avant-garde forms' but rejected any corresponding 'break with the past'.[138] Yet as Catherine Setz rightly argues, Jolas harnessed that contradiction, rather than attempting to suppress it. Jolas proposed 'a critical framework that starts with the very qualities for which it has traditionally been mocked' – an 'anachronistic zeitgeist' that articulated a 'European-American, "inter-racial synthesis" of language', which 'was activated through a series of untimely and clashing techniques'. These strategies sustained the journal 'as an active agent in transatlantic cultural formations right up to its final dissolution in 1938'.[139] One of those formations – or rather, as I argue in the next chapter, *meta*-formations – was Brown's readies project. Since the 1910s, Brown identified modernist avant-gardes as being merely one strand of a wide-ranging culture of Machine Age experimentation. He routinely exploited the humour and disruptive potential of juxtaposing proto-Dadaism, socialism and high finance, and the power of technics to mediate these specialist spheres. In *transition*, however, Brown identified a deliberately cross-formational strategy that made polyphony and divergent aims a strength, and which similarly identified technology and technicity as potential points of convergence between these groups. Yet he also identified grounds for dissent: Brown's bathetic technicities brought the 'Revolution of the Word' back down to earth, and to the mundane business of negotiating practical, disruptive change in socio-technical ensembles.

For Brown, as for Certeau, the emancipatory act of reading places 'autonomy in relation to the determinations of the text and a multiplication of spaces covered'.[140] The act of prototyping a working machine kept the practice of reading tethered to a stubbornly embodied experience, transformed but not supplanted by socio-technical augmentations. As I argue in the next chapter, the modernist archive and public record puncture the prevailing narrative that the Browns and their collaborators were dilettantes in both the avant-garde and in business. In fact, they were extraordinary strategists who envisaged a variegated media ecology in which multiple spheres and formations complemented each other's specialist strengths. Brown reached thousands and even millions of readers with his interventions in specialist and generalist periodicals, and he used his avant-garde credentials much as Loy did with her fashion designs: as a means of marketing innovation by folding it into the discourses of the everyday. The full account of the readies project, like the machine ensemble depicted in the blurry illustrations of his reading machine prototypes, has been hiding in plain sight for decades. Accordingly, the next chapter begins at the point at which the readies project supposedly failed: following the publication of *RFBBM* on 31 December 1931, and amid a string of technical, personal and financial failures unfolding against the backdrop of a resurgent left-wing political radicalism in the modernist transatlantic.

Notes

1. Bob Brown, *6BBB*.
2. Bob Brown, 'The Readies', *transition* 19–20 (June 1930): 167–73.
3. Ibid. p. 167.
4. Bob Brown, *Readies for Bob Brown's Machine*, ed. Bob Brown (Cagnes-sur-Mer: Roving Eye Press, 1931). Craig Saper's and my new critical facsimile edition of this text, *RFBBM*, preserves the original anthology's appearance and pagination.
5. See Jerome Rothenberg, *The Revolution of the Word: A New Gathering of American Avant-Garde Poetry, 1914–1945* (New York: Seabury Press, 1974); Hugh Ford, *Published in Paris: American and British Writers, Printers, and Publishers in Paris, 1920–39* (London: The Garnstone Press Limited, 1975); Cary Nelson, *Repression and Recovery: Modern American Poetry and the Politics of Cultural Memory, 1910–45, New Edition* (Madison: The University of Wisconsin Press, 1992 [1989]); Jerome McGann, *Black Riders: The Visible Language of Modernism* (Princeton: Princeton University Press, 1993); Tim Armstrong, *Modernism, Technology and the Body* (Cambridge: Cambridge University Press, 1998); Craig Dworkin,

'"Seeing Words Machinewise": Technology and Visual Prosody', *Sagetrieb* 18.1 (Spring 1999): 59–86; Michael North, *Camera Works: Photography and the Twentieth-Century Word* (Oxford: Oxford University Press, 2005); N. Katharine Hayles, *Electronic Literature: New Horizons for the Literary* (Notre Dame: University of Notre Dame Press, 2008); Craig Saper, 'The Adventures of Bob Brown and His Reading Machine', in Bob Brown, *The Readies*, ed. Craig Saper (Houston: Rice University Press/Literature By Design, 2009 [1930]), pp. 61–77; Paul Stephens, 'Bob Brown, "Inforg": The "Readies" at the Limits of Modernist Cosmopolitanism', *Journal of Modern Literature* 35.1 (Fall 2011): 143–64; Eric White, '"A Machine of Mirrors": Technology and American Identity in the Modernist Transatlantic', *Symbiosis* 17.1 (Spring 2013): 69–87; Jessica Pressman, *Digital Modernism: Making It New in New Media* (Oxford and New York: Oxford University Press, 2014); Robbie Moore, 'Ticker Tape and the Superhuman Reader', in *Writing, Medium, Machine Modern Technographies*, ed. Sean Pryor and David Trotter (London: Open Humanities Press, 2016), pp. 137–52; Saper, *Amazing Adventures* (2016); and Stephen Pasqualina, '"That Can Never Be History": Gertrude Stein and the Speed of the Reading Machine', *Modernism/Modernity* (March 2019): 19–42.
6. See North, *Camera Works*, p. 75.
7. Wambly Bald, 'La Vie de Bohème', *Chicago Tribune and the Daily News New York*, no. 5472 (12 July 1932), p. 4.
8. Craig Saper, 'Introduction and Notes on the Text', *RFBBM*, pp. ix–lvii (p. xx). Saper's relaunched Roving Eye Press has restored most of Brown's avant-garde publications to print; see the Abbreviations page in this book for further details of those editions.
9. Brown, 'The Readies', p. 171.
10. Bob Brown, 'Writing Readies', *Morada* 5 (December 1930): 16–19 (p. 16).
11. Simondon, *METO*, p. 43.
12. See Robert Carlton [Bob] Brown, *Tahiti: 10 Rhythms*, Bruno Chap Books 1.4 (March 1915); '[V Poems]', *Others: A Magazine of the New Verse* 1.2 (August 1915): 28–30; and *My Marjonary* (Boston: John W. Luce & Company, 1916).
13. See Bob Brown, 'Appendix', *RFBBM*, pp. 153–208 (pp. 160–9) and 'Notes for the Life of an American Writer', *Berkeley: a Journal of Modern Culture* 10 (1950): 1–4, 7. The *Berkeley* article draws on Brown's drafts for his unfinished late 1940s' typescript *I Don't Die: the Autobiography of Bob Brown*, Box 32, UCLA Brown. Extracts and a précis for a variant of that manuscript appear along with his timeline entitled 'Bob Brown: A Poet's Life' in B4, F1, SIU Kaplan-Brown.
14. Brown, 'Appendix', *RFBBM*, p. 160.
15. Robert Carlton [Bob] Brown, 'Eyes', *The Blind Man* 2 (May 1917): 3.
16. William Carlos Williams, 'America, Whitman, and the Art of Poetry', *The Poetry Journal* 8.1 (November 1917): 27–36 (p. 34).
17. Robert Carlton [Bob] Brown, 'Eyes', *The Blind Man* 2 (May 1917): 3.

18. Brown, 'Appendix', *RFBBM*, pp. 164–5.
19. Brown, *RDBBM*, p. 168.
20. Bob Brown, [Timeline], *I Don't Die*, B4, F1, SIU Kaplan-Brown.
21. Saper, *Amazing Adventures*, p. 115.
22. See Ibid. pp. 112–15.
23. Ibid. p. 142, also see pp. 111–45; and Caroline Burke, *Becoming Modern: The Life of Mina Loy* (New York: Farrar, Straus and Giroux, 1996), pp. 234–71. Brown produced a fictional account of this period in his 'Slacker novel' *You Gotta Live* (London: Desmond Harmsworth, 1932).
24. Brown , *I Don't Die*, UCLA Brown. Brown gives a similar account in 'Notes for the Life of an American Writer', p. 4.
25. See Saper, *Amazing Adventures*, pp. 141–5.
26. Brown, 'Appendix', *RFBBM*, p. 160,
27. Brown, *6BBB*.
28. Bob Brown, Untitled [aka 'My head in the clouds', or 'Self Portrait'], *1450–1950*, p. 83.
29. Brown, *6BBB*.
30. Paolo E. Coletta, *Admiral Bradley A. Fiske and the American Navy* (Lawrence, Kansas: Regents Press of Kansas, 1979), pp. 42, 179, 228–9.
31. See S. R. Winters, 'Stretching the Five-Foot Shelf: An Invention That May Reduce the Size of Our Books to a Fraction of Their Present Bulk', *Scientific American* 126.6 (June 1922): 407. Fiske eventually had at least eight patents for his reading machines.
32. See International Filmbook Corporation, 'The 7-in-1 Fiskeoscope' [advertising pamphlet ca. 1937], B8, F14, SIU Kaplan-Brown.
33. Brown, 'Appendix', *RFBBM*, p. 173.
34. W. B. Hislop, 'The Threatened Revolution in Printing', *Caxton Magazine* 25.3 (March 1923): 107–12 and 'Photo-Mechanical Typesetting', *Caxton Magazine* 25.12 (December 1923): 737–46. Hislop updated these accounts in 'August-Hunter Photo-Composing Machine', *Penrose's Annual* 28 (1926): 76–80.
35. Walter Clark, 'The Year's Progress in Applied Photography', *The Photography Journal*, 69 (November 1929): 463–70 (p. 468).
36. Anonymous, [untitled press clipping], n.d., B8, F15, SIU Kaplan-Brown.
37. J. R. C. August to Bob Brown, 27 November 1925, B1, F4, SIU Kaplan-Brown.
38. See Brown, *The Readies*, p. 38, and 'Appendix', *RFBBM*, pp. 173, 180.
39. Brown, 'Appendix', *RFBBM*, p. 173; Bob Brown to Rear-Admiral Bradley A. Fiske [copy], 5 January 1932, Box 32, UCLA Brown.
40. See Brown, 'Appendix', *RFBBM*, pp. 173–6, 180–3.
41. Ibid. p. 173. Brown sought out Fiske again in 1932, when the development of his reading machine faltered.
42. Ibid. p. 197.
43. See Saper, *Amazing Adventures*, pp. 141–5.

44. Brown self-published *The Readies* (Bad Ems: Roving Eye Press, 1930), *Globe-Gliding* (Diessen: Roving Eye Press, 1930), *Gems: A Censored Anthology* (Cagnes-sur-Mer, France: Roving Eye Press, 1931), *Readies for Bob Brown's Machine*, ed. Bob Brown (Cagnes-sur-Mer, France: Roving Eye Press, 1931) and *Demonics* (Cagnes-sur-Mer, France: Roving Eye Press, 1931). Harry and Caresse Crosby published Bob Brown, *1450–1950* (Paris: Black Sun Press, 1929) and he published *Words* (Paris: Hours Press, 1931) with Nancy Cunard. I cite Craig Saper's Roving Eye Press reissues, listed in the Abbreviations, in most cases.
45. Bob Brown, 'Writing', *Words*, pp. 16–19 (p. 19).
46. Bob Brown, 'An Anthology of Readies for Bob Brown's Machine [advertisement]', *RFBBM*, pp. lviii–lix. On the original *RFBBM* anthology publication date, see Edgar Marquess Branch, *A Paris Year: Dorothy and James T. Farrell, 1931–1932* (Athens, OH: Ohio University Press, 1998), p. 117.
47. Bob Brown, 'Japanese Print Rain Storm', *1450–1950*, p. 39.
48. Anonymous, 'Bob Brown, Who Used to Write "Diamond Dick" Stories, Debases His Art After Japanese Trip', *The New York Herald (European Edition)*, 27 April 1929, p. 9.
49. Brown, 'Appendix', *RFBBM*, p. 164.
50. Anonymous, 'Bob Brown, Who Used to Write "Diamond Dick" Stories', *The New York Herald (European Edition)*, 27 April 1929, p. 9.
51. Gertrude Stein to Bob Brown, 1931, in Gertrude Stein and Bob Brown, 'Letters of Gertrude Stein, Edited with an Introduction by Bob Brown', *Berkeley: A Journal of Modern Culture* 8 (1951): 1–2, 8 (p. 8).
52. Nancy Cunard refers to this diamond type in her letter to Bob Brown, n.d. [ca. October 1930], B1, F6, SIU Kaplan-Brown.
53. Bob Brown, 'Untitled' ['Without any whirr or splutter'], *1450–1950*, p. 30.
54. Bob Brown to Caresse Crosby, 1 October [1929], Caresse Crosby Papers, Special Collections Research Center, Southern Illinois University Carbondale, MMS 140, B34.
55. Montparno, 'Left Bankers Believe Bob Brown's Pill Box Book Reading Machine Will Help Them Absorb Dozen Gertrude Stein Novels in Afternoon', *Chicago Tribune and the Daily News New York* [aka *The Paris Tribune*], No. 4562 (13 January 1930), p. 3.
56. Sue Currell, 'Streamlining the Eye: Speed Reading and the Revolution of Words, 1870–1940', in *Residual Media*, ed. Charles R. Acland (Minneapolis: University of Minnesota Press, 2007), pp. 344–60 (p. 345).
57. Pressman, *Digital Modernism*, p. 72.
58. Montparno, 'Left Bankers Believe', p. 3.
59. Ibid.
60. Ibid.
61. Robbie Moore, 'Ticker Tape and the Superhuman Reader', pp. 149–50.
62. Ibid. p. 149.
63. Established in 1873, *The Publishers' Weekly* had a circulation of over 10,000 copies a week by 1944, even with the constraints of the Second

World War; see anonymous, [untitled editorial], *The Publishers' Weekly* 145.14 (1 April 1944): 1349, and Jay Satterfield, *The World's Best Books: Taste, Culture, and the Modern Library* (Amherst, MA: University of Massachusetts Press, 2002), pp. 81, 195 (note 72).
64. Bob Brown, 'My Reading Machine', *The Publishers' Weekly* 117.18 (3 May 1930): 2353–4 (p. 2253).
65. Ibid.
66. Ibid. pp. 2353–4.
67. Ibid. p. 2354.
68. See Satterfield, *The World's Best Books*, pp. 34–6.
69. Maria Jolas to Bob Brown, 4 October 1929, B1, F4, SIU Kaplan-Brown.
70. See Eugene Jolas to Bob Brown, 23 January 1930, B1, F5, SIU Kaplan-Brown.
71. Eugene Jolas, '*Transition*'s Revolution of the Word Dictionary', *transition* 21 (March 1932): 323–5.
72. Bob Brown/Roving Eye Press, 'The Roving Eye Press Announces: An Anthology of Stories for Bob Brown's Reading Machine [advertisement]', *transition* 21 (March 1932): 336.
73. Eugene Jolas, 'Logos', *transition* 16–17 (June 1929): 25–30 (p. 26).
74. Brown, 'The Readies', p. 173.
75. Ibid. p. 167.
76. Ibid. p. 173.
77. Ibid.
78. Brown, *The Readies*, p. 46. The Thereminovox, also known as the Theremin, is a gesture-controlled monophonic audio synthesiser, and was invented by the Russian scientist Léon Theremin in 1920 and patented in 1928; see Anonymous, 'Music from the Ether', *The London Mercury* 17.99 (1928): 225. Herman Spector referenced the Theremin in 'Nickel Artists', *RFBBM*, pp. 114–16 (p. 115).
79. Frank Scully to Bob Brown, 5 February 1932, B1, F16, SIU Kaplan-Brown; see Frank Scully, 'Chatter: Riviera', *Variety* 105.8 (2 February 1932): 39.
80. Pressman, *Digital Modernism*, p. 194.
81. See Pasqualina, '"That Can Never Be History"', p. 23.
82. Brown, 'Appendix', *RFBBM*, p. 168.
83. Unknown photographer [Bob or Rose Brown], [Photograph of Ross Saunders's Reading Machine Prototype], B5, F12, SIU Kaplan-Brown. I refer to this picture as the 'SIU Photograph' hereafter. The photograph is included, undocumented, in the same file as Brown's annotated copy of *The Readies*, which he used as a source for his *Readies Anthology* 'Appendix'.
84. Wambly Bald, 'La Vie de Bohème', *Chicago Tribune and the Daily News New York*, no. 5033 (19 May 1931): 4.
85. Kay Boyle to Bob Brown, 18 July 1931, B1, F11, SIU Kaplan-Brown.
86. Theodore Pratt to Philip Kaplan, 12 October 1940, B2, F11, SIU Kaplan-Brown.

87. See Bob Brown to Theodore Pratt, 16 September [1940], B2, F11, SIU Kaplan-Brown. Although Saunders was clearly influential in his time, no correspondence from him seems to exist in either Brown's or other archives, and only traces of information exist elsewhere. He resided in Cagnes until at least April 1936, when he returned 'after an exposition of recent paintings at New York'; Selina Yorke, 'Artists Abroad', *The New York Herald Tribune (European Edition)*, 8 April 1936, p. 4.
88. Bob Brown, *Reading Machines*; see the 'Abbreviations' section of this book for further details.
89. Robert Carlton Brown III, 'Reading by Machine' [TS, ca. 1931–2], B2, F9, The Robert Carlton Brown III Collection of Bob Brown Papers, Special Collections Research Center, Southern Illinois University Carbondale.
90. Brown, *Reading Machines V1*, p. 5. Images of 1920s–1930s 'biscuit boxes' can be found on auction and antiques websites.
91. Robert Carlton Brown III, 'Reading by Machine'.
92. A range of commercial gramophone motors might have been used, but it is also possible that the motor is a Meccano or Gilbert clockwork or electric motor, which had been produced since 1915.
93. Brown, *Reading Machines V2*, p. 7. See 'Woodstock Standard Typewriter, Model No. 5 by Woodstock Typewriter Co., 1922', Made in Chicago Museum <https://www.madeinchicagomuseum.com/single-post/2015/9/7/Woodstock-Standard-Typewriter-Model-No-5-by-Woodstock-Typewriter-Co-1921> (accessed 31 July 2018).
94. See Cecilia Tichi, *Shifting Gears: Technology, Literature, Culture in Modernist America* (Chapel Hill, NC, and London: University of North Carolina Press, 1987), pp. 3–16.
95. A range of such examples are included in Meccano Limited, *Meccano Instructions No. 19A* (Liverpool: Meccano Limited, 1919).
96. Douglas Hartree, 'Meccano differential analyser, [1934] 1947', Objects Collection [online database], Science Museum <https://collection.sciencemuseum.org.uk/objects/co531302/meccano-differential-analyser-1947-model-representation> (accessed 31 July 2018).
97. I am grateful to John Gardner, who has an engineering as well as a literary critical background, for discussing this assembly with me. I am also grateful to my collaborator Iulian Arcus of EOF Hackspace, with whom my Avant-Gardes and Speculative Technology (AGAST) Project has retro-engineered this mechanism in community workshops; examples of these models will be presented on my online scholarly resource *The AGAST Project Archive* (New York: electric.press, forthcoming).
98. Bob Brown, 'Story to be Read on the Reading Machine', *The Readies*, pp. 47–58, 'Appendix' on pp. 187–96.
99. See my discussion of these texts and their production in Eric White, 'Foreword', *RFBBM*, pp. vii–xviii (p. xii).
100. See Brown, 'Appendix', *RFBBM*, pp. 198–208.

101. Craig Saper's online simulation of the *RFBBM* anthology shows how its texts would have looked when 'readified'; *Readies.org* <http://readies.org/> (accessed 18 November 2018). For some readers, the scrolling text can introduce optical illusions such as motion-blurring and the apparent reversal of the texts' direction (an effect that Brown seems to have noticed as well, while speed-reading stock ticker tape). Scrolling texts on billboards, teleprompters, television news programmes, and now smart watches to some extent attest to the viability of Brown's idea, but not necessarily as a speed-reading technology in the traditional sense. As I discuss in the next chapter, however, Clare Brackett's solution to potential optical problems involved displaying the text at 'intervals' – a solution that resembles the format of some tachistoscopic speed readers; Clare Brackett to Bob Brown (copy), 22 March 1932, B32, UCLA Brown.
102. Robert Carlton Brown III, 'Reading by Machine'.
103. See Kay Boyle to Bob and Rose Brown, Sunday [October 1931], B1, F13, SIU Kaplan-Brown.
104. See Anonymous, 'Hiler Held in Nice as Death Driver', *The New York Herald (European Edition)*, 7 December 1930, p. 1, and 'Hiler to Declare Sobriety in Crash to Clear His Name', *The New York Herald (European Edition)*, 4 January 1932, p. 3.
105. Bob Brown, 'Reading Machines' [TS, version 1 ca. August–September 1937], p. 5.
106. Saper, *Amazing Adventures*, p. 177.
107. The legal requirement for patent models that demonstrated how an invention worked had been abolished in the United States in 1870, but they were still used in the twentieth century; see Alan Rothschild, *Inventing a Better Mousetrap: 200 Years of American History in the Amazing World of Patent Models* (San Francisco: Maker Media, 2015), p. 5.
108. Hilaire Hiler, 'Preface', *Readies Anthology*, pp. 5–8 (p. 5).
109. Ibid.
110. See especially Dworkin, '"Seeing Words Machinewise"', pp. 59–61, and North, *Camera Works*, pp. 79–82.
111. Craig Saper, 'The Adventures of Bob Brown and His Reading Machine', *The Readies*, pp. 61–77 (p. 70).
112. Brown, 'The Readies', p. 172.
113. Michael North, *Camera Works*, p. 81. Brown removed this colophon from his reissued edition published by Jonathan Williams; Bob Brown, *1450–1950* (New York: Jargon Books, 1959).
114. Ibid.
115. William Carlos Williams to Bob Brown, 11 May 1930 and Eugene Jolas to Bob Brown, 23 January 1930, B1, F5, SIU Kaplan-Brown.
116. Mark S. Morrisson 'The Call of the Southwest: *The Texas Review* (1915–24); *Southwest Review* (1924–); and *The Morada* (1929–30)', in *The Oxford Critical and Cultural History of Modernist Magazines* II: 538–57 (p. 555).

117. Ibid.
118. Walter Lowenfels, '[untitled readie]', in Ibid. p. 18.
119. Samuel Putnam to Bob Brown, 1 November 1930, Box 32, UCLA Brown.
120. See Mark Cirino, 'The Nasty Mess: Hemingway, Italian Fascism, and the *New Review* Controversy of 1932', *The Hemingway Review* 33.2 (Spring 2014): 20–47 (pp. 39–43).
121. North, *Camera Works*, p. 79.
122. Ibid., and Craig Saper, 'Invent(st)ory: The Contributors and Their Readies', *RFBBM*, pp. xxxviii–lxi, xlvi; also see Craig Dworkin's pioneering reading in '"Seeing Words Machinewise"', p. 60.
123. North, *Camera Works*, p. 79.
124. Craig Dworkin, '"Seeing Words Machinewise"', p. 60.
125. Nancy Cunard, 'Dlink', *RFBBM*, p. 124.
126. Nancy Cunard to Bob Brown, [n.d., ca. December 1930–January 1931], B1, F7, SIU Kaplan-Brown.
127. Kay Boyle, 'Change of Life [extract]', in Brown, 'Writing Readies', p. 18.
128. Nathanael West suggested to William Carlos Williams that the work of 'Archibald MacLeish, John Dos Passos, Murray Godwin' and 'Erskine Caldwell' exemplified what he 'meant by American Super-realism'; Nathanael West to William Carlos Williams, October 1931, quoted in Jonathan Veitch, *American Superrealism: Nathanael West and the Politics of Representation in the 1930s* (Madison: University of Wisconsin Press, 1997), p. 50.
129. Veitch, *American Superrealism*, p. 15.
130. Ibid.
131. Eric B. White, *Transatlantic Avant-Gardes: Little Magazines and Localist Modernism* (Edinburgh: Edinburgh University Press, 2013), p. 174.
132. Norman Macleod, 'Ready: Revelation', in Brown, 'Writing Readies', p. 18.
133. Norman Macleod, 'Ready: Revelation', *RFBBM*, pp. 53–4 (p. 53).
134. Ibid. p. 54.
135. Rose Brown, 'Dis', in Bob Brown, 'Writing Readies', p. 18.
136. Rose Brown, 'Dis', *RFBBM*, pp. 49–52 (p. 49).
137. Bob Brown, 'Writing Readies', p. 19.
138. Céline Mansanti, 'Between Modernisms: *transition* (1927–38)', in *The Oxford Critical and Cultural History of Modernist Magazines*, ed. Peter Brooker and Andrew Thacker, 3 vols (Oxford: Oxford University Press, 2009–2013), II, pp. 718–36 (pp. 724–5).
139. Catherine Setz, 'Transocean': *transition*'s Anachronistic Zeitgeists, *Modernist Cultures* 11.1 (2016): 65–85 (pp. 68–9).
140. *PEL*, p. 176.

Chapter 4

Ghosts in the Machine Age: Rose and Bob Brown's Reading Machines and the Socio-Technics of Social Change

Introduction

Fittingly for a book published on New Year's Eve, 1931, *Readies for Bob Brown's Machine (RFBBM)* is a modernist text caught in a transitional period. As the Great Depression deepened, the winter of 1931–2 proved to be a pivotal moment for transatlantic modernism. Expatriate communities in Europe began to disband, their participants returning (or emigrating) to America, and American writers who remained at home found previous allegiances and aesthetic commitments splintering. Projects and publications were re-imagined, set aside or abandoned altogether, and in the winter of 1932 Bob Brown's reading machine looked set to join the modernist casualties of the Great Depression. Indeed, that is the view most critics hold, and to a certain extent they are correct:[1] the reading machine was never manufactured commercially, and the delicate prototype constructed by Ross Saunders in Cagnes-sur-Mer during the summer of 1931 did not make the transatlantic journey to join the cultural vanguards back in America. However, evidence strongly suggests that Rose Brown led the development of a new working prototype after the Browns returned to New York. Although definitive prima facie evidence for Rose Brown's Reading Machine is predictably unavailable, the Browns' archive and the public record provide strong documentary evidence for its existence. Multiple references to (and recollections of) a second prototype appear at regular intervals in the Browns' archives in Special Collections at UCLA and SIU Carbondale, and in a host of mass-market, middlebrow and specialist publications spanning the 1930s–1950s. For the first time, this chapter tracks the evolution of the readies project on the other side of the Atlantic, and its journey from an avant-garde and commercial proposition to an instrument for social change. In doing so, it recovers the lost history of one of avant-garde modernism's most extraordinary long-term projects, which cuts across multiple literary and non-literary formations.

However, even the literary emphasis of *RFBBM* was cross-formational. The Browns had crafted a strategic coalition of individuals, most of whom were involved in publishing as well as creative writing and political activism. Indeed, the group most visibly represented in the collection was influential modernist (and/or political) writer-editors and writer-publishers, who, along with F. T. Marinetti, Ezra Pound, Gertrude Stein and William Carlos Williams, also included: Nancy Cunard (The Hours Press and *Negro: An Anthology*); Charles Henri Ford (*Blues: A Magazine of New Rhythms*); B. C. Hagglund (*The Anvil*); Richard Johns (*Pagany: A Native Quarterly*); Eugene Jolas (*transition* magazine); Alfred Kreymborg (*The Glebe*, *Others* and *Broom* magazines, plus the *American Caravan* anthologies); Walter Lowenfels (Carrefour Press); Norman Macleod (*Jackass, Palo Verde, Morada* and *Front* magazines); Robert McAlmon (*Contact* and Contact Editions Press); and Kathleen Tankersley Young (*The Echo*, *Blues* and the Modern Editions Press). These figures had been, or would shortly be, on the front lines of various revolutionary projects in the 1930s through their editing and publishing activities. Some of them, like John Banting, Kay Boyle, J. Jones, Walter Lowenfels, Samuel Putnam and Herman Spector, as well as Cunard, Hagglund and Macleod, would immerse themselves in radical left-wing politics. These efforts were allied to those of James T. Farrell, who found fame in the 1930s with his social realist *Studs Lonigan* trilogy. As I have argued, the brilliance of the Browns' approach owes a good deal to Jolas's strategy in *transition*, which avoided imposing a specific programme on the contributors while cultivating their experimental agendas. What they did instead was to impose a format on the contributors, with a clearly defined but capacious vision of a new media ecology, which correlated the various programmes of the cultural formations each represented.

Cultural formations involve collective cultural production defined by its 'internal' and 'external' relations.[2] Recently, critics in the field of periodical studies such as Matthew Chambers have added granularity to Raymond Williams's taxonomy of 'cultural formations', proposing more specific spheres of activity within particular contexts, such as 'periodical formations', without sacrificing the complexities of cultural production described by Williams.[3] I agree with this approach, but in considering the Browns' work, my focus, and terminology, tacks in the opposite direction. I use the term 'meta-formation' to describe interrelated cultural productions that take place across a number of distinct formations for a common purpose within a specific timeframe. Rather than collapsing the distinctions between formations, meta-formational activity is heterodox and polyvalent – it relies on, rather than is undermined by, different disciplines and approaches. In *RFBBM*, Browns's avant-garde meta-formation had already begun to confront the new politics of Depression-era America. By drawing together specialists in the field of writing, art, engineering, publishing and research to produce a new socio-technical ensemble and media ecology, they identified a basis for uniting a broad-based left-wing politics with a programme of aesthetic experimentation. And when they returned to America, they picked up where they left off, imagining new directions in which to develop the readies project.

The Great Depression had devastated the Browns' wealth on a scale they had not experienced since the end of their Greenwich Village days. Motivated by the need to earn a living as much as the need to complete a project, by the autumn of 1932 Rose had solved the problem of developing a readies medium, which had supposedly sunk the readies project. Working with Hugo Knudsen, a pioneering offset printer and brother-in-law of former *Others* editor and *RFBBM* contributor Alfred Kreymborg, she completed an electro-mechanical reading machine model built by Brown's cousin Clare Brackett, President of the National Machine Products Company (NMPC) in Detroit, and his chief engineer Albert Stoll. Rose also conceived of a plan to package classic and revolutionary texts for the age of mass communication, while Bob applied for a Guggenheim Fellowship to develop the project. Yet there were strong socio-political as well as aesthetic imperatives driving this next stage of the readies project. Many of the *RFBBM* contributors, including Rose, had already begun to chart a course beyond the binary orbits of dour social realism and 'ivory-tower' aestheticism. Binding the techno-socialist politics of Thorstein Veblen to the counter-servile technicities and energetic pedagogical strategies of Hilaire Hiler, the Browns began to re-imagine the reading machine as a device that could combine aesthetic and political revolution within the readies media ecology.

In 1934, the Browns joined the faculty of the radical labour institution Commonwealth College in Mena, Arkansas, where they applied meta-formational strategies to the Associated Little Magazines network, a clearing house for radical political and literary periodicals, and the Museum of Social Change, a legendary installation that dialectically critiqued capitalist society. At Commonwealth College, Bob also wrote the last surviving examples of his readie-style writing, which include an unpublished text about his travels through Russia with Rose, where they demonstrated her reading machine prototype to potential collaborators at Moscow Polytechnic Museum. Following their return to the United States in 1937, the Browns pursued new collaborations within the burgeoning microfilm industry, which had taken off while the Browns were in Russia. Unfortunately, their socio-technics were at odds with those of the industry leaders, Eastman Kodak, and smaller rivals, including the Filmbook Corporation and Albert Boni's Readex Microprint Corporation. The Browns' emphasis on affordable, portable and socially transformative technology was eclipsed by the industry's bulky, static and very expensive machines that were intended for libraries, governments and major corporations. Nevertheless, the Browns continued to argue that the Readies could enhance workers' access to writing, both materially and conceptually, and that such a medium could respond to and develop emergent technicities of reading across the social strata. The meta-formational readies project reaffirmed the tenacity, and technicities, of its multiple lives, cropping up in mass-market publications such as *Time* until the late 1940s. The readies stayed news because they interleaved the fortunes of larger-than-life personalities with the anonymous work and machinations of print culture. The untold story of these reading machines exposes the paper-thin boundaries between success and failure – between the national stage and the most intimate personal experiences.

'New-brains-kaleidoscoped': Prototyping a Commercial Reading Machine

Throughout its evolution, Bob's core concept for the readies project remained consistent with the one he originally proposed in his 1923 manuscript 'The Six Books of Bob Brown':[4] a cheap and portable, machine-assisted speed-reading device with directional and magnification controls for a micrographic medium, genre and media ecology he later called the Readies. As I discussed in the last chapter, when Bob fully articulated his readies project in the summer and autumn of 1930, he also laid the foundations for producing a commercial prototype with Brackett and Stoll at the NMPC. Brackett co-founded the NMPC in 1916, and as well as amassing a considerable personal fortune he held several leading roles in automotive industry associations. At its peak, his company had 300 workers manufacturing primarily nuts, bolts, rivets and other related products, for which Brackett held numerous patents.[5] Together with his chief engineer Albert Stoll and Brown's patent lawyer Ernest W. Bradford, as well as contacts at the New York-based optical technology firm Bausch and Lomb, NMPC elaborated the readies project with Brown across the Atlantic for nearly two years, investing considerable resources in the process.[6]

Brackett accepted Bob's basic design premise for the reading machine, and immediately identified its commercial potential. He wanted to 'develop a simple, compact, cheap device' and committed to 'developing a satisfactory mechanism for projecting or magnifying in accord with [Bob's] suggestions'.[7] This model was based on the commercial prototype design depicted on the flyleaf of *RFBBM*.[8] Although this reading machine never went into production, evidence strongly suggests that Brackett and the NMPC produced a semi-functional prototype by the spring of 1932 (which, as I discuss in the next section, Rose Brown completed with Hugo Knudsen in the summer and autumn). Brackett grasped the project's technical complexities, particularly the challenge of producing a transparent medium to carry the micrographically printed readies. However, it was his understanding of the readies format that made his brief partnership with the Browns so productive. This section details the evolution of that partnership between 1930–2, and the design principles underpinning the commercial reading machine prototype that the project team debated during this period. It also considers Bob's correspondence with the experimental writer and technology publisher Murray Godwin, and his work with Hilaire Hiler. Both Godwin and Hiler had engineering backgrounds, and their contributions to the readies project helped correlate the cultures of experiment that drove this transatlantic enterprise.

Unusually for a company executive – though not, perhaps, from one related to the Browns – Brackett appreciated that 'the modern trend demands new forms of expression'.[9] He eventually published his own readie in the *RFBBM Anthology*. 'Two Men 7 Duck No Luck' is a bathetic account of a failed duck hunt in the marshlands outside of Detroit,[10] but Brackett included a more explicit version in his September 1930 letter to Bob:

> Your-idea-drop-no-account-words-eye-translates-mind-absorbs-paragraphs-pages-books-simple-many-brilliant-thoughts-less-encumbered-no-use-phrases-hell-bent-election-time-saved-relaxing-dance-drink-jack-off-alone-together-what-Ho-new-brains-kaleidoscoped.[11]

Here, Brackett immediately adopts the taboo-flouting tone Bob had fostered in the readies, and, through his onanistic metaphor, understood how the machine might reconceptualise textual intimacies (or perhaps he was simply commenting on its potential laptop applications). Yet Brackett took seriously Bob's linguistic and literary innovations, and the bold strategy of promoting the device by using experimental writing produced by 'new-brains-kaleidoscoped'. Indeed, Brackett's readie captures the key features of the readies methodology, which included relentless punning, the use of punctuation to indicate motion, and the excision of pronouns, conjunctions and other words. He appreciated the bathetic technicity and aesthetics underpinning the revolutionary new media ecology, but also identified the serious commercial potential that the readies project could realise in the emerging market of domestic, business and academic information technology – and in that respect, he was not alone.

Brown had another contact in the Motor City with professional ties to its automotive industry. In the late 1920s, Murray Godwin was the editor of 'the house organ of the Ford Motor Company and live[d] in the Polish section of Detroit'.[12] Unlike Brackett, however, Godwin was also an avant-garde writer and *transition* contributor as well as a jobbing editor and left-wing political thinker. By the summer of 1930, Godwin had become the general editor of *Science and Invention Magazine*. When Brown sent *The Readies* to Godwin, the *Science and Invention* editor was impressed, and promised to profile the readies project in the magazine.[13] Godwin's editorial for the October 1930 issue featured a crisp synopsis of the reading machine and readies along with the first illustration of it in print (albeit in the magazine's house style caricature) (Fig. 4.1). From the plug 'connected with a current source', to the 'control' mechanism, to the scrolling texts 'exposed in a single unwavering line as they pass beneath a slot equipped with a magnifying glass to bring them up to readable size', the illustration accurately interpolates Brown's descriptions of the technical object in his manifestos.[14] By depicting a reader (however comically),

Reading By Machine

MY FRIEND Bob Brown, of South America, Paris, and at present Munich, sends me a little book, *The Readies,* in which he proposes to substitute rolls of printed tape, displayed to the eye by machine, for the book form of literature. His idea, as he has worked it out, is so logical and practical that it seems almost certain to be adopted. . . . Imagine the equivalent of an entire book printed in microscopic type on a roll of paper tape by a photographic process. The roll, about the size of a typewriter reel, is placed in a machine and connected with a winding spool. A plug is connected with a current source.

Figure 4.1 Murray Godwin, 'The Way I See It – [Editorial]', *Science and Invention* 18.6 (October 1930), p. 490.

the illustration comes closer to capturing the readies experience than either illustration in *RFBBM*. The forum was appropriate as well: *Science and Invention* was a high-circulation mass-market hobbyist/lifestyle journal produced by Radio-Science Publications, which quietly promoted a techno-cultural revolution in the United States. Godwin's journal imagined that people's everyday lives could be revolutionised by technology, not as passive consumers of industrial goods but as active participants in America's socio-technical innovation.

Given his expertise in several specialist discourse networks, Godwin was especially impressed by the interdisciplinary potential of the readies medium. He called it a 'new form, a marvellous acceleration and compression' that resulted in 'a vividness not achievable with the language as we know it'.[15] However, Godwin's editorial did not delve into his own experimental writing projects (Brown had invited him to contribute to the *RFBBM* anthology, but Godwin reluctantly turned down the opportunity). Godwin's themes and narrative experimentation connect him to the American superrealist mode proposed by Nathanael West and theorised by Jonathan Veitch (which I discussed in the last chapter),[16] while his site-specificity and ludic strategies dovetail with the new localist techniques emerging in *Blues*, *Pagany* and *Morada* magazines. As Jolas wrote in Godwin's biography for *transition*, 'his realistic viewpoint [. . .] has not lessened his appetite for the fantastic and Gargantuan'.[17] Although Godwin's writing engaged with dystopian urban landscapes favoured by the American realists, it more frequently evokes the techno-bathetic pastiches associated with New York Dada. His experimental piece 'A Day in the Life of a Robot' critiqued Detroit's burgeoning industrial infrastructure, which was already straining its civic infrastructure and social cohesion, whereas more speculative works, such as the 'The Wires Invisible', identified metaphysical resonances within and beyond urban technicities.[18] In this respect, Godwin also formed a direct point of contact between avant-garde practice, specialised technological discourse networks and a radical leftist politics that would find expression in 1930s' journals such as *The New Masses* (indeed, Godwin complained in a letter to Brown that the *New Masses* 'was not radical enough').[19]

Hinge figures like Godwin are not unique among the Browns' network of collaborators. Hilaire Hiler played a very similar role in Cagnes-sur-Mer, France. The Browns had been living in Bad Ems, a spa town in Rheinland Pfalz, Germany, in the summer, where Brown had completed and published *The Readies*.[20] They moved to Cagnes in the autumn, and invited Hiler, their new neighbour, to join them in producing the reading machine. In October 1930, Hiler tentatively agreed to illustrate and contribute to the *RFBBM Anthology* in a lavishly decorated letter.[21] That December, Bob published an extract from Hiler's readie 'H-A-N-G-O-V-E-R' in *Morada*.[22] Just at this pivotal moment, Hiler was arrested for killing a cyclist by vehicular manslaughter in Nice (the charges, as I explain in the previous chapter were eventually dropped). Nevertheless, in the summer of 1931, Hiler was able to assist the artist-engineer Ross Saunders in the construction and testing of his working patent model reading machine. Hiler's main focus, however, was the Commercial Design. A technical drawing of this reading machine appeared beneath the grainy photograph of the Saunders Prototype on the *RFBBM* flyleaf, and Hiler described its features in his 'Preface'. The illustration was probably made by Hiler and Saunders but may have been sketched out by the NMPC; it is sleek, but poorly reproduced due to the intaglio printing process, and as such, its labels are scarcely legible.[23] However, my annotated version in Figure 4.2 identifies the named parts and their specific roles more clearly. In this way, the components can be viewed as part of a functional whole rather than as a cryptic 'black box', whose illegibility transformed a straightforward technical diagram into an impenetrable (and to the suspicious, possibly deliberately inscrutable) puzzle.

Hiler's 'laptop'-style design elaborated the basic functions of the Saunders Prototype's. Brown imagined 'a machine as handy as a portable phonograph, typewriter or radio; compact, minute, operated by electricity'.[24] The illustration in *RFBBM* displays controls for motion, speed and direction in a clear interface on the lower right side of the 'aluminum hood'.[25] Hiler had been using this metal in his creative work around this time period, and it would give the Commercial Design the deco-inspired curves and lines of contemporaneous industrial and scientific equipment.[26] Unlike the exaggerated motor in the *Science and Invention* illustration, Hiler conceals his version beneath the hood at the rear of the unit, with the spool assemblies sitting towards the middle. The 'base' of the unit was actually the lid, and a case held the 'pill-box' reels underneath it.[27] At the top of the assembly beneath the handle, it also reveals the 'eight inch double adjustable lens' – a feature hidden on both existing pictures of the Saunders Prototype – with the 'tape with microscopic type' depicted as a straight black line through the centre of the rectangular viewing screen.[28]

As a polymath whose business involved 'industrial design', Hiler developed an evangelical passion for the applied sciences in the early 1930s.[29] Influenced by the writings of Karl Marx and Thorsten Veblen, Hiler advanced a counter-servile approach to technicity that encouraged artists to think of themselves as engineers, and vice versa, just as Wyndham Lewis had suggested in *Blast* nearly two decades previously.[30] In both his essays and art school, Hiler confronted the pervasive technological alienation and false consciousness spreading under capitalism in

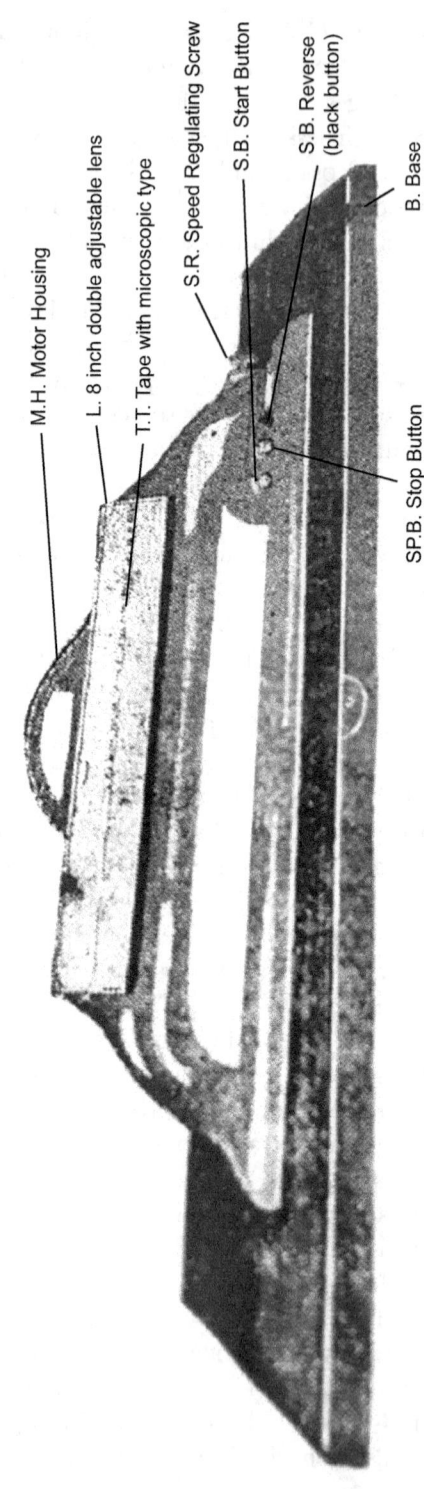

Figure 4.2 Eric White's annotated version of the Commercial Prototype Reading Machine illustration in *RFBBM* (p. 4).

the arts. According to Gilbert Simondon, this sense of alienation was not an inherent by-product of engaging with machines but resulted from the 'non-knowledge' of their 'nature' and 'essence'.[31] Hiler identified a practical, pedagogical method of confronting this kind of technological alienation in his radical art school Atelier Hiler. In an article for Samuel Putnam's *New Review*, Hiler demanded that artists reduce their 'childish trust' in art supply 'manufacturers' and embrace 'the discoveries of modern applied science'. He complained that '[t]he graphic fine arts are the only division of human activity which have escaped the effect of Thorsten Veblen's *Canon of Wasted Effort*, which stated simply means that the economic value of an object varies in direct ratio to the amount of labor expended in its creation'. Binding Marxist economics to Veblenist socio-technics, Hiler's conclusion was that, contrary to prevailing wisdom, 'the effect of surprise so sought after by modern artists may be attained not only by originality and extravagance of design, but also through the employment of a technical method capable of completely realizing their intention'.[32]

What Hiler describes here anticipates Walter Benjamin's account of the alienating effects of technology in 'Art in the Age of Mechanical Reproduction' (1936). Hiler similarly suggests that technological distancing can be productive, both aesthetically and politically, and his concept of 'surprise' is similar to Benjamin's use of 'distraction', 'shock effect' and the 'profound changes in apperception' that result from engaging with cinema technology. However, Hiler is less patient than Benjamin, and wanted to accelerate the means by which such 'changes' were 'mastered' by habituation, 'under the guidance of tactile appropriation'.[33] Hiler's solution interleaved 'social energetics' with artistic practice: through his teaching especially, he sought to create the conditions where, in Simondon's words, 'chance can produce the equivalent of a structural germ' that leads to paradigmatic change in a socio-technical ensemble.[34] Accordingly, Hiler's counter-servile engagement with socio-technics at Atelier Hiler was no mere 'DIY' aesthetic, but was an articulation of creative practice every bit as important as brushstrokes or perspective – technicity as *techné*. In his pamphlet *Technologie Matérial Des Arts Graphique* [*Material Technique in the Graphic Arts*], a prospectus for classes offered by his art workshop Atelier Hiler, he argued that '[t]he knowledge of the sound technical means and methods necessary to graphic expression gives confidence and self-respect to any artist', and that 'the knowledge of how the materials can be controlled and made to do that which we wish them to do' was best 'discover[ed] by working together'. Hiler embraced an ethos of co-creation in which there were 'no teachers, only students'.[35] In this co-operative model, he approached the material sciences as the basis, rather than a corollary, of artistic pedagogy.

At Atelier Hiler, he taught these skills in a pragmatist manner that broke down technical jargon and principles and focused instead on results. From this perspective, his detailed technical 'Preface' for *RFBBM* was not (or was not only) a heavy-handed attempt to convince investors of his technical expertise but a genuine engagement with a community of specialists that invited non-specialists to follow the discussion. In fact, the densest technical commentary comes from Albert Stoll, who Hiler quoted extensively in his preface.

Stoll discussed 'the different possibilities of magnification' with '[t]he local representative of Bausch and Lomb', who were then, as now, a major optical technology company specialising in lens production for military and scientific applications, as well as for the mass market.[36] They identified a few potential solutions using conventional microscope lenses, but Stoll had a better idea. He recommended a system of projecting, rather than magnifying, the micrographic text, which resembled the ground glass unit on 'a Graflex mirror camera'.[37] This system would permit 'reading on a translucent screen without being obliged to focus the eye to the magnifying glass, since the magnifying is done' with an artificial or natural light source 'through the projector'.[38] Stoll included meticulous calculations and detailed plans of his projection and text formatting systems in his summer 1931 letters, but Brown's patent lawyer, Ernest W. Bradford, summarised them crisply in the winter of 1932, when the team resumed work on the project following the publication of *RFBBM*:

> When the printing is only on one side a long type is required. Using a wide tape with six lines when running through with the use of a rectifying lens will print in regular position – the reversal of the ribbon would require an inversion of the type – by using a corresponding or correct type of lens the line would travel in the correct direction regarding the eyes while the ribbon is reversing, therefore reducing the length of ribbon or tape required. A hand-wound operating motor or an electric motor for propelling tape may be used.[39]

Brown, or possibly Stoll or Brackett himself, later mocked up a sketch of this format, which although slightly complex would allow sufficient space for the scrolling method Brown envisaged, and could be produced using standard 35 mm film stock (Fig. 4.3). The sketch is included in *Reading Machines V1*, and the narrative on the film sample in the sketch is a tongue-in-cheek riposte to critics of the readies, such as Ezra Pound and B. C. Hagglund.[40] Although they appreciated the concept, Pound and Hagglund echoed the concern of other critics, who felt that Brown's machine would speed up reading but slow down thinking, and ultimately disorientate the reader.

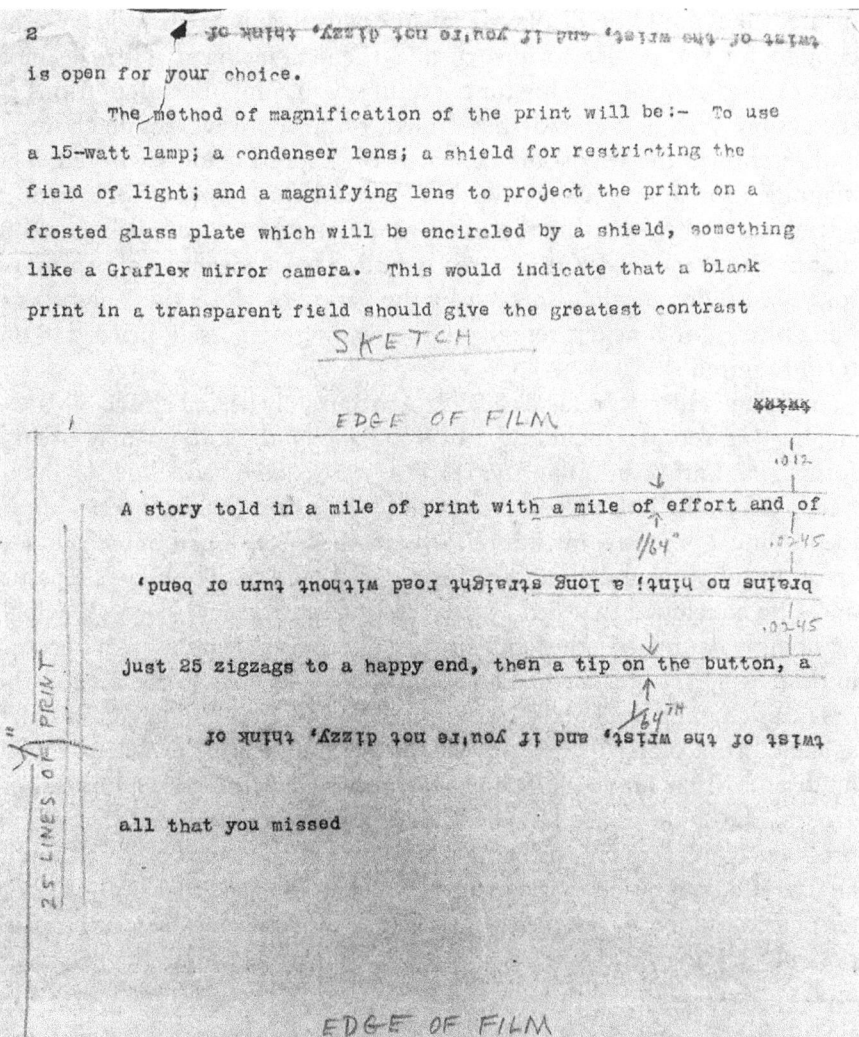

Figure 4.3 Bob Brown, [Readies prototype illustration, TS, ca. 1932–7], in *Reading Machines V1*, p. 5.

Brown playfully pastiches these arguments to play up the alternative possibilities for literacy that might result from such 'dizzy' reading (which his technical representation of the readies format amplified with its inversions of the text).[41] Nevertheless, Brackett proposed an elegant solution to this problem too. When he encountered a difference of opinion about 'whether a continuous flowing line of type' in the reading machine would prove 'tiresome or not', he proposed that 'parts of the printed line' could be displayed 'at intervals, leaving it stationary long enough for the reader to absorb and then replacing it with the next part of the sentence'.[42] This functionality would involve adaptations to the system they had already developed, rather than wholesale changes, and resembled the way some tachistoscopic speed readers worked. The magnification apparatus was well in hand, as was a system for creating, setting up and formatting the micrographic texts. Indeed, it is possible that by this stage NMPC had already built a basic mechanical prototype for the scrolling mechanism. But by the spring of 1932, the 'chief stumbling block' for Brackett remained 'the reading strip itself, printed in the form required'.[43]

Although Hiler's 'Preface' to *RFBBM* accurately described the NMPC's engineering reports, including Stoll's ingenious ideas about magnifying, formatting and positioning the readies, it also involved some sleight of hand. Crucially, Hiler glossed over the NMPC's serious concerns about identifying a potential medium for the readies.[44] Stoll had numerous reservations about sourcing a suitable material, and despite Hiler's reassurances he concluded that if they used existing nitrocellulose stock, which was highly flammable, the 'emulsion on photographic paper would result in destroying the surface' of the readies medium.[45] As I discussed in the previous chapter, Stoll and Brackett wanted something more stable, such as cellulose acetate, to use for the readies (and unbeknownst to Bob, his friend Mina Loy was using this same material in her lamp designs around the same time). However, they rejected commercially-available products like cellophane as being too rough for their purposes. Although he was still committed to the project, Brackett believed that Bob was better placed to 'obtain samples of this [film], for trial purposes, in France', possibly because Pathé was developing new stocks that might satisfy Stoll's specifications.[46] In fact, Bob had already been in touch with one such supplier.

The Eastman Kodak Company had been developing a cellulose acetate film since 1909, and had been working on a micrographic film reader since 1928.[47] They thanked Bob for exploring the 'photographic possibilities' of the readies project with them, but, unsurprisingly, did not tell him about their own developments.[48] Following an announcement in 1933, and a trial version installed in the New York Public Library in 1934, Kodak eventually launched the first commercially-available microfilm reader, the Recordak Library Projector, in 1935.[49] Huge, fixed and very expensive, the system used the same highly flammable nitrate film stock that Stoll had rejected for the readies project; the cellulose acetate 'safety film' that Kodak was developing was not rolled out until the late 1930s at the earliest, and not at commercial scale until the late 1940s.[50]

Unfortunately, it seems, Stoll had been overly cautious, and Hiler's advice was correct, as Rose and Knudsen would later prove.

For all of their concerns about the readies medium, however, the NMPC's major concern was probably with the patentability of the readies project. Ernest Bradford had revealed that Rear Admiral Fiske held at least eight patents for his various 'Fiskeoscope' reading machines. Bradford concluded that in 'Patent 1,476,290 (Fiske) suggests the idea which you describe', and five further patents seemed 'to be broad enough to clearly read on your proposition'.[51] As Fiske had predicted at the end of his meeting with Brown in 1926, these ideas were also under development in the film industry.[52] However, Bradford suggested that if Bob could be more specific about the mechanism, the novelty it introduced and the niche it would occupy, then a 'patentable subject matter' might be 'apparent'.[53] If not, then it would probably not be profitable to seek a patent for the reading machine, even if they were able to overcome the technical challenges involved in its production.[54] By the spring of 1932, it appeared that Bradford and the NMPC had exhausted the possibilities of developing the readies project.

If Bob had delved further into the specialised applications he envisaged for the device – for example, installed in waiting rooms, dentist's offices or airplanes, or used in scientific field research, automated Braille units, music readers, and pedagogical speed-reading trainers – then that narrower focus on any single application might have resulted in a patent.[55] Instead, he and Rose remained convinced that this revolutionary new media ecology could and should be implemented at a mass scale. The Browns would develop the reading machine in *collaboration* with specialist networks, but never exclusively *for* them. However, the economic crises engulfing America had rippled to expatriate Europe; rather than abandoning the readies project, as the consensus narrative supposes, the Browns considered how its meta-formational ensembles might respond to the realities of the Great Depression, rather than retreat from them. Although it produced some sceptical responses from contributors and critics alike, the *RFBBM* anthology had already begun to identify how this mode of engagement might be achieved.

Avant-Garde Engineering: Blueprinting Social Change in *Readies for Bob Brown's Machine*

Writing to James Farrell shortly after the publication of the *RFBBM* anthology, Bob Brown complained that '[t]he damned book cost over $300 and I went bust while it was coming out'.[56] In light of the deepening economic crisis, Farrell and other politically left-wing *RFBBM* contributors also began to question the cultural value of the readies project. The Minnesota-based socialist writer and publisher B. C. Hagglund worried that 'in a capitalist society', the reading machine might 'drown the sub-bourgeoisie in a sea of forgetfulness'.[57] The renowned Anarchist activist, intellectual, editor and memoirist Alexander Berkman, who Brown approached for an endorsement, harboured similar concerns.[58] Berkman praised Bob's innovation and resourcefulness, but preferred an invention 'that would cause people to read less and think more'.[59] Their correspondence indicates that a heated exchange ensued, and that Brown polemically defended his own socialist credentials, while attacking others'. However, Bob seems to have apologised, and Berkman praised him for his 'intellectual integrity' in acknowledging his error.[60] True to form, Brown used the setback as an opportunity to reconsider his trajectory and reformulate the readies project accordingly. Indeed, Hagglund thought that the readies could be re-imagined to provide the 'stepping stones to something better', and identified works by James T. Farrell his brother John as 'the real stuff' that might fuel such a project.[61] Combined with work by other vanguardists, the formal radicalism and technicities of the American superrealist readies might enhance rather than detract from the social realist impulse underpinning their vanguardism. Taking these readies as their blueprint, what if *transition*'s 'Revolution of the Word' could be aligned with revolutionary left-wing politics? What if, by shifting their priorities, the Browns could develop the counter-servile technicities of the readies into a socially transformative ensemble, as Hagglund had suggested?

The Browns would eventually pursue this strategy by taking the readies project to Russia in 1935–7. In the intervening period from 1932–4, however, they took other steps – both conceptual and practical – to bring their ideas, writing, publishing and politics into closer harmony. As Craig Saper argues, 'the readies variant of modernism' did not merely advance an apolitical aestheticism, or reactionary cultural elitism – it also 'create[d] a psychological social realism through experimental forms'.[62] This section focuses on the techno-bathetic works of writer-editors such as Gertrude Stein, and the new localist/American superrealist network of *Blues*, *Pagany*, *Contempo*, and *Contact* magazines; in *RFBBM*, these readies proposed counter-servile technicities and social energetics with which to oppose prevailing hierarchies of sex, race, ethnicity and class. The works of the Farrells epitomised the powerful but ethically fraught intersections between socio-technics and socio-politics in Machine Age American cities. Together, these works created a framework with which the Browns contextualised the continuing development of the readies in Russia and the United States throughout the 1930s.

In his correspondence with James T. Farrell, Bob observed a superficial levelling effect between 'experimental' texts and 'readified' conventional ones.[63] The disruptive impacts of reading 'machinewise' produced a slippage not only in aesthetic boundaries between avant-garde and mainstream print cultures, but, in some cases, between the dissenting politics and sexualities of those vanguards, and prevailing hegemonies in Western culture. In other words, because they scrambled standard semiotic contexts and hierarchies, the readies might be able to do the same thing to cultural ones. Laurence Vail and Ezra Pound responded to these Machine Age anxieties by identifying and attacking cultural difference, on the one hand, and hyperbolically reinstating gender and racial hierarchies, on the other. Nevertheless, the prospect of forging a new 'machine language' co-operatively, and transculturally, suggested a valuable opportunity to other contributors. The most prominent of these is the canonical, lesbian, Jewish American modernist Gertrude Stein.

Stein had self-published *Lucy Church Amiably* under her own 'Plain Edition' imprint in 1930, and corresponded enthusiastically with Brown about the conceptual and practical details concerning the readies and their other literary projects.[64] Her contribution to *RFBBM*, the historically revisionist narrative 'We Came', is unsurprisingly one of the strongest in the collection, not only because of its distinctive syntax and word play, but because of its riposte to various chauvinisms in the collection. As Paul Stephens argues, '[w]hereas Pound's translation parodically presumes that "Joe," his assumed everyman reader, will share his suspicion of "Persian buggahs," Stein's "We Came" offers a flexible "we".'[65] And whereas Pound was suspicious of the masses, Stein sardonically cautioned readers to '[b]e careful not at all=History is made by a very=Few who are important'.[66] Like the fragile machines of the New York Dadas, she presents history as a faulty apparatus rather than a well-oiled engine, which was 'open' and permeable, with its 'meaning' applicable to the quotidian rhythms of everyday life.

Unlike some readies, where tone is difficult to detect, Stein's well-known narrative strategies provide a useful context for decoding the rhetorical frame of 'We Came'. For example, while her anti-patriarchal argument is entirely serious, she skilfully deployed humour to perform her cultural critique. Her well-aimed quip, 'History must again be=Caught and taught and=Not be that it is tiring=To play with balls', identifies ridicule as a persistent vulnerability of phallocentrism.[67] Yet Stein's bathetic strategies also target her own personal history, which included the capacious but (by conventional measures) unsuccessful recent publication of her sprawling family history in *The Making of Americans*.[68] In this respect, 'We Came' was part of a bathetic crisis of representation in transatlantic discourse networks that many readies contributors struggled with. As part of a group that stood (to paraphrase Peter Nicholls) 'at a tangent' to 'other modernisms', where did groups outside the dominant hegemonies of high modernism fit into the wider arc of cultural history?[69] And could the readies provide a back door into its systems of representation?

Charles Henri Ford's readie 'Letter From the Provinces' strikes a similar challenge against gender and hetero-normativities as Stein's.[70] His camera eye pans the scene in soft focus, nurturing rather than attacking the gay subcultures it surveys. The readies format is central to this project, because in dispensing with capitals and transitional phrases Ford also undermines linguistic and grammatical hierarchies. The final readie that Brown received for the volume was 'Love Story' by the modernist writer and editor Kathleen Tankersley Young. Bisexual, feminist and politically progressive, Young was frequently associated with the Harlem Renaissance, but launched her career in the same Southwestern circles as Macleod and co-edited *Blues* with Ford and Parker Tyler.[71] The readies provided a socio-technical framework for Young's feminist critiques of cultural hierarchies, which frequently connected her affective landscapes and the non-human world. Her contribution 'Love Story' explores a failed transatlantic relationship unfolding against the bait-and-switch culture of the Caribbean tourist economy. Written in the past tense, the narrative dissolves in 'a fog of gulls', signalling that in the wake of the 1929 financial crash, escapist tourism was disappearing, along with the post-war prosperity of the 1920s.[72] As Young's example demonstrates, the technicity of the readies was particularly attuned to the effects of transportation and communications technologies, which assumed an intensely politicised valence in the Great Depression. In the *RFBBM* anthology, the communist writer Rue Menken's 'Cracked' depicted a high-risk 1930s' replay of Young's romance, but the travellers were illegal passengers on a freight train fleeing economic hardship, rather than tourists on vacation.[73] However, the most brutal accounts of life in Depression-era machine ensembles feature in James T. Farrell's readies 'Sylvester Mc Gullick' and 'Jeff', and his brother John's 'One of the Many'.

As I discussed in the previous chapter, critics have tended to overlook the socio-political agenda of the *RFBBM* anthology, and to focus instead on its articulations of essentialist, racist, sexist and other prejudices.[74] Stephens is correct when he insists that both the publisher and contributors 'should rightly be held to account for their content', but as he also points out, in some cases, the contributors actively contested and parodied the hierarchies and normativities that such discourses could articulate.[75] This can be true even when the readies incorporated bigoted language. Unlike some contributors who actively baited the censor, the Farrells negotiated carefully with Brown about how to avoid undue attention.[76] The Farrells' language in their readies *is* frequently racist and sexist, but it was essential to their social critique – as was the readies format, which made a virtue of the radical 'compression' of the readies genre criticised by other socialist writers such as Manuel Komroff, Berkman and Hagglund.[77] The socialist objection to the readies project was that although its mechanised texts might represent aspects of mass consciousness, the resulting cultural products could achieve neither the frictionless communion that Jolas called for in *transition*'s 'Revolution of the Word', nor the accessible political texts demanded by revolutionary communism. However, the Farrells were not necessarily interested in either of these outcomes as a main objective: their readies articulated a visceral *cri-de-coeur* from the classes enmeshed in the grimy cogs of Machine Age capitalism.

In James T. Farrell's readies, he takes a particular interest in white ethnic minorities, especially Irish, Catholic and Jewish groups, an interest he developed in his acclaimed *Studs Lonigan* trilogy. In the novels, he unflinchingly, and not unsympathetically, details the nativist, racist and increasingly fascist sympathies of Studs's anti-Semitic father Paddy Lonigan and his generation, and the more conflicted articulations of these tendencies in Studs's own.[78] As Ann Douglas rightly notes, the trilogy details 'Studs's miseducation as he is indoctrinated with the pseudo-facts of his own condition', namely 'that he is "white"', and thus, in both his neighbourhood and country, 'there was always someone the poorest, least successful European immigrant could feel superior to'. However, because 'the lines of ethnicity and race' were becoming 'permeable and shifting' in the Machine Age, Studs's 'insistence on this point of superiority becomes all the more critical'.[79] These brutally delineated hierarchies emerged in tandem with monopoly capitalism, because racism, misogyny and other forms of bigotry became entrenched and even permissible refuges from the inequities of capitalist society for various ethnic and socio-economic groups. The festering tensions in Studs's neighbourhood erupt frequently in the novel, just as they do in the Farrells' readies, as episodes of inter-ethnic, inter-racial and sexual violence.

The readies' deliberately rigid nativist perspective compresses and intensifies those episodes. In 'Sylvester Mc Gullick', James Farrell uses the readies format to interleave the protagonist's waking fantasies of financial and sexual conquest, misogynistic violence, salacious headlines and vague daydreams of 'freedom'. Unlike other readies, in Farrell's, mass transit is yet another form of servility rather than a form of liberation. Headlines from 'the Chicago Daily Tribune' scream about murders, and Sylvester uses them as an excuse to flirt with a female commuter as they are '[c]rushed in the I. C. train'.[80] Ironically, given the context, the woman explains that 'I'm uh private secretary an' I work for Mr. Young heze uh railroad president', while Sylvester explains that he works as a clerk for the 'Continental Screw Company'.[81] The characters' ties to industrial infrastructure and manufacturing elide with Sylvester's sexual desire and combine to suggest a system rigged against its workers, whom it 'screws' on a 'Continental' scale. The two make a date to meet at the Chicago Public Library, before 'Sylvester the slave go[es] back to his big books' of legers, which detail servile economic narratives that he apprehends only too well.[82]

Each one of Sylvester's encounters with print culture in urban spaces stimulates desire and anxiety, and he responds with an acute rage that unfolds only through the relentless, mechanised stream of free indirect discourse, and occasional bursts of dialogue. In the context of the dash-laden, telegraphic readies format, 'Sylvester Mc Gullick' provides a running ticker tape that charts the damaged psyches of a few citizens exploited by a mechanised, capitalist society. When the narrative is complete, it simply loops backs to the beginning, as the 'alarm clock shrieks . . . last night's sheiks become to-day's sheep'.[83] In keeping with the Naturalist idiom, Sylvester is both a product and victim of his environment. However, he is also a participant in its creation, as he splices the episodes together in a rhythmic '. . . tick tick tick . . .', which creates his own stilted take on Machine Age life, and allows for fleeting moments of individuating leisure, generosity and humour. Nevertheless, the mechanistic gait of his consciousness never abates, and he is unable to convert his intuitive understanding of the rhythms and infrastructure of Machine Age culture – tracked and instantiated in the readie itself – into a critical engagement with its vicissitudes.

Farrell's second readie explores the fate of another young man from a similar neighbourhood who, unlike Sylvester, actually becomes a criminal. The *bildung* charts the career of 'Jeff the fat jewboy . . . jeff the fatass of Fifty Eighth Street' who 'wanted to be like the other kids . . . wanted to be one of them' but 'was too big and fat'.[84] Of course, it's more likely that the kids bullied Jeff because he was Jewish, and that his physical difference serves as an analogy for his ethnic difference. Jeff endures the cruel ethnic stereotyping that he is subjected to by amplifying those characteristics in his own behaviour. By becoming a pimp, he not only extracts a kind of vengeance on his neighbourhood but also finds a way of asserting superiority over other oppressed minorities (including but not limited to African Americans). Inevitably, Jeff pays for his transgressions, as he contracts syphilis and dies.[85] Yet the narrative is a critique rather than an endorsement of anti-Semitism, racism and misogyny in Chicago's working-class neighbourhoods, which he would expand in the *Studs Lonigan* trilogy. The difference is that, shorn of the novels' broader Naturalist framework, the socio-political context for these readies is even harder to detect.

In keeping with their interstitial late modernist aesthetics, American superrealist and new localist formations did not view Naturalism and modernism as incompatible commitments but, rather, as equally valid and even complementary methods of navigating consciousness.[86] In Farrell's hybrid modernism, as Douglas rightly argues of *Studs Lonigan*, 'consciousness is not a delight, nor a refuge, for the large masses of people who have no real epistemological mastery over life'; rather, 'stream of consciousness serves instead as the anxious reflection of social programming and [the characters'] inchoate desire to escape it'.[87] For this reason, 'Farrell adopts, even respects, Paddy and Studs's limits as the novel's limits'; if Farrell supplied a clear alternative perspective, then how could 'the reader understand a point of view which posits a well-neigh alternativeless universe?'[88] Farrell had made this point even more forcefully in the readies. Using their compressed formal register and technicity, 'Sylvester' and 'Jeff' create myopic subjectivities that are inseparable from Farrell's critique of capitalist culture. However, his readies, and those of his brother, must be read in sequence for that critique to become apparent.

In 'One of the Many', the Farrell brothers adopt a common Naturalist trope of eliding commercial machinery with retail workers, and manufactured commodities with manufactured lives. One by one, they all 'wear down . . . like broken machines . . .'.[89] The readie is a direct and relentless critique of 'BUSINESS ACTIVITY', and even though he promotes social change, the 'everyman' narrator, John Smith, is inherently part of the problem.[90] For example, when he notices that workers appear to support the egregious claims of politicians that they hear on the radio, he mistakes their lack of criticism for ignorance. However, the Farrells suggest that in his privileged position, Smith cannot or will not recognise the risk that dissent poses to workers – a position made all the more untenable because of the precarious terms of his subordinates' employment, which he himself documents as part of his job. Rather than using technology to transcend the political pressures of the 1930s, then, this readie splices workers' experiences, present and historical, into the cultural narrative offered by the ruling classes, and the bourgeois management classes. In 'One of the Many', the ringing 'alarm clock' that condemned Sylvester Mc Gullick to another day of servility becomes a political wake-up call to Smith, alerting him to his own complicity in the system he ineffectually rails against.[91] In the context of the impending 1933 presidential elections, the Farrells' collaborative readie is a spur to convert documentary evidence into proportionate affective responses by harnessing workers' technicities. In doing so, they hoped to translate those responses – eventually – into targeted political action.

The techno-bathetic readies in *RFBBM* were an extended exercise in literary prototyping that envisaged a hybrid form of politically engaged avant-garde modernism. They practiced a kind of modernist cryptography designed to provoke and eventually defeat the censor and proposed new technicities with which to challenge the hierarchies articulated by post-war socio-technical ensembles, which had begun to break down in the Great Depression. Yet elements of this palpable work remained speculative, as the promise of a working readies ensemble remained a ghost in the Machine Age. The Browns sought to fulfil that promise. After the publication of *RFBBM*, they returned to America, forced back home by their increasingly desperate financial circumstances. There, they undertook the practical business of implementing their new Readies Revolution, and the future directions of social organisation that it augured.

Rose Brown's Reading Machine: Rebuilding the Readies Project in 1932

The Browns returned to New York via London in April 1932 and had settled in the Chelsea neighbourhood of Manhattan by June. After Bob's bruising exchange with Alexander Berkman, the Browns had a clearer vision of their socio-technical ambitions. In his *RFBBM* 'Appendix', Bob enumerated the enormous savings in 'paper, ink, binding and manual labour' the readies project could realise, and eliminating this burden could help writers and publishers 'become independent of advertising which today carries the cost of the cheap reading matter purveyed exclusively in the interests of the advertiser'.[92] The readies could radically expand access to knowledge for workers, while compressing the space occupied in their homes. Most importantly, they could also transliterate writing in a format that corresponded to workers' technicities of reading. Thanks to the ingenuity of Rose, her collaborator, Hugo Knudsen, and Bob's cousin, Clare Brackett, evidence suggests that she produced a working prototype micrographic reading machine by the autumn of 1932.

The Browns reconnected with many of their old friends in New York, including Stuart Davis and William Carlos Williams, and they made new ones, including Nathanael 'Pep' West, who edited the resurrected *Contact* magazine with Williams and first coined the term

'American Super-realism'.[93] They also held family reunions, and on 28 June 1932, Bob's cousin Clare Brackett wrote to arrange a meeting between the Browns and Stoll, which he hoped would help them 'come to a better understanding regarding the reading machine'.[94] No further details of that meeting survive, but it was probably here that Stoll presented the Browns with the NMPC's prototype model reading machine. This device had functional electro-mechanics, and possibly a magnification system, but did not include the micrographic readies medium, which Stoll abandoned work on. However, with help from the Danish offset printing pioneer Hugo Knudsen, Rose either completed or modified the NMPC prototype, and finally produced a micrographic readie using standard 35 mm nitrate film and an elaborate photo-composition method. The Browns' papers at UCLA and SIU Carbondale reveal a complex meta-formational project involving multiple collaborators, including high-profile members of the burgeoning microfilm industry with whom they were making contact following their return to New York.

In a letter to his friend and *RFBBM* contributor Theodore Pratt, who had seen the Saunders Prototype reading machine in Cagnes-sur-Mer in 1931 and was now based in New York, Bob described Rose's collaboration with Knudsen:

> My cousin in Detroit [Brackett] made a model, which I have and Rose made the first moving readie film - - all of [Voltaire's] *Candide* on a three or four foot roll, which is in the machine now. [. . .] Rose had it done in one line on Teletype, pasted it on a roll of wall paper and Knudsen photographed it down to invisibility. Better come out and see it.[95]

The teletype system could send and receive typed messages using the telephone system and electro-mechanical typewriting devices, which were fed by long reels of paper instead of single sheets.[96] In his unpublished August 1937 essay 'Reading Machines', Bob provided more details about how Rose 'got the idea' of combining her knowledge of interior design, craft, photography and writing with leading-edge technology to transform a classic text into a micrographic 'readie' film:

> It took her the entire length and breadth of a whole floor we occupied in 20th Street, seven pots of paste, eight rolls of white wallpaper and several weeks to get that monumental teletyped job pasted up, and then she was months working with camera experts, trying to get the white elephant photographed in miniature. Everyone said it couldn't be done, except for Hugo Knudsen, the offset man on Bleeker street, who took such an excited interest in it that he did the whole job for nothing.[97]

Bob's recollection of the Browns' Chelsea apartment is consistent with their activities in the summer of 1932, and together with evidence from Bob's Guggenheim Fellowship application, his correspondence and essays establish a fairly precise timeline for Rose and Knudsen's prototyping work. Following their meeting with Brackett and Stoll in July, Bob began work on a John Simon Guggenheim Fellowship application in the field of literature, dated 5 August 1932, in which he claimed to have produced 'a working model' of the reading machine.[98] Although it did not provide much technical detail, Bob's Guggenheim Fellowship application states that he was working on perfecting 'a reading machine' with a new speed-reading 'font' that would help 'writers develop a new optical technique which may be better suited to these radio-airplane-television times'.[99] Even in August, this would have been true, since Saunders had already produced a working prototype; however, Bob probably submitted a more complete version closer to the fellowship application deadline (1 November 1932).[100] Bob reported showing the new device to Watson Davis, the Director of the Science Service in Washington DC, who was also considered an important supporter of the microfilm industry, and Dr Robert G. Binkley of the American Council of Learned Societies' Joint Committee on Materials for Research who also reached out to Bob for further information about the reading machine for a report on micrographic technologies in October 1932.[101] If Bob's accounts in 'Reading Machines' are accurate – and the archival record suggests that they are – then Rose and Knudsen would have completed their work to produce a functional second reading machine before November 1932.

Based in his print shop on Bleeker Street, Knudsen was a 'pioneer in the field of photo-engraving' who invented the Knudsen process for 'photograph[ing] color images directly onto plates ready for printing by offset lithography'.[102] He held multiple patents for his work and was active in Greenwich Village's socialist politics and arts networks since 1913, which is how the Browns first met him. Crucially, he was also the brother-in-law of *Others* and *Broom* editor Alfred Kreymborg, and a good friend of Alfred Stieglitz, who relied on Knudsen's offset photo printing processes in his Pictorialist work.[103] Knudsen was also corresponding with the Eastman Kodak Company in 1932 during the same time period in which he was collaborating with Rose.[104] In fact, the technological solution that he helped Rose develop seems to have been an artisanal version of microphotography processes already being commercialised by Kodak, who were preparing to launch their Recordak microfilm reader with the New York Public Library the following year. An accomplished photographer herself, Rose had acquired a detailed knowledge of photography, both as art and as technology in the 1920s.[105]

Given her background in professional interior design, which she practised in the Browns' early days in South America, it is likely that she also collaborated with Hiler during her time in Cagnes, possibly as a visiting faculty member of Atelier Hiler. In fact, those interior design skills were just as important to the development of her machine as her photographic background, since she created the 'first moving readie film' by pasting it 'on a roll of wallpaper'.[106]

Rejecting Stoll's concerns about the instability of nitrate-based film, Rose and Knudsen seem to have used conventional stock in their readies prototype, which would have worked with existing plans and apparatus Bob developed with NMPC. On the sketch for the readies prototype in Figure 4.3, Bob provided a synopsis of the magnification apparatus. He describes 'a 15-watt lamp; a condenser lens; a shield for restricting the light; and a magnifying lens to project the print on a frosted glass shield'.[107] This ground glass system could be scavenged from any number of commercial cameras, and could be packaged by adapting existing designs for consumer information and home entertainment products. The light source was necessary, however, because the reel and motor assemblies would restrict the daylight, which most ground glass systems require. In Rose's reading machine, she used a battery to power the lamp for space efficiency (no mains transformer was necessary), to cut down on heat and to make the unit portable. When the Browns eventually took this model with them to Russia in the summer of 1935, Rose asked Bob's mother Cora Brown to send them 'the reading machine' along with two Kodak cameras and some other personal items before they departed. In her letter, Rose briefly described a 'blue metal cylinder which goes with [the reading machine] – about the size of a cigar'; she cautioned that 'the machine is useless for demonstration without this part' because it 'holds [a] battery which makes the light'.[108] Rose did not go into further detail about the mechanism, but this account confirms some of its key features, and gives some sense of its scale and functionalities. Given the level of technical information Rose provided, the urgency and frequency of their letters to Cora (Bob called the 'reading machine [. . .] indispensable' to their 'trip to the Soviet Union') and their subsequent development activities of the readies project, it seems difficult to imagine that a functional prototype did not exist.[109]

Neither Bob nor Rose provided any detail about the enclosure for the second machine, but an illustration for Ezra Pound's 1937 article 'Deflation Benefit' in the travel magazine *Globe* provides a possible clue about its form. In this essay, Pound wondered if anything concrete had ever resulted from 'Bob Brown's propaganda for a "reading machine"' – an invention that Pound 'unkindly summarised as "the conviction that if we

Figure 4.4 Anonymous [Hilaire Hiler], *Bob Brown's Readio*, in Ezra Pound, 'Deflation Benefit', *Globe* 1.5 (August 1937): 66–71 (p. 68).

only read FAST enough, we needn't bother to understand ANYthing"'.[110] Figure 4.4 is the second illustration of the Browns' reading machine to appear in a specialist periodical. Dubbed 'Bob Brown's Readio', the device resembles a consumer radio receiver, but instead of a frequency indicator the viewing screen displays a scrolling text behind the protective glass, which is flanked by two knobs to control speed and direction. This illustration might be dismissed as an interesting but irrelevant doodle except for two points: firstly, it closely resembles Bob's long-standing plans to market the readies project in a compact package similar to other consumer electronics; and, secondly, the illustration was almost certainly done by Hilaire Hiler, who had joined *Globe* as a staff illustrator and was credited with illustrations in that issue. Hiler visited New York and other US cities periodically following the Browns' return in the summer of 1932 for art exhibitions and other commitments, and moved back to the United States permanently in September 1934.[111] As a close friend and professional collaborator on the readies project, he probably would have seen any version of the machine the Browns had available, given the opportunity. Although Bob does not appear to have used the term 'Readio', in his 1937 'Reading Machines' essay drafts, he describes a unit with 'one continuous line' of text scrolling before 'the reader's eyes at a speed he can regulate with a knob just like the volume of sound on a radio'.[112] The similarity between this description and the functionalities Hiler depicts in 'Bob Brown's Readio' suggest that his illustration is a plausible representation of Rose Brown's reading machine.

In his readies manifestos, Bob connected the 'illuminated manuscripts'[113] of the Middle Ages and Renaissance to the 'huge illuminated letters' of outdoor commercial advertising.[114] However, it was Rose who provided the technology with which to flick the switch. Together with Knudson, she not only solved the problem of the readies medium that had supposedly sunk the project, but also used that process to demonstrate a potential market for the readies, as well as perform a kind of social critique. In this respect, readiefying *Candide* was a canny decision by Rose. Her selection dovetailed with industry-wide initiatives to repackage canonical literature in affordable formats, which was led by influential publishers such as Boni & Liveright, who also had a track record of publishing modernist writers.[115] There were also practical advantages: the novella is relatively short and episodic, so the 'three or four foot roll' of microfilmed text that Bob described is realistic, given that the text occupied multiple lines (see Fig. 4.3).[116] In addition, *Candide* had broader thematic and political resonances in the Great Depression. The Enlightenment political satire was a picaresque featuring a privileged protagonist who travelled the world (including several ports of call, such as Buenos Aires, where the Browns had lived). In his quest for '*paradis terrestre*', Candide navigated a range of catastrophes that exposed the brutal corruption throughout Western societies and institutions, as well as in their colonial outposts. However, Candide also made attempts to alleviate those injustices, and, however naively, to suggest alternatives to Western imperialism.[117] Rose had a particular interest in the escalating global crises resulting from ongoing colonial rule. While in Paris, she had launched a new career as a journalist, and wrote on both culinary and political topics. Indeed, she often combined the subjects in articles that 'did not simply describe the food but showed how it appears in a web of relations, practices, and economies'.[118] Throughout 1931, she drew on her academic background in sociology and economics in frequent discussions with her mentor Emma Goldman as she surveyed the fall-out of their adopted country's colonial policies. She had researched and published an account of the 1931 famine in Niger, which claimed over 15,000 lives, and which was partly caused by the French government's negligence. For Rose, Voltaire's narratives no doubt cast light on Bob's precarious situation, and how unpredictable reversals of personal fortune could have far-reaching consequences that extended far beyond the individual, to fold in the legacies of their broader sociopolitical milieu.

Rose's readie 'Dis', as I discussed in the previous chapter, was a feminist expression of American superrealism that details working-class life in Hell's Kitchen. Like Kay Boyle's and the Farrell Brothers' readies, 'Dis' performed a documentary critique of Machine Age urban culture rooted in the quotidian and embodied technicities of the readies. Rose insisted that Machine Age technicities such as those augured by the readies could liberate rather than further marginalise women and involve them in future technical innovations. Her adaptation of Voltaire was an extension of this practice, since she, like Bob, conceived of the reading machine as a means of disseminating canonical texts to working-class Americans, with a view to priming them for social revolution. For such 'classics', the readies could, in theory, help transliterate an otherwise inaccessible text by virtue of its contemporary format. Voltaire rendered as a billboard-style ticker might one day reach people like the 'Rousseau-shy-Canadian-family-in-Hells - - - - Kitchen', whom the 'ladylibrarians' – custodians of literature in the neighbourhoods Rose writes about, whose own ability to assist needy families was constrained by their own desperate circumstances – currently could not.[119] The radio could reach out to millions, so why not a Readio?

Accordingly, the Readio accompanied the Browns on an extraordinary journey across the length and breadth of America, the Atlantic, through Russia, and quite possibly through South America. The Readio itself appears to have been lost in the early 1940s. For a time, it resided in the personal collection Max Sherover. A polymath inventor, socialist activist and brilliant multilinguist, Sherover became president of the Linguaphone Corporation in America, which sold language instruction courses on records, and he employed the Browns as sales agents in the mid-1930s. Sherover also introduced Bob to key players in the microfilm industry, and exhibited the Readio at a microfilm industry trade show at the Waldorf Astoria in 1937 (as I discuss in later sections, his involvement with the readies did not end there).[120] The machine was either lost or abandoned when the Browns travelled between North and South America in the early 1940s, but Rose's readie film survived until her death in 1952.[121] However, in the mid-1930s, the device still had a crucial role to play in the Browns' socio-political project. Voltaire famously concluded *Candide* with his protagonist's declaration, '*il faut cultiver notre jardin*'.[122] In 1933–4, the Browns took a similar but slightly broader approach when they rejected their metropolitan literary careers for a rural life that combined hard labour, pedagogy and socio-political organisation with

Commonwealth College, a new socialist college with strong ties to the Communist Party, organised labour and civil rights movements.

'The Russian Double-Cross': the Readio, Commonwealth College and the 'Soviet of Technicians'

In December 1932, the Browns moved to the affluent neighbourhood of Atlantic Highlands, New Jersey. Their correspondence from the period suggests that, although they were initially doing well after the move, by the spring of 1933 Bob began spiralling into depression and alcoholism, and their relationships with friends and family were beginning to strain.[123] Corresponding with like-minded and increasingly politicised peers such as Manuel Komroff, who had moved to Cuba (but soon relocated to Hollywood), the Browns balanced culinary writing projects with their political commitments. Bob made a breakthrough when the publishers Farrar and Rhinehart paid him a substantial advance to write 'a book about living on a commune that eventually appeared with the commune's own publishing arm as *Toward a Bloodless Revolution*'.[124] In the spring and summer of 1934, the Browns worked the commune's land in New Llano, Louisiana, in exchange for food and board, and continued this arrangement when they joined the faculty at the newly-relocated Commonwealth College at Mena, Arkansas, in November 1934.[125] On the surface, the Browns' departure from the city appeared to be a classic rejection of their techno-modernism in favour of a gritty proletarian realism grounded in practical experience. In reality, it was actually a shift in emphasis, which prioritised the development of revolutionary social assemblages over (but not at the expense of) technological ones. At Commonwealth, the reading machine continued its evolution, not in other guises, but in coeval forms. The college provided the Browns with the ideal platform for developing an idea they had harboured since leaving France: building the readies project in collaboration with Soviet Russia.

Commonwealth College was 'a center of communitarian farm and labor efforts', but upon their arrival the Browns transformed its modest in-house publication *The Commonwealth Fortnightly* into the Associated Little Magazines network, an extraordinary literary-political clearing house with more than 100 journals with a subscriber base of over 22,000 readers.[126] Bob identified a common 'United Red Front stretching from Brooklyn Heights to Beverly Hills' that merged in a number of fugitive journals, but because of their 'erratic' publishing schedules and disparate, overlapping subscriber and advertising bases, he concluded that 'a clearing house of information concerning them is badly needed'.[127] The Browns were ideally placed to create Associated Little Magazines, and they set about transforming the *Fortnightly* into a meta-formational 'nucleus' combining political advocacy and business intelligence – cross-promotion and content development.[128] The Museum of Social Change was an equally ambitious enterprise. Designed and curated by the Browns in collaboration with a wide network of influential cultural figures, and pictured here for the first time since it burned down on 16 April 1939 (Fig. 4.5), the Museum exposed the insidious effects of industrial capitalism through a dialectical and dialogic arrangement of photographs, tools, collages, posters, books and other objects.[129] Although it was destroyed by a lightning strike, the Museum transformed the literary capital of the modernist archive into a multimodal critique of monopoly capitalism. It was, in effect, a vernacular machine for reading society, and for stimulating revolution.

Figure 4.5 Harris W. Nowell, The Museum of Social Change [Photograph], in Anonymous, 'A Red College in the Bible Belt Where Future Labor Leaders Work to Pay Way', *Milwaukee Journal*, 5 May 1935: n.p.; clipping from B5, F3, UCLA Brown. The 'students' are the Browns.

A few years earlier, B. C. Hagglund had written that 'the value of such a [reading] machine in a socialistic society cannot be questioned', and recommended that Bob 'get the machine started in Russia'.[130] When the Browns were settled in Arkansas at Commonwealth with Cora, they began planning their first educational group tour of the Soviet Union.[131] As they did, Bob's thoughts turned back to the Readio they brought with them from New York, and to the revolution they hoped it would stimulate. In December 1934, he wrote to Bennett Cerf, the Vice President of Boni & Liveright, to propose 'a new anthology for my Reading Machine', together with a range of other potential projects. He explained that his 'reading machine will be used first in Russia, as soon as the cultural program gets going. I feel sure I could get our leading writers to contribute reading machine experiments, as the expatriates did in my French edition' of *RFBBM*.[132] The two trips that the Browns organised to Russia with the World Tourists travel agency united nearly every strand of their cultural and political work. They were also a means of making money: by 1935, Russo-American tours had become well-worn and reasonably profitable tourist destinations, as well as 'showcases' of revolutionary Russia, taking in factories, farms, galleries and Museums of the Revolution. In March 1935, World Tourists Inc. offered a new series of tour packages to Russia in the radical left-wing journal *The New Masses*, led by the Browns and the Russian-born American Constructivist artist Louis Lozowick.[133] The Browns' trip included four weeks of study at the Summer Session of Moscow University, departing on 29 June on the *SS* Britannic and returning on the *SS* Aquitania on 31 August. Travellers on the tour included the commercially and critically acclaimed Armenian-American novelist William Saroyan, and Nancy Cunard, who briefly joined en route. In addition to the usual range of cultural destinations, their group visited 'workers' clubs', which sounded rather like the Museum for Social Change, since they featured 'the relics of another day in sharp contrast to the new';[134] the new tours also marketed Russia's rapid technological development.

Although Russians often fetishised America's technological superiority, the Soviets were seen increasingly as technological revolutionaries as well as political ones. As Barnaby Harran has incisively noted, there was a certain irony involved in the Russo-American cultural exchanges taking place in the 1920s to early 1930s, since American artists who embraced revolutionary communism often did so to protest the excesses of their own nation's industrial complexes. By undertaking a 'Russian journey, many former Americans in Paris [. . .] confronted an intellectual, political, and cultural discourse that saw the keys to Soviet success in industrialization, rationalization and efficiency. Fleeing America in Paris, they found that "Amerikanizm"', with its zeal for 'standardization' and 'technological modernity', was actually 'inescapable in Russia'.[135] However, many Americans began to share in the Soviets' sublime enthusiasm for technology. Indeed, in the twilight of such exchanges in the mid-1930s, professional tour leaders such as Lozowick and the Browns actively tapped into this technophilic zeitgeist. Promotional material for the World Tourists emphasised the Browns' technical credentials, including their connections with Max Sherover's Linguaphone company.[136] In one pamphlet, Bob also announced that he was 'the inventor of the Reading Machine'.[137] The pedagogical emphasis of the tours also focused on science and technology, and one of the highlights of the trip was a series of seminars at Moscow University and the Moscow Polytechnic Museum, where the Browns hoped to identify Russian collaborators for the next phase of the readies project. Although the tour ended in August, the Browns stayed on until September as they investigated the partnership further.[138]

For the travellers on the Browns' Russian tour, the trip seems to have been a resounding success. According to their correspondence, the group was particularly impressed by technical developments they witnessed in Russia, and with the Moscow Polytechnic Museum in particular.[139] This institution was attractive not only because it was a repository of science and engineering advances, but also because its lecture theatre was a forum for a wide array of cultural debate. This included not only the expected debates about science and engineering, but also served as a forum for the Moscow Inventors' Society and a wide spectrum of artistic activities, including early avant-garde performances by the Russian Futurist poet Vladimir Mayakovsky.[140] Although many American visitors projected their own fantasies on the carefully managed, pre-packaged experiences, in many respects the Moscow Polytechnic Museum lived up to the billing. It hosted a permeable, co-creative environment in which inventions could be debated and developed based on their merits and not the amount of financial or social capital behind them.

In an unpublished manuscript written in Cagnes-sur-Mer, Brown had previously imagined that 'in Russia some writer is tinkering with a motor and a roll of text, trying to help reading out of the book into a larger sphere'.[141] In Russia, he found that the Constructivist movement, as Harran points out, 'heralded a Soviet machine age, a technophile workers' state in which artists were producers and in which art was an everyday life currency of the masses'.[142] However, these ideas had first taken root in America, where Veblen had developed a related strain of argument in 1919. His writing was rediscovered by the left as the impacts of the Great Depression began to deepen, particularly in

The New Masses, where Brown placed several articles. Many left-wing writers noted that Veblen's pragmatist vision of a heterogeneous techno-proletariat closely matched the experiences of their peers, as specialised workers were forced to cross and change specialisations out of practical necessity rather than a sense of revolutionary zeal. As such, his proposal for a 'soviet of technicians' resonated with many skilled workers across multiple disciplines.[143] Writing in *The New Masses* in 1934, Earl Browder, the leader of the Communist Party USA (CPUSA), argued that '[u]nrealistic as Veblen's dream was, he should by no means be saddled with responsibility for the recurrent vulgarization of his suggestions that are propagated by the technocrats [. . .] The engineers and technicians are themselves a most heterogeneous group.' Browder goes on to describe how, since the Great Depression, many of this group 'have become taxi-drivers, doormen at night clubs and hotels, waiters, etc., displacing former workers in these positions and throwing them into the ranks of the unemployed'. Browder reminds his readers that Veblen called for workers to unify in the face of such class struggle: 'their only future lies in identifying themselves with the working class'.[144]

As Cecilia Tichi rightly states, Veblen depicted a 'world in class conflict', but 'not between those who control the means of production and a proletariat empowered only by its capacity to work'. Rather, Veblen saw classes 'divided by their habits of thinking', and aligned business managers, and their wider professional networks, against scientists, workers and technicians 'whose way of thinking' had 'evolved' in tandem 'with the machine process itself'.[145] In doing so, Veblen recognised a point that Simondon would later develop: under capitalism, business managers and bankers were in some ways more susceptible to technological alienation than workers.[146] As management principles grew less context specific, managers frequently did not have first-hand experience with or detailed knowledge of the machines that generated value in organisations.

Veblen's account of class struggle, although it involved dialectics, surmounted the traditional binaries coupling class and profession with more flexible accounts of class and *technicity*. As Browder recognised, Veblen's approach emphasised the granularity and fluidity, rather than the intractable dialectics, of both class and professional affiliation. Instead of a utopian technocracy, then, Veblen's 1921 book *The Engineers and the Price System* called for 'solidarity of sentiment between the technicians and the working force engaged in transportation and in the greater underlying industries of the system', and beyond it.[147] However, this collective assemblage relied on non-servile relationships with technology – ways of working and being that had been diminished by monopoly capitalism and processes of cultural diffusion. Browder also pointed out that Veblen's concept of a 'technocracy' elided just as easily with the tenets of fascism as with those of communism. Later articles in the *New Masses* also identified how Veblen's sympathies with 'pure-racialists and anti-Semites' were at odds with the mainstream CPUSA policies, and how they provided a fillip to technocrats and the emergent far-right.[148] Nevertheless, those same articles argued against the pervasive caricatures of Veblen's theories and dialectics, which had emerged on both sides of the political divide.

Walter Ralston reminded *New Masses* readers that '[t]he social change which Veblen desired can be achieved not through the isolation of a limited group in society but through the extensive cooperation of all working groups which suffer from the system of business enterprise, or capitalism'.[149] Yet Veblen also stressed that any such change was dependent upon 'bring[ing] the underlying population to a reasonable understanding of what it is all about'.[150] Although he did not use the term, the non-servile relationship with technology that he advocated, and the pedagogical systems it required, became the foundation for the kind of socio-technical revolution he imagined. For Americans travelling to Russia, the Moscow Polytechnic Museum was the closest they would get to seeing a 'Soviet of Technicians' in action. The Browns hoped that the readies project could become the technological catalyst for such institutions in America, and according to their correspondence they had grounds for optimism.

In a 10 September 1935 letter written from Moscow to Cora Brown at Commonwealth College, Rose wrote that '[i]t looks like the Soviet would make a new model of the Reading Machine. They are meeting with us next week to consider final plans and are very enthusiastic. If they are successful [then they] will put it into mass production.'[151] Following a trip to show 'a model of our machine' to 'Tov. Cooley of the Polytechnic Museum' and the 'Inventors Society', Bob indicated that Cooley was 'working to have [the reading machine] adopted in some form or other', and the Browns were justifiably confident that their project would be taken forward.[152] This Russo-American reading machine collaboration came tantalisingly close to fulfilment, but it faltered as the idea worked its way up the Soviet hierarchy. Unfortunately, the '*Hayka n Texhnka* [sic]' rejected the readies project as unsuitable, citing nine technical and subjective objections.[153] In an undated reply, Brown answered all of these objections point by point, and added refinements to the practical functions he envisaged in the reading machine. He described a device 'equipped with notches, like a mechanical piano music roll, so certain passages can be found by pressing a button and repeating the chapter that contains it'. Acknowledging that it was bespoke technology, Brown argued that any investment in new manufacturing infrastructure would be repaid almost immediately by savings in paper, binding and storage costs, as well as the cultural benefits of reading the socialist literature distributed by these new means.

The Browns had also arranged a return tour to Russia in 1936 with the Compass Travel Bureau, so he promised to demonstrate 'a perfected model' then.[154] There does not seem to be any evidence that the Browns followed up these plans in their second visit to Russia – in fact, in a later unpublished essay he noted that after he and Rose 'lugged our latest model over to Moscow and tried to give it away', they 'found the comrades way ahead of us, for they were hitching up their own reading machines to go with television boxes, even as talkie tape has come to be the sidekick of the silent film'.[155] The 'televistic future' Bob had long anticipated in his readies writing was apparently already underway in Russia, even as the microfilm industry in the United States was taking micrography in a new direction. Nevertheless, he still wrote a piece inspired by the ongoing readies project.

Ironically – yet typically – Bob wrote his unpublished mid-1930s essay 'What the Soviet Union Means to Humanity' with a strong financial motive. The piece was for a contest run by *Soviet Russia Today* with a first prize of $500, and its title was stipulated by the judging panel, led by the novelist Erskine Caldwell. With an American superrealist involved in the contest, Bob perhaps felt encouraged to return to his readies format, which he used to describe his trip to Russia.[156] The piece preserves the vocabulary, run-on sentences, technicities and superrealist mode of his readies writing, but only occasionally features em-dashes, generally using them as connectives or in hyphenated words. In this respect, the 'Soviet Union' essay picks up the idea Bob pitched to Cerf while at Commonwealth – that a re-launched readies anthology could adapt its distinctive literary style to more explicitly social realist narrative conventions.[157] Bob performs this hybridisation in the essay as he imagines an originary technicity developing in childhood and suffusing both the human and non-human ecologies of a communist society.

In the essay, Bob describes a trip 'on a train out of Moscow', where his 'gaze became fixed on the deep crystal pools that actually were the eyes of a little Soviet citizen about two years old [. . .] and in them unrolled a televistic continuity of all that the Soviet means to everybody'.[158] The child's eyes become lenses through which a Soviet propaganda narrative plays out via tachistoscopic 'optical flash[es]' (perhaps reflecting the modifications to the scrolling mechanism he discussed with Brackett, in which word clusters could be paused and flash-scrolled, rather than streamed). Bob identifies a series of 'flashing pageant[s]' that play out the child's life, all of which emerge from 'a Pageant of Freedom from Greed'. The child is eventually 'marching free, with millions of comrades [. . .] working with tools fashioned by the collective toil of Old Social Pioneers, creating machines to make machines' and 'seeking new sciences to conquer'.[159] In an earlier draft, Brown also describes 'Young Pioneers at their self-managed building in Rostov' who made him 'understand in Esperanto how life was thrusting out for them, through their self-run radio plant, miniature railways system, shows and games'.[160] Again, Brown describes a communist revolution of the word wedded to a Veblenist vision of non-servile techno-socialism. Characteristically, his 'Soviet Union' essay suggests that technology should augment rather than blunt affective communication, especially humour. For example, he refers to the 'laughing pool of [the child's] eyes' and 'exchang[ing] a confident wink' with him.[161] Technicity passes between them as an affective impulse rather than a pedagogical exchange. This resurgent techno-bathetic impulse is an instrument of building critique as well as comradery, as he reflects in another manuscript that 'The Soviet Taught Us Democracy'. The us/US pun in that essay is typical of his contrarian strategies, which take common assumptions, such as the assumed technological superiority of America, and upend them.[162]

American superrealists frequently deployed the slippery tactics of late modernism to lace orthodox dialectics with complicating strands of irony, paradox, humour, pastiche and satire. Yet Bob's unpublished mid-1930s essays also demonstrate how techno-bathetic strategies could forge productive alignments between disciplines, generations and classes. In an unpublished lecture delivered at Commonwealth College entitled 'The Arrowhead', Brown produced a compelling synthesis of his socialist and communist politics, and the interdisciplinary aesthetics he advocated during *transition*'s 'Revolution of the Word'. Citing examples as diverse as Boyle, Caldwell, Joyce, West and Williams, Brown argued that 'art depends on good material and besides its three material dimensions has a fourth [. . .] This intangible quality, this dialectic of art is the thing itself, and this onward and upward surge is the essence by which we recognize all creative expression.'[163] Unpicking the dialectic between modernist experiment and social realist doctrine, he insisted that writing 'isn't creative if it stands still, it isn't creative if it's mere realism - - - it must be socialist realism, social realism, in faithful flux with all mind and matter if it contains the germ of creation'.[164] In this respect, the 'Revolution of the Word' had a very similar 'purpose as the Bolshevik revolution, but was much less vitally important, for it fought to free words instead of fellow-working. But don't think its purpose was at all piffling, for we are made by our words much more than they by us.'[165] Eliding the specialist discourse networks of writers and engineers, Brown laced his argument with figurative references to aeronautics and information technology to support his correlations. However, his broader point was that technicity served as a point of mediation between creative and spatial practices, not as a barrier to them. Nevertheless, in configuring technicity as an affective impulse, he neglected the practical business of technical pedagogy, which as Hiler had suggested, was essential to inculcating non-servile relationships with technology.

Like many attempts to bolt modernist experimentation onto sociopolitical projects, the results of the Browns' mid-1930s readies experiment remained provisional, and did not result in a widely-available technical object or media ecology. But they came very close on several occasions to achieving this goal. Brown felt that the treatment that they received from the Soviets amounted to a 'Russian double-cross',[166] and although some critics consider that rejection to be the tragi-comic finale of the readies project,[167] there were good reasons for the Browns to feel aggrieved. They remained behind in Russia, at considerable expense, to develop the readies project with their 'comrades' in 1935, and continued to develop the project when they returned to the United States. Nevertheless, it was just as well that the plan collapsed, because the Browns' rose-tinted view of the Soviet Union was swiftly colliding with political reality. As Cary Nelson notes, 'the aggressive strain of proletarian poetry identified with revolutionary world communism largely collapsed under pressure from historical events – particularly the notorious Moscow "show" treason trials of the years following 1935' – which were gathering pace at a time when the Browns were most engaged with Russia.[168] The former *Masses* editor Max Eastman echoed many literary figures of the left when in the mid-1930s he 'expressed sympathy with the USSR but strongly opposed Stalin's increasingly draconian treatment of actual and perceived dissenters'.[169] For once, the Browns' work was slightly behind the curve, as they still embraced the heavily edited vision of the Soviet Union their minders presented them with in Russia. Indeed, they continued to seek a consilience between their reading machine and their political commitments until the prospect became unsustainable. Yet when their plans finally collided with practical and political reality in 1936, the Browns adapted their readies project to a new context: the burgeoning microfilm industry.

The Afterlives of the Readies: Filmbooks, Microfilm and Readios

When the Browns returned to New York, they were once again patching their lives together. Brown had lost his daughter Cornelia (from his first marriage with Lillian Fox) in 1935, but he and Rose took some solace in renewing their correspondence with Kay Boyle, whose daughter Clotilde had also recently died.[170] In urgent need of funds, the Browns turned again to the idea of developing the readies project alongside their mainstay of cookery writing, because micrographic reading machines had become a major new field of business while they were travelling, and other pioneers, such as their old rival Rear Admiral Bradley Fiske, were being paid as consultants in the field. Following their return from Russia in autumn 1935, their correspondence began to swell with references to and articles about new micrographic reading technologies, largely through the agency of Phillip Kaplan.[171] Born in Grodno, Belarus, in 1903, Kaplan was a designer, 'advertisement art director, self-taught painter, book and art collector' who worked in Cleveland and New York.[172] He had a passionate interest in visual poetry that led him to Brown, and they collaborated on several exhibitions of calligrammes and concrete poetry; eventually, Kaplan became Brown's literary agent, as well as his good friend.[173] Reviewing adverts by Kodak and the new Filmbook Corporation that Kaplan sent him in Spring 1937, Brown complained that commercial reading machines had 'progressed to a multi-million company without me'. In addition,

> five or six clumsy machines are now being manufactured for the market by Filmbook in New York. Trouble is, they stick to the old fashioned column and page and I can't get a patent on my moving one because all type in motion has been patented by the movie people, so I guess my machine, which is still with Max Sherover of the Linguaphone, will only be a museum piece.[174]

Brown had accurately predicted the advent of micrographic machine reading, but not in the form he anticipated. Kodak's Recordak Library Projector catered for major libraries, government departments, corporations and publishing agencies.[175] Although it was a boon to libraries, it was only available in restricted reading rooms. The Browns had previously corresponded with Kodak, but the impressive new Filmbook organisation, which included their friend and business associate Max Sherover as well as Admiral Fiske, looked like more promising collaborators. Verneur Edmund Pratt (no relation to *RFBBM* contributor Theodore Pratt) was the founder of the International Filmbook Corporation and had bought up all of Fiske's reading machine patents. Unlike the cheap and portable Fiskeoscope, Pratt's 'Optigraph' reading machines targeted the business and high-end consumer market with exquisitely designed (but expensive and unreliable) mid-sized devices. The heart of the system was the 'Filmbook cartridge', which would drop 'into the Optigraph like a penny in a slot' and then (in theory) operate like a more streamlined Recordak. The larger Optigraph Models B and C were for smaller libraries and companies, but Pratt marketed the Model A, which was 'not quite as large as the average table radio', to the consumer and small-business market Bob had originally imagined in Cagnes.[176]

Operating from the artist's colony of Silvermine Connecticut, Pratt launched a new trade journal with a micrograph industry leader W. Wadsworth Wood entitled *Microfilm* to promote his product and the industry in general. Pratt and Wood organised a trade show of reading machines at the Waldorf Astoria in New York in the summer of 1937, where Sherover reportedly demonstrated Rose Brown's Readio (and where Brown and Fiske had met a decade earlier to discuss reading machines).[177] After the event, Pratt was interested in including 'the two models of your machine' in his 'historic collection', and wanted to pursue projects 'of common interest' with the Browns.[178] Bucking industry trends, the Browns persisted with their plans to create a cheap, electrically-powered, mass-market reading machine with moving text. In August 1937, Bob wrote to Pratt to report that he was attempting to locate the Saunders Prototype in Cagnes, and invited Pratt and his team 'to see the model I have'. Bob wanted 'to work on a practical reading machine for the masses', but preferred to focus on the medium in an 'editorial' capacity, as he wanted to concentrate on producing 'more experimental writing' for the machine with 'other writers'.[179] However, Pratt did not include the Browns and Sherover in the post-exhibition marketing campaign because he had bigger problems. Pratt had released the Optigraph before it was perfected, and with customers' models failing his business began to collapse. By 1939, Optigraphs were no longer in production and Pratt had made and lost a fortune. Bob had seen this coming in 'Reading Machines', but also thought he and Rose had missed their chance. 'We're through with inventing', he wrote, but he and Rose still wanted 'the chance to write the first reel' when their idea did reach the marketplace – probably as someone else's concept.[180] The problem was, with the advent of the Optigraph, the industry had shifted decisively to the Recordak's micrographic reading format. And when the Optigraph failed, another semi-affordable alternative was emerging to take its place.

The famous publisher behind Boni & Liveright, Albert Boni, had been working on a machine called the Readex since the mid-1930s. Boni's device used a unique micro-opaque process that captured texts on 35 mm microfilm and reproduced them on paper cards using offset lithography.[181] As a 1940 article in *The Saturday Review* reported, Boni's 'Readex looks like a large typewriter case. Pull out a narrow drawer in the bottom of it, insert the small sheet of microprint, and turn on a light inside the machine.'[182] Boni marketed the Readex to both consumers and businesses, using a nearly identical promotional strategy as Pratt had (and as Rose envisaged), featuring microfilmed literary 'classics'. Boni had known the Browns since their Greenwich Village days, but the similarities to the Optigraph's marketing in particular were not accidental: Boni served as a consultant for one of Filmbook's major investors, Lessing Rosewald, the heir to the Sears Roebuck fortune.[183] According to Bob, the organisations were 'quietly buying up a score of patents on reading machines', and the Rosewald Foundation was planning major interventions in the market via a number of channels.[184] When Pratt failed, Boni could simply absorb his infrastructure. After a succession of technical setbacks in the 1940s, Boni eventually formed highly successful partnerships with the American Antiquarian Society, the Library of Congress and several university libraries so that the Readex became the Recordak's only serious rival. From the 1950s, the Readex Corporation became embedded in the micrographic (and later, digital) archival publishing industry, which continues today as a division of Newsbank.

In the late 1930s, the only serious competition for the Recordak, the Optigraph and the Readex, had carried forward Fiske's, and not Brown's, vision of micrographic reading: while the media and mechanisms varied, the emphasis on stationary and static reading machines became the technical orthodoxy at the highest levels of the industry – with a new emphasis on the technical objects' major size and cost. Nevertheless, there were remarkable similarities between the Browns', Pratt's and Boni's respective reading machine projects. Boni began developing the Readex in 1934, when he renewed his friendship with Manuel Komroff, an original Greenwich Village socialist and sceptical contributor to *RFBBM*. According to one Readex foundation narrative, Boni hatched the idea at a Greenwich Village party hosted by Komroff in 1934, at which Komroff showed his guests a series of photographic enlargements of Komroff's eye – an uncanny parallel with Brown's enlarging 'eyes on the half-shell' anecdote.[185] Komroff may have relayed ideas about the Readies to Boni, but Brown claimed elsewhere that he had been discussing reading machines with Boni since their Greenwich Village days.[186] However, the more fascinating parallel was with Boni's prototyping process, which used scavenged components to create a working device. His initial Readex 'reading machine' was 'a cigar-box contraption' that used a 'six-volt current' and 'a dome-shaped reflector' for providing a light source.[187] From their quirky meta-formational origins (which combined Greenwich Village/arts-colony radicalism with big business) to their technical prototyping stages (which combined basic patent-model constructions and state-of-the-art engineering techniques), Boni's, Pratt's and Brown's reading machine projects followed remarkably similar trajectories, operating among several leading cultures of experiment simultaneously. But of course, by 1940, Boni was the only member of the industry's 'also-rans' to have produced a successful commercial product and distribution network.

When the *Saturday Review* article about the Readex was published in September 1940, Bob wrote to Boni and several of his own friends to complain that the Readies had not received proper credit.[188] However, the following year, Theodore Pratt finally realised his ambition to set that right and document Brown's achievement, in a very prominent (albeit anonymous) illustrated article on the microfilm industry for *The American Weekly* entitled 'Science Makes Libraries Pocket-Sized'. With a purported circulation of up to fifty million, this was the largest circulating Sunday supplement in the world, and in the article Pratt mentioned both Fiske and Bob as the industry's pioneers.[189] This acknowledgement no doubt was some source of satisfaction to Bob, but the article ignored the contributions of Rose, who Bob consistently identified with the readies in his later letters and unpublished essays. Although Bob had at last received national recognition for the readies, after a year in Brazil and the death of Cora Brown, he and Rose had moved on to other projects. The Browns relocated to Hollywood in 1941, seeking to join friends such as Hiler, S. J. Perelman, Man Ray and Nathanael West (who died in a car accident weeks before the Browns' move) to work in the film industry.[190] By 1942, the Browns had relocated to Mexico, and then to South America, staying either at their twelve-acre plantation in Petropolis, Brazil, or travelling through the continent. They would remain there until Rose's unexpected death by sudden illness in 1952, conducting research for various books and Hollywood film projects on South American culture, and producing cookbooks and (in Rose's case) political articles.[191]

Although Bob managed to hang onto Rose's readie film of *Candide*, her Readio, like their original certificate for Duchamp's *Monte Carlo Bond* roulette system and the chess set he handcrafted for them in Brazil in 1919, was either lost, misplaced, stolen or simply set aside.[192] Their readies project remained forgotten until an extraordinary feature appeared in the Education section of the pre-eminent American mass-market weekly *Time* magazine on 2 February 1948. The subject of the *Time* article was Sherover's latest pedagogical project, 'hypnopedia', a process of sleep-learning that he hoped to encourage with his latest invention, the '"cerebrograph" (mind-writer)'. When he discussed his next project, however, he seemed to veer from prototyping to plagiarism:

If Max Sherover has his way no U.S. household will be without his latest invention: the "Readie" (pronounced reedy). This is a gadget to let people read without turning a page. Books will be printed on long tapes, run through a machine. The strips will be adjustable to the reader's normal eyespeed. Maybe even the Readies will be too much trouble for lazy readers. If so, Sherover would have a voice ("Why not Lowell Thomas?") fill the room, reading aloud.[193]

Sherover's description of the 'readies project', in which he had played such an important role, appeared to be a brazen act of theft, as many correspondents pointed out to Bob. On 22 February 1948 Bob wrote to Sherover from Brazil to complain, and Sherover replied that in the interview he had not claimed to have invented the readies project, just that he hoped to bring it back to public attention for future development, and that the article misrepresented this subtlety.[194] Bob knew the magazine business well enough to recognise the plausibility of Sherover's account. However, Bob's disappointment was compounded by the news that after a protracted illness, Clare Brackett, who Brown described as his 'millionaire cousin' and credited with help in 'making the second model' of the reading machine, died of a stroke around the time the *Time* article appeared.[195] Yet mitigating this tragedy was Sherover's accidental revelation that the anonymous interviewer was Bruce Barton, Jr. This turned out to be an extraordinary coincidence, even by Bob's standards: the *Time* journalist was the son of his first fiancée, Esther Randall.

Bob had been engaged to Randall in the early 1900s, but she chose to marry his boyhood friend and business partner Bruce Barton Sr, who went on to co-found the highly successful advertising agency BBDO.[196] Bob relayed the story to Randall and Kaplan, and once again the reading machine became a central feature of his interior life as well as his public one, as he reconnected with old friends.[197] The re-emergence of the readies project also prompted Bob to resume work on his autobiography, and to consider other, more experimental, endeavours, including the production of more calligrammes for a new edition of *1450–1950*, and another 'televistic' iteration of the readies.[198] Boni's success had demonstrated that avant-garde connections were no barrier to commercial innovation, yet Bob's experience suggested that he needed to be more strategic in finding his niche, and to be more agile in his responses to evidence and feedback from experts in other fields. Technicians had a lot to learn from the avant-gardes, but the reverse was also true. Nevertheless, the technicities and visuality of reading and writing continued to intrigue and sustain Bob until his death in 1959, even when the rest of his life risked falling apart.

Conclusion

Perhaps most remarkable aspect of this penultimate episode in the story of the Browns' and other reading machines is the power of microfilm technology to stay news for nearly three decades. From the first *Scientific American* report on Fiske's inventions in 1922, to the *Time* story in 1948, the technology remained a fascinating innovation that had diffused into culture without having entered widespread production. Its potent combination of science and literature, publishing and technology, speed and reading, and plausibility and speculation continued to captivate the imaginations of inventors and the general public alike. Yet its revolutionary potential for mass culture resided in its simplicity. As Brown, Pratt and Boni argued, by combining existing technologies from multiple fields, packaged in a form consistent with other consumer information technologies, new devices had the potential to transform an everyday act like reading. Although their ideas were squeezed out by industry leaders, another reading machine device announced in 1948 finally *did* transform American popular culture, on a scale commensurate with the Browns' predictions.

In Hollywood, the actor-turned-inventor Fred Barton constructed a device that unrolled scripts printed in half-inch letters vertically on 'a roll of waxed butcher's paper' mounted in half a suitcase 'and cranked by hand' off camera.[199] Starting out in 1948 as a functional proof-of-concept model even more humble than Brown's and Boni's reading machines, Barton founded the TelePromTer Corporation, and began producing the ubiquitous teleprompter.[200] The device displayed up to half a page of text, and it was developed and perfected because of a clearly-defined need in a lucrative industry. It also depended on other technical objects (television cameras and production equipment) to perform its role, and it performed that role best when it drew no attention to itself. The technology marked a defining moment in the advent of what Mark Hayward calls 'neoliberal optics', a phenomenon in which technology creates an intense bond between 'vision, identity, and intersubjectivity'.[201] In a way, this technology realised Brown's vision of 'seeing words machine-wise', not by enhancing and expanding the visual and literary impact of texts, but by reducing it to a purely instrumental mnemonic device.

On the teleprompter, texts became radically simplified for the actor, and as the technology improved, producers and audiences became less aware of the actors' doubled gaze at the camera and teleprompter, intensifying the affective bond between viewer and actor. Brown learned about this 'revolution of the word' in a 1952 letter from Theodore Pratt, who wrote from a Hollywood studio to enthuse about its 'foot control' interface and its similarity to 'your reading machine'.[202] Knowing that Bob was in a deep depression, and in the process of returning to the United States following the sudden illness and tragic death of Rose in Brazil, Pratt promised to look into the teleprompter further as a means of boosting Bob's spirits (and possibly his depleted finances). However, Brown was already reconceptualising the readies project as a screenplay involving animated words and letters.[203] He returned to Greenwich Village to open a bookshop with his new wife Eleanor Phillips, whom he had known as a slacker in Mexico, and had become reacquainted with in New York. However, until the end of his life in 1959, Bob focused on his calligrammes and autobiography rather than the readies project – perhaps because it was Rose's story too.[204]

The prototypes the Browns, Boni and Fred Barton used were cobbled together from the most banal of everyday objects – a cracker box, a cigar box and a suitcase filled with butcher's paper – but proposed nothing less than a revolutionary transformation of text. As Bob and Rose Brown's reading machines reveal, when we delve into the avant-gardes' interventions in socio-technical ensembles, stable boundaries that separate individual writers, formations and even chronologies begin to break down. Exploiting the bathetic possibilities of obsolescence even as they fretted about sustaining the cultural capital of innovation, late modernist avant-garde formations especially strained to make sense of increasingly complex socio-technical ensembles, while proposing alternative, energetic technicities to transform those ensembles, and the hierarchies they sustained. However, throughout that century, experimental black writers in America have told a different story – one in which breakdowns, systematic injustices and liminal or unintended spaces generated by technical ensembles are exposed and exploited with ingenuity, and unique meta-formational strategies. The next chapter details the technicities and creative spatial practices of black writers who engaged with rail technologies and their wider socio-technical ensembles, from the modernist period to the Black Arts Movement.

Notes

1. See Hugh Ford, *Published in Paris: American and British Writers, Printers, and Publishers in Paris, 1920–39* (London: The Garnstone Press Limited, 1975), p. 311; Michael North, *Camera Works: Photography and the Twentieth-Century Word* (Oxford: Oxford University Press, 2005), p. 75; and Jessica Pressman, *Digital Modernism: Making It New in New Media* (Oxford and New York: Oxford University Press, 2014), p. 194.

2. Raymond Williams, *Culture* (London: Fontana, 1981), pp. 68–70.
3. Matthew Chambers, *Modernism, Periodicals, and Cultural Poetics* (New York: Palgrave Macmillan, 2015), pp. 2, 19.
4. Bob Brown, *6BBB*.
5. Anonymous, 'Clare L. Brackett', in *The Michigan Alumnus* 47.1 (5 October 1940): 418.
6. The first letter in the sequence is Clare Brackett to Bob Brown, 24 September 1930, and the final letter, which arranged for a meeting between Brown and Stoll on 6 July in New York, is dated 27 June 1932; B32, UCLA Brown. A few letters from Brackett to Cora Brown, Bob's mother and Clare's aunt, appear in B2, F1–3, SIU Kaplan-Brown.
7. Clare Brackett to Bob Brown, 24 September 1930, B32, UCLA Brown.
8. Anonymous, [untitled illustrations of reading machines], *RFBBM*, p. 4.
9. Clare Brackett to Bob Brown, 24 September 1930.
10. Clare Brackett, 'Two Men 7 Duck No Luck', *RFBBM*, p. 130.
11. Clare Brackett to Bob Brown, 24 September 1930.
12. Eugene Jolas, 'Glossary', *transition* 4 (July 1927): 179–82 (p. 180).
13. Murray Godwin to Bob Brown, 13 July 1930, B1, F5, SIU Kaplan-Brown.
14. Murray Godwin, 'The Way I See It – [editorial]', *Science and Invention* 18.6 (October 1930): 490.
15. Ibid.
16. See Veitch, *American Superrealism: Nathanael West and the Politics of Representation in the 1930s* (Madison: University of Wisconsin Press, 1997).
17. Jolas, 'Glossary', p. 180.
18. Murray Godwin, 'A Day in the Life of a Robot: A Prose Pantomime in Four Parts', *transition* 13 (summer 1928): 148–71, and 'The Wires Invisible: A Tale of Two Worlds', *transition* 19–20 (June 1930): 151–65. 'The Wires Invisible' was published in the same issue of *transition* as Bob Brown's essay 'The Readies' (pp. 167–73).
19. Murray Godwin to Bob Brown, 13 July 1930.
20. The Browns travelled regularly to health spas in Germany to treat Brown's various ailments, which included agoraphobia, stomach complaints and depression; see Saper, *Amazing Adventures*, pp. 155–7.
21. Hilaire Hiler to Bob Brown, 20 October 1930, B1, F6, SIU Kaplan-Brown.
22. Hilaire Hiler, 'H-A-N-G-O-V-E-R', in Bob Brown, 'Writing Readies', *Morada* 5 (December 1930): 16–19 (p. 19).
23. Intaglio prints are produced from images on copper plates that are either incised or etched by photogravure, rotogravure or other photo-mechanical process; see Geoffrey Ashall Glaister, *Encyclopedia of the Book, Second Edition* (New Castle, DE: Oak Knoll Press, 1996), pp. 250, 374–6, 425.
24. Bob Brown, 'The Readies', *transition* 19–20 (June 1930): 167–73 (p. 167).
25. Hilaire Hiler, 'Preface', *RFBBM*, pp. 5–8 (p. 5).
26. Anonymous, 'American Artist Here Shows Work Done in New Medium on Aluminum', *The New York Herald (European Edition)*, 2 October 1932, p. 4.

27. Hilaire Hiler, 'Preface', p. 5.
28. Ibid.
29. Hilaire Hiler, [business card], B1, F20, SIU Kaplan-Brown.
30. See Wyndham Lewis, 'Futurism, Magic and Life', *B1*, pp. 132–5 (p. 135); I discuss this article in Chapter 1.
31. Simondon, *METO*, p. 16.
32. Hilaire Hiler and C. F. Colin, 'Method, Moderne and Medieval', *The New Review* 1.4 (Winter 1931–2): 320–1 (p. 321).
33. Walter Benjamin, 'Art in the Age of Mechanical Reproduction', in *Illuminations*, ed. Hannah Arendt, trans. Harry Zorn (London: Pimlico, 1999), 211–244 (pp. 232–3).
34. Gilbert Simondon, *L'individuation psychique et collective* (Paris: Aubier, 1989), p. 63; also see Muriel Combes's compelling account of social energetics in Gilbert Simondon and the *Philosophy of the Transindividual*, trans. with a preface and afterword by Thomas LaMarre (Cambridge, MA and London: The MIT Press, 2013), pp. 52–53.
35. Hilaire Hiler, *Technologie Matérial des Arts Graphique* [*Material Technique in the Graphic Arts*] [pamphlet prospectus, 14 October 1932] (Atelier Hilaire Hiler: Paris, 1932), n.p.
36. Albert Stoll to Bob Brown, 3 June 1931, B32, UCLA Brown.
37. Brown, *Reading Machines V1*, p. 5.
38. Hiler, 'Preface', pp. 6–7.
39. Ernest W. Bradford to Robert [Bob] Carlton Brown, 13 February 1932, B32, UCLA Brown.
40. Ezra Pound, 'Deflation Benefit', *Globe* 1.5 (August 1937): 66–71 (p. 68), and B. C. Hagglund to Bob Brown, 8 February 1932, B32, UCLA Brown.
41. Brown, *Reading Machines V1*, p. 5.
42. Clare Brackett to Bob Brown (copy), 22 March 1932, B32, UCLA Brown.
43. Clare Brackett to Bob Brown, 11 February 1932, B32, UCLA Brown.
44. Hiler, 'Preface', p. 6.
45. Albert Stoll to Bob Brown, 3 June 1931, B32, UCLA Brown.
46. Clare Brackett to Bob Brown, 22 March 1932, B32, UCLA Brown.
47. National Film Preservation Foundation, *The Film Preservation Guide: The Basics for Archives, Libraries and Museums* (San Francisco: National Film Preservation Foundation, 2004), p. 9.
48. O. W. Cook (Eastman Kodak Company Production Department) to Bob Brown, 27 August 1930, B1, F5, SIU Kaplan-Brown.
49. D. H. Litchfield and M. A. Bennett, 'Microfilm Reading Machines: Part III', *Special Libraries* 34.5 (May–June 1943): 157–64 (p. 157).
50. National Film Preservation Foundation, *The Film Preservation Guide*, p. 9.
51. Ernest W. Bradford to Robert Carlton [Bob] Brown, 13 February 1932. The other US Patent numbers were: 107,969; 1,149,383; 1,745,718; 1,730,045; and 1,684,309.
52. Bob Brown to Rear Admiral Bradley A. Fiske, 5 January 1932, B32, UCLA Brown; on Fiske's and Brown's meeting, see Chapter 3.

53. Ernest W. Bradford to Bob Brown, 13 February 1932.
54. Ernest W. Bradford to Robert Carlton [Bob] Brown, 28 March 1932, B1, F17, SIU Kaplan-Brown.
55. Brown, 'Appendix', *RFBBM*, pp. 198–204. In the mid-1960s, tachistoscopic machines for personal and institutional speed reading training were manufactured by many companies (including SVE, EDL, Keystone, Rheem-Califone, and Reading Laboratories), and these niche products grew into a small industry; see Charles R. Acland, 'The Swift View: Tachistoscopes and the Residual Modern, *Residual Media*, ed. Charles R. Acland (Minneapolis: University of Minnesota Press, 2007), pp. 361–84 (p. 371–77).
56. Bob Brown to James Farrell, 7 January 1932, B31, F33, UPenn Farrell.
57. B. C. Hagglund to Bob Brown, 8 February 1932, B32, UCLA Brown.
58. See Alexander Berkman, *Memoirs of an Anarchist*, ed. Barry Pateman and Jessica Moran (Edinburgh: AK Press, 2017).
59. Alexander Berkman to Bob Brown, 8 January 1932, B1, F16, SIU Kaplan-Brown.
60. Alexander Berkman to Bob Brown, 15 and 19 January 1932, B1, F16, SIU Kaplan-Brown.
61. B. C. Hagglund to Bob Brown, 8 February 1932.
62. Craig Saper, 'Introduction and Notes on the Text', *RFBBM*, pp. ix–lvii (p. xlvii).
63. See James Farrell to Bob Brown, 14 and 19 June 1931, B1, F11, SIU Kaplan-Brown.
64. See Gertrude Stein and Bob Brown, 'Letters of Gertrude Stein, Edited with an Introduction by Bob Brown', *Berkeley: A Journal of Modern Culture* 8 (1951): 1–2, 8. Stein wrote a privately-printed prose 'portrait' of Brown entitled *Absolutely Bob Brown, Or Bobbed Brown* (Pawlet, VT: Addison M. Metcalf Collection, 1955).
65. Paul Stephens, 'Bob Brown, "Inforg": The "Readies" at the Limits of Modernist Cosmopolitanism', *Journal of Modern Literature* 35.1 (Fall 2011): 143–64 (p. 160).
66. Gertrude Stein, 'We Came', *RFBBM*, pp. 99–104 (p. 100).
67. Ibid.
68. Gertrude Stein, *The Making of Americans* (Paris: Contact Editions and the Three Mountains Press, 1925).
69. Peter Nicholls, *Modernisms: A Literary Guide* (London: Macmillan, 1995), p. 197.
70. Charles Henri Ford, 'Letter from the Provinces', *RFBBM*, pp. 132–3 (p. 133).
71. See Eric B. White, *Transatlantic Avant-Gardes: Little Magazines and Localist Modernism* (Edinburgh: Edinburgh University Press, 2013), pp. 187–90 for the first critical account of Young's career, which will be developed substantially in a forthcoming article. Saper adds valuable new information about Young in 'Invent(st)ory', *RFBBM*, pp. 238–9.
72. Kathleen Tankersley Young, 'Love Story', *RFBBM*, pp. 133–5 (p. 135).
73. Rue Menken, 'Cracked', *RFBBM*, pp. 104–5.

74. North, *Camera Works*, p. 78, and Craig Dworkin, '"Seeing Words Machine-wise": Technology and Visual Prosody', *Sagetrieb* 18.1 (Spring 1999): 59–86 (pp. 59–61).
75. Stephens, 'Bob Brown, "Inforg"', p. 162.
76. See James Farrell to Bob Brown, 14 and 19 June 1931, B1, F11, SIU Kaplan-Brown; Bob Brown to James Farrell, 12, 19 and 30 June, and 1 and 22 July 1931, B31, F33, UPenn Farrell; and Edgar Marquess Branch, *A Paris Year: Dorothy and James T. Farrell, 1931–1932* (Athens: Ohio University Press, 1998), p. 62.
77. Manuel Komroff, 'The Writies', *RFBBM*, pp. 110–13 (p. 110).
78. See Ann Douglas, 'Studs Lonigan and the Failure of History in Mass Society: A Study in Claustrophobia', *American Quarterly* 29.5 (Winter 1977): 487–505 (p. 492).
79. Ann Douglas, 'Introduction', in James T. Farrell, *Young Lonigan* (New York and London: Penguin Books, 2001), pp. vii–xxvi (p. xvii).
80. James T. Farrell, 'Sylvester Mc Gullick', *RFBBM*, pp. 16–25 (pp. 16–17).
81. Ibid. p. 19.
82. Ibid. p. 22.
83. Ibid. p.25.
84. James T. Farrell, 'Jeff', *RFBBM*, pp. 25–30 (p. 25).
85. Ibid. p. 29.
86. See especially Erik M. Backman, *Literary Obscenities: U.S. Case Law and Naturalism After Modernism* (University Park: The Pennsylvania State University Press, 2018), p. 48.
87. Ann Douglas, 'Introduction', p. xx.
88. Ibid. p. xv.
89. John A. Farrell and James T. Farrell, 'One of the Many', *RFBBM*, pp. 30–6 (p. 32).
90. Ibid. p. 33.
91. Ibid. p. 30.
92. Bob Brown, 'Appendix', pp. 179–80.
93. See Nathanael West to Bob Brown, 13 August 1932, B1, F20, SIU Kaplan-Brown.
94. Clare Brackett to Bob Brown, 27 June 1932, B32, UCLA Brown.
95. Bob Brown to Theodore Pratt, 16 September 1940, B2, F11, SIU Kaplan-Brown.
96. See Anton A. Huurdeman, *The Worldwide History of Telecommunications* (Hoboken: John Wiley & Sons, Inc., 2003), pp. 300–7.
97. Bob Brown, *Reading Machines V1*, p. 6.
98. Bob Brown, 'John Simon Guggenheim Memorial Foundation Fellowship Application Form', 5 August 1932, B28, UCLA Brown.
99. Bob Brown, 'Plans for Study [Guggenheim Application]', B28, UCLA Brown. Pages two and three of the 'Plans for Study' are included in Brown's *Reading Machines V1* (pp. 7–8) at SIU Carbondale.
100. Ibid.

101. Bob mentions the visit by Watson Davis in Bob Brown to W. Wadsworth Wood, 16 August 1937, B2, F11, SIU Kaplan-Brown; also see Robert G. Binkley to Bob Brown, 14 September and 15 October 1932, B1, F20. Binkley's report was considered 'the bible of the microfilm industry', and his correspondence with Brown indicates that he took the readies project seriously; W. Wadsworth Wood, 'We Nominate for Stars of a New Industry', *Microfilm* 1.1 (July 1937): 2.
102. Hagley Museum and Library, *Finding Aid: Inter-Society Color Council Records (Accession 2188)*, Hagley Museum and Library, Wilmington, Delaware <https://findingaids.hagley.org/xtf/view?docId=ead/2188.xml&doc.view=content&brand=default&anchor.id=0#series7> (accessed 24 May 2018).
103. Alfred Kreymborg dedicated his poem 'Rainy Cycle' to Knudsen in *No More War: And Other Poems* (New York: Bookman Associates, 1950), p. 15.
104. Hugo Knudsen, 'Correspondence – Eastman Kodak Company, 1932, 1949–51', B226, Inter-Society Color Council records (Accession 2188), Hagley Museum and Library, Wilmington, Delaware.
105. Rose Brown's published photographs appear in various untitled newspaper clippings in the 'Commonwealth College' Folder in UCLA Brown; see Rose Brown and Bob West, [untitled photos], in 'Labor College Exhibits', [unknown newspaper clipping ca. 1934–5], B5, UCLA Brown.
106. Bob Brown to Theodore Pratt, 16 September 1940, B2, F11, SIU Kaplan-Brown.
107. Bob Brown, *Reading Machines V1*, p. 5.
108. Rose Brown to Cora Brown, June 1935, B32, UCLA Brown.
109. Bob Brown to Cora Brown, 18 June 1935, B32, UCLA Brown. Bob also makes urgent mention of the reading machine in his 9 and 15 June letters to her, prior to their departure to Russia on 29 June 1935.
110. Pound, 'Deflation Benefit', p. 68. This article was preceded by a terse exchange of letters between Brown and Pound earlier that summer; see Ezra Pound to Bob Brown, 14 June 1937, B6, F264, Ezra Pound Papers, YCAL MSS 43, Beinecke Library, Yale University.
111. See Anonymous, 'H. Hiler, Lonely, Leaving for U.S.', *The New York Herald (European Edition)*, 4 September 1934, p. 5.
112. Bob Brown, 'Reading Machines [Alt. Draft 2]', B5, F13, SIU Kaplan-Brown.
113. Brown, *The Readies*, p. 45.
114. Ibid. p. 39.
115. See Jay Satterfield, *The World's Best Books: Taste, Culture, and the Modern Library* (Amherst, MA: University of Massachusetts Press, 2002), pp. 34–6. Bennett Cerf purchased a vice-presidency in Boni & Liveright which came with the Modern Library 'classics': in partnership with Random House, the series eventually sold millions of volumes.
116. Bob Brown, 'Reading Machines [Alt. Draft 2]', B5, F13, SIU Kaplan-Brown.

117. Voltaire, *Candide ou l'Optimisme*, Édition de Frédéric Deloffre (Paris: Éditions Gallimard, 2003), p. 30. I am grateful to Nicole Pohl for discussing *Candide* with me; any errors are my own.
118. Saper, *Amazing Adventures*, pp. 201, 255.
119. Rose Brown, 'Dis', *RFBBM*, pp. 49–52 (pp. 50–1).
120. See Bob Brown to Phillip Kaplan, 11 May 1937, B2, F7, SIU Kaplan-Brown.
121. See Bob Brown to Theodore Pratt, 6 February 1948, B3, F3, SIU Kaplan-Brown.
122. Voltaire, *Candide*, p. 154.
123. See Theodore Pratt to Bob Brown, 1 April 1933, and Kay Boyle to Bob Brown, 10 May 1933, B2, F1, SIU Kaplan-Brown. Brown fell out with Boyle in the Spring over perceived 'disloyalty' to her then husband Laurence Vail.
124. Saper, *Amazing Adventures*, p. 204.
125. For an indispensable history of Commonwealth College, see William H. Cobb's *Radical Education in the Rural South: Commonwealth College 1922–1940* (Detroit: Wayne State University Press, 2000).
126. Ibid. pp. 206–9, and Abbott Cohen, 'Associated Little Magazines', *Commonwealth College Fortnightly* 9.8 (15 April 1935): 3.
127. Bob Brown, 'Little Mag, What Now', *Commonwealth College Fornightly* 10.21–22 (15 November 1934): 1.
128. Bob Brown, Untitled, [bibliographical statement], B32, UCLA Brown.
129. See Bob Brown, 'Workers Museum Opened', *Commonwealth College Fortnightly* 11.1 (1 January 1935): 4. For Saper's discussion of the Museum for Social Change, see *Amazing Adventures*, pp. 209–13. I also discuss the Museum of Social Change in my digital project *The AGAST Archive* (New York: electric.press, forthcoming).
130. B. C. Hagglund to Bob Brown, 8 February 1932, B32, UCLA Brown.
131. See Rose Brown to Cora Brown, [June 1935], B32, Folder 'Soviet Union Trip', UCLA Brown. It appears that Cora Brown remained at Commonwealth College during this period.
132. Bob Brown to Bennett Cerf, 7 December 1934, B2, F3, SIU Kaplan-Brown. Brown was still in touch with many *RFBBM* contributors during this period, including Boyle, Cunard, James Farrell, A. L. Gillespie, J. Jones, Pound, Williams and others (see B2, F2–3), and corresponded with Cerf throughout the decade.
133. Anonymous, 'Tour Leaves June 29', *Commonwealth College Fortnightly* 11.10 (15 May 1935): 1.
134. World Tourists, Soviet Union Tour advert, *The New Masses* 14.11 (12 March 1935): 2.
135. Barnaby Harran, *Watching the Red Dawn: The American Avant-Garde and the Soviet Union* (Manchester: Manchester University Press, 2016), pp. 2–4.
136. World Tourists, 'Spend this Summer in Moscow [advert, 29 June 1935]', B2, F5, SIU Kaplan-Brown.

137. Bob Brown, 'Spend this Summer in Moscow [advertising circular, n.d.]', B5, UCLA Brown. Four pamphlets in this box advertise trips with a technological emphasis, and feature agricultural machinery, transmission lines and a reflector telescope.
138. See Rose Brown to Cora Brown, 10 September 1935, B25, UCLA Brown.
139. See ibid.
140. See Dennis Ioffe, 'The Posthumous Legacy of Khlebnikov Versus Mayakovsky Sub Specie Avant-Garde Performance of Scandal: Debating the Semiotic Pragmatics of Avant-Garde Behavior and Life-Creation', *Neohelicon* 39.2 (December 2012): 453–73 (p. 464).
141. Bob Brown, 'Spawn', [TS, n.d.], B32, Bob Brown Papers.
142. Harran, *Watching the Red Dawn*, p. 3.
143. Thorsten Veblen's treatise on 'A Memorandum of a Practicable Soviet of Technicians' was the sixth chapter in *The Engineers and the Price System* (New York: B. W. Huebsch, Inc., 1921), pp. 138–69.
144. Earl Browder, 'What Is Communism?: 3. Who Will Lead the Revolution?', *The New Masses* 15.8 (21 May 1935): 18–19 (p. 19).
145. Cecilia Tichi, *Shifting Gears: Technology, Literature, Culture in Modernist America* (Chapel Hill, NC, and London: University of North Carolina Press, 1987), p. 133.
146. *METO*, pp. 17–18.
147. Veblen, *The Engineers and the Price System*, p. 169.
148. Walter Ralston, 'Veblen and Revolution', *New Masses* 19.2 (7 April 1936): 41–2 (p. 41).
149. Ibid.
150. Veblen, *The Engineers and the Price System*, p. 168.
151. Rose Brown to Cora Brown, 10 September 1935, B25, UCLA Brown.
152. Bob Brown to Cora Brown, 1 August 1935, B32, UCLA Brown.
153. Bob Brown to Hayka n Texhnka [sic., n.d.], B32, UCLA Brown.
154. Ibid.
155. Bob Brown, *Reading Machines* V2, p. 8.
156. Anonymous, '[*Russia Today* Prize Contest]', undated newspaper clipping, B32, UCLA Brown.
157. Bob Brown to Bennett Cerf, 7 December 1934, B2, F3, SIU Kaplan-Brown.
158. Bob Brown, 'What the Soviet Union means to Humanity' [TS, third draft, ca. 1935–6], B32, UCLA Brown.
159. Ibid.
160. Bob Brown, 'What the Soviet Union means to Humanity' [TS, second draft, ca. 1935–6], B32, UCLA Brown.
161. Bob Brown, 'What the Soviet Union means to Humanity' [TS, third draft, ca. 1935–6], B32, UCLA Brown.
162. Bob Brown, 'The Soviet Taught Us Democracy', [TS, n.d.], B32, UCLA Brown.
163. Bob Brown, 'An Arrowhead: A Poem', B32, UCLA Brown.
164. Ibid.

165. Ibid.
166. Bob Brown to Hayka n Texhnka [*sic.*, n.d.], B32, Folder 'Reading Machine – correspondence, clippings [1930–1940]', UCLA Brown.
167. See Hugh Ford, *Published in Paris*, p. 311, and North, *Camera Works*, p. 75.
168. Cary Nelson, *Repression and Recovery: Modern American Poetry and the Politics of Cultural Memory, 1910–45, New Edition* (Madison: The University of Wisconsin Press, 1992), p. 159.
169. Harran, *Watching the Red Dawn*, p. 176.
170. See Rose Brown to Cora Brown, n.d. [May–June 1935], Box 25, UCLA Brown, and Kay Boyle to Bob and Rose Brown, 5 February 1936, B2, F6, SIU Kaplan-Brown. Cornelia apparently died from complications related to anemia; see [unknown] to Ray Young, 2 April 1939, B2, F9, SIU Kaplan-Brown.
171. See B2, F5–8, SIU Kaplan-Brown.
172. Southern Illinois University Special Collections Research Center, 'Historical Note: Kaplan, Philip, (1903–1990)', <https://archives.lib.siu.edu/?p=creators/creator&id=288> (accessed 1 October 2019).
173. Phillip Kaplan to Bob Brown, 25 October 1934, B2, F3, SIU Kaplan-Brown.
174. Bob Brown to Philip Kaplan, 11 May [1937], B2, F7, SIU Kaplan-Brown.
175. Recordak Corporation, 'Recordak Library Projector', *Microfilm* 1.1 (July 1937): 14–15.
176. V. E. Pratt, 'The Day of the Reading Machine is Here!', *Microfilm* 1.1 (July 1937): 24–5.
177. Bob Brown to V. E. Pratt, 16 August 1937, B2, F11, SIU Kaplan-Brown.
178. V. E. Pratt to Bob Brown, 20 August 1937, B32, UCLA Brown.
179. Bob Brown to V. E. Pratt, 21 August 1937, B2, F7, SIU Kaplan-Brown.
180. Bob Brown, 'Reading Machines [Alt. Draft 2]', B5, F13, SIU Kaplan-Brown.
181. Marvin Lowenthal, 'Too Small to See but Not to Read', *The Saturday Review* 22.20 (7 September 1940): 11–13 (p. 12).
182. Ibid. p. 11
183. August A. Imholtz, Jr, 'Albert Boni: A Sketch of a Life in Micro-Opaque', *Proceedings of the American Antiquarian Society* 115 (October 2005): 253–77, p. 269.
184. Bob Brown, *Reading Machines V2*, p. 4.
185. Imholtz, 'Albert Boni', p. 268. On Brown's calligramme, see 'Appendix', *RFBBM*, p. 168 and the previous chapter.
186. Bob Brown to Theodore Pratt, 16 September 1940, B2, F11, SIU Kaplan-Brown.
187. Marvin Lowenthal, 'Too Small to See but Not to Read', p. 12.
188. Multiple letters address this subject in B2, F11, SIU Kaplan-Brown.
189. See Anonymous [Theodore Pratt], 'How Science Makes Libraries Pocket-Sized', *The American Weekly* (23 March 1941): 2. See annotations by Pratt on Carl Goodkind to *American Weekly* (23 March 1941), B32, UCLA Brown.

190. See Saper, *Amazing Adventures*, pp. 251–5.
191. See Ibid. pp. 257–8.
192. Bob describes the lost Duchamp items in his 6 May 1948 letter to Philip Kaplan and mentions the *Candide* film in his 6 February 1948 letter; B3, F3, SIU Kaplan-Brown.
193. Anonymous [Bruce Barton, Jr], 'Learn While You Sleep', *Time* 51.5 (2 February 1948): 21.
194. Bob Brown to Max Sherover, 22 February 1948, and Max Sherover to Bob Brown, 27 February 1948, B3, F3, SIU Kaplan-Brown.
195. Bob Brown to Philip Kaplan, 12 February 1948, B3, F3, SIU Kaplan-Brown.
196. See Saper, *Amazing Adventures*, p. 11.
197. See Bob Brown to Philip Kaplan, 6 February 1948, SIU Kaplan-Brown, B3, F3, and Bob Brown to 'Woozy' [Esther Randall], 4 March 1948, B12, F2, UCLA Brown.
198. See Bob Brown's proofs and drafts for *1450–1950* in B4, F8, SIU Kaplan-Brown.
199. Erik H. Arctander, 'How a Teleprompter Works', *Popular Science Monthly* 177.1 (July 1960): 104–5 (p. 104).
200. Ibid. pp. 104–5.
201. Mark Hayward, 'ATMs, Teleprompters and Photobooths: A Short History of Neoliberal Optics', *New Formations* 80 (2013): 194–208 (p. 202).
202. Theodore Pratt to Bob Brown, 5 August 1952, B32, UCLA Brown.
203. Bob Brown, [Screenplay: 'I But Bend my Finger'], in Bob Brown to Bertha Case, 21 October 1951, B108, UCLA Brown. I discuss this project further in *The AGAST Project Archive*.
204. See Saper, *Amazing Adventures*, pp. 257–68.

Chapter 5

'Our Technology Was Vernacular': Radical Technicities in African American Experimental Writing

Introduction

Since their inception in the early-nineteenth century, rail technologies have co-evolved with America's spaces, infrastructure, economy and cultural imaginaries. Their tracks have remained deeply embedded in its national mythology, and the rhetoric of the technological sublime, ever since.[1] For African American communities, the symbolic capital of railways remained tangled in those national narratives. On the one hand, the 'freedom trains' and the Underground Railroad networks that slaves used to escape the slaveholding states extended fairly seamlessly to the narratives of the Great Migration, where African Americans travelled from the agrarian South into the industrialised North in search of greater opportunities.[2] Yet on the other, Jim Crow rail cars, a 'boxcar' subculture in the Great Depression, and incidents such the Scottsboro trials of the 1930s began to expose the lingering dilemmas that rail technologies both exemplified and disguised in American culture. Cumulatively, rail systems served both as socio-technical instruments for implementing Jim Crow segregation policies, and potent metaphors for the wider effects of segregation and racism in the United States. For black writers such as Langston Hughes, Gwendolyn Bennet, Pauli Murray, Ralph Ellison, Amiri Baraka and others, bathetic critiques and 'tactical' appropriations of rail systems and other infrastructure technologies became linked directly to specific strains of resistance to institutional racism. Out of sight and on the periphery of most major settlements, the physical infrastructures of this socio-technical ensemble form part of a grid that becomes visible again only when it fails, or when vulnerabilities in normal operations are exploited for alternative purposes, such as 'riding the rails', squatting and vernacular modifications to power supplies. Accordingly, black experimental writers and artists identified these socio-technical assemblages as key arenas in which to diagnose the vicissitudes of everyday life behind the colour line, and to re-invent a future beyond it.

In his 1920s–1930s writing, Hughes created a diagnostic framework for the revolutionary poetics and spatial practices of African American avant-gardes, who both reclaimed and newly articulated a black vernacular technicity in response to ongoing segregationist practices and the Scottsboro trials. Drawing on this framework, this chapter then considers how two under-explored black voices – Gwendolyn Bennett, a leading figure of the Harlem Renaissance, and Pauli Murray, a student who wrote about her illegal rail travels before launching an extraordinary career as a civil rights activist and Professor of Law – produced what were among the most powerful, yet disguised, articulations of vernacular socio-technical critique to emerge in the 1930s. They added their voices to Hughes's critiques of Scottsboro, as well as the steady stream of ephemeral print projects organised by white Americans (including *Contempo*, *The New Masses* and Nancy Cunard's *Negro: An Anthology*) in probing the inequities and cultural blind spots that American rail networks had helped entrench. A new generation of black writers grew up in the shadow of Scottsboro and produced equally powerful socio-technical as well socio-political responses. In the summer of 1933, Ralph Ellison 'rode the rails' from Oklahoma across the Midwest to Alabama to take up his music scholarship at the Tuskegee Normal School and Technical Institute. The journey itself left an indelible impression on him, and his first surviving fictional manuscripts are scored with the marks of rail tracks, and associated injuries, as well as the techno-signifyin(g) strategies of his mentor Hughes. Like the unnamed 'thinker tinker' narrator of *Invisible Man*, Ellison's early unpublished writing reflect his technological expertise, and his interventions in radical left-wing journals reveal that technology was inseparable from his socio-poetics.[3] The chapter concludes with a discussion of Amiri Baraka, and in particular how he revised and refined generations of black modernists' engagements with rail networks, and identified technicity as a viable route to challenging racist hegemonies embedded in socio-technical infrastructure.

When Ellison claimed in a 1969 interview that '[o]ur technology was vernacular', the signifyin(g) link he makes between technology and language is more than a convenient metaphor.[4] Although he includes the entirety of American culture in his possessive adjective, the valence that Ellison identifies between language, technology and strategies of adaptation and appropriation over an extended time period elides closely with Rayvon Fouché's conception of 'black vernacular technological creativity' and Henry Louis Gates, Jr's definition of motivated signifyin(g). Fouché has brilliantly analysed the role and development of technology in African American culture, and how vernacular technologies in particular have found expression in the twentieth century, and beyond. Developing Ron Eglash's concept of technological 'appropriation', and with reference to the aesthetics of Amiri Baraka, Fouché's formulation of 'black vernacular creativity' 'enables African American people to reclaim different levels of technological agency'.[5] In this chapter I consider how the trans-historical, interrelated and complexly interdependent contexts of the New Negro Movement, ethnic avant-gardes and Black Arts Movements fold into practices of 'motivated signifyin(g)' identified by Gates. Motivated signifyin(g) 'functions to redress an imbalance of power, to clear a space rhetorically' for 'alter[ing] fundamentally the way we read the tradition'.[6] Gates's emphasis on space is crucial here, because in some cases the textual practice of motivated signifyin(g) forms analogues with the *spatial* practices of African American cultural production. As I argued in the book's Introduction, those spatial practices are expressed powerfully in technicities articulated by African American cultural formations.

In this configuration, technology serves as a hinge between rhetorical and spatial practice – it acts as a figurative device, certainly, but one which connects insistently with the world beyond or (in writing that links the production of material texts with other socio-technical ensembles) actually *on* the page. My argument is that technology's doubled voice in African American writing surfaces with particular intensity among African American avant-gardes, and especially in their treatment of rail technology. Embodying the paradoxical ubiquity, specificity and persistence of America's infrastructure, railroads became a signifyin(g) machine for the everyday technicities of black life throughout the twentieth century. Drawing on decades of tradition, these writers dragged the invisible and over-determined rail networks, and the spaces that framed them, back into plain sight, and made them the targets of a sustained attack.

'Lookin' for a box car': Railway Politics and Vernacular Technicities in Langston Hughes's Early Writing

When he launched his career in the Harlem Renaissance, Langston Hughes began to read urban spaces as crucibles in which the oppression of working classes, ethnic minorities and a broad range of people marginalised by American capitalism could be examined. In the mid-1920s, he had identified the rail networks as a literal groundwork that expressed social policies connected to race, class and economic status.

In his early collections of poetry, *The Weary Blues* and *Fine Clothes to the Jew*, but most particularly in his contributions to periodicals such as *The Workers Monthly*, *Fire!!* and *The Messenger*, Hughes harnessed the dormant power of railway infrastructure and redeployed it with an emergent black voice. His work became a signifyin(g) prototype for black populations in the United States, and beyond, who negotiated these networks. In particular, Hughes identified the individuating power of technology using a range of strategies, including the 'locomotive onomatopoeia' of blues and African American folk culture as a means of enhancing rather than supressing black technicities.

By the 1920s, the sublime ensembles of the nineteenth century had produced a patchwork of spaces and objects that spoke a new, bathetic language. The term 'Railroad Avenue' had taken an actual street name in many American cities to describe generically neighbourhoods adjacent to rail infrastructure. These areas were often settled by lower-income communities, including African American and other ethnic minority and/or working-class populations, who often had connections to the rail industry. Sometimes by accident, but often very deliberately by design, these areas frequently dovetailed with Jim Crow urban planning policies. As 'direct segregation became untenable', authorities often used 'residential segregation, generated and protected by municipal land-use laws' to achieve the same ends.[7] Hughes was far ahead of many contemporaries in identifying socio-technical segregation as another version of racist planning policies, but he also identified instances and strategies of potential resistance, calibrating his work carefully for each intended audience. For example, he placed his poem 'God to Hungry Child' in *The Workers Monthly*, a radical left-wing journal that fostered social revolution. In the poem, the speaker sardonically declaims to the 'Hungry Child': 'I didn't make this world for you. / You didn't buy stock in my railroad', or 'invest in my corporation'.[8] Here, Hughes styles the construction of corporate and state infrastructure in America as a supreme act of collusion rather than a divine act of creation. He was adept at harmonising his socio-political activism and aesthetic experimentation across multiple periodicals, but in *The Workers Monthly*, his poetry was formally orthodox, and his subject position clearly working class. Opportunities to connect his multiple subject positions – working class, queer and African American – were rare. However, the little magazine *Fire!!* provided a powerful exception.

Joining Wallace Thurman, Zora Neale Hurston, Gwendolyn Bennett and Richard Bruce Nugent, Hughes helped produce the influential avant-garde journal *Fire!!*, which was an attempt to explore those energies collectively, but beyond the upper-class 'uplift' sensibility's of Locke's *The*

New Negro anthology. The self-consciously avant-garde *Fire!!* engaged overtly with the contingencies of black working-class experience and other marginalised cultures, and enabled him to develop the focus on rail and infrastructure technologies he had identified in *The Crisis* and *The Workers Monthly*. As I have argued elsewhere, the motif of rail transport became a means by which *Fire!!* contributors negotiated the colour lines that they encountered in urban America.[9] Hughes's poem 'Railroad Avenue' uniquely identifies the spectres of obsolescence and marginalisation in urban areas embedded in the rail network.[10] In it, an abandoned 'box-car' becomes a totemic metonym for the community's vivisection by modern transportation links. Hughes's strategic references to a discarded 'player piano' and 'victrola' (a large manual gramophone) compounds his vision of progress in decline.[11] David Suisman has argued that 'the player piano and phonograph transformed the "aural environment"' of the home in a way analogous to the 'railroads, [. . .] [which] transformed both the physical landscape and the way people experienced it'.[12] However, by 1926, the player piano was viewed as outmoded, and phonographs such as Victrolas were becoming smaller, portable and increasingly automated, making earlier models (such as the unit with the conspicuously low serial number '942' that Hughes identifies here) less desirable. With the advent of 'planned obsolescence' in the early-1920s,[13] there was a sense in which communities, like these technical objects, could be rendered obsolete and/or marginalised as a normal part of these ensembles' operations. These patterns reinforced the sense in which economic (and literal) 'progress' in the United States often came at the expense of black and other minority workers and communities, who were forced to find ways of coping with these iniquities. However, Hughes does not accept this decline as inevitable and identifies sociotechnical means of pushing back.

In 'Railroad Avenue', as elsewhere, the signifyin(g) power of affective expression in black working-class neighbourhoods transforms a stagnant urban space into an energetic one. When the sound of sudden laughter, 'Like a taught drum', transfigures the street by 'Shaking the lights in the fish joints' and 'Rolling white balls in the pool rooms', it fuses with the locomotive power of the rail networks that surround the neighbourhood. Hughes quite literally mobilises the self-contained fields in the poem by harnessing this unifying force. A 'boy / lounging on the corner' and a 'passing girl / With purple powdered skin' are the only people identified in the poem, and, though passive, Hughes invests them with latent potential.[14] As Jason M. Baskin argues, 'laughter has a collective origin in the radical African American struggle against the material structures of racism in American society'.[15] The laughter coursing through Hughes's poem suggests an unsanctioned community-level broadcast emerging from live networks littered with obsolete technology. Devices change, but the networks – both technical and social – remain live, and volatile.

In Fouché's terminology, the assemblages that Hughes maps out in 'Railroad Avenue' could be redeployed or reconceived as tools for potential social transformation (which, in Gilbert Simondon's terms, would be called social energetics). According to Fouché, 'Black vernacular technological creativity is characterized by innovative engagements with technology based upon black aesthetics', and is articulated in three major ways – 'redeployment, reconception, and re-creation'; in this formulation,

> Redeployment is the process by which the material and symbolic power of technology is re-interpreted but maintains its traditional use and physical form, as with blues musicians extending the perceived capability of a guitar without altering it. Reconception is the active redefinition of a technology that transgresses that technology's designed function and dominant meaning, as in using a police scanner to observe police activities. Re-creation is the redesign and production of a new material artifact after an existing form or function has been rejected, as in the case of DJs and turntablists developing new equipment.[16]

In black and other minority communities, such strategies have, as Fouché's definitions make clear, involved adapting existing or past technologies, and/or 'artifactual culture', for new uses, across the long twentieth century. Hughes, anticipating Fouché, explicitly connected the blues to his vernacular technicities and strategies of redeployment, and also identified related spatial practices that extended to other areas of cultural production.

In his 1927 collection *Fine Clothes for the Jew* (which takes its title from his blues-inflected poem 'Hard Luck'), Hughes identified the intimate connections between the socio-technical ensembles of rail technology, vernacular technicity and the emergence of working-class black voices. In the eight-poem section entitled 'Blues', and thirteen-poem sequence 'Railroad Avenue', Hughes remained preoccupied with the coercive forms of power embedded in transportation infrastructure and the tactical vernaculars black artists used – or might use – to reflect and confront them.[17] In the last poem in the 'Blues' sequence, 'Homesick Blues', the speaker declares, 'I went down to de station. / Ma heart was in ma mouth.'[18] Seeking to overcome his despair, he is 'Lookin' for a box car' to reverse his own Great Migration, and 'roll me to de South'. In doing so, he amplifies its dialectical rhythms with the mechanical sounds generated by railroads. A blast from a train whistle on the 'railroad bridge's' span' creates 'A sad song in de air', but rather than pure elegy, Hughes's poetry suggests a tactical redeployment of technical objects in railways. In his hands, the shrieking sounds resulting from the routine operation of an impersonal and mechanised transportation system become tools for creative individuation.

In 1883, rail companies imposed time zones across the United States to help co-ordinate their networks and timetables, and the system was consolidated legally in 1918 in response to the logistical demands of the First World War.[19] Train whistles became the voice of this mechanised and standardised temporal order. However, these long-distance signals could be customised because of their simple construction. Most whistles contained a battery of narrow tubes that produced tones when a blast of steam passed through them. These tubes could be customised through a process known as 'quilling', in which 'each engineer made his own whistle and developed a distinctive tone and technique' for its operation.[20] In this sense, engineers effectively wrote, or quilled, themselves into the vernacular of the onrushing Machine Age by appropriating a specific technical object. As James McPherson notes, the sound of 'a quilling whistle' could, 'in the right hands', suggest both 'unrestrained freedom and power' and intense loneliness, 'a fit of blues' that had at last found a means of expression.[21] According to rail historians, the quilling technique was respected by African American musicians in particular,[22] who invented redeployment strategies using similar methods. As a result, the train whistle and other rail technologies became a lexicon embedded in African American music, from its technical foundations to its lyrical and sonic vocabulary. For example, techniques such as playing guitar with a bottleneck could produce a portamento that recreated the Doppler effect of passing train whistles. Building on a term originally coined by Albert Murray,[23] Joel Dinerstein describes such processes in African American cultural production as 'locomotive onomatopoeia'. In blues and swing music in particular, this technique articulates the 'symbiotic relationship of machine aesthetics and individual artistic power'.[24] In Hughes's work, the signifyin(g) potential of this framework emerged on the margins of American culture while remaining deeply (if scarcely visibly) connected to the centres of its socio-technical ensembles.

In Hughes's *Fine Clothes* sequence 'Railroad Avenue', such poems as 'The New Cabaret Girl', 'Closing Time', 'Crap Game', 'Ballad of Gin Mary', 'Elevator Boy', 'Porter' and 'Sport' depict black populations that apparently subsist as little more than cogs in a machine. In these vignettes, the dehumanising work these communities perform necessitates affective release in the only entertainments available: the black and grey market economies of juke joints, jazz cabarets, speakeasies and gaming establishments. These zones facilitate both self-expression and cultural subversion, but with the attendant risks of economic ruin, prison, harm and even death. Throughout the sequence, Hughes evokes the paradoxical doublings of locomotive onomatopoeia (especially hope and despair, and joy and pain) using blues and other cultural motifs. The final poem in the sequence, 'Saturday Night', charts a gin-fuelled downward spiral in a speakeasy. Hughes intensifies the euphoric staccato rhythms with proleptic scatting. The ellipsis in 'Hey! Hey! / Ho . . . Hum' disrupts the bathetic, mechanical routines explored in other parts of 'Railroad Avenue' with a potentially electrifying 'hum'. 'Do, it, Mr. Charlie', the speaker urges, 'Till de red dawn come'.[25] The 'red dawn' is a red stoplight bringing a halt to the self-destructive behaviour, but in the mid-1920s it was also strongly associated with the Russian Revolution. Although the subjects in 'Saturday Night' seem 'culturally active' but 'politically passive',[26] Hughes's speaker, and the formal apparatus of the poem, show how the inhabitants of 'Railroad Avenue' form a scarcely-visible network of latent political agency. Each injury, dead-end and death that an African American suffers in the sequence trips a switch, which will eventually complete a circuit and activate a social revolution.[27] The 'red dawn' that Hughes imagines is emergent but inevitable because, as he clearly documents in 'Railroad Avenue', African Americans were in the process of redeploying the technical assemblages of civic infrastructure, re-imagining and re-engineering a new social order that was hiding in plain sight.

Of course, Hughes did not passively await that 'red dawn' – he actively pursued its intellectual and social foundations, in print culture and beyond. In forging an allegiance with *The Messenger*, a prominent socialist magazine founded in 1917 by A. Phillip Randolph and Chandler Owen, Hughes found important validation among its black working-class readership. In 1925, *The Messenger* became the official magazine of the newly founded Brotherhood of Sleeping Car Porters, which was led by Randolph and was the first and largest African American-led labour organisation to be granted a charter by the American Federation of Labor. The magazine did not emphasise matters of cultural production to the same extent as *Opportunity* or *The Crisis*, but thanks to Randolph and Owen, who frequently extolled Hughes's working-class credentials as well as his middle-class education,[28] readers of *The Messenger* embraced him as 'our folk poet' – a ringing endorsement from trade unionists, which would be echoed later by socialists and the Communist Party USA (CPUSA).[29]

Hughes's short stories 'Bodies in the Moonlight' and 'The Little Virgin' drew on his personal experience working on *The West Hesseltine*, a freighter that travelled from Manhattan to the West Coast of Africa in 1923. They explored in detail the experience of 'humble toilers of the sea', rather than the railroad workers who read *The*

Messenger, but focused on the ability of even 'the most heterogeneous crew imaginable' to 'stick together like brothers in a fight in a foreign port'.[30] Hughes's short fiction for *The Messenger* tackled encounters with race, gender, sexuality and illicit economies at the sharp end of working-class life. In its support for Hughes, *The Messenger* helped inculcate an African American modernism intimately connected to urban, working-class experience. Theophilus Lewis, the theatre critic for the magazine explained how Hughes's socially engaged modernist writing fitted into the political work of *The Messenger*. 'The task for the Negro artist', Lewis wrote, was to represent 'the convulsions of a world breaking down in chaos' and simultaneously, 'the nuclei of a new world forming in incandescence [. . .] This condition of doubt will find its esthetic expression in dissonances of sound and color.'[31] By 1931, Hughes had immersed himself in those dissonances with revolutionary zeal, and turned increasingly to drama to channel his political thought.[32] During this pivotal year, the themes of sex, class, gender and race he explored in his avant-garde and periodical writing collided in a boxcar in Scottsboro, Alabama.

'A moving freight train': Langston Hughes, the Scottsboro Trials and the Redeployment of Rail Technology

On 25 March 1931 nine young African American boys and men aged twelve to nineteen – Clarence Norris (19); Olen Montgomery (17); Haywood Patterson (18); Ozie Powell (16); Willie Roberson (16), Charlie Weems (19); Eugene Williams (13); and brothers Andy Wright (19) and Roy Wright (12) – were accused by a group of white men of raping two white women, Victoria Price and Ruby Bates. All of the travellers were illegal passengers on freight cars seeking work in Alabama by 'riding the rails' on a Southern Railway Corporation freight train departing from Chattanooga to Memphis via Alabama. A fight had broken out on the train between the white and black travellers, which resulted in all but one white traveller being thrown from the train before it reached the station in Paint Rock, Alabama. All were eventually arrested, and the charges of rape were made by the women while they were in police custody. As Estelle Freedman notes, by making these charges, the plaintiffs could claim 'the status of a southern white woman worthy of protection from black men' rather than working-class itinerant workers who transgressed the South's strict social codes concerning inter-racial contact.[33] Despite flimsy and inconsistent evidence, all defendants excepting the youngest, Roy

Wright, were convicted, and initially sentenced to death. The CPUSA and the International Labor Defence (ILD) led the defence, and they were later joined by the NAACP and other organisations who formed the Scottsboro Defense Committee in 1935. The long-running series of retrials, mistrials and sentencing hearings resulted in acquittals for four of the nine defendants, but extended periods in prison for the rest, who belatedly received pardons (the latest arriving posthumously on 19 April 2013, when all of the Scottsboro Nine were exonerated by the Alabama legislature). The cases epitomise the miscarriages of justice perpetrated in the Jim Crow South, but they also reveal the intricate socio-technical ensembles underpinning (and, frequently, working at cross purposes with) American law.[34] Langston Hughes was a crucial hinge figure in mobilising both cultural and political advocacy against what was in effect a state-sanctioned lynching.[35] By referring directly to the infrastructures that the defendants illicitly navigated, and those that helped 'railroad' them in the long-running trials, Hughes's political works of the 1930s attempted to recover a voice for the Scottsboro Nine, and others affected by their plight.

The incident in Paint Rock, Alabama transgressed the rigid boundaries of race, sex, gender and class. However, the travellers' ability to move secretly across the country by appropriating technology pointed to an equally systemic threat to the white hegemony in the South. John Lennon argues that the illegal travellers, or hobos, were also 'itinerant workers whose mobility offered possible disruptions' to the 'ideological narrative of white, patriarchal capitalism'.[36] Indeed, cultural anxieties about the hobo yoked a range of marginalised subcultures together, since in the 1930s 'sex workers', itinerant 'mill workers, and African Americans' tended to share 'the same economic base and social capital'.[37] Yet the trials also tacitly acknowledged the important role that migrant workers played in the US economy. In addition, the cases also formed an implicit critique of the capitalist structures that drove unprecedented numbers to risk injury and death by riding the rails: of the hundreds of thousands riding the rails in search of employment each year, between 1929–39 a 'total of 24,647 trespassers were killed and 27,171 injured on railroad property'.[38] Those who survived risked persecution and incarceration, particularly if they were African American. But they also developed an extraordinary set of skills to survive, and these vernacular socio-technics formed part of their overall threat to cultural hegemonies. The expertise and spatial practices of these economic migrants, and their ability to appropriate not only the technological infrastructure of rail transport but also the social assemblages that sustained it, were dangerous because they developed within but beyond the regulatory frameworks of state law. Far from the nostalgic and unsophisticated stereotype that circulates in contemporary popular culture, hobos were often, to use an anachronism, fairly advanced 'hackers' of key economic and legal systems, with their own specialist techniques, jargon and other social codes that formed a crucial part of their subculture. Scottsboro brought this invisible group out of the shadows, and interleaving visual culture, revolutionary poetics and vernacular technicities, Hughes used his work to help amplify their voices.

Initially, Hughes attempted to rally support for the Scottsboro Nine in the South. The editors of the little magazine *Contempo*, a fortnightly journal based at the University of North Carolina, published two special numbers on the Scottsboro trials in July and December 1931. Milton Abernethy and Tony Buttitta invited Hughes to visit the campus in advance of the second issue's publication, which featured Hughes's poem 'Christ in Alabama', his essay 'Southern Gentlemen, White Prostitutes, Mill-Owners and Negros', and a stark, modernist illustration by Zell Ingram, which towers above the poem but also mediates the various elements of the page. Exposing the racial injustice of the case, Hughes's essay draws particular attention to the deterministic sociotechnical apparatuses that sealed the fate of both groups of economic migrants. He cites the 'State's electric chair' and its rail network as two mechanisms that 'Southern gentlemen' used to rig the socio-economic system against the working classes and African Americans alike.[39] These levers let 'Alabama's Southern gentlemen amuse themselves [by] burning 9 young black boys till they're dead'. Furthermore, Hughes indicts 'the mill-owners of Huntsville [who] continue to pay women workers too little for them to afford the price of a train ticket to Chattanooga', claiming that he 'never knew until now that white ladies (the same color as Southern gentleman) travelled in freight trains'.[40] By referring directly to the infrastructures that helped 'railroad' the defendants, Hughes argued that the case crossed economic, racial and gender lines, while still adhering to the narrative set forth in defence attorney Carol Weiss King's article 'Facts About Scottsboro', which *Contempo* reprinted in the December issue featuring Hughes's work. As King demonstrated in her article, the stereotypes connecting sex workers, African Americans and itinerant workers were prevalent in the South, and proved too tempting for the Scottsboro defence team.[41] Although his arguments demonstrated 'sensitivity to class', in his own essay Hughes's sympathies did not extend to sexual agency or convention; as Freedman argues, '[w]hile blaming capitalists for driving working women to desperation, Hughes nonetheless excluded these women from legal protection in his closing question, "And who ever heard of raping a prostitute?"'[42]

Although he failed to appreciate fully the Scottsboro trials' fraught dynamics of sex and gender in his essay for *Contempo*, in his poem 'Christ in Alabama' Hughes focused on a group of women ignored by most writers: the mothers of the Scottsboro Nine. In Scottsboro, the Christ figure is 'Beaten and black', while 'Mary is His Mother --' and 'God's his father', taking the form of a '*White Master Above*'.[43] While the focus is on the 'Most holy bastard / Of the bleeding mouth', the poem's narrative actually remains open with possibility, especially for its witnesses – and, in particular, for the African American women represented by Mary. These women played an important role in rallying support for the Scottsboro Nine in the black community and beyond. They are the point of contact between the victims and their wider social grouping – the black working classes – who are also, by extension, on trial. Mary's silence is not a given, and in 'Christ in Alabama' Hughes establishes the wider public voice she embodies as a point of contact between the poem and his essay 'Southern Gentlemen, White Prostitutes, Mill-Owners and Negros'. In that article, he demands that '12 million Negro Americans [. . . .] raise such a howl that the doors of Kilbee Prison Shake until the 9 youngsters come out'. The train lurks in the background of the essay and serves as a potential connection between the disparate American voices speaking out in support of the Nine. Would those who could 'afford the price of a train ticket to Chattanooga' now speak up for those who 'travelled in freight trains'?[44] The answer, in the case of *Contempo* magazine, was 'No'.

After the promised third issue on Scottsboro did not appear in January, Hughes published 'The Town of Scottsboro' in the 13 February 1932 issue. In that poem, the '*mob*' has drowned out the '*court*'. Yet the poet's eyes remain firmly rooted 'At Scottsboro', implying that the struggle was not over, and not limited, either by geography or the disappointing precedent set by *Contempo*, which capitulated to local pressure and quietly abandoned the cause.[45] However, by this stage Hughes had already turned his attention to journals more attuned to his communist politics. He published his one-act agitprop verse play *Scottsboro, Limited* in the left-wing journal *The New Masses* in November 1931, just before the second Scottsboro issue of *Contempo* appeared. An overt expression of communist propaganda, the play featured 'Red voices' that matched the tenor of *The New Masses* perfectly: 'The Communists will fight for you, / Not just black – but black and white'.[46] In an accompanying illustration which depicted a police officer pushing forward a rural gunman, William Gropper underscored the collusion between the mob and judicial system in the South.[47] In the deluxe edition of *Scottsboro, Limited* published by the Golden Stair Press in 1932, which also featured four Scottsboro-themed poems, Hughes enlisted Prentiss Taylor to expand the visual and socio-technical frame of the ensemble.[48]

Taylor produced four lithographs for *Scottsboro, Limited*. The *mis-en-page* of the Golden Stair edition connects the bodies of the Nine not only to the train, but also to the broader technical ensemble of the rail network, which mediates the play's political call-and-response. The cover illustration also introduces the play, except on the cover it is flanked by two red columns, signalling its communist affiliations, and a 'red alert' for the urgency of the case (Fig. 5.1). Michael Thurston has noted that the power lines connecting to the figures on the boxcar in the illustration suggest both 'electrocution' and 'lynching'.[49] However, from the late 1910s to the early 1930s, power lines were also used for telephony.[50] Taylor's *Scottsboro* illustration forms a telling dialogue with his lithograph for 'Christ in Alabama', which depicts the Christ figure's mouth opened in a silent scream, suggesting the parted lips of some of the defendants on the cover (Fig. 5.2). Rather than sentimentally 'tam[ing]' Hughes's poem 'Scottsboro Limited' 'to advance the pamphlet's fundraising agenda', as Thurston argues, Taylor's images extend Hughes's own strategies, harnessing communications infrastructure to amplify (and signify) both the work's socio-political commentary, and the voices of the Nine. In this way, the text performs an affective, and figurative, call to arms, activating the conscientious network of (African) American voices he invited to join him in his defence of the Scottsboro Nine.

Hughes's typographical strategies in *Scottsboro, Limited* echo his sparse but tactical staging. In the stage directions, the actors' bodies mimic the motion of the train, evoking the symbolic power of the rail network as well as the literal scene of the incident. In this respect, he implements Theophilus Lewis's earlier demand in *The Messenger* for black drama that registered both 'the convulsions of a world breaking down in chaos' and simultaneously, 'the nuclei of a new world forming in incandescence'.[51] The 'rocking boxcars' that the actors recreate on stage may have been invisible, but in Taylor's illustration they become an iron platform and conductor for their voices. In the widely performed play, the actors literally embodied that space and infrastructure through their gestures (and as I discuss at the end of the chapter, Amiri Baraka developed this technique in his attempted re-staging of *Scottsboro, Limited*). Hughes amplified the collective power of the black voice using vernacular technicities, completing a trajectory begun in his early poems, which focused on individuating the black voice by redeploying rail and other infrastructure technologies. The Scottsboro trials continued to generate a concerted effort across the modernist left to enlist support for the Nine, and they produced a rare consilience

Figure 5.1 Prentiss Taylor, Cover, in Langston Hughes, *Scottsboro, Limited* (New York: Golden Stair Press, 1932); Yale Collection of American Literature, Beinecke Rare Book and Manuscript Library.

Fig 5.2 Prentiss Taylor, *Christ in Alabama*, in Langston Hughes, *Scottsboro, Limited* (New York: Golden Stair Press, 1932), n.p.; Yale Collection of American Literature, Beinecke Rare Book and Manuscript Library.

between black and white formations across the modernist transatlantic, which peaked in the mid-1930s. As usual, Langston Hughes was at the centre of this activity, but equally he facilitated the rise of several young black voices with unique perspectives on Scottsboro and its broader contexts, including Pauli Murray.

Pauli Murray and the Transatlantic Boxcar: Covert Travel in Nancy Cunard's *Negro Anthology*

In an unpublished letter to Nancy Cunard of 30 September 1931, Hughes championed the work of a young African American woman 'named [Anna] Pauline Murray, 437 Manhattan Ave., New York, [who] has some poems and stories that I liked. Never been published. Not racial stuff', but, nonetheless, the work she eventually submitted had a clear relevance to Cunard's *Negro Anthology*, and was included in the collection.[52] Pauli Murray eventually became a prominent civil rights activist, law professor and Episcopal priest, but she was a student when she wrote 'Three Thousand Miles on a Dime in Ten Days' and 'The Song of the Highway'. In these works she addressed her experience of travelling illegally from San Francisco to New York on the rail network (the 'dime' in the title of the short story referred to the subway fare she paid on the final part of her journey). Although she did not address Scottsboro directly, she provided a critique of the cultural hierarchies and gender normativities underpinning the trials, which she connected to the suppressed contexts and technicities of riding the rails. And while they were not as overtly 'racial' as other contributions to Cunard's *Negro Anthology*, they did address racial diversity among the hobo subculture, and specific risks to young African Americans. As John Lennon rightly notes, 'authentic female voices writing of their own road experiences are noticeably absent' in the historiography of boxcar culture because such 'deviant mobility [. . .] could not be officially acknowledged'.[53] Murray's story has remained a crucial but hidden account of this period. But it also dovetails with the avant-garde's encounter with the 'boxcar politics' of the Great Depression, and the ways in which those discourses were mediated by modernist formations.

As an emerging writer, Murray's appearance in *Negro Anthology* was certainly a coup for her, yet she exerted an impressive level of control over that appearance, and Hughes had briefed her on the context. Originally entitled *COLOR*, Cunard's *Negro Anthology* showcased a wide range of black and white cultural commentators, as well as modernist avant-garde writers, in a meta-formational civil rights and political advocacy campaign.[54] Cunard founded her influential modernist publishing house The

Hours Press in 1927, and after beginning a relationship with the black jazz musician Henry Crowder she became intensely invested in the human rights of black people, particularly in America and British colonies. A white member of the British aristocracy and an heir to the Cunard ocean liner fortune, Cunard conflated avant-garde practice with her socialite celebrity, while cultivating a programme of political advocacy inflected by her increasingly radical left-wing views. Motivated by the Scottsboro trials, she began assembling the *Negro Anthology* in 1931, and published it in 1934. Her article 'Scottsboro – and other Scottsboros' summarised a range of evidence from the trial to mount a sustained attack on the numerous miscarriages of justice across the United States, especially in the South.[55] Other references to the trials appeared regularly throughout *Negro Anthology*, including Cunard's discussion of Hughes's appearance in *Contempo*, but they featured especially in its pro-communist sections, which she co-ordinated with her collaborators Tiemoko Garang Kouyaté and George Padmore.[56] As Peter Kalliney astutely argues, 'in place of political consensus, Cunard relied on shared aesthetic principles and professional attitudes to secure participation from a wide range of intellectuals'.[57] The debates between Cunard and the communist contributors, on the one hand, and W. E. B. Du Bois and his NAACP associates, on the other, showed how the Scottsboro trials cut across boundaries of race, ethnicity and political affiliation, without compromising particular subject positions.[58] Hughes played a key role in facilitating these exchanges, however. Like Cunard, he had travelled to Russia (on a failed filmmaking expedition), but he also maintained enormous pedigree in mainstream, left-wing and working-class African American print cultures.[59] He formed an important point of contact between the anthology's literary and political formations, and, of course, he was vital in securing contributions from lesser-known figures, who explored channels of American culture that more prominent contributors could not. And Cunard was particularly impressed by Murray.

In the years between Hughes's recommendation to Cunard and the publication of *Negro Anthology*, Pauline Murray increasingly identified as what we might now call gender non-binary and began using the name Pauli Murray in her published work. Cunard's policy was to publish photographs of the anthology's black contributors alongside their work, and she included one of Murray. Strikingly, however, Murray was not identified in the picture: instead, she appeared as 'Pete', the travelling companion of the unnamed (and apparently male) narrator dressed in male clothing (Fig. 5.3). 'Pete' was a persona she cultivated in her travels, and a shortened form of 'Peter Pan': an ageless adventure-seeker protected by his naivety and Boy Scout uniform ('the dude' was a variant of this persona,

Pete

Figure 5.3 Anonymous, *Pete* [Photograph of Pauli Murray], illustrates Pauli Murray, 'From "Three Thousand Miles on a Dime in Ten Days"', in *Negro Anthology*, ed. Nancy Cunard (London: Nancy Cunard at Wishart & Co., 1934), pp. 90–3 (p. 90).

and wore a sailor's suit instead). The narrator of 'Three Thousand Miles' was more experienced and analytical, however, with a detailed knowledge of the various systems that Murray would navigate in her future career as Professor of Law at Brandeis University in the 1960s. Yet even in 'Three Thousand Miles', Murray's semi-autobiographical characters reflect her precocious and subversive intellect, as well as her counter-servile technicities – but they also preserve her anonymity while rendering her gender ambiguous.

Murray relocated from Durham, North Carolina to attend high school in New York, eventually graduating with BA in English from Hunter College in 1933, shortly after completing the story.[60] The brief epigraph for 'Three Thousand Miles' provides an accurate autobiographical context for the narrative, but it withholds the crucial detail that Murray and her travelling companion had 'jumped the rails' by dressing in male clothes.[61] Cunard was delighted by the narrative, since she herself famously dressed in male clothing as part of her avant-garde challenge to the patriarchy. However, Murray requested that Cunard withhold the details about her sex.[62] Whereas Cunard's cross-dressing was provocative, and undertaken from a position of relative cultural strength, Murray's was protective – both on the rails and in print. Before she moved to New York in 1928, Murray had become adept at navigating the daily grind of the segregated infrastructure in Durham, NC where the transport network subjected her and her fellow black travellers to constant humiliation. As Kenneth Mack argues, 'her ongoing struggles with boundaries that sorted people by color' helped frame 'Murray's invention of the term "Jane Crow" to describe the illogic of sex discrimination'.[63] In this respect, her impulse to travel in the overtly liminal spaces of the open road, or the railroad, under a new name and gender identity was motivated by her politics as much as her practical need to travel quickly from San Francisco to New York to visit her aunt Pauline, who was ill and needed care.

In her response to Murray's submission, Cunard wrote that '[y]ou are the only one in the book not represented by a purely racial piece of writing'.[64] This is true, to a certain extent: although the photograph identifies 'Pete' as black, the narrative does not, and the narrator's identity in 'Three Thousand Miles' remains ambiguous. When race does feature in the story, however, it is either to showcase the varied backgrounds of illegal travellers, or to emphasise the particular dangers that African Americans faced. A drifter tells Pete and the narrator 'a wild tale about a "dick" [police officer] who kicked a colored boy off a freight', and 'then shot at him'.[65] In self-defence, '[t]he wounded man in turn pumped him with six bullets from a hidden gun', and '[t]he cop rolled off dead. Since then the whole country was hostile to "niggers."' A 'second fellow said two fellows had been lynched at Marion, Ohio, on this line a couple of hundred miles up the road, not along ago'.[66] As Rosalind Rosenberg notes, *The New York Times* carried a story about the charges arraigned against the Scottsboro Nine immediately before Murray departed for California; upon her return 'from her own harrowing freight-train ride, twenty-four days later, she discovered that the nine teenagers had been summarily tried, convicted, and sentenced to death'.⁶⁷ In 'Three Thousand Miles', direct references to Scottsboro are conspicuous by their absence; however, the brutal judicial and extra-judicial treatment meted out to black men in Murray's narrative is clearly informed by the trials.

The characters in 'Three Thousand Miles' do not offer direct commentary on the events their travelling companions report. Nevertheless, the dialogic arrangement of *Negro Anthology* made the social context of this story inescapable, and Murray's narrative tactics were highly appropriate to their bibliographical contexts. The *Negro Anthology*'s 'America' section provided a range of exegeses on geography, law and African American slang, among other topics, and had a broadly pedagogical thrust. The section featured many instances in which African Americans engaged with high-profile media technologies, including 'the gramophone, radio, and vitaphone (sound) film', as well as the 'new economy of celebrity enabled by them'.⁶⁸ However, it also addressed the bathetic, everyday technologies and marginalised groups central to the Scottsboro trials, and in this respect Murray's story carried an urgent pedagogical imperative. Written from the perspective of new members (or temporary interlopers) in its growing community, and strewn with detailed, accurate footnotes, the piece explains the strategies, jargon and technicities experienced in the subcultures that rode the rails – and those agencies who attempted to stop them. 'Three Thousand Miles' serves not only as a practical guide for a new generation of African Americans in search of economic opportunity, but as an exploration of the multiple risks and possibilities that travel in this liminal cultural zone entailed.

After receiving some guidance from 'a hobo with a mean reputation', the narrator provides detailed instructions for slotting a body into a machine that wasn't designed to carry it for extended periods – all under the gaze of professional organisations devoted to keeping it out:

> Right in the face of a 'dick' I caught the back end of a box car, the most dangerous thing I could have done. She [the train] swung me around under the wheels, my ribs crashed into a rod but my feet hung clear. I got to the flat in time to glimpse the 'bull' [cop] just behind me. Two 'brakies' [Brakeman, one of a crew] were running up from the rear. I jumped from one flat on to another, took a leap and found myself lying on top of Pete underneath a car-load of hot new machines.⁶⁹

This passage reveals the multiple physical risks that 'riding the rails' posed, and the feats of strength, knowledge and improvisational wit necessary to surmount them. Yet to any reader with knowledge of Murray's background – including *Negro Anthology* contributors such as Langston

Hughes, Countee Cullen and Alain Locke – it also manages to interleave those practices and vocabularies with the survival strategies of queer culture. Successfully evading authority figures with phallocentric ('dicks' and 'bulls') or excessively didactic ('brakies') sounding names results in bodily injury, but also a recuperative homosocial/homoerotic embrace, 'lying on top of Pete underneath a car-load of hot new machines'. The setting for this embrace is also relevant. The automobiles in the freight train are the flagship products of a new consumer culture promising liberty and autonomy, which stands in stark contrast to the heavily regulated machine ensemble of rail travel. Protected for transport, these machines represent pure potential, and suggest a technicity that might enhance, rather than restrict, other (and othered) forms of being, if only by providing another layer of disguise or another means of escape. The threat of exposure is always present, however, as in the stops on their journey, 'the yards were full of brakies, and the headlights of switch engines played on our flattened bodies'.[70] In these moments, the narrator and Pete attempt to become ghosts in the machine, haunting the interstices of the nation's infrastructure, but constantly returning, often violently, and bathetically, to the bodily traumas of riding the rails.

The barrage of technical and lexical detail in 'Three Thousand Miles' provides Murray's characters the means of their survival. From prying oranges from a crate in a 'reefer' (an 'ice cell of a refrigerator carriage') with frozen, injured hands, to hauling a numbed leg onto a 'high-ball' (or 'non-stop fast express freight') in time to dodge a policeman's bullet, Pete and the narrator barely survive their journey to New York. Following a hitchhiked journey from Jersey City to the 'Seventh Avenue subway', the pair take a final rail journey to Pete's mother's (actually Murray's aunt's) home, and they pay the dime required.[71] The journey underground, into the cover of the city's purportedly neutral zone of mass transit, provides a poignant backdrop to 'The Song of the Highway', the poem with which Murray concludes the story. Written from the perspective of the road, the refrain, 'I am the Highway / Long, white winding Highway' constitutes a warning about – as much as a celebration of – life on the 'open' road.[72] Accessible and lyrical, the poem uses a complex and variable rhyme scheme reminiscent of Hughes's early 1930s work, and it is equally ambivalent in its encounter with socio-technical infrastructure. After elegising the open spaces and connective power of America's travel routes, the penultimate stanza memorialises those 'Who bartered with famine – thirst – / And death – to give me birth'.[73] Here, Murray gives a voice to those (non-'white') workers who died producing America's infrastructure, which 'go[es] on in silence', its 'Long, white' expanse erasing that violent past, and perpetuating its present myth of opportunity and connection.[74] Her detailed attention to that infrastructure, and to the people who negotiate its grey and black expanses, provides a kind of Baedeker for these zones – but one whose guidance she ciphers through multiple registers of race, class and gender.

Although 'The Song of the Highway' parrots the sublime symbolic register associated with roads, railroads and subways, Murray's diptych in *Negro Anthology* provides a section of its readership alert to her codes with bathetic critiques and tactical blueprints for navigating them. In *The Practice of Everyday Life*, Michel de Certeau also invokes the technological sublime without identifying it as such; he calls rail networks a 'gridwork of technocratic discipline' in which '[t]he machine is the *primum mobile*, the solitary god from which all action proceeds'. Nevertheless, he also identifies a countervailing 'speculative' presence that inheres 'in the heart of the mechanical order', which constantly produces temporary 'spectators and transgressors of space'.[75] The transgressive act of riding the rails lurks as latent possibility in the background of Certeau's analysis of rail travel, a blasphemy that he dares not utter. Although critics have not fully considered this possibility, Garret Ziegler has incisively connected Certeau's 'analysis of spatial pracitices' to 'the mass movements of individuals on the routes of public transit' and subways.[76] Ziegler argues that some modernist poets 'articulate[d] a discourse of tactical resistance to the dominant power systems of the functionalist subway through a rhetoric of technological sublimity'.[77] However, in Ziegler's argument, the technological sublime becomes a means of *undermining* the 'functionalist dynamics' of rail systems, rather than as a means of *expressing* them, as Certeau and many modernist poets do. Zielger's emphasis on 'the everyday speech practices of the subway's passengers' is a more convincing articulation of the 'oblique politics of resistance' that modernist writers deployed in their encounters with machine ensembles;[78] however, Murray's techno-bathetic strategies not only provide a pedagogical account of illegally navigating the railroads – they also critique the rhetorical and conceptual operations of the sublime *itself*. 'Three Thousand Miles' counters the railroad's functionalism with a kind of realist hyper-functionalism – a 'speculative' strategy of resistance that does not seek to impede the railroad's efficiency of movement, only the toll extracted for that movement. 'The Song of the Open Road' opens out her bathetic critique of the dynamic technological sublime underpinning this vast machine. In a paean to its open, 'Binding' expanses, Murray conceals a warning to the culturally marginalised who sought to navigate its networks.[79]

Gwendolyn Bennett, Infrastructure and the Legacies of Scottsboro

Although they were not aware of each other's work at the time, Gwendolyn Bennett developed Murray's tactical engagement with America's transportation networks throughout the 1930s in different forms. A rising star of the Harlem Renaissance, Bennett's work had appeared in *Opportunity, Crisis, Fire!!* and other influential journals and anthologies in the 1920s. She won a scholarship to study art in Paris in 1925, and her subsequent work combined a deft command of poetics with strategic flashes of avant-garde experimentation. Her short stories set in Paris especially create disjunctive temporal frameworks to match the defamiliarised experiences she encountered as a black expatriate. For example, in 'Wedding Day' she showed how the colour line still persisted for African Americans in Paris, and articulated its presence through the bathetic movements of the metro.[80] Her 1927 short story 'Tokens' also developed her interest in timekeeping and transportation technologies, where multiple chronologies intersected and blurred around fragile, convalescent bodies in a hospital on the banks of the Seine.[81] Bennett's radical politics and increasingly experimental style also inflected her column 'The Ebony Flute' in *Opportunity*, and, like her friends Langston Hughes and Zora Neale Hurston, she seemed ideally placed to join the black vanguards responding to the socio-economic crises of the 1930s.

Unfortunately, due to a complex series of personal and professional crises in the mid–late 1920s, her writing career suffered multiple setbacks. In 1926–7, she not only witnessed the probable suicide of her father, who died when he fell in front of a subway train, but also experienced the loss of her major artworks in a house fire. She was compelled to resign from the Art faculty at Howard University when she came under pressure for her engagement to Alfred Jackson, a medical student she met there.[82] Taking on work in batik fabric production to support herself, she relocated to Tennessee and then Florida between 1928–32, before returning to New York. Despite occasional readings and appearances, her public engagement with the arts in the 1930s was largely administrative. As Belinda Wheeler and Louis Parascandola note, in many ways Bennett 'sacrificed her own artistic talents in order to further the advancement of others' during this period when she was employed as Director of the Harlem Community Art Center, the flagship Federal Art Project sponsored by Works Progress Administration (WPA).[83] Nevertheless, Bennett's archives confirm that she *did* join the 1930s literary vanguard, developing her poetic voice with an assured and polemical force. Combining documentary social realism, vernacular versification and the diachronic technicities and 'locomotive onomatopoeia' of her more avant-garde works of the 1920s, her 1930s poetry evolved in parallel with other politically activist work. During this period, Bennett came under severe pressure from the House Un-American Activities Committee, which accused her of communist affiliations.[84] The Art Center supported her, and she was eventually acquitted, but the controversy may explain why Frank Horne, at the WPA, never published the manuscript of poems she sent him in 1939.[85] Nevertheless, Bennett's archive survived as a kind of blueprint, privately circulating in pedagogical networks, and bridging the generational divide between African American vanguardists until its very recent publication.

In her 1938 poem 'I Build America', Bennett reverses the emphasis of Murray's 'The Song of the Highway', and gives a voice to the multitudes of ethnically, racially and economically marginalised 'dead, / Building America'. The present participles throughout the poem emphasise not only the enduring material evidence of those workers' labour, but, through a material fusion of bodies and technologies, the hierarchies that dominate the ensembles it built:

> I died in a smelting furnace
> White-hot and shining molten, I,
> To make a bridge or singing rail[86]

Technology is clearly not neutral for Bennett: the workers are black, the originary technical object is 'White-hot', and the resulting ensemble continues to victimise 'weeping Negros' by using the infrastructures they helped create to oppress them. They are '[t]hat riddled thing', the black mass of exploited workers, 'Lowered [. . .] From a lynching tree'. However, by locating the black voice in the 'singing rail', Bennett recovers the oral and material vernacular histories they embedded in the infrastructure they constructed.[87] Railroads were also a synecdoche for the industrialised socio-technical ensembles that proliferated in the Machine Age, which in turn formed an archive of American culture, evoking the country's past and future simultaneously. As the cultural historian Julie Cohn explains, in addition to 'bricks, mortar, pipes, or wires', 'infrastructure also encompasses more abstract entities, such as protocols (human and computer), standards, and memory'.[88] These 'protocols' are anything but neutral, and throughout their evolution these systems represent the partnerships and collusions articulated through spatial apparatus, both visible and invisible, that shape the practice of everyday life and the hierarchies that proliferate within it. As Bennett had done previously with her writing about colour lines, her strategy of embodiment deliberately stress-tests the boundaries between the socio-technics, race and class – and between the dead and the living – as the 'sightless eyes' of black workers 'Survey the plains and chart railways'.[89]

In the specific context of 'I Build America', Bennett's references to the rail technologies and the 'lynching tree' also echo the 'legal lynching' of the Scottsboro trials, while maintaining the silence around its specific contexts. By 1933, those sessions had shifted to Decatur, Alabama, and continued until 1937, ending predictably in convictions, which the defence appealed.[90] Written one year later, 'I Build America' emphasises the ongoing, disproportionate price paid by African Americans in the regular operation of the country's industrial ensembles. Yet Bennett also acknowledges the collective sacrifice by 'red men, the black, the white', who together have formed a techno-necropolis of the working classes, who quite literally support America's living cities:

> I, underneath the ground,
> And rumbling through the air,
> At work at machines,
> Guiding roaring motors,
> And teaching unborn children –
> I am the dead,
> Building America.[91]

Bennett insists that black working-class culture is encoded in American socio-technics, and that readers can recover its oral and material histories by attending to specific codes. Like Hughes and Murray, Bennett locates those ciphers both in visual signifiers – for example the oppressive 'whiteness' that dominates her descriptions of forges and concrete structures – and the aurality that articulates black sacrifice for and resistance to those structures. By reactivating that dialogue and re-presenting it as a living and unified black working-class voice, Bennet encourages African Americans to reclaim and recalibrate their sense of technological agency and innovation. Her counter-servile strategies 'Breathe a living song / Into the nation that I build', and create an explicit bond between folk vernacular and technicity.[92] Her redeployment of Scottsboro-era socio-technics is an important but, until recently, largely unknown link in the tradition of motivated signifyin(g) from the Machine Age to the Information Age. In 'I Build America' especially, Bennett's articulation of black voices across the *longue durée* of industrial modernity creates a foundation of technical pedagogy that diffuses laterally across culture, as well as vertically between generations.[93]

For Bennett, as for other black writers, the standardised temporal orders that governed train schedules and the noise of the day-to-day operations of rail networks dominated the seemingly static infrastructure that sustained it. By giving voice to that infrastructure, Bennett articulates what Michael Germana calls the 'multiple heterogeneous durations' experienced by black Americans and other minority and marginalised groups.[94] 'I Build America' makes a diachronic spectacle of 'the grid', the network (and patchwork) of infrastructure that powers and moves the United States; Bennett legitimises those alternative temporalities with her strategic re-deployment of infrastructure and socio-technical signifyin(g). Although her poetry was only privately circulated, her influence diffused in Harlem's cultural scene in other ways. According to the archive at the Amistad Research Center, Frank Horne, an optometrist and Harlem Renaissance poet who also directed the WPA in Harlem, enthusiastically supported Bennett's work, and although he was unable to publish it he continued to collaborate with Bennett on a number of art education projects, including the Harlem Art Centre, throughout the 1930s.[95] Bennett's own work from this period has only recently been recovered, but her influence on other artists and writers, including Jacob Lawrence, has been felt indirectly through her work with the WPA.

By 1940, the Scottsboro trials themselves had receded from public attention as retrials continually shifted venues, but by then motifs connecting rail networks with the diachronic technicities of African American experience had become embedded in American systems of cultural production, particularly in the radical left. The railroad justice of the Scottsboro trials crossed boundaries of race, class, gender, region and time, and connected Harlem Renaissance luminaries such as Bennett, Murray and Hughes to a new generation of black left-wing technomodernists. Bennett's emphasis on vernacular folk culture also forged clear correlations between technology and black working-class men and women in particular. Her 1938 poem 'Sweat' embodied their technicity as fluid, hard-won knowledge that flowed between generations. From the agrarian South to the industrialised North, Bennett traces the progress of 'black women' working at 'brightly polished stoves' and 'black men' working in 'stevedore gang[s]', 'Mines, boiler rooms', 'and Pullman trains'. Combined, their 'story' is 'burned in sweat', but Bennett configures this work itself *as infrastructure*; as such, the 'sweat' that creates it is a redemptive and baptismal force for 'living things', which, 'nurtured and tended', has made subsequent generations 'rich and strong'.[96]

The Switch Engine: Riding the Rails and Radical Technicities in Ralph Ellison's Early Fiction

Like Langston Hughes and Pauli Murray before him, in the summer of 1933 Ralph Ellison was a young African American with academic opportunities but limited means who rode the rails to pursue opportunities and meet obligations. However, his experience proved to be even more dangerous. He was travelling through Decatur, Alabama, the site of the first Scottsboro retrials, when the freight train on which he had stowed away pulled into the rail yard. Two 'bulls' carrying guns 'came into the cars looking for girls', and then rounded up the illegal travellers.[97] In interviews, Ellison claimed to have narrowly escaped by charging the guards with a group of white hobos, and then hiding under a stockyard shed before 'flipping' another boxcar to complete his journey to Tuskegee College.[98] However, his fictional accounts of the events are actually closer to the truth. As Lawrence Jackson has deduced, Ellison was not only caught in Decatur, but also seriously beaten, receiving two head wounds – a fact that Ellison omits from his essays and interviews about the incident.[99] Ellison kept the source of his injuries secret in public, but he replays versions of the incident throughout his early published and unpublished fiction. His drafts for *Invisible Man* include a scene where the narrator 'would be badly beaten up by railroad police – as was Ellison himself [en route to] Tuskegee – and flee to a nearby funeral home'.[100] In his proletarian short story 'Hymie's Bull', the narrator also discloses that '[o]nce a bull hit me across the bridge of my nose and I felt like I was coming apart like a cigarette floating in a urinal'.[101] For Ellison, the incident articulated the cultural fall-out from the Scottsboro trials at a personal level, and made him acutely conscious of the judicial, socio-economic and socio-technical ensembles at work behind the scenes of his early short stories, including 'Hymie's Bull' (1937) and 'I Did Not Learn Their Names' (ca. 1940).[102] These works established a template for the sustained campaign of motivated techno-signifyin(g) that he undertook in his early writing, including 'Slick Gonna Learn' (1939), 'A Hard Time Keeping Up' (ca. 1937–8), 'King of the Bingo Game' (1944), and various essays. Scottsboro and rail technologies emerge like ciphers in these works, in which Ellison elides emergent counter-servile technicities with patterns of vernacular speech, under intensely pressurised socio-political contexts. Of course, Ellison achieved the fullest articulation of these practices in *Invisible Man*. But like the unnamed 'thinker tinker' narrator Invisible, the protagonist who would later define his professional career, Ellison's early unpublished fiction reveals that technicity was an integral component of the signifyin(g) system embedded in his programme of social change.[103]

Ellison's accounts of rail travel in his early fiction, like Pauli Murray's, were rich with technical details and jargon. Ellison grew up near the Rock Island Roundhouse in Oklahoma City, where the sounds of 'switch engines' comingled with the sounds of blues music emerging from nearby venues.[104] Under the tutelage of 'Charlie', an experienced black hobo who could pass for white, Ellison learned techniques for 'flipping' (boarding a fast-moving freight train), reading manifests (documents tacked to the 'sides of the boxcars' with details of destinations) and protecting himself against aggression and predation.[105] In his fiction, he quickly integrated this technical language with vernacular technicity as part of his long-term project, which he honed during an intense burst of work with the WPA's New York Writer's Project in 1937–8. 'Hymie's Bull' stages a contest between two groups of technical specialists, hobos and bulls, in which the illegal travellers achieved a temporary victory (in Hymie's case, killing a bull), but in full knowledge that the bulls had a clear and usually unassailable advantage. Hymie and the narrator both negotiate constant illness, injury and bodily discomfort, but the narrator is visibly black, and despite his skill he is at a clear disadvantage: on the rails or off, when a flashpoint occurred, 'the main thing' for the bulls was 'to make some black boy pay for it'.[106]

In 'I Did Not Learn Their Names', Ellison explores hobo socio-technics in more extensive detail than 'Hymie's Bull', developing a more complex commentary on inter-racial and inter-generational relationships in the process. The narrator discovers a pair of elderly white travellers in the same freight car who were forced to ride the rails to visit their son in jail because of the economic hardships of the Great Depression. Initially, he maintains a hostile distance and overt lack of deference as a self-preservation tactic. This response reflects the narrator's own sense of double consciousness, which is acute, even within the liminal zone of the hobo community. However, in keeping with the social realist mode, the characters' shared circumstances presented some opportunity for a new relationship. As the train rolls on, the narrator's suspicions break down as he begins to admire the Texan couple's sophisticated grasp of technological appropriation, as well as the altruistic impulses that motivate it:

> I had gone down to see the old man stripping the car of its brown-paper lining to make a bed for the old lady. It was an ingenious thing for him to do. I wondered why no one had thought to do it before. The floor of a boxcar is hard, and the paper used to line the walls of cars in which automobiles are shipped is the softest thing about them.[107]

Here, the couple redeploys the buffer between two machine ensembles as a shield for their own bodies, which both protects and conceals their illegal infiltration. In a strategy reminiscent of Murray's, in this scene

Ellison not only reveals the means by which appropriated technologies spread through hobo communities – he also creates a blueprint for redeploying infrastructure technologies against the hegemonies they instantiate, both individually and collectively. Among the marginalised group of illegal rail travellers, class and economic relations sometimes transcended issues of race, especially when the opportunity to share tactics presented itself. However, Certeau cautioned that a spatial 'tactic' used to insinuate 'itself into the other's place' maintains 'no base where it can capitalize on its advantages [. . .] Whatever it wins, it does not keep.'[108] Although he sought continually to consolidate and extend such moments of tactical cohesion throughout his fiction, Ellison also acknowledged that they were generally only temporary, and were prone to rupture by unexpected encounters with legal and regulatory frameworks. In such moments, standard hierarchies were reinstated, and, due to the illicit context of riding the rails, often violently. Ellison often used references to rail technology as a means of signifyin(g) on such encounters, even where the narrative did not directly involve trains.

For example, in his 1939 work 'Slick Gonna Learn', an extract from an abandoned novel project published in the WPA journal *Direction*, Ellison's working-class African American protagonist 'Slick' is released from jail after accidentally striking a white police officer in an altercation. Slick was simply in the wrong place at the wrong time, but police protocol required his arrest. Following a discussion, Slick is released, but not before breaching social convention: he does not show deference to the arresting officers, and they almost immediately seek retribution. In the moments before they attack him in the street, Ellison evokes a white/black binary in Slick's immediate surroundings, in which 'a switch engine with a string of cars puffed behind a building with steam hissing as it poured from its valves, sweeping in a tumbling white cloud against the dark night'.[109] The 'white cloud' of steam from the switch engine merges with the sound of the police car, which 'pulled quietly to the curb as he came to a corner, its motor pulsating rhythmically, smoothly' and 'blocked his way'.[110] A switch engine is a powerful locomotive built for moving trains around stockyards, but this 'switch' also connects to the invisible socio-technical apparatus that sustains the colour line, even in the Industrialised North. This machinery could be switched on at a moment's notice, as it is in this case, when Slick is bundled into a police car. The police take Slick on an extended, silent trip in the car to intimidate him, but before they can administer the beating they abandon him to break up a strike at a factory in Baltimore. A white Irish truck driver later rescues Slick, identifying himself as a union member as they listen to reports of the strike on the radio. He expresses sympathy for the strikers and with Slick, and their temporary comradeship suggests a shared bond of class. Just as in 'I Did Not Learn Their Names', however, Ellison concludes this seemingly archetypical social realist narrative with ambivalence, as Slick studies the face of the driver and tries 'to connect him with the experiences of the day'.[111] Slick remains suspicious about whether class and economic affiliation can ever transcend the colour line, or the socio-technical systems that sustain it.

Ellison analysed similar encounters in other works, gradually raising the stakes and brutality involved in political activism. In his *New Masses* essay 'Judge Lynch in New York', he describes a racist attack on Harry Smith, Marvin Jackson and Edward Meggs, three black economic migrants from the South who recently moved to New York City. Shortly before the incident 'they saw an Amsterdam Avenue street car passing', and are immediately set upon by a white lynch mob until 'a crowd gathered and the mobsters ran'.[112] The streetcar here invokes state-enabled extra-judicial violence, which plays out at the local level, just as it did in 'Slick'. Ellison pointedly concludes the essay by asking 'why the mob turned up so soon after the police searched [Smith, Jackson and Meggs] and sent them up the street' before the attack, and 'why no arrests were made'?[113] The implied answer is fairly clear – as was the case in his earlier short story 'The Birthmark', the police were helping the lynch mob.[114] And just as in that story, this sort of thing supposedly didn't happen anymore.

Ellison constantly coupled the interior mediations of double consciousness with exterior infrastructures, which instantiated the sense of 'two-ness' that W.E.B. Du Bois associated with color lines in socio-technical ensembles.[115] In Ellison's untitled 1937–8 short story posthumously published as 'A Hard Time Keeping Up', rail tracks criss-cross its introductory passages, as a group of friends catch a streetcar across town. As they exit the train, the narrator discovers that the fallen 'snow had turned to ice, and under the streetlights the rusting rails made it look like a cigarette stain', which reminds him 'of the first snow I'd seen with blood on it'.[116] After carefully priming the Naturalistic narrative for a sublime and brutal conclusion, Ellison undermines readers' expectations with a bathetic turn. He reveals that an apparent racially motivated barroom shooting turns out to be an elaborate practical joke. Ketchup, rather than blood, soaks a naked black man who the group sees running through the streets, apparently mortally wounded. The witnesses' anger and fear, and the narrator's relief at learning the truth, reinforce how this surreal exception proved the rules outlined in Ellison's other works: that racial binaries in the United States conditioned behaviour as profoundly as its civic infrastructure did, largely because that infrastructure helped implement and normalise segregationist policies. Mirroring the diffusion of such ensembles in culture, Ellison embedded that infrastructure in his fiction; it is generally detectable only in moments of crisis, but is always present, and always signifyin(g). Nevertheless, his experiments with narrative structure and temporality helped probe those deeply entrenched socio-technical relationships for weak points. He pushed this tactic to a new extreme in 'King of the Bingo Game', which completed his transition from social (or super-) realist to avant-garde intra-modernist.

Like *Invisible Man*, in 'King of the Bingo Game' Ellison does not abandon the bathetic technicities of his proletarian fiction but, rather, amplifies and triangulates them. Also like the novel, the unnamed protagonist in the short story is a black man from the South, but in this case he is impoverished and desperately anxious about his critically ill wife, Laura. Watching a film in a Harlem theatre, he tries to distract himself as he awaits an all-important bingo game that will be played in the intermission. The modest prize money will be enough for a doctor to treat Laura. Transfixed by the movie, and its technical apparatus, the narrator takes a swig of whiskey and enters a sort of fugue state, in which his deeply embedded experiences of asymmetrical power become externalised.[117] Predictably, rail technology plays a pivotal role in this reverie:

> he was a boy again walking along a railroad trestle down South, and seeing the train coming, and running back as fast as he could go, and hearing the whistle blowing, and getting off the trestle to solid ground just in time, with the earth trembling beneath his feet, and feeling relieved as he ran down the cinder-strewn embankment onto the highway, and looking back and seeing with terror that the train had left the track and was following him right down the middle of the street, and all the white people laughing as he ran screaming.[118]

In this instance, the narrator's childhood act of trespass on a railway bridge is re-inscribed by the racially valenced media environment in which he is trapped. As Richard Dyer and Rayvon Fouché have argued, in its most basic photochemical processes cinema 'technology was constructed to privilege and perfect representations of whiteness'.[119] Ellison was a professional photographer, and he identifies how cinema technology re-inscribes a cultural narrative of white supremacy as the light beam literally projects a form of historical determinism, with the black subject position suggested by the 'specks of dust dancing' in the screen's expansive 'whiteness'.[120] In the theatre, subjected to its deterministic temporalities, the narrator becomes trapped in a vicious circuit, in which spinning train and bingo wheels, and film reels, all form part of the same inescapable socio-technical ensemble. As his screams merge with those of the train whistle, the narrator's nightmarish vision of the past foreshadows his forthcoming humiliation, terror and injury, all for the amusement of 'white people'.

The protagonist believes he might change his luck when he is called to play the bingo game. However, as he takes the switch that controls the bingo wheel he refuses to release it, and keeps the wheel spinning, stepping outside of the acceptable temporal boundaries and social codes governing the game in the process. In his incisive reading of 'King of the Bingo Game', Michael Germana argues that '[t]he protagonist's desire to discover possibility (and agency) within the deterministic narrative of the motion picture comes to fruition' during the bingo game.[121] That agency revolves around 'the dynamic time of the spinning wheel [which] coincides with the suspension of historical determinism'.[122] Germana is correct to accentuate the temporal dynamics of the scene, but he understates the significance of the narrator's literal grip on the switch, a instrument of technological control, which extends to the signifyin(g) power of the socio-technical assemblages that Ellison (re-)deploys throughout the narrative. By seizing control of the spinning wheel, the protagonist becomes King-of-the-Bingo-Game; he not only disrupts the temporal order of a heavily regulated event but also (in Fouché's terminology) reconceptualises and redeploys that leisure technology as a disruptive tool of individuation. His technique is improvisational and experimental but evolves rapidly in tandem with his ambitions. In this sense, 'King of the Bingo Game' is Ellison's first fully developed case study in vernacular rapid prototyping, in which he embraces bathetic technicity as an instrument of social critique, and self-actualisation.

As Fouché argues, expressions of 'black vernacular technological creativity' frequently articulate a 'resistance to existing technology and strategic appropriations of the material and symbolic power and energy of technology'.[123] Although the narrator's strategy ultimately ends in humiliation and tragedy, his gesture is not instinctual but tactical, and technical:

> He squeezed the button until his fist ached. Then, like the sudden shriek of a subway whistle, a doubt tore through his head. Suppose he did not spin the wheel long enough? What could he do, and how could he tell? And then he knew, even as he wondered, that as long as he pressed the button, he could control the jackpot. He and only he could determine whether or not it was to be his. Not even the man with the microphone could do anything about it now.[124]

In his state of hyper-stimulation, the narrator not only 'grasps' the interdependency of socio-technical ensembles, but also the vulnerability of the points of connection that control them. He seizes that control by appropriating a switch, or relay point, and becoming its living actuator. Unfortunately, his revelation arrives just as he realises that temporary disruption does not equal lasting change. Although he understands the work, significance and basic functionalities of the system that he has 'hacked', King-of-the-Bingo-Game does not have a firm grip on the extent of its technical operations – and, particularly, the ways in which it has been rigged to maintain its primary output, i.e. social control. 'Like the sudden shriek of a subway whistle', this realisation dramatically re-imposes standard mechanical 'clock time' on his diachronic reveries.[125] As it becomes clear that he cannot sustain his experiment, the locomotive from his past takes the form of 'an A train' bearing down on him with 'Laura in his arms', as he runs 'down the tracks of the subway'. The narrator is about to be overrun in both his virtual world and his actual one. Nevertheless, he modulates his response to intense pain when he transforms his scream into a quiet 'confidential tone' as a security guard crushes his wrist. King-of-the-Bingo-Game tells the guards, '"Boys, I really can't give it up"', and in doing so, creates a crucial moment of individuation by dissociating himself from the electromechanical 'screams' of the ensemble.[126]

Ellison's crucial modulation of the protagonist's voice is one of the most important points in the narrative. As well as sustaining King-of-the-Bingo-Game's battle for the button, it marks a break in the circuit. The narrator is in control of the machine ensemble, but more importantly he has also decoupled some of his interior thought processes from its operations. In this context, although his experiment in vernacular rapid prototyping has failed to alter his material circumstances, he has created a machine for transforming his personal narrative – and, by extension, potentially those of other working-class black men in his predicament. As the narrator finally loses consciousness and (by implication) control of his bowels when the security guards finally knock him out, 'he knew even as it slipped out of him that his luck had run out on the stage'.[127] He is contained, humiliated and denied this chance to save his wife, but in a sense the conclusion is not entirely tragic. His humiliation is a punishment, but it is a survivable one, and it carries its own form of dignity as an expression of physical and spiritual exertion. King-of-the-Bingo-Game has ultimately failed to alter the sublime power of white supremacist socio-technics, but, briefly, he also exposed the fragility of such systems, and the power of socially marginalised communities to challenge them. Ellison would deploy the same strategy in the 'Battle Royal' chapter of *Invisible Man*, where Invisible is tortured with an electrified mat. The experience teaches him that he can 'conduct electricity'.[128] This short-hand assertion of non-servile technicity is an important part of the process that enables Invisible to reclaim 'all past humiliations' as 'precious parts of my experience' that 'defined me'.[129] 'King of the Bingo Game' provided his blueprint: if you confront and rewire social machinery, don't get caught, but if you do, survive, take notes, tell the tale and be prepared for the next inevitable encounter.

'Experimentation is Prometheus': Prototyping *Invisible Man*

In his childhood, Ellison developed a foundation in electronics 'by obsessively mastering the techniques and concepts of crystal-set circuitry, vacuum tubes, and winding coils'.[130] By adulthood he could read electronic schematics, and his acquisition of technical expertise was relentless.[131] Shifting from 'riding the rails' in the 1930s to 'becom[ing] a compulsive experimenter' with audio and visual technology, Ellison eventually financed his fiction writing by selling custom-made 'high-fidelity sound systems' in the late 1940s.[132] He was also a professional photographer, and assembled 35 mm and Polaroid photomontages from portraits and still lifes in the 1940s–1970s.[133] However, locomotive onomatopoeia continued to suffuse his engagements with technology in *Invisible Man*. Indeed, his nickname for his protagonist, generally known as 'Invisible', is 'Jack-the-Bear', a generic folk character in African American oral tradition.[134] However, in railroad slang 'jack' is a term for a 'locomotive',[135] while in electronics a jack is a receptacle for plugs, and a point of contact, or circuit interface, between various parts of an ensemble, generally in communications networks (*OED*). Developing his technological discourse and locomotive onomatopoeia, in *Invisible Man* Ellison continued to equate technology, and technicity, with vernacular. But equally, and inversely, a crucial part of Ellison's project is to reconsider the individuating power of African American technicities, and how they diffuse through culture. As he stated in his notes for the novel based on his short extract 'Slick Gonna Learn', 'Experimentation is Prometheus' – it is 'the inspired application of experimental method' and 'the will to discover new knowledge'.[136] The 'thinker tinker' Invisible describes how his acts of technological 'sabotage'– illegally tapping electricity from 'Monopolated Light & Power' and modifying media technology to articulate his experiences of time-space dynamics – are actually part of a political experiment that makes him 'kin to Ford, Edison and Franklin' (and, through signifyin[g] strategies, the African American inventors Lewis H. Latimer and Granville T. Woods).[137] By the end of the novel, Invisible has begun the process of formulating a black vernacular technicity that converts his acts of redeployment and reconception throughout the novel into a framework for technological recreation on a grand scale. As Fouché states, 're-creation is the redesign and production of a new material artifact after an existing form or function has been rejected'.[138] However, Invisible's emergent programme is not limited to 'artifacts' but addresses entire ensembles. As Ellison's references to American legislators, inventors and corporate structures make clear, Invisible seeks to disrupt and then overthrow white supremacist socio-technics one system at a time.

Drawing on the blueprints in his earlier fiction, Ellison threads sociotechnics into Invisible's socio-political consciousness throughout his *bildung*. As I have argued, this process begins with the infamous 'Battle Royal' scene, but its more intense articulations are also less visible, and often occur when Invisible attempts to get to grips with transportation infrastructure. Rail tracks first appear in the novel when Invisible drives the college's white trustee, Mr Norton, towards the infamous 'Golden Day' bar. It is Ellison's first clear signal that space, time and hegemony are about to intersect.[139] When he brings Norton to the Golden Day bar, Ellison reveals that Invisible's socio-technical education is just beginning. Critics have long identified the bar as a chronotope that invokes Lewis Mumford's 1926 book *The Golden Day*, a study of society and technology.[140] Jennifer Lieberman has argued that the veterans' verbal abuse of Invisible contains key terms from Mumford's study, such as 'mechanical man', 'automaton' and '*slave*'; together, they 'describe how machines have hindered the Transcendentalist aspiration for greatness' in America. Furthermore, '[b]y using Mumford's terms to describe the arrested development of the novel's protagonist, Ellison draws an analogy between racism and machine-age utilitarianism' that Invisible only scarcely perceives at this stage.[141] This is because Invisible has been indoctrinated to accept a servile relationship with technology. As I noted in the book's Introduction, Mumford had diagnosed post-industrial techno-servility in his 1934 work *Technics and Civilization* as a collapse in key distinctions between machine and worker. Unless they mastered technical objects, he argued, workers would become 'dumb, servile, [and] abject' machines themselves.[142] Although he rejected the 'binarizing logic that glorifies utilitarianism and denigrates romanticism', Mumford nevertheless perpetuated a master-slave dialectic characteristic of his Young American associates, which casually glossed the reality of slavery for African Americans, and the socio-technical ensembles that sustained the institution.[143] Ellison took serious exception to this omission, and (in my view) the servile conceptual framework of the technological sublime that sustained it. He agreed with Mumford's conclusion that 'it is not industrial progress per se which damages peoples or cultures', but argued that 'when industrialism is linked to political doctrine which has as its goal the subjugation of the world', then its dominant, servile technicities resulted in the routine 'exploitation of peoples'.[144] His task in *Invisible Man* was to transform Invisible's reflexive actions into deliberated strategies and technicities. To do so, he delved into the histories and contexts of socio-technical signification in the South, and, for Ellison, that involved rail transportation.

The first extensive reference to trains in *Invisible Man* occurs in Reverend Homer A. Barbee's sermon about the death of the founder of Invisible's college, which Ellison models on the African American civil rights pioneer Booker T. Washington. Succumbing to a sudden illness on a Pullman train during a speaking tour, Barbee links 'the cry of that train and the pain too big for tears!'[145] In this evocation of a quintessential technological sublime, Ellison connects a train whistle to an articulation of pain, but also of individuation, since this is the moment that Dr Bledsoe 'takes on the burden' of leading the college.[146] Here, Ellison acknowledges the signifyin(g) locomotive onomatopoeia that suffuses Machine Age African American writing. Unlike 'King of the Bingo Game', however, in *Invisible Man* he almost always locates references to rail technology in the external world. Rail technology still serves as a ligature between socio-technical hierarchies and the rhythms of daily life, but for Invisible they are also a point of mediation between individuals and assemblages – between socio-political policies and embodied experience – and, crucially, they signify moments in which his past experiences with those assemblages condition his forthcoming encounters with them.

For example, after the son of his prospective employer Mr Emerson discloses to Invisible that Dr Bledsoe's reference letters describe Invisible's expulsion, rather than his suspension, from college, Invisible takes a subway ride to consider his fate. Eventually, Invisible decides to accept the job at Liberty Paints that has been suggested to him by Emerson's son. The subway emits a 'drone' at this stage,[147] but that grows into a 'roar' in an iconic superrealist scene that follows his employment at the factory.[148] At Liberty Paints, Invisible and the other black workers become '*machines inside the machine*', until he inadvertently causes an explosion.[149] Confined to the factory hospital, he is subjected to electroshock therapy, which induces a state of profound dissociation. The process does not subdue Invisible in the way that the doctors hope it will, however, and instead it has the opposite effect: he was 'no longer afraid' of 'important men, not of trustees and such'.[150] Tellingly, the scene ends, not in the hospital, but in the subway, the arterial network connecting New York City. In keeping with the social realist conventions I discuss earlier in the chapter, throughout the novel the 'roaring' of the subway expresses a pervasive narrative in which its Taylorist spatial dynamics assert an all-pervasive democratic anonymity. However, as Amiri Baraka would later point out, that narrative is a 'modern myth' that conceals hegemonies of race, class, gender and sexuality beneath its spatial systems and rigid codes of behaviour.[151] As Invisible enters the subway after leaving the hospital, Ellison's brief reference to the blonde woman who 'nibbled at a red Delicious apple as station lights rippled past her' accrues a proleptic as well as allegorical significance. Invisible now has eaten of the fruit, as it were: he recognises that race, class, gender and other markers of power and status are embedded in the foundations of America's socio-technical infrastructure.

As Invisible begins his career of political activism with the Brotherhood, a political organisation loosely modelled on the CPUSA, Invisible begins to identify similar dynamics at play in its party machinery – that is, an invisible framework of white patriarchal hegemony dominates its daily operations, and, eventually, is turned against him. Just as it did for 'Slick', the steam from a 'switch engine' signals to Invisible that racial hegemonies dominate the Brotherhood, even if Invisible can't or won't recognise the warning.[152] Later, in a hallucination, Invisible imagines his former mentor Brother Jack and his colleagues circling him 'with their knives, looking for the slightest excuse [. . .] to "ball the jack,"'.[153] In railroad terminology 'balling the jack' means making 'a fast run' in a locomotive,[154] while in gambling slang it means 'staking everything on a single bet'.[155] Techno-signifyin(g) on the term 'jack', Invisible creates a signal path between these two meanings, and the adopted names of himself and his mentor. In doing so, he describes how the Brotherhood had used him as a pawn to provoke a race riot in Harlem, which the Brotherhood could exploit to gain power in the ensuing chaos. It was a high-stakes but calculated gamble, because Brother Jack had already learned how to probe civic infrastructure for weak points and racial valences; he could use the black community as pawns in his attempts at social engineering, but he only partially succeeded, because Jack-the-Bear had also grasped that strategy and was nearly ready to formulate his own.

When one of his African American former Brotherhood colleagues, Brother Tod Clifton, is chased and shot down by a police officer, Invisible feels 'the subway vibrating underground' as '[t]he sun seemed to scream an inch above my head'.[156] Riding in the subway in the aftermath of the shooting, Invisible equates Clifton's death with a decision 'to step off the platform and fall beneath the train' in a suicidal 'plunge outside of history'.[157] In this passage, Ellison once again connects rail technology with a persistent form of sociotechnical temporality, in which trains stand in for hegemonic, deterministic histories. As 'the trains [plunge] in and out' of the tunnel, 'throwing blue sparks', Invisible considers the 'transitory ones' who stand on the peripheries of history – those who 'shoot up from the South into the busy city like wild *jacks*-in-the box broken loose from our springs [my emphasis]', 'standing noisy in their very silence [and] harsh as a cry of terror in their quietness'.[158] For Invisible, these black youths are 'men outside of historical time', 'running and dodging the forces of history instead of making a dominating stand'. This realisation triggers another key revelation for Invisible: '[w]hat if history was a gambler, instead of a force in a laboratory experiment, and the boys his ace in the hole?' With these 'boys [as] his agents', could Invisible exact his 'own revenge' against those who would 'ball the jack'?[159]

Once again Ellison produces a consilience of socio-technical ensembles, which connect rail technologies, media ecologies and specific forms of African American cultural expression, bound together by the vernacular language of the blues, which he evokes with references to 'grooves' on a vinyl disc. Invisible concludes that black youth operates 'outside the groove of history, and it was my job to get them in, all of them'.[160] Here, he begins to envisage himself as a sort of retro-engineer who seeks to mix his community's experience with the dominant 'groove of history', preserving its unique rhythms but changing American history as a whole using improvisational strategies. However, Ellison has still lodged Invisible in the deterministic rhythms of the dominant socio-technical hegemony. As the subway scenes in *Invisible Man* make clear, the key to completing his work resides in re-formulating black technicities collaboratively with the community. However, that work is impossible until Invisible is able to overcome his own sense of techno-servility. Threatened by Ras the Destroyer, a civil rights activist turned extremist, and chased by the police, Invisible escapes through a manhole cover into an underground coal storage depot. He retreats underground, to the domain of the subway, but also to a wellspring of black vernacular creativity.

Invisible is able to make his subterranean home quite comfortable due to his extensive technical knowledge and social connections within Harlem. As part of his research for Roi Ottley's and William Weatherby's WPA project *The Negro in New York: An Informal Social History*, Ellison became acquainted with a network of basement-level and subterranean dwellings in Harlem where poor black families were forced to reside, relying on their ingenuity to subsist while paying 'exorbitant rents' to live in 'these run-down sections' of town.[161] Importing tactics from the 'Hooverville' shantytowns that Ellison alludes to in *Invisible Man*,[162] these residents illegally tapped power lines and shorted gas and electricity meters to avoid paying for utilities (a practice that Ellison engaged in himself).[163] Invisible, of course, goes several steps further and engages in his reconception and redeployment of grid technologies. He tactically siphons electricity from 'Monopolated Light & Power' (which is surely a *détournement* of the 'United Electric Light and Power Company' in New York City) to power 1,339 'filament type' light bulbs and his hi-fi equipment – as well as devices to enhance his comfort, such as remote-controlled coffee machines.[164] As John Wright notes, the 'filament' bulbs that 'shed light on [the narrator's] invisibility' are a crucial technical reference to an invention by Lewis H. Latimer.[165] Together with his collaborators, Latimer invented a carbon filament that improved upon the one in Edison's light bulbs (and as Fouché notes, Latimer was also an aspiring poet).[166] In a draft of the 'Prologue' to *Invisible Man*, Ellison originally refers to 'Monopolated Light & Power' as 'Consolidated Edison'; in doing so, he signifies on the invisibility of black inventors such as Latimer and Granville T. Woods, whose technological creativity was occluded from history by a socio-technical framework dominated by white men.[167]

As Ellison himself wrote in *The Negro in New York*,[168] 'despite disclaimers to the contrary which rendered black technological innovators historically *invisible* [my emphasis], the bewildering array of technical inventions, which altered human life within a brief span, found Negroes in the vanguard' of the Machine Age.[169] They were also left beyond the groove of history: Ellison reported that African Americans were frequently denied proper credit and due payment for their inventions, or even their capacity to invent, despite 'reports that more than four thousand patents [were] held' by African Americans by the late 1930s.[170] Fouché also shows how 'inventions by black individuals can be interpreted as subverting and resisting the dominant American society'. Operating from the 'periphery', a 'key site for the production and sustenance of counterhegemonic discourse', black inventors 'shap[ed] American material culture' through the 'invention of technological artefacts'. In effect, 'inventive creativity by African Americans [contested] the structural exclusion of black people' by allowing them to become 'visible metaphorically and materially through technological production'.[171] Like King-of-the-Bingo-Game, Invisible identifies the socio-technical assemblages that create the 'grooves' of history from which he and his community have been excluded. Hijacking those assemblages, and co-opting those grooves, the characters are determined variously to disrupt, supplant and/or reconfigure those cultural narratives, but on their own terms, and with their own technicity.

In the penultimate chapter before the novel's 'Epilogue', a chance encounter with the white trustee from his former college, Mr Norton, prompts Invisible to complete his journey from Mumfordian automaton to underground vernacular technologist. When he accosts Norton,

Invisible assures him that '[y]ou're safe. Take any train; they all go to the Golden D –.'[172] Norton escapes before Invisible can complete his sentence, reinforcing the ambivalence of this relationship. For both characters, the connection between the past and the present is a continuous circuit, but an incomplete and glitchy one, subject to revision and reinterpretation. However, the advantage that Invisible holds is that he now recognises these glitches and understands how they can be exploited. Invisible's encounters in the subway routinely place him between two socio-technical 'grooves', and two orders of time: one associated with black culture, and the other with the dominant white hegemony. However, Ellison continually disrupts these dialectical encounters by short-circuiting their binary modalities through Invisible's acts of redeployment and reconception. When the time comes to emerge from the underground spaces he inhabits, Invisible is no longer content to ride the rails or work on the margins. Instead, he has found a way to access the frameworks that N. Katherine Hayles calls the nation's 'cognitive assemblages'. These intricate networks combine 'human and nonhuman cognizers' with 'material agents' to amplify and articulate 'the flow of information through a system and the choices and decisions that create, modify, and interpret that flow'.[173] Hayles's discussion focuses on highly complex information systems of the late twentieth century, such as traffic control networks, which frequently incorporate artificial intelligence. However, Ellison had a detailed familiarity with the systems that laid the groundwork – and indeed, which still forms a part – of this advanced communications network. In *Invisible Man*, he also identifies a non-servile technicity with which to access it.

In the final sentence of the novel, Invisible asks the reader, 'Who knows but that, on the lower frequencies, I speak for you?'[174] As many critics have noted, this cryptic conclusion suggests a pirate radio broadcast, an 'underground' signal in a literal sense. Invisible's shift from physical to electronic communications infrastructure brilliantly synthesizes multiple registers and discourses that Ellison negotiates over the course of the novel. Bounded by geographic region but accessible locally and internationally, wireless communication operates polyphonically, simultaneously and, in certain applications, dialogically. However, Ellison's reference is technically specific, and worth further attention. Low frequency (aka LF, 'low band', or 'kilometre band') radio waves are simply frequencies in the 30–300 kilohertz range, and are mainly used in long-distance communications. In Europe and Africa, that includes AM broadcast radio, but in the United States, where AM frequencies start at 300 khz, LF bands are for reserved for point-to-point broadcasting and specialised military, emergency, aviation, navigation, clock time and weather communications systems, as well as for amateur radio.[175] In other words, these frequencies are not necessarily a platform for *illicit* communication – rather, they are for *specialised* communication. These bands facilitate transportation, security, agriculture and other vital sectors of national infrastructure, but they are also available to trained amateurs, who can access these systems, and, potentially, intervene in them. Rather than a form a sabotage, then, Ellison imagines low frequency communication as both the means and the metaphor for a profound reconception of America's socio-technical ensembles. His narrator seeks invisibly to co-opt the nation's burgeoning cognitive assemblages, and redirect them: in effect, he, like the socio-technical organisations he targets, speaks for 'you' before 'you' realise that he has done so.

Figuratively (but in mid-century America sometimes quite literally), key socio-technical ensembles operate on 'the lower frequencies', articulating cognitive processes through a sequence of electro-mechanical operations. *Invisible Man* charts the progress of an individual who becomes adept at negotiating the reticulated strata of socio-technical systems, from railways to broadcast technologies. In Ellison's socio-technical vision, double consciousness can serve as a potential advantage in the emergent cognitive assemblages of the Information Age. As he was aware, these new assemblages were built on and symbiotic with (and not, somehow, sweeping aside) deeply entrenched and compromised Machine Age infrastructures. By the end of the novel, Invisible had identified the points in which those assemblages intersect as areas for potential transformation. He becomes an expert in navigating and subverting socio-technical hierarchies that engender and exploit mass techno-servility, while considering alternative ensembles in which marginality could provide a platform for energetic innovation and individuation, rather than powerlessness. In this way, Ellison shifts black vernacular technicity from a mere survival strategy to an ontological imperative. The challenge was to become a cultural agent capable of driving that change, and Invisible does this at ground level, cultivating a voice in one neighbourhood, Harlem, before expanding across America.

Conclusion: (In)Visible Legacies – African American Avant-Gardes and Counter-Servile Technicities

Across the arc of the modernist, late modernist and inter-modernist periods, rail technologies continued to embed the deep network of signifyin(g) themes and practices for (and between) generations of black experimental writers. For the writers I have discussed in this chapter, they are ciphers for repressive cultural binaries, which rearticulate long-standing problems of socio-technical segregation, which were consolidated in the Machine Age. For Ralph Ellison, the bathetic rhythms of rail technology invisibly connected those ongoing crises to the emergent infrastructures of the post-Second World War Information Age. As a new generation of writers emerged, the trans-generational strategy of motivated signifyin(g) on the theme of railways, and the counter-servile technicities that emerged from the liminal spaces they occupied in culture, continued to develop. As Matthew Luter notes, Amiri Baraka's 1964 play *Dutchman*, set in 'the flying underbelly of the city', contains telling parallels with the conclusion of chapter eleven in Ellison's *Invisible Man*.[176] 'The salient features of this brief scene – white temptress [the antagonist Lula], unassuming black man [the protagonist Clay], subway, apple – are the same', and as such constitute a prime example of motivated signifyin(g).[177] Baraka's play is thus a 'revision of Ellison in order to advance an alternate aesthetic that more directly attacks white (especially white liberal) racism'.[178] The subway is a potent spatial frame for this project; however, a technical reading of the play's title, *Dutchman*, also folds the work into a tradition of techno-bathetic critique rearticulated by black avant-garde writers in the 1960s.

In the technical trades, the term 'dutchman' refers to a makeshift repair, or a device used to cover a flaw or 'badly made joint' (*OED*), while in the field of stage management, it refers to a piece of fabric 'stuck over a scenery joint and painted in to conceal it'.[179] On the aging rail networks of the early twentieth century, however, a 'dutchman' was a method of repairing worn tracks with 'fishplates' and 'welding steel'.[180] By 1964, when *Dutchman* was first performed, New York's subway system itself had become riddled, literally and metaphorically, with such short-term fixes, and had begun its decline from a Taylorist iteration of the technological sublime into 'an international symbol of post-industrial decay and governmental ineffectiveness' that reached its nadir in the 1970s and early 1980s.[181] Since the 1930s, New York City had also been undertaking subtle yet powerful policies of racial segregation in several of its boroughs, which proliferated via Jim Crow hiring, banking and zoning policies, and, in particular, via the segregationist planning designs of Robert Moses.[182] By the early 1960s, the various 'dutchmen' that had maintained New York City's rail infrastructure and its behind-the-scenes policies of racial and social segregation began to strain to breaking point. Techno-signifyin(g) on Ellison's fiction, Baraka's *Dutchman* explored Lula's and Clay's tactical responses to the socio-technics of race and gender as articulated in New York's subway system in more detail than Ellison. The play concludes less optimistically than *Invisible Man*, but with an entirely consistent result: the humiliation, serious injury and death of its protagonist, who naively misreads the racially valenced machine ensemble in which he is trapped.

In *Dutchman*, Baraka sharpened his techno-bathetic critique into brutal satire to emphasise the increasingly dire consequences of servile technicities, and the segregationist politics that exploited them. However, whereas Ellison drifted away from from the politics of the radical left, Baraka took the opposite tack as he delved more deeply into signifyin(g) railways. In 1977–9 Baraka attempted to re-stage Langston Hughes's *Scottsboro, Limited* with the Anti-Imperialist Cultural Union.[183] The play intersected with Baraka's own Marxist politics at the time and revived his interest in vernacular technicities. His production never reached the stage, but explaining his attraction to the play he cited the 'ingenious props that Hughes has written in to be created by the actors through the use of motion. The scene on the train, for example, is created by the way the actors stand and sway.'[184] Identifying a point at which 'one of the Scottsboro Boys sounds as though he might capitulate to the racist judicial system', Baraka notes how 'suddenly, the tide turns and he says the group must fight and struggle unremittingly against it', evoking the Red Train of revolution with a vocal and bodily locomotive onomatopoeia.[185] The sparse dynamism of the staging prompted Baraka's 'serious re-evaluation' of Hughes as an 'avant-garde' figure in American culture.[186] Baraka's proposed adaptation evinces a sustained interest in the human body's capacity to evoke and intervene in both machine and social ensembles, so it is no surprise that he rediscovered this aspect of Hughes's work as he recovered the signifyin(g) technicities of African American culture.

Using strategies of reconception, redeployment and recreation – and, as I have suggested, rapid prototyping and tactical vernacular technicity – writers such as Langston Hughes, Pauli Murray, Gwendolyn Bennett, Ralph Ellison and Amiri Baraka articulated a nuanced vernacular technicity articulated across the *longue durée* of industrial modernity. Rejecting the late capitalist discourses of controlled obsolescence, they critiqued the means by which its technicities persisted as instruments of a racist hegemony. From urban planning to the space race, discourses of innovation could implement socio-technical segregation, sometimes invisibly, just as effectively as the obverse: by the breakdown of quotidian infrastructure, degraded by those same segregationist policies. However, black writers proposed innovative prototypes for augmenting, undermining and supplanting those technicities with tactical interventions. Their radical technicities form a vernacular infrastructure every bit as important as other cultural products taken to define experimental black writing. To paraphrase Ellison, their engagement with 'technology' was strategically 'vernacular', and therefore adaptable, and, above all, resilient.

Notes

1. See David E. Nye, *American Technological Sublime* (Cambridge, MA, and London: The MIT Press, 1994), p. 45.
2. For representative case studies see Darcy A. Zabel, *The (Underground) Railroad in African American Literature* (New York: Peter Lang Publishing, 2004).
3. Ralph Ellison, *Invisible Man* (London: Penguin Books, 2001), p. 7.
4. Ralph Ellison and Alan Macpherson, 'Indivisible Man', in Ralph Ellison, *CERE*, pp. 359–99 (p. 373).
5. Rayvon Fouché, 'Say It Loud, I'm Black and I'm Proud: African Americans, American Artifactual Culture, and Black Vernacular Technological Creativity', *American Quarterly* 58.3 (September 2006): 639–61 (p. 641).
6. Henry Louis Gates, Jr, *The Signifying Monkey: A Theory of African-American Literary Criticism* (New York and Oxford: Oxford University Press, 1988), p. 124.
7. Jessica Trounstine, *Segregation by Design: Local Politics and Inequality in American Cities* (Cambridge: Cambridge University Press, 2018), p. 104.
8. Langston Hughes, 'God to Hungry Child', *Workers Monthly* 4.5 (March 1925): 234.
9. See Eric B. White, *Transatlantic Avant-Gardes: Little Magazines and Localist Modernism* (Edinburgh: Edinburgh University Press 2013), pp. 165–71.
10. Langston Hughes, 'Railroad Avenue', *Fire!!* 1.1 (November 1926): 21.
11. Ibid.
12. David Suisman, *Selling Sounds: The Commercial Revolution in American Music* (Cambridge, MA: Harvard University Press, 2009), p. 92.
13. Giles Slade, *Made To Break: Technology and Obsolescence in America* (Cambridge, MA, and London: Harvard University Press, 2006), p. 5.
14. Langston Hughes, 'Railroad Avenue', p. 21.
15. Jason M. Baskin, *Modernism Beyond the Avant-Garde: Embodying Experience* (Cambridge: Cambridge University Press, 2018), pp. 112–13.
16. Fouché, 'Say It Loud, I'm Black and I'm Proud', p. 642.
17. Langston Hughes, 'Blues' [sequence], *CWLH 1*, pp. 75–80.
18. Langston Hughes, 'Homesick Blues', *CWLH 1*, p. 80.
19. See James Alan McPherson, 'Some Observations on the Railway and American Culture', in *Railroad: Trains and Train People in American Culture*, ed. James Alan McPherson and Miller Williams (New York: Random House, 1976), pp. 3–17 (pp. 14–15).
20. Ibid. p. 14.

21. Ibid. p. 15.
22. Ibid. pp. 14–15.
23. Albert Murray, *Stomping the Blues* (New York: Da Capo, 1976), p. 106.
24. Joel Dinerstein, *Swinging the Machine: Modernity, Technology, and African American Culture Between the World Wars* (Amherst: University of Massachusetts Press, 2003), p. 25.
25. Langston Hughes, 'Saturday Night', *CWLH 1*, pp. 90–1 (p. 91).
26. Anthony Dawahare, *Nationalism, Marxism, and African American Literature Between the Wars* (Jackson: University Press of Mississippi, 2003), p. 59.
27. See especially Langston Hughes, 'Closing Time', *CWLH 1*, p. 85, and 'Porter', *CWLH 1*, pp. 89–90 (p. 90).
28. [A. Phillip Randolph and Chandler Owen], 'Langston Hughes', in 'Aframerican Academy', *The Messenger* 9.4 (April 1927): 115, 135 (p. 135).
29. Lewis Alexander, [Letter to the Editors], *The Messenger* (November 1927): 328.
30. Langston Hughes, 'The Little Virgin', *The Messenger* (November 1927): 327–8 (p. 327).
31. Theophilus Lewis, 'The Theatre: The Souls of Black Folk', *The Messenger* 7.6 (June 1925): 230.
32. See Joseph McLaren, *Langston Hughes: Folk Dramatist in the Protest Tradition, 1921–1943* (Westport, CT, and London: Greenwood Press, 1997), pp. 2–6.
33. Estelle B. Freedman, *Redefining Rape: Sexual Violence in the Era of Suffrage and Segregation* (Cambridge, MA, and London: Harvard University Press, 2013), p. 259.
34. See Dan T. Carter, *Scottsboro: A Tragedy of the American South* (Baton Rouge: Louisiana State University Press, 1979), pp. 8–9.
35. See James A. Miller, *Remembering Scottsboro: The Legacy of an Infamous Trial* (Princeton and Oxford: Princeton University Press, 2009), p. 17.
36. John Lennon, *Boxcar Politics: The Hobo in U.S. Culture and Literature* (Amherst, MA: University of Massachusetts Press, 2014), pp. 143–4.
37. Ibid. p. 136.
38. Ibid. p. 137.
39. Langston Hughes, 'Southern Gentlemen, White Prostitutes, Mill-Owners and Negros', *Contempo* 1.13 (1 December 1931): 1.
40. Ibid.
41. Carol Weiss King, 'Facts about Scottsboro', *Contempo* 1.13 (1 December 1931): 1, 4 (p. 4).
42. Freedman, *Redefining Rape*, p. 261.
43. Langston Hughes, 'Christ in Alabama', *Contempo* 1.13 (1 December 1931): 1.
44. Langston Hughes, 'Southern Gentlemen', p. 1.
45. See Suzanne Churchill et al., '"Mammy of the South/Silence Your Mouth": The Silencing of Race Radicalism in *Contempo* Magazine',

Modernism/Modernity Print Plus, vol. 1, cycle 1 (2 March 2016) <https://doi.org/10.26597/mod.0000> (accessed 8 January 2018).
46. Langston Hughes, *Scottsboro, Limited: A One Act Play*, in *The New Masses* 7.6 (November 1931): 18–21 (p. 19).
47. William Gropper, [untitled illustration], in Ibid. p. 19.
48. Langston Hughes and Prentiss Taylor, *Scottsboro Limited* (New York: Golden Stair Press, 1932). The poems in the unpaginated pamphlet are 'Justice', 'Scottsboro', 'Christ in Alabama' and 'The Town of Scottsboro' (n.p.).
49. Michael Thurston, 'Black Christ, Red Flag: Langston Hughes on Scottsboro', *College Literature*, 22.3 (October 1995): 30–49 (p. 40).
50. See Mischa Schwartz, 'Carrier-wave Telephony Over Power Lines: Early History', *IEEE Communications Magazine* 47.1 (January 2009): 14–18.
51. Theophilus Lewis, 'The Theatre: The Souls of Black Folk', *The Messenger* 7.6 (June 1925): 230.
52. Langston Hughes to Nancy Cunard, 30 September 1931, HRC Cunard.
53. Lennon, *Boxcar Politics*, pp. 25–6.
54. See Langston Hughes to Nancy Cunard, 27 December 1931, B15, F11, HRC Cunard.
55. Nancy Cunard, 'Scottsboro – and Other Scottsboros', *Negro Anthology*, pp. 245–71.
56. See Nancy Cunard, 'A Note on *Contempo* and Langston Hughes', *Negro Anthology*, pp. 141–2.
57. Peter Kalliney, *Commonwealth of Letters: British Literary Culture and the Emergence of Postcolonial Aesthetics* (Oxford: Oxford University Press, 2013), p. 40.
58. See especially Nancy Cunard, 'A Reactionary Negro Organisation: A Short Review of Dr. Dubois, *The Crisis*, and the NAACP in 1932', *Negro Anthology*, pp. 142–7.
59. On Langston Hughes's work on the failed Soviet film *Chernye i belye* [*Black and White*], and his various accounts of it, see Steven S. Lee, *The Ethnic Avant-Garde: Minority Cultures and World Revolution* (New York: Columbia University Press, 2015), especially pp. 121–30, 135–6, 141–8.
60. The definitive account of Pauli Murray's extraordinary career is Rosalind Rosenberg's *Jane Crow: The Life of Pauli Murray* (Oxford: Oxford University Press, 2017), but Kenneth W. Mack's chapter on Murray in *Representing the Race: The Creation of the Civil Rights Lawyer* (Cambridge, MA: Harvard University Press, 2012) also presents a richly detailed if more synoptic account (pp. 207–32).
61. Pauli Murray, 'From "Three Thousand Miles on a Dime in Ten Days"', in Cunard, *Negro Anthology*, pp. 90–3 (p. 90).
62. Nancy Cunard to Pauli Murray, 15 January [n.d.], quoted in Mack, *Representing the Race*, p. 212.
63. Mack, *Representing the Race*, p. 210.
64. Nancy Cunard to Pauli Murray, 15 January [n.d.], cited in Ibid. p. 212.

65. Ibid. p. 92.
66. Ibid.
67. Rosenberg, *Jane Crow*, p. 44.
68. Jeremy Braddock, 'Media Studies 1932: Nancy Cunard in the Archive of Claude McKay', *Modernism/Modernity Print Plus*, vol. 3, cycle 2 (30 May 2018) <https://doi.org/10.26597/mod.0050> (accessed 16 September 2018).
69. Murray, '"Three Thousand Miles"', p. 91.
70. Ibid.
71. Ibid. p. 92.
72. Murray, 'The Song of the Highway', in Ibid. pp. 92–3 (p. 92).
73. Ibid. p. 93.
74. Ibid.
75. *PEL*, p. 113.
76. Garrett Ziegler, 'Subjects and Subways: The Politics of the Third Rail', *space & culture* 7.3 (August 2004): 283–301 (p. 285).
77. Ibid. p. 292. See Nye, *American Technological Sublime*, p. 77.
78. Ziegler, 'Subjects and Subways', p. 291.
79. Murray, 'The Song of the Highway', p. 92.
80. Gwendolyn Bennett, 'Wedding Day', *HHRB*, pp. 46–52.
81. Gwendolyn Bennett, 'Tokens', *HHRB*, pp. 53–7.
82. Belinda Wheeler and Louis J. Parascandola, 'Introduction', *HHRB*. pp. 1–17 (pp. 9–12).
83. Ibid. p. 14.
84. Ibid.
85. Belinda Wheeler and Louis J. Parascandola, 'Poetry: Introduction', *HHRB*, pp. 107–10 (p. 109); also see William J. Maxwell, *F.B. Eyes: How J. Edgar Hoover's Ghostreaders Framed African American Literature* (Princeton: Princeton University Press, 2015), p. 88.
86. Gwendolyn Bennett, 'I Build America', *HHRB*, pp. 115–17 (p. 115).
87. Ibid.
88. Julie A. Cohn, *The Grid: Biography of an American Technology* (Cambridge, MA, and London: The MIT Press, 2017), p. 7.
89. Ibid. p. 116.
90. Despite Judge William Callahan's decision to ban any form of journalism from the retrials, strong public interest in the Scottsboro trials persisted, and the case continued to reverberate through left-wing vanguardist literature; see Carter, *Scottsboro: A Tragedy of the American South*, p. 297.
91. Bennett, 'I Build America', p. 117.
92. Ibid.
93. I draw here on Wai Chee Dimock's use of '*longue durée*', a term first coined by the historian Fernand Braudel, to describe 'a scale enlargement along the temporal axis' in which history is organised and explored diachronically, by 'centuries' as well as being 'periodized by decades'; Wai Chee Dimock, *Through Other Continents: American Literature Across Deep Time* (Princeton, and Oxford: Princeton University Press, 2006), p. 4.

94. Michael Germana, *Ralph Ellison, Temporal Technologist* (Oxford: Oxford University Press, 2018), p. 54.
95. See Wheeler and Parascandola's notes on 'Unpublished Poetry', in Bennett, *HHRB*, p. 235.
96. Bennett, 'Sweat', *HHRB*, pp. 117–19 (pp. 118–19).
97. Ralph Ellison, 'I Did Not Learn Their Names', *FH*, pp. 89–96 (pp. 95–6).
98. See Ralph Ellison, 'Perspective of Literature', *CERE*, pp. 770–85 (pp. 772–4).
99. Lawrence Jackson, *Ralph Ellison: The Emergence of Genius* (New York: John Wiley and Sons, Inc., 2002), pp. 93–4.
100. See Barbara Foley, *Wrestling with the Left: The Making of Ralph Ellison's Invisible Man* (Durham, NC: Duke University Press, 2010), pp. 162–3. Drafts for *Invisible Man* which reference Scottsboro and the CPUSA include 'Woodridge', B146; 'Notes 1942–50', B1, F151; and 'New York', B145, LOC Ellison; see Foley, p. 162.
101. Ralph Ellison, 'Hymie's Bull', *FH*, pp. 82–8 (p. 83). Ellison's injuries were around his eyes rather than the nose – a slight alteration but enough to shield the specifics.
102. See John Callahan, 'Introduction', *FH*, pp. i–xxxviii (pp. x, xxi–xxii).
103. Ellison, *IM*, p. 7.
104. Jervis Anderson, 'Profiles: Ralph Ellison – Going to the Territory [Interview]', *New Yorker* 52.40 (22 November 1976): 55–108 (p. 88).
105. Ibid. p. 88.
106. Ellison, 'Hymie's Bull', p. 84.
107. Ibid. p. 90.
108. Certeau, *PEL*, p. xix.
109. Ralph Ellison, 'Slick Gonna Learn: From an Unpublished First Novel', *Direction* 2.5 (September 1939): 10–11, 14, 16 (p. 11).
110. Ibid. p. 11.
111. Ibid. p. 16.
112. Ralph Ellison, 'Judge Lynch in New York', *New Masses* 32.8 (15 August 1939): 15–16 (p. 16).
113. Ibid.
114. Ralph Ellison, 'The Birthmark', *New Masses* 36.2 (2 July 1940): 16–17.
115. W. E. B. Du Bois, *The Souls of Black Folk*, ed. Brent Hayes Edwards (Oxford: Oxford University Press, 2007), p. 8.
116. Ellison, '[A Hard Time Keeping Up]', *FH*, pp. 97–109 (pp. 98–9).
117. Ellison, 'King of the Bingo Game', *FH*, pp. 123–36 (p. 124).
118. Ibid. p. 125.
119. Fouché, 'Say It Loud, I'm Black and I'm Proud', p. 649; also see Richard Dyer, *White* (New York: Routledge, 1997), p. 90.
120. Ellison, 'King of the Bingo Game', *FH*, p. 125.
121. Germana, *Ralph Ellison, Temporal Technologist*, p. 172.
122. Ibid. p. 173.
123. Fouché, 'Say It Loud, I'm Black and I'm Proud', p. 641.

124. Ellison, 'King of the Bingo Game', *FH*, p. 130.
125. Ibid.
126. Ibid. p. 135.
127. Ibid. p. 136.
128. Ellison, *IM*, p. 27.
129. Ibid. pp. 507–8.
130. John Wright, *Shadowing Ralph Ellison* (Jackson: University Press of Mississippi, 2006), p. 152.
131. Ralph Ellison, 'Living with Music', *CERE*, pp. 227–36 (p. 233).
132. Ralph Ellison, 'Introduction to the Thirtieth-Anniversary Edition of *Invisible Man*', *CERE*, pp. 475–89 (p. 478).
133. Ralph Ellison, 'Living with Music', *CERE*, p. 234.
134. Ellison, *IM*, p. 6.
135. James Alan McPherson and Miller Williams, 'Sidetrack: The Language', in *Railroad*, pp. 140–1 (p. 141).
136. Ralph Ellison, 'Notes', in 'Slick', Box 159, LOC Ellison; cited in Foley, *Wrestling With the Left*, p. 130.
137. Ellison, *IM*, p. 7.
138. Fouché, 'Say It Loud, I'm Black and I'm Proud', p. 642.
139. Ellison, *IM*, p. 71.
140. Lewis Mumford, *The Golden Day: A Study in American Experience and Culture* (New York: Horace Liveright, 1926).
141. Jennifer L. Lieberman, *Power Lines: Electricity in American Life and Letters, 1882–1952* (Cambridge, MA, and London: The MIT Press, 2017), p. 197.
142. Lewis Mumford, *Technics and Civilization* (London: Routledge & Kegan Paul Ltd, 1934), pp. 324–5.
143. Lieberman, *Power Lines*, pp. 171, 174.
144. Ralph Ellison, 'Some Questions and Some Answers', *CERE*, pp. 291–301 (p. 294).
145. Ellison, *IM*, p. 129.
146. Ibid.
147. Ibid. p. 193.
148. Ibid. p. 250.
149. Ibid. p. 217.
150. Ibid. p. 249.
151. Amiri Baraka, *Dutchman*, in Baraka, *The LeRoi Jones/Amiri Baraka Reader, Second Edition*, ed. William J. Harris (New York: Basic Books, 2009), pp. 76–99 (p. 76).
152. Ellison, *IM*, pp. 336–7.
153. Ibid. p. 576.
154. Freeman H. Hubbard, *Railroad Avenue* (New York and London: McGraw-Hill Book Company, Inc., 1945), p. 436.
155. Jason Puskar, 'Risking Ralph Ellison', *Daedalus* 138.2 (Spring 2009): 83–93 (p. 90).
156. Ellison, *IM*, p. 436.

157. Ibid. pp. 438–9.
158. Ibid. pp. 439–40.
159. Ibid. pp. 440–1.
160. Ibid. p. 443.
161. Roi Ottley and William Weatherby (eds), *The Negro in New York: An Informal Social History* (New York: New York Public Library, 1967), pp. 266–7.
162. Ellison, *IM*, pp. 336–7.
163. See Foley, *Wrestling With the Left*, p. 245 (note 15); Jackson, *Ralph Ellison*, pp. 280–1; and Cheryl Lynn Greenberg, *Or Does It Explode? Black Harlem in the Great Depression* (Chapel Hill: University of North Carolina Press, 1991), pp. 175–8.
164. Ellison, *IM*, p. 7.
165. John Wright, *Shadowing Ralph Ellison* (Jackson: University Press of Mississippi, 2006), pp. 157–8.
166. Rayvon Fouché, *Black Inventors in the Age of Segregation: Granville T. Woods, Lewis H. Latimer, and Shelby J. Davidson* (Baltimore, MD, and London: The Johns Hopkins University Press, 2003), pp. 93–102, 107.
167. Ralph Ellison, 'Prologue', Box 147, LOC Ellison; see Foley, *Wrestling With the Left*, p. 245 (note 15).
168. See Wright, *Shadowing Ralph Ellison*, p. 159.
169. Ottley and Weatherby, *The Negro in New York*, p. 140.
170. Ibid. p. 143.
171. Fouché, *Black Inventors*, pp. 24–5.
172. Ellison, *IM*, p. 578.
173. N. Katherine Hayles, *Unthought: The Power of the Cognitive Nonconscious* (Chicago and London: The University of Chicago Press, 2017), pp. 115–16.
174. Ellison, *IM*, p. 581.
175. Robert S. Fortner, 'Frequency Allocation', in *The Concise Encyclopedia of American Radio*, ed. Christopher H. Sterling, Cary O'Dell and Michael C. Keith (New York and London: Routledge, 2010), pp. 312–15.
176. Amiri Baraka, *Dutchman*, in Baraka, *The LeRoi Jones/Amiri Baraka Reader*, pp. 76–99 (p. 76).
177. Matthew Luter, '*Dutchman*'s Signifyin(g) Subway: How Amiri Baraka Takes Ralph Ellison Underground', in *Reading Contemporary African American Drama: Fragments of History, Fragments of Self* (New York: Peter Lang Books, 2007), pp. 21–38 (pp. 21–2).
178. Ibid. p. 22.
179. Daniel Bond, *Stage Management: A Gentle Art* (2nd edn) (New York: Theatre Arts Books/Routledge 1998), p. 135.
180. P. Ney Wilson, 'Making the Old Track Last a Little Longer: What the Connecticut Company Did to Extend the Life of a Stretch of Track in New Haven, With Particular Reference to Arc Welding', *Electric Railway Journal* 52.24 (14 December 1918): 1053–4 (p. 1053).

181. Ziegler, 'Subjects and Subways', p. 284.
182. See Thomas Heisse, *Urban Underworlds: A Geography of Twentieth-Century American Literature and Culture* (New Brunswick, NJ, and London: Rutgers University Press, 2011), p. 239.
183. Amiri Baraka and VèVè Clark, 'Restaging Langston Hughes' *Scottsboro Limited* (1979)', in Amiri Baraka, *Conversations with Amiri Baraka* (Jackson: University Press of Mississippi, 1994), pp. 157–67 (p. 157).
184. Ibid. p. 161.
185. Ibid. p. 163.
186. Ibid. pp. 163, 161.

Afterword: The Robot Does (Not) Exist

A nineteenth-century journalist writing in the August 1847 issue of *Scientific American* declared that technological innovation was nothing less than 'reaching up after our divine title, "lords of the creation" [. . .] It is truly a sublime sight to behold a machine performing nearly all the functions of a rational being'. This familiar claim identifies technical creativity as a near-mystical power, which could elevate machines to the status of sentient beings, and inventors to the status of gods. However, the anonymous journalist was actually harnessing this hyperbolic rhetoric to accentuate the 'sublime sadness' of 'poor inventors' who had been ridiculed, impoverished and exploited while others profited from or ignored their expertise.[1] As I have argued throughout this book, unearthing the wider contexts of the technological sublime not only exposes the potent grip that its servile dialectics exert on the Western imagination, but also the bathetic contexts of their articulation in culture, which are often occluded or repressed by their sublime counterparts. Despite (or perhaps even because of) the interventions of the techno-bathetic avant-gardes, alternative narratives about socio-technical relations in the West have struggled to come into being. Few authors illustrate the dynamics of these transductive processes more powerfully than Ralph Ellison in the penultimate chapter of *Invisible Man*. After locating his underground refuge, Invisible flies into a rage after discovering the extent to which Brother Jack has manipulated him. Eventually Invisible collapses and enters a fugue state, and his ensuing hallucination bolts his *bildung* onto the *longue durée* of the American Machine Age, and the racially valenced transduction of the technological sublime.

Configuring American history as a '*river of black water*' running near '*an armored bridge*' that '*arched sharply away to where I could not see*', Invisible imagines himself lying prostrate, tortured by a group of his antagonists, including Brother Jack, '*all of whom had run*' and deceived him. As *'they came forward with a knife'*, he feels *'the bright red pain'* as they castrate him. They take *'two bloody blobs'* of the flesh that remained of his testicles *'and cast them over the bridge'* where they hang *'dripping down through the sunlight into the dark red water'*. Invisible looks *'up through a pain so intense now that the air seemed to roar with the clanging of metal, hearing, HOW DOES IT FEEL TO BE FREE OF ILLUSION'*.[2] His answer is that he feels *'painful and empty'*, and yet he laughs, *'[b]ecause at a price I now see what I couldn't see'*: suspended from the bridge *'there hang not only my generations wasting on the water'* but also *'your sun'*, *'your moon'* and *'your world'*. Invisible's affective response reveals the extent to which he experiences technology as an inherited and embodied expression of culture. It also reveals how dominant hegemonies sustain their power by manipulating processes of coming into hiding. As Invisible learns, those agencies use technology, and technicity, to control the dialectics of revelation, and the means of enforcing brutally who sees what, and when. By exposing this sublime narrative, and how the dominant parties lose control of it, everyone involved is now vulnerable, as Invisible explains:

> ["]*that drip-drop upon the water is all the history you've made, all you're going to make. Now laugh, you scientists. Let's hear you laugh!"*
> *And high above me now the bridge seemed to move off to where I could not see, striding like a robot, an iron man, whose iron legs clanged doomfully as it moved. And then I struggled, full of sorrow and pain, shouting, "No, no, we must stop him!"*[3]

As the bridge morphs into an electro-mechanical and, finally, a robotic entity, Ellison tracks the evolution of the technological sublime through its geometrical, dynamic and cybernetic stages.[4] Although saturated in the dystopian awe we would expect from a rendering of the technological sublime, and although Invisible is wounded, *'full of sorrow and pain'*, he is not terrified. He remains hyper-critical and defiant, struggling, on the one hand, to control his own affective feedback mechanisms, but, on the other, using that struggle to rope his oppressors into his critique, and his alternative vision of America's technological future.

For Ellison, the *'robot'* is a cultural creation that fused technical discourses in engineering with industrial alienation and narratives of the technological sublime. As Ron Eglash points out, the term 'robot' actually began to modify discourses in technical literature.[5] Like Karel Čapek's protagonist Alquist in his 1921 play *R.U.R.* (which, as Eglash argues, contributed to the consolidation of the master-slave dialectic in technical literature), Invisible has an affective crisis as he witnesses the hybridisation of flesh and machine taking on a life of its own in robotic form. Invisible's *'pain and sorrow'* announces his own profound attachment to the cultural tropes of the technological sublime, and the social hierarchies they instantiate, as well as the intricate, painful process of identifying and critiquing them as such. As the robot strides off into the distance, the ambivalence of Invisible's cry, '*No, no, we must stop him!*' articulates both an imperative (i.e. the robot *must* be stopped before it does any more damage) and a crisis (the robot *cannot* be stopped because even if we separate ourselves from the servile technicities it articulates, we have no alternative vision of technology or technicity with which to replace it).

For Gilbert Simondon, 'the robot does not exist' because it represents a conceptual failure: 'it is not a machine, no more so than a statue is a living being' because 'it is merely a product of the imagination and of fictitious fabrication, of the art of illusion'.[6] For Ellison, the robot exists, but only, as Scott Selisker points out, as 'a point of unsettling confusion between people and objects' – a confusion also found in the automata and figurines that evoke institutional slavery elsewhere in the novel, such as Brother Clifton's 'Sambo doll', or the racist caricature of an African American man on a mechanical coin bank.[7] Like armoured bridges between the metaphysical and physical worlds, tropes of the technological sublime fused with the socio-technical infrastructure of America, from the Machine Age to the Information Age. In this configuration, techno-servility operates like a form of double consciousness. Shortly after he published *Invisible Man*, Ellison argued that this cultural phenomenon evolved alongside the 'technological expansion' of the 'United States' and had reached an apotheosis with 'the invention of the Atom Bomb'. At this point in history, the 'problem of personal and democratic integrity symbolized by the Negro was pushed into the underground of the American conscience and...ignored'. Any potential social uplift that US techno-supremacy might have generated was therefore short-circuited because 'the so-called race issue became like a stave driven into the American system of values'. The terrifying capacity of nuclear weapons to unleash mass destruction was therefore a sublime symbol for the age. For Ellison, their blinding power was analogous to (and brought into hiding by) the white hegemony's hypocritical 'violation[s]' of America's 'most sacred principles; holding that all men are created equal they treated the members of America's minority peoples as though they were neither human nor equal'.[8] By exposing the means with which techno-servility entered culture, and yoking it to racial difference, Ellison 'plung[es] outside history' to engender new modes of technological agency, in the US and beyond.[9]

As I have argued throughout the book, this has been the task of the techno-bathetic avant-gardes: to propose the intermediary stage of disaggregation before alternative narratives can gain traction in the public sphere. Although this work and these models have remained in a provisional state throughout that century (and, in some ways, to the present day), they have emerged continually, across a wide range of technicities, narratives and interrelated fields. Indeed, libraries, Maker groups, schools, and other organisations dedicated to diffusing technical knowledge in the community have made remarkable progress in this respect, while fledgling academic networks (including my own) are attempting to catch up.[10]

In drawing such correlations, it is traditional at such points in modernist studies monographs to begin identifying analogies between the world the modernists inhabited and the present day. In this case, however, such figurative translations aren't necessary. The technological sublime and techno-servile frameworks codified in the early twentieth century continue to thrive in current digital media ecologies, much as they did in the modernist period. Untold numbers of cultural commentators have transformed online consortia, artificial intelligence (AI), virtual reality, mixed and augmented reality, social media, and a host of other socio-technical ensembles into metaphysical forces, before folding them into the 'black boxes' that mediate our (utopian) hopes and (dystopian) fears. These accounts stoke the proliferation of narratives that style massive tax avoidance organisations with publishing, retail, infrastructure and/or manufacturing arms as 'tech companies'; or which read AI as an amorphous, 'bloodless' entity, rather than the product of human choices and values that are (or should and can be) accountable to the people they affect.[11] The horrors of nuclear weapons and technologically-facilitated genocide have helped encourage us to keep these black boxes closed. However, these socio-technical realities only underscore the urgency with which we should be prying them open. Techno-bathetic responses, and dissenting counter-servile technicities, can help us do this. As the techno-bathetic avant-gardes understood so well, the technicities of everyday life are linked to a series of choices and behaviours that cumulatively affect our lives, cultures and planet. Alternatives to prevailing technicities existed then, and they exist now. As Iain Sinclair recently wrote in response to the work of Bob Brown, perhaps we need to rediscover them – perhaps 'the future's future is in the past'.[12]

Notes

1. Anonymous, 'Poor Inventors', *Scientific American* 2.49 (28 August 1847): 389. Leo Marx cited this article in *The Machine in the Garden: Technology*

and the Pastoral Ideal in America* (New York: Oxford University Press, 2000 [1964]), p. 194, and other commentators continue to do so, without addressing the context of the article itself.
2. Ralph Ellison, *IM*, p. 569. Note that all italic in this and Ellison's following quotations is as in the original text.
3. Ibid. Ellison's tone in this passage is crucial: his use of the term 'scientists', for example, is not generic, but context-specific, and therefore ironic. Invisible's antagonists have abused technics in the service of a malevolent social agenda, and Invisible mocks them accordingly.
4. See my discussion of the technological sublime and cybernetics in the book's Introduction; and on the 'dynamic technological sublime' see David Nye, *The American Technological Sublime* (Cambridge, MA, and London: The MIT Press, 1994), p. 77, on the 'electrical sublime', see p. 152.
5. Ron Eglash, 'Broken Metaphor: The Master-Slave Analogy in Technical Literature', *Technology and Culture* 48.2 (April 2007): 360–9 (p. 364).
6. Gilbert Simondon, *METO*, p. 16.
7. Scott Selisker, '"Simply by Reacting?": The Sociology of Race and Invisible Man's Automata', *American Literature* 83.3 (2011): 571–96 (p. 584).
8. Ralph Ellison, 'Undated Notes', Box 173, folder '"The Role of the Novel in Creating the American Experience", Salzburg Seminar in American Studies, Salzburg, Austria, 1953–1955', LOC Ellison; quoted in M. Cooper Harriss, *Ralph Ellison's Invisible Theology* (New York: New York University Press, 2017), p. 76.
9. *IM*, p. 377.
10. In partnership with such community initiatives, my Avant-Gardes and Speculative Technology (AGAST) Project team is working with academic, library, and third sector groups to co-create new digital tools based on the non-servile technicities advanced by Bob and Rose Brown, Luigi Russolo, Mina Loy, Amiri Baraka and others. Its outputs will be presented in my digital publication *The AGAST Project Archive* (New York: electric.press, forthcoming).
11. Ed Pilkington, 'Digital Dystopia: How Algorithms Punish the Poor', *The Guardian*, 13 October 2019 <https://www.theguardian.com/technology/2019/oct/14/automating-poverty-algorithms-punish-poor> (accessed 15 October 2019).
12. Iain Sinclair, *The Reading Machine 2017* [MAR Performance Exhibition], Oxford Brookes University, 17 March 2017.

Index

Adorno, Theodor, 76
African American culture
  black working-class
    experiences, 217–18, 220–2,
    237–9
  engagement with technology,
    218, 233, 238–9
  inventions, 252
  locomotive onomatopoeia,
    220–1
  symbolic capital of the
    railroads, 21, 214
alienation, 13–14, 169–71, 193
American superrealism, 150,
  152, 168, 176, 196
American technological sublime
  Alfred Stieglitz's contribution
    to, 73–4, 76, 85
  concept of, 8–10
  diffusion of technology, 10–12,
    69–70
  language of, 68
  mystic nationalism, 76, 109
  the nationalist technological
    sublime, 74, 76
  servile technicities of, 8, 75,
    249, 267
  Young American's imaginary
    of, 74
  see also technological sublime

Anderson, Sherwood, 74
artist-engineer figures
  Baroness Elsa von
    Freytag-Loringhoven, 90–1,
    98
  in Dadaism, 90–1
  Duchamp, Marcel, 88, 90,
    103
  Loy, Mina, 68, 90, 99, 103–5,
    109
  in Vorticism, 44, *59*
assemblages
  concept, 16
  cognitive assemblages (Hayles),
    253–4
  human/non-human
    assemblages, 14, 15–16, 68,
    249
  individuating potential of,
    74
  rail technology as, 74,
    214–15
  tactics of intervention for, 23,
    245
Associated Little Magazines
  network, 189–90
August, J. R. C., 127
August-Hunter Photo-Composing
  machine, 127, *128*,
  136

avant-garde
  and the development of dazzle camouflage, 30–1, 57
  as an 'ism', 75–6
  military technology of camouflage and, 23–4, 57
  relationship with military technology, 1–3
  spatial practice of technicity, 32
  understandings of technology, 4–6, 22–4
  use of bathetic technicities, 7, 19, 21–3, 69, 87
  use of dazzle strategies, 30–2
  visual language of, 82–3

Baraka, Amiri
  Dutchman, 255–6
  on *Invisible Man* (Ellison), 250
  staging of *Scottsboro, Limited* (Hughes), 226, 256
Barton, Fred, 203
bathos
  bathetic critique, 18–19
  in Picabia's mechanomorphic portraits, 77, 79–81
  poetics of, 17–18
  and the sublime, 18, 77, 265
  see also techno-bathetic framework
Benjamin, Walter, 171
Bennett, Gwendolyn
  career of, 236–7, 239
  in the Harlem Renaissance, 21, 215, 236
  'I Build America', 237–9
  involvement with *Fire!!* 217
  locomotive onomatopoeia, 237
  'Sweat', 239
  'Wedding Day', 21, 236
Black Sun Press, 129, 132–3

black vernacular technicity
  in African American culture, 215–16
  in Bennett's poetry, 238–9
  counter-servile strategies of, 7
  in *Invisible Man* (Ellison), 247–9, 254
  locomotive onomatopoeia, 220–1, 237–8, 247, 249
  redeployment of quilled train whistles, 220
  of riding the rails, 241
  socio-technical ensembles in Hughes's work, 217–20
  strategies of redeployment, 219–20, 242, 251–3
black vernacular technological creativity (Fouché)
  concept of, 219, 245–6
  redeployment, reconception, and re-creation strategies, 245, 247–8, 252–4, 256
Blast
  Edward Wadsworth and, 52–3
  human-machine interaction, 39–40, 169
  in relation to Futurism, 37–9
  Rock Drill (Epstein), 40
  title, 38
  'A Vision of Mud' (Saunders), 42–3
  Vorticist technicity, 38, 39, 40
  War Number, 32, 38, 39, 40, 43, 52–3
The Blind Man
  'Eyes' (Brown), 123
  Fountain by R. Mutt, 83–5, 84, 93
  'O Marcel - - - Otherwise I Also Have Been to Louise's' (Loy), 85–6
  Williams's review of, 87, 123

bodies
  as circuits of commodities, 35
  commercial and military technicities, 39
  in Mina Loy's work, 100
  relationship with technology, 77
Boni, Albert, 199–201, 203
Boyle, Kay
  career of, 144, 163
  'Change of Life', 150, 151, 152
  as a contributor to *RFBBM*, 118
  correspondence with the Browns, 197–8
  Saunders Prototype, 140
Brackett, Clare
  co-founder of the NMPC, 164, 165
  commercial potential of the reading machine, 165–7
  as a contributor to *RFBBM*, 166
  death of, 202
  reading machine prototype, 182, 183
  Readio prototype, 120
Bradford, Ernest W., 165, 172, 175
Browder, Earl, 193–4
Brown, Bob
  article in *The New York Herald (European Edition)*, 130–2, *131*
  capacity for collaboration, 129, 144–5, 163–4
  career of, 122
  correspondence with J. R. C. August, 127
  cultural tours to Russia, 191–2
  exile in South America, 103, 110, 123–5

expatriate published works, 129–30
'Eyes', 123, 129, 130, *131*, 132
1450–1950, 123, 126, 129, 132–3, 147, 202
friendship with Mina Loy, 86, 101
Guggenheim Fellowship application, 164, 184
introduction to Gertrude Stein, 3
invention of the reading machine, 3
move to Commonwealth College, 189
Museum of Social Change, 189–90, *190*
patent problems, 127
possible collaboration with Admiral Fiske, 127, 129
publishing business, 125, 129
'The Readies', 129, 130, 133, 136–8, 148
'Reading Machines', 140, 141, 145, 183, 184
scholarship on, 119
'The Six Books of Bob Brown', 125, 127, 165
Untitled [aka 'Self Portrait'], 125, *126*
'What the Soviet Union Means to Humanity', 195–6
see also readies project; reading machines
Brown, Cora, 191, 194, 201
Brown, Robert Carlton ('Carlton') Brown III
  archival evidence from, 140, 143
  'Reading By Machine', 140–2
Brown, Rose (neé Watson)
  cultural tours to Russia, 191–2

death of, 201, 204
'Dis', 152–3, 188
exile in South and Central America, 103
feminist poetics of, 152, 187–8
friendship with Mina Loy, 100
move to Commonwealth College, 189
Museum of Social Change, 189–90, *190*
readiefication of *Candide*, 187–8, 201
Readio prototype, 120, 145, 162, 164, 182–7, 190, 199, 201
solution to the readies' medium problem, 4, 144, 164, 187
Bull, Maclolm
coming into hiding, 10–11, 12, 17
Burke, Edmund, 9

camouflage
of disruptive technology, 11–12
function of, 31
naval camouflage, 28, *29*
Stein's camouflaged cannon anecdote, 1–3, 5, 23
technical innovation of, 23–4
see also dazzle camouflage
camouflage techniques, 2
Carrà, Carlo, *Guerrapitura*, 37
Certeau, Michel de, 23, 88–90, 93, 101, 109, 235, 242
cinema technology, 244–5
class
black working-class experiences, 217–18, 221–2, 237–9
class conflict during the Great Depression, 192–4
and a non-servile relationship with technology, 193–4
and the Scottosboro trials, 225
technicity and, 193
techno-proletariat, 192–4
Coburn, Alvin Langdon
as a Vorticist, 52
Vortoscope, 43–4, 47–51, *49*
Combes, Muriel, 13–14
coming into hiding
anticipated in Pope's 'Peri Bathous', 18
and the technological sublime, 10–11, 12
Commonwealth College, Arkansas, 164, 189–90, 194, 196
communism
Bob Brown's views on, 195–7
Gwendolyn Bennett's suspected affiliations with, 237
Langston Hughes's *Scotsboro, Limited*, 225–6
and the *Negro Anthology*, 230
consumer culture
circuits of commodities, 35
commercial fashion as transformative technology, 100–3
in *De Zayas! De Zayas!* (Picabia), 79–81
'Mass Production on 14th Street' (Loy), 108
and military tropes in Vorticism, 35, 41, 42–3
planned obsolescence, 105, 218
Contempo, 224–5, 230
counter-servile strategies
approaches to technicity, 169–71
bathetic technicity in The Baroness's poetry, 97–8

counter-servile strategies (*cont.*)
  of black vernacular technicity, 7, 238–9
  counter-servile strategies in Mina Loy's work, 108–9
  non-servile relationship with technology, 15, 193–4, 246–7
  of reading machines, 122, 176
  in *RFBBM*, 176
  in techno-bathetics, 22, 69, 98
  see also techno-servility
Crane, Stephen, 'Black Riders', 132, 146
Crangle, Sara, 18, 19, 79, 103
Cravan, Arthur, 69, 86, 99, 107, 123–4
Crosby, Caresse, 132–3
cultural formations, 153–4, 163–4
culture
  cultural tours to Russia, 191–2
  fears over cultural homogeneity, 88–9
  technics/humanity dialectic in, 12–13
  see also African American culture; consumer culture
Cunard, Nancy
  as a contributor to *RFBBM*, 118, 148, 163
  cross-dressing, 232
  cultural tour to Russia, 191
  "Dlink," 149–50
  experiments in micrographic printing, 129, 143
  friendship with the Browns, 133
  human rights work, 230
  Negro Anthology, 229–33
  'Scottsboro – and other Scottsboros,' 230

cybernetics, 13, 95, 103
cyborg theory
  The Baroness's work and, 95, 96
  Futurism and, 34, 37
  human/non-human relations, 95–6
  overview of, 95

Dadaism
  artist-engineer figure in, 89–90
  bathetic technicities of, 69–70, 82, 83, 100, 103, 108–9
  found art, 85
  horse figure in, 102
  machine ensembles, 68, 78, 81, 90
  Mina Loy, 99, 102
  and techno-bathetics, 69–70, 79, 82, 83, 100, 103, 108–9
  see also 291 magazine
dazzle camouflage
  avant garde dazzle strategies, 31–2
  and avant-garde visual art, 30–1, 57
  Dazzle-ships in Drydock at Liverpool (Wadsworth), 55, 56
  early version of, 126
  HMS Industry, 54
  HMS Mauretania, dazzle-painted, 30
  legacy of, 57–9
  as a sensory augmentation tactic, 31
  Ship Being Dazzle Camouflaged by Edward Wadsworth's Crew, 1918, 54–6, 55
  as a situated technical object, 31

use by the Navy, 28–30, 29, 58
and Vorticism, 23–4, 28–9, 52, 54
Wadsworth's development of, 23, 28–9, 53, 54–5, 58
dazzle poetics
  anxieties of, 35, 37
  concept of, 32
  within the Futurist manifesto, 33–5
  of Helen Saunders, 42–3
  of Jessica Dismorr, 41–2, 43
  of Vorticism, 39, 42
De Zayas, Marius, 73–4, 76, 79–80
Deleuze, Gilles, 15
diffusion
  in the American technological sublime, 69, 70–1
  of disruptive technology, 11–12
Dismorr, Jessica
  dazzle techniques, 40–1
  'London Notes', 41
  'Monologue', 41, 42–3
Du Bois, W. E. B., 10, 230, 243
Duchamp, Marcel
  Anémic Cinéma, 145
  artist-engineer figure, 90
  The Blind Man, 83–4
  Discs Inscribed with Puns, 88
  Fountain by R. Mutt, 83–5, 84, 93
  The Large Glass, 81–3
  and the Machine Age, 68, 81, 82, 83
  Monte Carlo Bond project, 87–8
  a new technicity of literacy, 88–9
  Nude Descending a Staircase, No. 2, 19, 123

Once More to This Star (Duchamp), 19, 20
Portrait of Marcel Duchamp (The Baroness), 92–3, 94, 95
Williams's dialogue with, 87–9

Eastman Kodak Company, 30–1, 59, 165, 174, 184, 198
elements, defined, 15–16
Ellison, Ralph
  cinema technology, 244–5
  color lines in socio-technical ensembles, 241–4
  early unpublished works, 215, 240–1
  'A Hard Time Keeping Up', 243–4
  'Hymie's Bull', 240, 241
  'I Did Not Learn Their Names', 241–2, 243
  'Judge Lynch in New York', 243
  'King of the Bingo Game', 244–7, 252
  locomotive onomatopoeia, 247, 249
  non-servile relationship with technology, 246–7
  riding the rails, 215, 240, 241
  'Slick Gonna Learn', 242–3, 247
  technical proficiency of, 247
  techno-bathetics, 243–4
  on techno-servility, 248–9
  see also Invisible Man (Ellison)
Emerson, Ralph Waldo, 9
energetics, 15, 16, 17, 34, 95, 96, 171, 219
ensembles
  American advanced industrial ensembles, 76, 77
  animal ensembles, 103

ensembles (*cont.*)
  color lines in socio-technical ensembles, 241–4
  defined, 15–16
  foregrounding of, 75–6
  socio-technical ensembles in Hughes's work, 219–20
  socio-technical ensembles in the Baroness's work, 94–5, 98
  see also machine ensembles
Epstein, Jacob, *Rock Drill*, 40, 47–8

Farrell, James T., 150, 152–3, 163, 175–6, 178–82
Farrell, John, 176, 178–9, 181–2
feminism
  'Change of Life' (Boyle), 150, 151, 152
  'Dis' (Brown), 152, 187–8
  feminist satire, 96–8, 100, 108–9, 152
  'Love Story' (Young), 178
  in the work of Gwendolyn Bennett, 239
  in the work of Mina Loy, 90, 99–100, 108–9
  in the work of Pauli Murray, 229, 230–2, 234–5
  in the work of the Baroness, 90–1, 92–4, 98
Fire!! 21, 217–18
Fiske, Rear Admiral Bradley
  and the Filmbook Organisation, 198
  as an inventor, 127, 198
  meeting with Bob Brown, 127, 129
  non-motorised micrographic reading device, 125
  patent applications, 145, 175

Ford, Charles Henri, 148, 150, 163, 178
Fouché, Rayvon, 6, 215–16, 219, 244, 245, 248, 252
Frank, Waldo, 74, 76, 88
Freytag-Loringhoven, Baroness Elsa von
  alignment with cyborg theory, 95, 96
  American culture and, 91–2, 96
  artist-engineer figure, 68, 90–1, 98
  attack on Williams, 92
  'Cast-Iron Lover', 92–3
  counter-servile bathetic technicity, 97–8
  as a Dadaist, 90–1
  on discipline of engineering, 91
  Enduring Ornament, 91, 95
  'Filmballad', 96–7
  God, 85, 91
  involvement in *Fountain*, 84–5
  'Love – Chemical Relationship', 92
  'A Modest Woman', 91
  'Narcissus Icarus', 95
  Portrait of Marcel Duchamp, 92–3, *94*, 95
  socio-technical ensembles, 95–6, 98
  'Stagnation', 97–8
  subversion of hegemonies, 91–2
  techno-bathetics critique of, 96–7, 98
  vernacular technicity in, 96–7
  'X-Ray', 97
Futurism
  advent of, 32–4
  Anglo-Italian alliance, 37
  Blast, 37–9

contrasted with Vorticism, 38–40
dazzle strategies, 45
emphasis on speed, 33
foundation narrative, 33–4, 103
human/machine relationship, 39
innovations of, 43–5
internal rivalries, 36
Lacerba, 37
Mina Loy's critique of, 100
time-space flux, 33–5, 36
use of contrast and contradiction, 36
see also Marinetti, F. T.

Gates, Jr, Henry Louis, 216–17
Geels, Frank, 15
gender
  challenges to in readies, 177–8
  gender identity of Pauli Murray, 230–2
  hierarchies of, 177
  sex, gender, sexuality and ethnicity narratives in the Machine Age, 146–7, 152, 178
  sex workers and the Scotsboro trials, 224
  women's experiences of boxcar culture, 229
Godwin, Murray
  'A Day in the Life of a Robot', 168
  and the readies project, 166
  Science and Invention Magazine, 167–8, *167*
  as a superrealist, 168
Goody, Alex, 10, 85–6, 91
Gouel, Eva ('Eve'), 1
Great Depression

class conflict during, 192–4
impact on transatlantic modernism, 162
readies project adaptation to, 175–6, 178
Guattari, Félix, 15
Guggenheim, Peggy, 97, 104, 105, 144
Guirand de Scévola, Lucien-Victor, 2

Hagglund, B. C.
  as a contributor to *RFBBM*, 152–3, 163
  criticism of readies, 172, 176
  reading machines in socialist societies, 191
Haraway, Donna, 95
Hayles, N. Katherine, 96, 253
Hiler, Hilaire
  accidental killing of a cyclist, 144–5, 169
  Atelier Hiler, 144, 171–2, 184
  career of, 144
  Commercial Design, 120, *121*, 169, *170*
  as a contributor to *RFBBM*, 168
  counter-servile strategies, 169–72
  description of the Saunders Prototype, 143, 145–6, 169
  involvement in the readies project, 119, 138, 166, 168–9
  'Preface' for *RFBBM*, 143, 169, 172, 174–5
  as a readie contributor, 148
  sketch of the 'Readio', 145, 185–6, *186*, 187

Hughes, Langston
  association with *The Messenger*, 221–2
  black vernacular technicity, 215
  black working-class experiences, 217–18, 221–2
  'Bodies in the Moonlight', 221–2
  'Christ in Alabama', 224–5, 226, 228
  Fine Clothes for the Jew, 219–20
  'God to Hungry Child', 217
  'The Little Virgin', 221–2
  locomotive onomatopoeia, 220–1
  rail networks in the works of, 216–17, 219–20
  'Railroad Avenue', 21, 218–19, 220–1
  recommendation of Pauli Murray, 229
  and the Scottosboro trials, 215, 223, 224, 227–9
  Scottsboro, Limited, 225–6, 227, 256
  'Southern Gentlemen, White Prostitutes, Mill-Owners and Negros', 224, 225
  strategies of redeployment, 219
  'The Town of Scottsboro', 225
  work in *Contempo*, 224, 230
Hunter, E. Kenneth, 127
Hurston, Zora Neale, *Color Struck*, 21

individuals, defined, 15–16
infrastructure
  Alfred Stieglitz's industrial structures, 71–2
  critiques of urban infrastructure, 21–2
  'I Build America' (Bennett), 237–9
  redeployment of technology, 241–2, 251–3
  segregationist infrastructure, 21, 217–18
  'The Song of the Highway' (Murray), 234–5
  see also rail technology
International Filmbook Corporation, 198
intonarumori (noise intoner), 43–6, 46, 47
Invisible Man (Ellison)
  black vernacular technicity, 247–8
  broadcast technology, 253–4
  early drafts, 240
  non-servile technicity, 246–7
  redeployment of technology, 215, 251–3
  techno-servility, 248–9
  train technology, 249–52
  transduction, 265–7

Jim Crow urban planning policies, 217
Jolas, Eugene
  as a contributor to *RFBBM*, 119, 136, 163
  fears over cultural homogeneity, 89
  see also transition

Kaplan, Philip, 139, 140, 198, 202
King, Carol Weiss, 224
Knudsen, Hugo
  reading machine prototype, 164, 182, 183, 184

solution to the readies medium problem, 144
Kodak's Recordak Library Projector, 198
Komroff, Manuel, 200
Kroiz, Lauren, 79, 80

Lacerba (journal), 36, 37, 43
lacerbiani (Florentine avant-garde), 36
Laforgue, Jules, 19
LaMarre, Thomas, 14, 96
language
  avant-garde visual language, 82–3
  in the Baroness's poetry, 97–8
  in *De Zayas! De Zayas!* (Picabia), 79–81
  Loy and machine writing, 85–6
  'O Marcel - - - Otherwise I Also Have Been to Louise's' (Loy), 85–6
  taboo-flouting in readies, 146, 149–50, 166, 178–9
  technology and, 215
  Williams's translinguistic punning, 87
  in 'Writing(s)' (Williams), 88–9
  see also black vernacular technicity; military language; vernacular technicity
Latimer, Lewis H., 247, 252
Le Corbusier, 33
Lewis, Theophilus, 222
Lewis, Wyndham, 37, 38–40; *see also* Blast
The Little Review
  Anglo-Mongrels and the Rose (Loy), 104–5
  The Baroness's work in, 91, 92–3, 94, 95
  Ezra Pound as editor, 58
  Marcel Duchamp's work in, 82, 88
  Mina Loy's work in, 104
  vernacular aesthetics of, 147
  Vorticism in, 58
Lowenfels, Walter, 148, 163
Loy, Mina
  on American consumer culture, 108–9
  Anglo-Mongrels and the Rose, 104
  artist-engineer figure, 68, 90, 99, 103–5, 109
  'Auto-Facial-Construction' project, 100–1
  The Blind Man, 83–6
  career of, 99–101
  counter-servile strategies, 108–9
  as a Dadaist, 99, 102
  design business, 103–4
  exile to Mexico, 86, 99, 103, 107, 124
  fashion as transformative, 100–4
  on Futurism, 100
  'Horse Ear Hat' design, 101, *102*, 103–4
  interior lighting designs, 99, 103, 104–7
  as an inventor, 99, 100, 104–5, 107–8
  marriage to Arthur Cravan, 69
  'Mass Production on 14th Street', 108
  Mexican Bloom design, 107
  'Novel Floral Decorations That Light Up Modern Interiors', 105, *106*, 107
  'O Marcel - - - Otherwise I Also Have Been to Louise's', 85–6

Loy, Mina (*cont.*)
  The Pamperers, 100, 101
  Peggy Guggenheim's patronage of, 104, 105, 144
  technicity, 100
  as techno-bathetic critic of the Machine Age, 100, 109
  verrovoile invention, 99, 105–8, 144
  'Would You Be "Different?" Madame Loy Shows How', 101, *102*, 103–4

machine, defined, 9
Machine Age
  fears over cultural homogeneity, 88–9
  gear and girder aesthetics, 141
  in Russia, 192
  sex, gender, sexuality and ethnicity narratives, 146–7, 152, 178
  techno-bathetic critiques of, 100, 109–10
machine ensembles
  in Dadaism, 68, 77–8, 81, 90
  'King of the Bingo Game', 244–7
  in *The Large Glass* (Duchamp), 82
  Picabia's machine ensembles, 78
  the railroad as, 16
Mackenzie, Adrian, 6, 12, 31
Macleod, Norman, 119, 147, 151–2, 163; see also *Morada*
Marcus, Laura, 4–5
Mare, André, 2
Marinetti, F. T.
  'Centaur', 103
  as a contributor to *RFBBM*, 118, 148, 163
  'Destruction of Syntax – Wireless Imagination – Words-in-Freedom', 33
  fascist politics of, 148–9
  'The Founding and Manifesto of Futurism', 33–4, 103
  military language, 34–5
  relationship with technology, 34–5
  'Technical Manifesto of Futurist Literature', 34
  technicity, 100
  time-space flux, 33–5
  'Vital English Art', 37–8
Marx, Karl
  alienation, 13–14, 169–71
  human/non-human assemblages, 14
  non-servile relationships with technology, 15
Marx, Leo, 8–9, 17
Master-Slave Dialectic, 10
Mazza, Armando, '*Transatlantico*', 35–6, 57
Meccano sets, 141–2
The Messenger, 221–2
meta-formations
  Associated Little Magazines network, 189–90
  concept of, 163–4
  Negro Anthology, 229
  the readies project as, 164–5, 175, 183
metastability, 95
Meyer, Agnes E., 75
milieu, defined, 16
military language
  'Cast-Iron Lover' (The Baroness), 92
  of F. T. Marinetti, 34–5

'O Marcel - - - Otherwise I Also Have Been to Louise's' (Loy), 86
see also Blast
military technology
  'Armory Show' and, 73
  and avant-garde visual art, 73
  Russolo's *intonarumori* as quasi-military, 44–6
  Vortography and, 50
  see also dazzle camouflage
modernism
  expatriate modernists, 109–10
  speed reading of modernist literature, 133–4
  and the technological sublime, 5, 69
  technology as a cipher for, 1
Morada
  avant-garde readership of, 135, 147–8
  Commercial Design reading machine in, 120
  coverage of the reading machine, 120
  'Ready: Revelation', 151–2
  'Writing Readies', 129, 148–50, 151–2
motivated signifying(g)
  concept of, 216
  Langston Hughes and the rail network, 216–17
  locomotive onomatopoeia, 220–1, 237–8, 247, 249
  in Pauli Murray's work, 238–9
  rail technology, 255–6
Mumford, Lewis, 8, 11, 15, 74, 248
Murray, Pauli
  career of, 215
  engagement with the Scotsboro trials, 229, 232–3
  experiences of the rail network, 229
  gender identity of, 230–2
  in *Negro Anthology*, 229, 235
  'Pete' persona, 230, *231*
  'The Song of the Highway', 229, 234–5
  techno-bathetics in, 235
  'Three Thousand Miles on a Dime in Ten Days', 229, 230–4, 235
Museum of Social Change, 190–1, *190*

National Machine Products Company (NMPC), 164–6
Naturalism, 180–1
Nevinson, C. R. W., 37–8
The New Masses
  on American culture, 215
  'Judge Lynch in New York' (Ellison), 243
  leftist politics, 168
  Russo-American cultural exchanges, 191
  Scottsboro, Limited (Hughes), 225
  Veblen's techno-proletariat, 192–4
The New York Herald (European Edition), 130–2, *131*
Nicholls, Peter, 18, 19, 35–6
North, Michael, 146, 149
Norton, Allen, 86, 99, 123
Norton, Louise, 85, 99
Nugent, Richard Bruce, 21
Nye, David, 4–5, 8, 74

Optigraph, 198–9

Papini, Giovanni, 36
Piatti, Ugo, 45

Picabia, Francis
 De Zayas! De Zayas!, 78, 79–81
 Ici, C'est Ici Stieglitz, 77, 78
 mechanomorphic portraits, 76–7, 78–81
 Portrait D'une Jeune Fille Américaine Dans L'État de Nudité, 81
Picasso, Pablo, 1–2, 23
Pictorialism, 71
Pope, Alexander, 17–18, 19, 74
Pound, Ezra
 as a contributor to *RFBBM*, 118, 163
 criticism of readies, 172, 185
 'The Death of Vorticism', 58, 59
 'Deflation Benefit', 185
 Mauberly, 59–60
 readies project and social hierarchies, 177
 relationship with Alvin Coburn, 52
 on Vorticism, 53
 Vortoscope, 43–4, 47–51, 49
Pratt, Theodore, 140, 201, 201, 203–4
Pratt, Verneur Edmund, 198–200
The Publishers' Weekly, 135–6
Putnam, Samuel, 119, 148–9, 163, 171

race
 Jim Crow urban planning policies, 217
 racial essentialism, 146, 151
 racism in readies, 146–7, 149–50, 177, 178–9
 racism/machine-age analogy, 248

'Ready: Revolution' (Macleod), 151–2
 segregationist infrastructure, 217–18
 sex, gender, sexuality and ethnicity narratives in the Machine Age, 146–7, 152, 178
 superrealism and, 152–3
rail technology
 illicit uses of by migrant workers, 223–4
 in *Invisible Man* (Ellison), 249–52
 in Langston Hughes's work, 216–17, 219–20, 226
 liminal zones of rail travel, 21, 214–15, 223–4, 235
 locomotive onomatopoeia, 220–1, 237–8, 247, 249
 national narratives of, 214
 New York City's rail infrastructure, 255–6
 Pauli Murray's experiences of, 229, 232
 railroads as machine ensembles, 16
 riding the rails, 214, 215, 222, 223, 229, 233–4, 235, 240, 241
 segregationist infrastructure, 21, 217–18
 as a signifyin(g) machine, 216–17, 255–6
 as socio-technical assemblages, 214–15
 the technological sublime of, 235
 train whistles, 220
 women's experiences of boxcar culture, 229
Railroad Avenue, term, 217

Randall, Esther, 202
Randolph, A. Phillip, 221
Ray, Man, 51, 75, 87, 88, 133, 145, 201
Readies for Bob Brown's Machine: A Critical Facsimile Edition (RFBBM)
  bigotry in, 146–7, 149, 178–9
  Browns's avant-garde meta-formation, 163–5
  'Change of Life' (Boyle), 150, 151, 152
  the Commercial Design on the flyleaf of, 120, *121*, 139, 145
  contributors for, 3, 118, 136, 137, 138, 148, 152–3, 163–4, 166
  cost of, 175
  counter-servile technicities, 176
  'Dis' (Rose Brown), 152, 187–8
  'Eyes' (Bob Brown), 123, 132
  'Jeff' (Farrell), 180–1
  'Letter From the Provinces' (Ford), 178
  'Love Story' (Young), 178
  micrographic sample readies, 143
  modernist practices in, 150–1, 176–77
  'One of the Many' (James T. Farrell and John Farrell), 181
  'Preface' (Hiler), 143, 169, 171, 173–4
  publication of, 130
  reading machine foundation narrative, 122–3, 125, 129
  superrealism in, 150–3, 176
  'Sylvester Mc Gullick' (Farrell), 179–80
  'Two Men 7 Duck No Luck' (Brackett), 166

'We Came' (Stein), 177–8
readies project
  anthology of readie scripts, 147, 148
  avant-garde print contexts, 129–30
  the basic design, 125
  bigotry in, 146–7, 152
  as catalyst for socio-technical revolution, 194
  cellulose acetate, 144, 174
  Clare Brackett and, 120, 165–7, 182, 183, 202
  criticism of, 172, 175–6, 185–6
  foundation narrative, 122–3, 125–6
  1450–1950 and, 129, 132–3, 146–7
  as an instrument of social change, 162, 164, 175–82, 187–9, 203
  medium for the texts, 4, 144, 164, 174, 187
  medium of, 3, 118
  meta-formational ensembles of, 164–5, 175, 183
  micrographic sample readies, 143
  NMPC collaboration on, 165–6
  the photo-compositing machine and, 127
  racism and bigotry in the contributions, 146, 149–50, 177, 178–9
  readiefication of *Candide*, 187–8, 201
  'Ready: Revelation' (Macleod), 151–2
  'The Six Books of Bob Brown', 125, 127, 165

readies project (*cont.*)
  'Story to be Read on the Reading Machine', 143
  technical proofs-of-concept, 143–4
  term, 120
  texts and technicities of, 120–2
  Time magazine feature, 201–2
  in *transition*, 133, 135, 136–8, 153
  see also reading machines
reading machines
  archival evidence for, 139–41, 162, 165, 172–4, 183–8, 194, 198–9
  August-Hunter Photo-Composing machine, 127, *128*, 136
  basic design, 125
  Commercial Design, 120, *121*, 138–9, 169, *170*
  commercial potential of, 165–7
  core concept of, 165
  'Eyes' as inspiration for, 123
  first working prototype model background, 119
  foundation narrative, 3, 118, 122–3, 125–6, 129, 132
  within Machine-Age modernism, 3, 109, 110
  magnification mechanism, 172–4, 183–5
  Meccano components in, 141–2
  mechanically-assisted speed reading, 133–4
  micrographic reading technologies, 197–8
  'My Reading Machine' in *The Publishers' Weekly*, 135–6
  non-motorised micrographic reading device (Fiske), 127
  Optigraph, 198–9
  The Paris Tribune article, 130, 133, 134, 135, 136
  patent applications, 175
  public fascination with, 203–4
  Readex, 199–201
  Readio prototype, 120, 145, 162, 185–7, 188, 191, 199, 201
  Recordak Library Projector, 174, 184, 198, 199, 200
  in Russia, 191
  Saunders Prototype, 120, 139–44, *140*, 145, 169, 199
  scepticism over the existence of, 3–4, 119, 138–9
  scholarship on, 119
  in *Science and Invention Magazine*, 167–8, *167*
  scrolling mechanism, 172–4, *173*
  'The Six Books of Bob Brown', 125, 127, 165
  within a socialist society, 190
  Soviet model of, 194–5, 197
  specialist/mass market readership crossover, 133–5
  Taylorist efficiencies of, 136, 145, 146
  techno-bathetic tactics, 122
  teleprompters, 203–4
  training for the use of, 133–5
  working prototype, 182–5
Recordak Library Projector, 174, 184, 198, 199, 200
Rodker, John, 91
Rogue, 99
Russia
  cultural tours to, 191–2
  Russo-American reading machine collaboration, 194–5, 197

technology in, 191, 192
'What the Soviet Union Means to Humanity' (Brown), 195–6
Russolo, Luigi
The Art of Noises, 43, 44, 103
cultural confrontations, 46–7
intonarumori (noise intoner), 43–6, 46, 47
militaristic technology, 45
publicity photographs, 45–6, 46

Saper, Craig, 119–20, 146, 149, 176
Saunders, Helen
dazzle techniques, 40–1
'A Vision of Mud', 42–3
Saunders, Ross, 119, 138, 139–43, 145, 169
Schamburg, Morton, 85
Science and Invention Magazine, 167–8, *167*
Scottsboro trials
'Christ in Alabama' (Hughes), 224–5, 226, *228*
critiques of, 215, 229
cultural crises following, 214, 215
influence on Ralph Ellison, 240
Langston Hughes's work and, 215, 222, 224, 227–9
mothers of the Scottsboro Nine, 225
overview of, 222–3
Pauli Murray's engagement with, 229, 232–3
Scottsboro, Limited (Hughes), 225–6, 227, 256
'Scottsboro – and other Scottsboros' (Cunard), 230
socio-technical aspects of, 224

'Southern Gentlemen, White Prostitutes, Mill-Owners and Negros' (Hughes), 224, 225
sensory augmentation
concept of, 6, 31
dazzle camouflage as, 31
in F. T. Marinetti's work, 45
in Futurism, 36–7
intonarumori (noise intoner), 45
in Luigi Russolo's work, 45
technicity of, 31, 32, 39, 40, 42–3
and technological innovations, 43–4
via reading machines, 134–5
sexuality
in *De Zayas! De Zayas!* (Picabia), 79–81
liminal zones of rail travel, 21
sex, gender, sexuality and ethnicity narratives in the Machine Age, 146–7, 152, 178
sexual satisfaction and consumer activity, 35, 42
superrealism and, 152–3
Sherover, Max, 188, 192, 198, 199, 201–2
Simondon, Gilbert
human/non-human interactions, 15–16
METO, 13, 15
non-servile relationship with technology, 15
social energetics, 171, 219
technological alienation, 13–14, 169–71, 193
theory of technology, 12–13
on unfinished inventions, 122

286 Index

socio-technics
  in African American literature, 21–2
  black working-class experiences, 217–18, 221–2, 237–9
  color lines in socio-technical ensembles, 241–4
  counter-servile engagements, 14–15, 17, 169–71
  human/non-human assemblages, 14, 16–17, 68
  in *Invisible Man* (Ellison), 248–9, 251–2, 253–4
  of Mina Loy's lighting designs, 104–8
  of the reading machines, 164–5
  of the Scottsboro trials, 224
  segregationist infrastructure, 21, 217–18
  socio-technical ensembles in Langston Hughes's work, 219–20
  socio-technical ensembles in The Baroness's work, 93–5, 98
Soffici, Ardengo
  'Crocicchio', 36
  Lacerba, 36
space
  in African American literature, 216
  spatial practices of rail networks, 223–4, 235
  time-space compression, 33
  time-space flux of Futurism, 33–5, 36
Stein, Gertrude
  camouflaged military equipment anecdote, 1–3, 5, 11–12, 23
  as a contributor to *RFBBM*, 118, 163, 177
  introduction to Bob Brown, 3
  Lucy Church Amiably, 177
  production of a readie, 3
  speed reading of, 133, 134
  techno-bathetic work, 176, 177–8
  'We Came', 177–8
Stiegler, Bernard, 15
Stieglitz, Alfred
  and the American technological sublime, 71–4, 75, 76, 85
  'Armory Show', 70–3
  Camera Work, 73, 74
  De Zayas's critique of in *291*, 73–4, 75, 76, 77–8
  dialectical urban studies, 71
  Fountain by R. Mutt, 83–5, 84, 93
  Ici, C'est Ici Stieglitz (Picabia), 77, 78, 79
  Old and New York, 71, 72
  The Steerage, 71
  techno-servility and, 74–5
  291 Gallery, 73, 74, 75, 83
  291 magazine, 73, 75, 76
  and the Young Americans, 74–6
Stoll, Albert, 120, 164, 165, 172, 174–5, 183–4
Sutherland, Keston, 18–19

Taylor, Prentiss, 225–6, 227, 228
Taylorism, 4, 70, 81, 97, 98, 133, 134, 136, 145, 146
technical objects, 15–16, 31
technicity
  for the augmented self, 32
  bathetic technicity, 19
  class and, 193

counter-servile strategies, 169–71
of dazzle camouflage, 31
defined, 6, 16, 31
humanity/machine relationship, 39–40
of literacy, 88–9
in literary modernism, 137
of sensory augmentation, 31, 32, 39, 40, 42–3
situated technical objects, 31
socio-technical interactions and, 16–17
and *techné*, 171
transduction and, 6, 16
in Vorticism, 38, 39, 40
see also socio-technics; vernacular technicity
techno-bathetic framework
in African American literature, 21–2
bathetic technicity, 19
concept of, 34, 68–70
counter-servile strategies, 22, 69, 97–8
in *De Zayas! De Zayas!* (Picabia), 79–81
feminist satire, 96–8, 100, 108–9, 152
Francis Picabia's bathetic machines, 78
Francis Picabia's mechanomorphic portraits, 76–7, 78–9
in Gertrude Stein's work, 176, 177
inter-disciplinary applications, 196
The Large Glass (Duchamp), 81–3

Marcel Duchamp's bathetic negotiations with Laforgue, 19–21
the New York Dada movement, 69–70, 79, 82, 83, 100, 108–9
overview of, 5–6
in Pauli Murray's work, 235
in Ralph Ellison's work, 243–4
of reading machines, 122
as a spatial practice, 21
use by the avant-garde, 23
in Williams's works, 87
technological sublime
coming into hiding, 10–11, 12
concept, 5, 8–9, 17–18
in Futurism, 34
Gertrude Stein's camouflaged cannon anecdote, 11–12
and modernism, 5, 69
of the railroads, 235
techno-servility and, 8, 15, 17
transduction of, 22
see also American technological sublime
technology
African American engagement with, 218, 233, 238–9
black box effect, 11–12, 79
as a cipher for modernity, 1
coeval nature of, 6
language and, 215
public engagement with, 8
relationship with avant-garde practice, 4, 6
servile discourses of, 10–11
Simondon's theory of, 13–15
technological alienation, 13–14, 193
time-space compression, 33
Western culture's relationship with, 12–13

techno-proletariat, 192–4
techno-servility
  Alfred Stieglitz, and, 74–5
  cyborg theory and, 95, 96
  defined, 14, 75, 248
  in *Invisible Man* (Ellison), 248–9
  servile discourses of technology, 10–11
  techno-bathetics and, 22, 69, 96–8
  technological sublime and, 8, 15, 17
  see also counter-servile strategies
Thurman, Wallace, 21
Tichi, Cecilia, 9–10, 93
time-space compression, 33
time-space flux, 33–5, 36
transduction
  concept, 6
  in *Invisible Man* (Ellison), 265–7
  in Picabia's mechanomophic portraits, 80–1
  socio-technical interactions and, 16–17
  technicity and, 6, 16
  of the technological sublime, 22
transition
  association with the readies, 153
  counter-narrative of, 147
  critical framework of, 153–4
  race as subject in, 146
  'The Readies' (Brown), 129, 130, 133, 136–8, 147–8
  'Revolution of the Word', 3, 109–10, 119, 130, 136–7, 146–7, 152, 153, 176, 196
  utopianism of, 110, 119
  'X-Ray' (The Baroness), 97

291 magazine
  Alfred Stieglitz's contributions to, 76
  De Zayas! De Zayas! 79–81
  De Zayas's critique of Stieglitz, 73–4, 76, 77–8
  experimental methods in, 75
  fifth issue, 76–7
  Francis Picabia's mechanomorphic portraits, 73, 76–7, 78–81
  launch of, 73

the uncanny, 1–3, 5
United States of America (USA)
  American identity, 146
  anti-war sentiment, 86, 123–5
  Russo-American cultural exchanges, 191–2
  Stieglitz's nationalist technological sublime, 74, 76
  WWI American nationalism, 86
  see also African American culture; American technological sublime
utopianism, 109–10

Vail, Lawrence, 144–5, 149, 151–2, 177
Veblen, Thorsten, 169, 171, 192, 193–4
Veitch, Jonathan, 150, 152
vernacular technicity
  in African American literature, 215
  in The Baroness's work, 96–7
  riding the rails, 223–4
  of train whistles, 220
  see also black vernacular technicity
Villon, Jacques, 2

visibility/concealment dialectic
  black box effect, 11–12, 79
  coming into hiding, 10–11
Viviani, Alberto, '*Partenza aeroplano + concerto vieuxtemps*', 36
Vorticism
  in America, 60
  artist-engineer figure, 44, 59
  commercial culture and war, 35, 41, 42–3
  contrasted with Futurism, 38–9
  dazzle camouflage, 23–4, 28–9, 52, 54
  dazzle poetics, 39, 42
  'The Death of Vorticism' (Pound), 58, 59
  dualistic logic, 39–40, 49, 53
  within the Establishment, 58
  innovations of, 43–4, 51–2
  manifestos, 37, 39
  relationship with technology, 38, 39
  technicity in, 38, 39, 40
Vortography
  Camera Club exhibition, 48, 50
  and military technology, 50, 52
  Vortograph No. 8, 50, 51
Vortoscope, 43–4, 47–51, 49

Wadsworth, Edward
  dazzle camouflage, 23, 28–9, 52, 53, 54–5, 58
  Dazzle-ships in Drydock at Liverpool, 55, 56
  In Dry Dock (1918), 57
  Dry-docked for Painting and Scaling, Liverpool (1918), 55
  friendship with Coburn, 52
  involvement in *Blast*, 52–3
  Rotterdam, 53
  as a Vorticist, 52–3, 57
  Vorticist alphabet, 59
  War-Engine, 53
West, Nathanael, 168, 182, 201
Wiener, Norbert, 95
Wilkinson, Norman, 28–30, 31, 54–5, 58–9
Williams, William Carlos
  as an American superrealist, 150
  the Baroness's attack on, 92
  contribution of a readie, 118
  as a contributor to *RFBBM*, 163
  dialogue with Marcel Duchamp, 87–9
  fears over cultural homogeneity, 88–90
  review of *The Blind Man*, 87, 123
  'Writing(s)', 87, 88–9
Woods, Granville T., 247, 252
The Workers Monthly, 217

Young, Kathleen Tankersley, 150, 163, 178
Young Americans, 70, 72, 73, 74–5, 76, 88, 248

EU representative:
Easy Access System Europe
Mustamäe tee 50, 10621 Tallinn, Estonia
Gpsr.requests@easproject.com

www.ingramcontent.com/pod-product-compliance
Lightning Source LLC
Chambersburg PA
CBHW071829230426
43672CB00013B/2794